Robert Browning

Christmas-Eve and Easter Day Men and Women in Balcony

Robert Browning

Christmas-Eve and Easter Day Men and Women in Balcony

ISBN/EAN: 9783741117756

Manufactured in Europe, USA, Canada, Australia, Japa

Cover: Foto ©Andreas Hilbeck / pixelio.de

Manufactured and distributed by brebook publishing software (www.brebook.com)

Robert Browning

Christmas-Eve and Easter Day Men and Women in Balcony

CHRISTMAS-EVE AND EASTER DAY
MEN AND WOMEN: IN A BALCONY
DRAMATIS PERSONÆ: BALAUSTION'S
ADVENTURE: PRINCE HOHENSTIEL-
SCHWANGAU: FIFINE AT
THE FAIR

BY

ROBERT BROWNING

WITH THE AUTHOR'S LATEST CORRECTIONS

BOSTON AND NEW YORK
HOUGHTON, MIFFLIN AND COMPANY
The Riverside Press, Cambridge
1896

CONTENTS

	PAGE
CHRISTMAS-EVE AND EASTER-DAY.	
CHRISTMAS-EVE	1
EASTER-DAY	31
MEN AND WOMEN.	
TRANSCENDENTALISM: A POEM IN TWELVE BOOKS	57
HOW IT STRIKES A CONTEMPORARY	58
ARTEMIS PROLOGIZES	61
AN EPISTLE, CONTAINING THE STRANGE MEDICAL EXPERIENCE OF KARSHISH, THE ARAB PHYSICIAN . . .	64
JOHANNES AGRICOLA IN MEDITATION	71
PICTOR IGNOTUS	72
FRA LIPPO LIPPI	74
ANDREA DEL SARTO	83
THE BISHOP ORDERS HIS TOMB AT SAINT PRAXED'S CHURCH	89
BISHOP BLOUGRAM'S APOLOGY	91
CLEON	115
RUDEL TO THE LADY OF TRIPOLI	123
ONE WORD MORE	124
IN A BALCONY	131
DRAMATIS PERSONÆ.	
JAMES LEE'S WIFE: —	
I. JAMES LEE'S WIFE SPEAKS AT THE WINDOW .	153
II. BY THE FIRESIDE	154
III. IN THE DOORWAY	155
IV. ALONG THE BEACH	156
V. ON THE CLIFF	157
VI. READING A BOOK, UNDER THE CLIFF . .	158
VII. AMONG THE ROCKS	101
VIII. BESIDE THE DRAWING-BOARD . . .	161
IX. ON DECK	163

CONTENTS

GOLD HAIR: A STORY OF PORNIC	165
THE WORST OF IT	170
DIS ALITER VISUM; OR, LE BYRON DE NOS JOURS	173
TOO LATE	178
ABT VOGLER, AFTER HE HAS BEEN EXTEMPORIZING UPON THE MUSICAL INSTRUMENT OF HIS INVENTION.	182
RABBI BEN EZRA	185
A DEATH IN THE DESERT	191
CALIBAN UPON SETEBOS; OR, NATURAL THEOLOGY IN THE ISLAND	207
CONFESSIONS	214
MAY AND DEATH	215
DEAF AND DUMB: A GROUP BY WOOLNER	216
PROSPICE	216
EURYDICE TO ORPHEUS: A PICTURE BY LEIGHTON	217
YOUTH AND ART	217
A FACE	219
A LIKENESS	220
MR. SLUDGE, THE MEDIUM	222
APPARENT FAILURE	257
EPILOGUE	259
BALAUSTION'S ADVENTURE, INCLUDING A TRANSCRIPT FROM EURIPIDES	263
PRINCE HOHENSTIEL-SCHWANGAU, SAVIOR OF SOCIETY	331
FIFINE AT THE FAIR	381

CHRISTMAS-EVE AND EASTER-DAY

FLORENCE, 1850.

CHRISTMAS-EVE.

I.

Out of the little chapel I burst
Into the fresh night-air again.
Five minutes full, I waited first
In the doorway, to escape the rain
That drove in gusts down the common's centre
At the edge of which the chapel stands,
Before I plucked up heart to enter.
Heaven knows how many sorts of hands
Reached past me, groping for the latch
Of the inner door that hung on catch
More obstinate the more they fumbled,
Till, giving way at last with a scold
Of the crazy hinge, in squeezed or tumbled
One sheep more to the rest in fold,
And left me irresolute, standing sentry
In the sheepfold's lath-and-plaster entry,
Six feet long by three feet wide,
Partitioned off from the vast inside —
I blocked up half of it at least.
No remedy; the rain kept driving.
They eyed me much as some wild beast,
That congregation, still arriving,
Some of them by the main road, white
A long way past me into the night,
Skirting the common, then diverging;
Not a few suddenly emerging
From the common's self through the paling-gaps,
— They house in the gravel-pits perhaps,
Where the road stops short with its safeguard border
Of lamps, as tired of such disorder; —
But the most turned in yet more abruptly
From a certain squalid knot of alleys,
Where the town's bad blood once slept corruptly,

Which now the little chapel rallies
And leads into day again, — its priestliness
Lending itself to hide their beastliness
So cleverly (thanks in part to the mason),
And putting so cheery a whitewashed face on
Those neophytes too much in lack of it,
That, where you cross the common as I did,
And meet the party thus presided,
"Mount Zion" with Love-lane at the back of it,
They front you as little disconcerted
As, bound for the hills, her fate averted,
And her wicked people made to mind him,
Lot might have marched with Gomorrah behind him.

II.

Well, from the road, the lanes or the common,
In came the flock: the fat weary woman,
Panting and bewildered, down-clapping
Her umbrella with a mighty report,
Grounded it by me, wry and flapping,
A wreck of whalebones; then, with a snort,
Like a startled horse, at the interloper
(Who humbly knew himself improper,
But could not shrink up small enough)
— Round to the door, and in, — the gruff
Hinge's invariable scold
Making my very blood run cold.
Prompt in the wake of her, up-pattered
On broken clogs, the many-tattered
Little old-faced peaking sister-turned-mother
Of the sickly babe she tried to smother
Somehow up, with its spotted face,
From the cold, on her breast, the one warm place;
She too must stop, wring the poor ends dry
Of a draggled shawl, and add thereby
Her tribute to the door-mat, sopping
Already from my own clothes' dropping,
Which yet she seemed to grudge I should stand on:
Then, stooping down to take off her pattens,
She bore them defiantly, in each hand one,
Planted together before her breast
And its babe, as good as a lance in rest.
Close on her heels, the dingy satins
Of a female something, past me flitted,
With lips as much too white, as a streak
Lay far too red on each hollow cheek;

And it seemed the very door-hinge pitied
All that was left of a woman once,
Holding at least its tongue for the nonce.
Then a tall yellow man, like the Penitent Thief,
With his jaw bound up in a handkerchief,
And eyelids screwed together tight,
Led himself in by some inner light.
And, except from him, from each that entered,
I got the same interrogation —
"What, you the alien, you have ventured
To take with us, the elect, your station?
A carer for none of it, a Gallio!" —
Thus, plain as print, I read the glance
At a common prey, in each countenance
As of huntsman giving his hounds the tallyho.
And, when the door's cry drowned their wonder,
The draught, it always sent in shutting,
Made the flame of the single tallow candle
In the cracked square lantern I stood under,
Shoot its blue lip at me, rebutting
As it were, the luckless cause of scandal:
I verily fancied the zealous light
(In the chapel's secret, too!) for spite
Would shudder itself clean off the wick,
With the airs of a Saint John's Candlestick.
There was no standing it much longer.
"Good folks," thought I, as resolve grew stronger,
"This way you perform the Grand-Inquisitor
When the weather sends you a chance visitor?
You are the men, and wisdom shall die with you,
And none of the old Seven Churches vie with you!
But still, despite the pretty perfection
To which you carry your trick of exclusiveness,
And, taking God's word under wise protection,
Correct its tendency to diffusiveness,
And bid one reach it over hot ploughshares, —
Still, as I say, though you 've found salvation,
If I should choose to cry, as now, 'Shares!' —
See if the best of you bars me my ration!
I prefer, if you please, for my expounder
Of the laws of the feast, the feast's own Founder;
Mine 's the same right with your poorest and sickliest,
Supposing I don the marriage vestiment:
So, shut your mouth and open your Testament,
And carve me my portion at your quickliest!"
Accordingly, as a shoemaker's lad

With wizened face in want of soap,
And wet apron wound round his waist like a rope,
(After stopping outside, for his cough was bad,
To get the fit over, poor gentle creature,
And so avoid disturbing the preacher)
— Passed in, I sent my elbow spikewise
At the shutting door, and entered likewise,
Received the hinge's accustomed greeting,
And crossed the threshold's magic pentacle,
And found myself in full conventicle,
— To wit, in Zion Chapel Meeting.
On the Christmas-Eve of 'Forty-nine,
Which, calling its flock to their special clover,
Found all assembled and one sheep over,
Whose lot, as the weather pleased, was mine.

III.

I very soon had enough of it.
The hot smell and the human noises,
And my neighbor's coat, the greasy cuff of it,
Were a pebble-stone that a child's hand poises,
Compared with the pig-of-lead-like pressure
Of the preaching man's immense stupidity,
As he poured his doctrine forth, full measure,
To meet his audience's avidity.
You needed not the wit of the Sibyl
To guess the cause of it all, in a twinkling:
No sooner our friend had got an inkling
Of treasure hid in the Holy Bible,
(Whene'er 't was the thought first struck him,
How death, at unawares, might duck him
Deeper than the grave, and quench
The gin-shop's light in hell's grim drench)
Than he handled it so, in fine irreverence,
As to hug the book of books to pieces:
And, a patchwork of chapters and texts in severance,
Not improved by the private dog's-ears and creases,
Having clothed his own soul with, he 'd fain see equipt
    yours, —
So tossed you again your Holy Scriptures.
And you picked them up, in a sense, no doubt:
Nay, had but a single face of my neighbors
Appeared to suspect that the preacher's labors
Were help which the world could be saved without,
'T is odds but I might have borne in quiet
A qualm or two at my spiritual diet,

Or (who can tell?) perchance even mustered
Somewhat to urge in behalf of the sermon:
But the flock sat on, divinely flustered,
Sniffing, methought, its dew of Hermon
With such content in every snuffle,
As the devil inside us loves to ruffle.
My old fat woman purred with pleasure,
And thumb round thumb went twirling faster,
While she, to his periods keeping measure,
Maternally devoured the pastor.
The man with the handkerchief untied it,
Showed us a horrible wen inside it,
Gave his eyelids yet another screwing,
And rocked himself as the woman was doing.
The shoemaker's lad, discreetly choking,
Kept down his cough. 'T was too provoking!
My gorge rose at the nonsense and stuff of it;
So, saying like Eve when she plucked the apple,
" I wanted a taste, and now there's enough of it,"
I flung out of the little chapel.

IV.

There was a lull in the rain, a lull
In the wind too; the moon was risen,
And would have shone out pure and full,
But for the ramparted cloud-prison,
Block on block built up in the West,
For what purpose the wind knows best,
Who changes his mind continually.
And the empty other half of the sky
Seemed in its silence as if it knew
What, any moment, might look through
A chance gap in that fortress massy:—
Through its fissures you got hints
Of the flying moon, by the shifting tints,
Now, a dull lion-color, now, brassy
Burning to yellow, and whitest yellow,
Like furnace-smoke just ere flames bellow,
All a-simmer with intense strain
To let her through,—then blank again,
At the hope of her appearance failing.
Just by the chapel, a break in the railing
Shows a narrow path directly across;
'T is ever dry walking there, on the moss—
Besides, you go gently all the way up-hill.
I stooped under and soon felt better;

My head grew lighter, my limbs more supple,
As I walked on, glad to have slipt the fetter.
My mind was full of the scene I had left,
That placid flock, that pastor vociferant,
— How this outside was pure and different!
The sermon, now — what a mingled weft
Of good and ill! Were either less,
Its fellow had colored the whole distinctly ;
But alas for the excellent earnestness,
And the truths, quite true if stated succinctly,
But as surely false, in their quaint presentment,
However to pastor and flock's contentment!
Say rather, such truths looked false to your eyes.
With his provings and parallels twisted and twined,
Till how could you know them, grown double their size
In the natural fog of the good man's mind,
Like yonder spots of our roadside lamps,
Haloed about with the common's damps?
Truth remains true, the fault 's in the prover ;
The zeal was good, and the aspiration ;
And yet, and yet, yet, fifty times over,
Pharaoh received no demonstration,
By his Baker's dream of Baskets Three,
Of the doctrine of the Trinity, —
Although, as our preacher thus embellished it,
Apparently his hearers relished it
With so unfeigned a gust — who knows if
They did not prefer our friend to Joseph?
But so it is everywhere, one way with all of them!
These people have really felt, no doubt,
A something, the motion they style the Call of them ;
And this is their method of bringing about,
By a mechanism of words and tones,
(So many texts in so many groans)
A sort of reviving and reproducing,
More or less perfectly, (who can tell?)
The mood itself, which strengthens by using:
And how that happens, I understand well.
A tune was born in my head last week,
Out of the thump-thump and shriek-shriek
Of the train, as I came by it, up from Manchester ;
And when, next week, I take it back again,
My head will sing to the engine's clack again,
While it only makes my neighbor's haunches stir,
— Finding no dormant musical sprout
In him, as in me, to be jolted out.

'T is the taught already that profits by teaching;
He gets no more from the railway's preaching
Than, from this preacher who does the rail's office, I:
Whom therefore the flock cast a jealous eye on.
Still, why paint over their door " Mount Zion,"
To which all flesh shall come, saith the prophecy?

v.

But wherefore be harsh on a single case?
After how many modes, this Christmas-Eve,
Does the self-same weary thing take place?
The same endeavor to make you believe,
And with much the same effect, no more:
Each method abundantly convincing,
As I say, to those convinced before,
But scarce to be swallowed without wincing
By the not-as-yet-convinced. For me,
I have my own church equally:
And in this church my faith sprang first!
(I said, as I reached the rising ground,
And the wind began again, with a burst
Of rain in my face, and a glad rebound
From the heart beneath, as if, God speeding me,
I entered his church-door, nature leading me)
— In youth I looked to these very skies,
And probing their immensities,
I found God there, his visible power;
Yet felt in my heart, amid all its sense
Of the power, an equal evidence
That his love, there too, was the nobler dower.
For the loving worm within its clod
Were diviner than a loveless god
Amid his worlds, I will dare to say.
You know what I mean: God's all, man's nought:
But also, God, whose pleasure brought
Man into being, stands away
As it were a handbreadth off, to give
Room for the newly-made to live,
And look at him from a place apart,
And use his gifts of brain and heart,
Given, indeed, but to keep forever.
Who speaks of man, then, must not sever
Man's very elements from man,
Saying, " But all is God's " — whose plan
Was to create man and then leave him
Able, his own word saith, to grieve him,

But able to glorify him too,
As a mere machine could never do,
That prayed or praised, all unaware
Of its fitness for aught but praise and prayer,
Made perfect as a thing of course.
Man, therefore, stands on his own stock
Of love and power as a pin-point rock:
And, looking to God who ordained divorce
Of the rock from his boundless continent,
Sees, in his power made evident,
Only excess by a million-fold
O'er the power God gave man in the mould.
For, note: man's hand, first formed to carry
A few pounds' weight, when taught to marry
Its strength with an engine's, lifts a mountain,
— Advancing in power by one degree;
And why count steps through eternity?
But love is the ever-springing fountain:
Man may enlarge or narrow his bed
For the water's play, but the water-head —
How can he multiply or reduce it?
As easy create it, as cause it to cease;
He may profit by it, or abuse it,
But 't is not a thing to bear increase
As power does: be love less or more
In the heart of man, he keeps it shut
Or opes it wide, as he pleases, but
Love's sum remains what it was before.
So, gazing up, in my youth, at love
As seen through power, ever above
All modes which make it manifest,
My soul brought all to a single test —
That he, the Eternal First and Last,
Who, in his power, had so surpassed
All man conceives of what is might, —
Whose wisdom, too, showed infinite,
— Would prove as infinitely good;
Would never, (my soul understood,)
With power to work all love desires,
Bestow e'en less than man requires;
That he who endlessly was teaching,
Above my spirit's utmost reaching,
What love can do in the leaf or stone,
(So that to master this alone,
This done in the stone or leaf for me,
I must go on learning endlessly)

Would never need that I, in turn,
Should point him out defect unheeded,
And show that God had yet to learn
What the meanest human creature needed,
— Not life, to wit, for a few short years,
Tracking his way through doubts and fears,
While the stupid earth on which I stay
Suffers no change, but passive adds
Its myriad years to myriads,
Though I, he gave it to, decay,
Seeing death come and choose about me,
And my dearest ones depart without me.
No: love which, on earth, amid all the shows of it,
Has ever been seen the sole good of life in it,
The love, ever growing there, spite of the strife in it,
Shall arise, made perfect, from death's repose of it.
And I shall behold thee, face to face,
O God, and in thy light retrace
How in all I loved here, still wast thou!
Whom pressing to, then, as I fain would now,
I shall find as able to satiate
The love, thy gift, as my spirit's wonder
Thou art able to quicken and sublimate,
With this sky of thine, that I now walk under,
And glory in thee for, as I gaze
Thus, thus! Oh, let men keep their ways
Of seeking thee in a narrow shrine —
Be this my way! And this is mine!

VI.

For lo, what think you? suddenly
The rain and the wind ceased, and the sky
Received at once the full fruition
Of the moon's consummate apparition.
The black cloud-barricade was riven,
Ruined beneath her feet, and driven
Deep in the West; while, bare and breathless,
North and South and East lay ready
For a glorious thing that, dauntless, deathless,
Sprang across them and stood steady.
'T was a moon-rainbow, vast and perfect,
From heaven to heaven extending, perfect
As the mother-moon's self, full in face.
It rose, distinctly at the base
With its seven proper colors chorded,
Which still, in the rising, were compressed,

CHRISTMAS-EVE AND EASTER-DAY

Until at last they coalesced,
And supreme the spectral creature lorded
In a triumph of whitest white, —
Above which intervened the night.
But above night too, like only the next,
The second of a wondrous sequence,
Reaching in rare and rarer frequence,
Till the heaven of heavens were circumflexed,
Another rainbow rose, a mightier,
Fainter, flushier and flightier, —
Rapture dying along its verge.
Oh, whose foot shall I see emerge,
Whose, from the straining topmost dark,
On to the keystone of that arc?

VII.

This sight was shown me, there and then, —
Me, one out of a world of men,
Singled forth, as the chance might hap
To another if, in a thunderclap
Where I heard noise and you saw flame,
Some one man knew God called his name.
For me, I think I said, "Appear!
Good were it to be ever here.
If thou wilt, let me build to thee
Service-tabernacles three,
Where, forever in thy presence,
In ecstatic acquiescence,
Far alike from thriftless learning
And ignorance's undiscerning,
I may worship and remain!"
Thus at the show above me, gazing
With upturned eyes, I felt my brain
Glutted with the glory, blazing
Throughout its whole mass, over and under,
Until at length it burst asunder
And out of it bodily there streamed,
The too-much glory, as it seemed,
Passing from out me to the ground,
Then palely serpentining round
Into the dark with mazy error.

VIII.

All at once I looked up with terror.
He was there.
He himself with his human air,

On the narrow pathway, just before.
I saw the back of him, no more —
He had left the chapel, then, as I.
I forgot all about the sky.
No face : only the sight
Of a sweepy garment, vast and white,
With a hem that I could recognize.
I felt terror, no surprise ;
My mind filled with the cataract
At one bound of the mighty fact.
" I remember, he did say
Doubtless that, to this world's end,
Where two or three should meet and pray,
He would be in the midst, their friend ;
Certainly he was there with them ! "
And my pulses leaped for joy
Of the golden thought without alloy,
That I saw his very vesture's hem.
Then rushed the blood back, cold and clear,
With a fresh enhancing shiver of fear ;
And I hastened, cried out while I pressed
To the salvation of the vest,
" But not so, Lord ! It cannot be
That thou, indeed, art leaving me —
Me, that have despised thy friends !
Did my heart make no amends ?
Thou art the love of God — above
His power, didst hear me place his love,
And that was leaving the world for thee.
Therefore thou must not turn from me
As I had chosen the other part !
Folly and pride o'ercame my heart.
Our best is bad, nor bears thy test ;
Still, it should be our very best.
I thought it best that thou, the spirit,
Be worshipped in spirit and in truth,
And in beauty, as even we require it —
Not in the forms burlesque, uncouth,
I left but now, as scarcely fitted
For thee : I knew not what I pitied.
But, all I felt there, right or wrong,
What is it to thee, who curest sinning ?
Am I not weak as thou art strong ?
I have looked to thee from the beginning,
Straight up to thee through all the world
Which, like an idle scroll, lay furled

To nothingness on either side :
And since the time thou wast descried,
Spite of the weak heart, so have I
Lived ever, and so fain would die,
Living and dying, thee before !
But if thou leavest me " —

IX.

Less or more,
I suppose that I spoke thus.
When, — have mercy, Lord, on us !
The whole face turned upon me full.
And I spread myself beneath it,
As when the bleacher spreads, to seethe it
In the cleansing sun, his wool, —
Steeps in the flood of noontide whiteness
Some defiled, discolored web —
So lay I, saturate with brightness.
And when the flood appeared to ebb,
Lo, I was walking, light and swift,
With my senses settling fast and steadying,
But my body caught up in the whirl and drift
Of the vesture's amplitude, still eddying
On, just before me, still to be followed,
As it carried me after with its motion :
What shall I say ? — as a path were hollowed
And a man went weltering through the ocean,
Sucked along in the flying wake
Of the luminous water-snake.
Darkness and cold were cloven, as through
I passed, upborne yet walking too.
And I turned to myself at intervals, —
" So he said, so it befalls.
God who registers the cup
Of mere cold water, for his sake
To a disciple rendered up.
Disdains not his own thirst to slake
At the poorest love was ever offered :
And because my heart I proffered,
With true love trembling at the brim,
He suffers me to follow him
Forever, my own way, — dispensed
From seeking to be influenced
By all the less immediate ways
That earth, in worships manifold,
Adopts to reach, by prayer and praise,
The garment's hem, which, lo, I hold ! "

X.

And so we crossed the world and stopped.
For where am I, in city or plain,
Since I am 'ware of the world again?
And what is this that rises propped
With pillars of prodigious girth?
Is it really on the earth,
This miraculous Dome of God?
Has the angel's measuring-rod
Which numbered cubits, gem from gem,
'Twixt the gates of the New Jerusalem,
Meted it out, — and what he meted,
Have the sons of men completed?
— Binding, ever as he bade,
Columns in the colonnade
With arms wide open to embrace
The entry of the human race
To the breast of . . . . what is it, yon building,
Ablaze in front, all paint and gilding,
With marble for brick, and stones of price
For garniture of the edifice?
Now I see; it is no dream;
It stands there and it does not seem:
Forever, in pictures, thus it looks,
And thus I have read of it in books
Often in England, leagues away,
And wondered how these fountains play,
Growing up eternally
Each to a musical water-tree,
Whose blossoms drop, a glittering boon,
Before my eyes, in the light of the moon,
To the granite lavers underneath.
Liar and dreamer in your teeth!
I, the sinner that speak to you,
Was in Rome this night, and stood, and knew
Both this and more. For see, for see,
The dark is rent, mine eye is free
To pierce the crust of the outer wall,
And I view inside, and all there, all,
As the swarming hollow of a hive,
The whole Basilica alive!
Men in the chancel, body and nave,
Men on the pillars' architrave,
Men on the statues, men on the tombs
With popes and kings in their porphyry wombs,

All famishing in expectation
Of the main-altar's consummation.
For see, for see, the rapturous moment
Approaches, and earth's best endowment
Blends with heaven's; the taper-fires
Pant up, the winding brazen spires
Heave loftier yet the baldachin;
The incense-gaspings, long kept in,
Suspire in clouds; the organ blatant
Holds his breath and grovels latent,
As if God's hushing finger grazed him,
(Like Behemoth when he praised him)
At the silver bell's shrill tinkling,
Quick cold drops of terror sprinkling
On the sudden pavement strewed
With faces of the multitude.
Earth breaks up, time drops away,
In flows heaven, with its new day
Of endless life, when He who trod,
Very man and very God,
This earth in weakness, shame and pain,
Dying the death whose signs remain
Up yonder on the accursed tree, —
Shall come again, no more to be
Of captivity the thrall,
But the one God. All in all,
King of kings, Lord of lords,
As His servant John received the words,
" I died, and live forevermore! "

XI.

Yet I was left outside the door.
" Why sit I here on the threshold-stone,
Left till He return, alone
Save for the garment's extreme fold
Abandoned still to bless my hold? "
My reason, to my doubt, replied,
As if a book were opened wide,
And at a certain page I traced
Every record undefaced,
Added by successive years, —
The harvestings of truth's stray ears
Singly gleaned, and in one sheaf
Bound together for belief.
Yes, I said — that he will go
And sit with these in turn, I know.

Their faith's heart beats, though her head swims
Too giddily to guide her limbs,
Disabled by their palsy-stroke
From propping mine. Though Rome's gross yoke
Drops off, no more to be endured,
Her teaching is not so obscured
By errors and perversities,
That no truth shines athwart the lies:
And he, whose eye detects a spark
Even where, to man's, the whole seems dark,
May well see flame where each beholder
Acknowledges the embers smoulder.
But I, a mere man, fear to quit
The clue God gave me as most fit
To guide my footsteps through life's maze,
Because himself discerns all ways
Open to reach him: I, a man
Able to mark where faith began
To swerve aside, till from its summit
Judgment drops her damning plummet,
Pronouncing such a fatal space
Departed from the founder's base:
He will not bid me enter too,
But rather sit, as now I do,
Awaiting his return outside.
— 'T was thus my reason straight replied
And joyously I turned, and pressed
The garment's skirt upon my breast,
Until, afresh its light suffusing me,
My heart cried — " What has been abusing me
That I should wait here lonely and coldly,
Instead of rising, entering boldly,
Baring truth's face, and letting drift
Her veils of lies as they choose to shift?
Do these men praise him? I will raise
My voice up to their point of praise!
I see the error; but above
The scope of error, see the love. —
Oh, love of those first Christian days!
— Fanned so soon into a blaze,
From the spark preserved by the trampled sect,
That the antique sovereign Intellect
Which then sat ruling in the world,
Like a change in dreams, was hurled
From the throne he reigned upon:
You looked up and he was gone.

Gone, his glory of the pen!
— Love, with Greece and Rome in ken,
Bade her scribes abhor the trick
Of poetry and rhetoric,
And exult with hearts set free,
In blessed imbecility
Scrawled, perchance, on some torn sheet
Leaving Sallust incomplete.
Gone, his pride of sculptor, painter!
— Love, while able to acquaint her
While the thousand statues yet
Fresh from chisel, pictures wet
From brush, she saw on every side,
Chose rather with an infant's pride
To frame those portents which impart
Such unction to true Christian Art.
Gone, music too! The air was stirred
By happy wings: Terpander's bird
(That, when the cold came, fled away)
Would tarry not the wintry day, —
As more-enduring sculpture must,
Till filthy saints rebuked the gust
With which they chanced to get a sight
Of some dear naked Aphrodite
They glanced a thought above the toes of,
By breaking zealously her nose off.
Love, surely, from that music's lingering,
Might have filched her organ-fingering,
Nor chosen rather to set prayings
To hog-grunts, praises to horse-neighings.
Love was the startling thing, the new:
Love was the all-sufficient too;
And seeing that, you see the rest:
As a babe can find its mother's breast
As well in darkness as in light,
Love shut our eyes, and all seemed right.
True, the world's eyes are open now:
— Less need for me to disallow
Some few that keep Love's zone unbuckled,
Peevish as ever to be suckled,
Lulled by the same old baby-prattle
With intermixture of the rattle,
When she would have them creep, stand steady
Upon their feet, or walk already,
Not to speak of trying to climb.
I will be wise another time,

And not desire a wall between us,
When next I see a church-roof cover
So many species of one genus,
All with foreheads bearing *lover*
Written above the earnest eyes of them;
All with breasts that beat for beauty,
Whether sublimed, to the surprise of them,
In noble daring, steadfast duty,
The heroic in passion, or in action, —
Or, lowered for sense's satisfaction,
To the mere outside of human creatures,
Mere perfect form and faultless features.
What? with all Rome here, whence to levy
Such contributions to their appetite,
With women and men in a gorgeous bevy,
They take, as it were, a padlock, clap it tight
On their southern eyes, restrained from feeding
On the glories of their ancient reading,
On the beauties of their modern singing,
On the wonders of the builder's bringing,
On the majesties of Art around them, —
And, all these loves, late struggling incessant,
When faith has at last united and bound them,
They offer up to God for a present?
Why, I will, on the whole, be rather proud of it, —
And, only taking the act in reference
To the other recipients who might have allowed it,
I will rejoice that God had the preference."

XII.

So I summed up my new resolves:
Too much love there can never be.
And where the intellect devolves
Its function on love exclusively,
I, a man who possesses both,
Will accept the provision, nothing loth,
— Will feast my love, then depart elsewhere,
That my intellect may find its share.
And ponder, O soul, the while thou departest,
And see thou applaud the great heart of the artist,
Who, examining the capabilities
Of the block of marble he has to fashion
Into a type of thought or passion, —
Not always, using obvious facilities,
Shapes it, as any artist can,
Into a perfect symmetrical man,

Complete from head to foot of the life-size.
Such as old Adam stood in his wife's eyes, —
But, now and then, bravely aspires to consummate
A Colossus by no means so easy to come at,
And uses the whole of his block for the bust,
Leaving the mind of the public to finish it,
Since cut it ruefully short he must :
On the face alone he expends his devotion,
He rather would mar than resolve to diminish it,
— Saying, "Applaud me for this grand notion
Of what a face may be ! As for completing it
In breast and body and limbs, do that, you !"
All hail ! I fancy how, happily meeting it,
A trunk and legs would perfect the statue,
Could man carve so as to answer volition.
And how much nobler than petty cavils,
Were a hope to find, in my spirit-travels,
Some artist of another ambition,
Who having a block to carve, no bigger,
Has spent his power on the opposite quest,
And believed to begin at the feet was best —
For so may I see, ere I die, the whole figure !

XIII.

No sooner said than out in the night !
My heart beat lighter and more light :
And still, as before. I was walking swift,
With my senses settling fast and steadying.
But my body caught up in the whirl and drift
Of the vesture's amplitude, still eddying
On just before me, still to be followed,
As it carried me after with its motion.
— What shall I say ? — as a path were hollowed,
And a man went weltering through the ocean,
Sucked along in the flying wake
Of the luminous water-snake.

XIV.

Alone ! I am left alone once more —
(Save for the garment's extreme fold
Abandoned still to bless my hold)
Alone, beside the entrance-door
Of a sort of temple, — perhaps a college,
— Like nothing I ever saw before
At home in England, to my knowledge.
The tall old quaint irregular town !

It may be . . . though which, I can't affirm . . . any
Of the famous middle-age towns of Germany;
And this flight of stairs where I sit down,
Is it Halle, Weimar, Cassel, Frankfort,
Or Göttingen, I have to thank for 't?
It may be Göttingen, — most likely.
Through the open door I catch obliquely
Glimpses of a lecture-hall;
And not a bad assembly neither,
Ranged decent and symmetrical
On benches, waiting what's to see there;
Which, holding still by the vesture's hem,
I also resolve to see with them,
Cautious this time how I suffer to slip
The chance of joining in fellowship
With any that call themselves his friends;
As these folks do, I have a notion.
But list — a buzzing and emotion!
All settle themselves, the while ascends
By the creaking rail to the lecture-desk,
Step by step, deliberate
Because of his cranium's over-freight,
Three parts sublime to one grotesque,
If I have proved an accurate guesser,
The hawk-nosed, high-cheekboned Professor.
I felt at once as if there ran
A shoot of love from my heart to the man —
That sallow virgin-minded studious
Martyr to mild enthusiasm,
As he uttered a kind of cough-preludious
That woke my sympathetic spasm,
(Beside some spitting that made me sorry)
And stood, surveying his auditory
With a wan pure look, wellnigh celestial, —
Those blue eyes had survived so much!
While, under the foot they could not smutch,
Lay all the fleshly and the bestial.
Over he bowed, and arranged his notes,
Till the auditory's clearing of throats
Was done with, died into a silence;
And, when each glance was upward sent,
Each bearded mouth composed intent,
And a pin might be heard drop half a mile hence, —
He pushed back higher his spectacles,
Let the eyes stream out like lamps from cells,
And giving his head of hair — a shake

Of undressed tow, for color and quantity —
One rapid and impatient shake,
(As our own young England adjusts a jaunty tie
When about to impart, on mature digestion,
Some thrilling view of the surplice-question)
— The Professor's grave voice, sweet though hoarse,
Broke into his Christmas-Eve discourse.

XV.

And he began it by observing
How reason dictated that men
Should rectify the natural swerving,
By a reversion, now and then,
To the well-heads of knowledge, few
And far away, whence rolling grew
The life-stream wide whereat we drink,
Commingled, as we needs must think,
With waters alien to the source;
To do which, aimed this eve's discourse;
Since, where could be a fitter time
For tracing backward to its prime,
This Christianity, this lake,
This reservoir, whereat we slake,
From one or other bank, our thirst?
So, he proposed inquiring first
Into the various sources whence
This Myth of Christ is derivable;
Demanding from the evidence,
(Since plainly no such life was livable)
How these phenomena should class?
Whether 't were best opine Christ was,
Or never was at all, or whether
He was and was not, both together —
It matters little for the name,
So the idea be left the same.
Only, for practical purpose' sake,
'T was obviously as well to take
The popular story, — understanding
How the ineptitude of the time,
And the penman's prejudice, expanding
Fact into fable fit for the clime,
Had, by slow and sure degrees, translated it
Into this myth, this Individuum, —
Which, when reason had strained and abated it
Of foreign matter, left, for residuum,
A Man! — a right true man, however,

Whose work was worthy a man's endeavor:
Work, that gave warrant almost sufficient
To his disciples, for rather believing
He was just omnipotent and omniscient,
As it gives to us, for as frankly receiving
His word, their tradition, — which, though it meant
Something entirely different
From all that those who only heard it,
In their simplicity thought and averred it,
Had yet a meaning quite as respectable:
For, among other doctrines delectable,
Was he not surely the first to insist on
The natural sovereignty of our race? —
Here the lecturer came to a pausing-place.
And while his cough, like a droughty piston,
Tried to dislodge the husk that grew to him,
I seized the occasion of bidding adieu to him,
The vesture still within my hand.

XVI.

I could interpret its command.
This time he would not bid me enter
The exhausted air-bell of the Critic.
Truth's atmosphere may grow mephitic
When Papist struggles with Dissenter,
Impregnating its pristine clarity,
— One, by his daily fare's vulgarity,
Its gust of broken meat and garlic;
— One, by his soul's too-much presuming
To turn the frankincense's fuming
And vapors of the candle starlike
Into the cloud her wings she buoys on.
Each, that thus sets the pure air seething,
May poison it for healthy breathing —
But the Critic leaves no air to poison;
Pumps out with ruthless ingenuity
Atom by atom, and leaves you — vacuity.
Thus much of Christ does he reject?
And what retain? His intellect?
What is it I must reverence duly?
Poor intellect for worship, truly,
Which tells me simply what was told
(If mere morality, bereft
Of the God in Christ, be all that's left)
Elsewhere by voices manifold;
With this advantage, that the stater

Made nowise the important stumble
Of adding, he, the sage and humble,
Was also one with the Creator.
You urge Christ's followers' simplicity:
But how does shifting blame evade it?
Have wisdom's words no more felicity?
The stumbling-block, his speech — who laid it?
How comes it that for one found able
To sift the truth of it from fable,
Millions believe it to the letter?
Christ's goodness, then — does that fare better?
Strange goodness, which upon the score
Of being goodness, the mere due
Of man to fellow-man, much more
To God — should take another view
Of its possessor's privilege,
And bid him rule his race! You pledge
Your fealty to such rule? What, all —
From heavenly John and Attic Paul,
And that brave weather-battered Peter,
Whose stout faith only stood completer
For buffets, sinning to be pardoned,
As, more his hands hauled nets, they hardened, —
All, down to you, the man of men,
Professing here at Göttingen,
Compose Christ's flock! They, you and I,
Are sheep of a good man! And why?
The goodness, — how did he acquire it?
Was it self-gained, did God inspire it?
Choose which; then tell me, on what ground
Should its possessor dare propound
His claim to rise o'er us an inch?
Were goodness all some man's invention,
Who arbitrarily made mention
What we should follow, and whence flinch, —
What qualities might take the style
Of right and wrong, — and had such guessing
Met with as general acquiescing
As graced the alphabet erewhile,
When A got leave an Ox to be.
No Camel (quoth the Jews) like G, —
For thus inventing thing and title
Worship were that man's fit requital.
But if the common conscience must
Be ultimately judge, adjust
Its apt name to each quality

Already known, — I would decree
Worship for such mere demonstration
And simple work of nomenclature,
Only the day I praised, not nature,
But Harvey, for the circulation.
I would praise such a Christ, with pride
And joy, that he, as none beside,
Had taught us how to keep the mind
God gave him, as God gave his kind,
Freer than they from fleshly taint:
I would call such a Christ our Saint,
As I declare our Poet, him
Whose insight makes all others dim:
A thousand poets pried at life,
And only one amid the strife
Rose to be Shakespeare: each shall take
His crown, I'd say, for the world's sake —
Though some objected — "Had we seen
The heart and head of each, what screen
Was broken there to give them light,
While in ourselves it shuts the sight,
We should no more admire, perchance,
That these found truth out at a glance,
Than marvel how the bat discerns
Some pitch-dark cavern's fifty turns,
Led by a finer tact, a gift
He boasts, which other birds must shift
Without, and grope as best they can."
No, freely I would praise the man, —
Nor one whit more, if he contended
That gift of his from God descended.
Ah friend, what gift of man's does not?
No nearer something, by a jot,
Rise an infinity of nothings
Than one: take Euclid for your teacher:
Distinguish kinds: do crownings, clothings,
Make that creator which was creature?
Multiply gifts upon man's head,
And what, when all's done, shall be said
But — the more gifted he, I ween!
That one's made Christ, this other, Pilate,
And this might be all that has been, —
So what is there to frown or smile at?
What is left for us, save, in growth
Of soul, to rise up, far past both,
From the gift looking to the giver,

And from the cistern to the river,
And from the finite to infinity,
And from man's dust to God's divinity?

XVII.

Take all in a word: the truth in God's breast
Lies trace for trace upon ours impressed:
Though he is so bright and we so dim,
We are made in his image to witness him:
And were no eye in us to tell,
Instructed by no inner sense,
The light of heaven from the dark of hell,
That light would want its evidence, —
Though justice, good and truth were still
Divine, if, by some demon's will,
Hatred and wrong had been proclaimed
Law through the worlds, and right misnamed.
No mere exposition of morality
Made or in part or in totality,
Should win you to give it worship, therefore:
And, if no better proof you will care for,
— Whom do you count the worst man upon earth?
Be sure, he knows, in his conscience, more
Of what right is, than arrives at birth
In the best man's acts that we bow before:
This last knows better — true, but my fact is,
'T is one thing to know, and another to practise.
And thence I conclude that the real God-function
Is to furnish a motive and injunction
For practising what we know already.
And such an injunction and such a motive
As the God in Christ, do you waive, and "heady,
High-minded," hang your tablet-votive
Outside the fane on a finger-post?
Morality to the uttermost,
Supreme in Christ as we all confess,
Why need we prove would avail no jot
To make him God, if God he were not?
What is the point where himself lays stress?
Does the precept run " Believe in good,
In justice, truth, now understood
For the first time"? — or, " Believe in me,
Who lived and died, yet essentially
Am Lord of Life"? Whoever can take
The same to his heart and for mere love's sake
Conceive of the love, — that man obtains

A new truth; no conviction gains
Of an old one only, made intense
By a fresh appeal to his faded sense.

XVIII.

Can it be that he stays inside?
Is the vesture left me to commune with?
Could my soul find aught to sing in tune with
Even at this lecture, if she tried?
Oh, let me at lowest sympathize
With the lurking drop of blood that lies
In the desiccated brain's white roots
Without throb for Christ's attributes,
As the lecturer makes his special boast!
If love's dead there, it has left a ghost.
Admire we, how from heart to brain
(Though to say so strike the doctors dumb)
One instinct rises and falls again,
Restoring the equilibrium.
And how when the Critic had done his best,
And the pearl of price, at reason's test,
Lay dust and ashes levigable
On the Professor's lecture-table, —
When we looked for the inference and monition
That our faith, reduced to such condition,
Be swept forthwith to its natural dust-hole, —
He bids us, when we least expect it,
Take back our faith, — if it be not just whole,
Yet a pearl indeed, as his tests affect it,
Which fact pays damage done rewardingly,
So, prize we our dust and ashes accordingly!
"Go home and venerate the myth
I thus have experimented with —
This man, continue to adore him
Rather than all who went before him,
And all who ever followed after!" —
Surely for this I may praise you, my brother!
Will you take the praise in tears or laughter?
That's one point gained: can I compass another?
Unlearned love was safe from spurning —
Can't we respect your loveless learning?
Let us at least give learning honor!
What laurels had we showered upon her,
Girding her loins up to perturb
Our theory of the Middle Verb;
Or Turk-like brandishing a scimitar

O'er anapæsts in comic-trimeter ;
Or curing the halt and maimed "Iketides,"
While we lounged on at our indebted ease :
Instead of which, a tricksy demon
Sets her at Titus or Philemon !
When ignorance wags his ears of leather
And hates God's word, 't is altogether ;
Nor leaves he his congenial thistles
To go and browse on Paul's Epistles.
— And you, the audience, who might ravage
The world wide, enviably savage,
Nor heed the cry of the retriever,
More than Herr Heine (before his fever), —
I do not tell a lie so arrant
As say my passion's wings are furled up,
And, without plainest heavenly warrant,
I were ready and glad to give the world up —
But still, when you rub brow meticulous,
And ponder the profit of turning holy
If not for God's, for your own sake solely,
— God forbid I should find you ridiculous !
Deduce from this lecture all that eases you,
Nay, call yourselves, if the calling pleases you,
Christians,"— abhor the deist's pravity. —
Go on, you shall no more move my gravity
Than, when I see boys ride a-cockhorse,
I find it in my heart to embarrass them
By hinting that their stick 's a mock horse,
And they really carry what they say carries them.

XIX.

So sat I talking with my mind.
I did not long to leave the door
And find a new church, as before,
But rather was quiet and inclined
To prolong and enjoy the gentle resting
From further tracking and trying and testing.
"This tolerance is a genial mood :"
(Said I, and a little pause ensued.)
"One trims the bark 'twixt shoal and shelf,
And sees, each side, the good effects of it,
A value for religion's self,
A carelessness about the sects of it.
Let me enjoy my own conviction,
Not watch my neighbor's faith with fretfulness,
Still spying there some dereliction

Of truth, perversity, forgetfulness!
Better a mild indifferentism,
Teaching that both our faiths (though duller
His shine through a dull spirit's prism)
Originally had one color!
Better pursue a pilgrimage
Through ancient and through modern times
To many peoples, various climes,
Where I may see saint, savage, sage
Fuse their respective creeds in one
Before the general Father's throne!"

XX.

— 'T was the horrible storm began afresh!
The black night caught me in his mesh,
Whirled me up, and flung me prone.
I was left on the college-step alone.
I looked, and far there, ever fleeting
Far, far away, the receding gesture,
And looming of the lessening vesture! —
Swept forward from my stupid hand,
While I watched my foolish heart expand
In the lazy glow of benevolence,
O'er the various modes of man's belief.
I sprang up with fear's vehemence.
Needs must there be one way, our chief
Best way of worship: let me strive
To find it, and when found, contrive
My fellows also take their share!
This constitutes my earthly care:
God's is above it and distinct.
For I, a man, with men am linked
And not a brute with brutes; no gain
That I experience, must remain
Unshared: but should my best endeavor
To share it, fail — subsisteth ever
God's care above, and I exult
That God, by God's own ways occult,
May — doth, I will believe — bring back
All wanderers to a single track.
Meantime, I can but testify
God's care for me — no more, can I —
It is but for myself I know;
The world rolls witnessing around me
Only to leave me as it found me;
Men cry there, but my ear is slow:

Their races flourish or decay
— What boots it, while yon lucid way
Loaded with stars divides the vault?
But soon my soul repairs its fault
When, sharpening sense's hebetude,
She turns on my own life! So viewed,
No mere mote's-breadth but teems immense
With witnessings of providence:
And woe to me if when I look
Upon that record, the sole book
Unsealed to me, I take no heed
Of any warning that I read!
Have I been sure, this Christmas-Eve,
God's own hand did the rainbow weave,
Whereby the truth from heaven slid
Into my soul? — I cannot bid
The world admit he stooped to heal
My soul, as if in a thunder-peal
Where one heard noise, and one saw flame,
I only knew he named my name:
But what is the world to me, for sorrow
Or joy in its censure, when to-morrow
It drops the remark, with just-turned head,
Then, on again, "That man is dead"?
Yes, but for me — my name called, — drawn
As a conscript's lot from the lap's black yawn,
He has dipt into on a battle-dawn:
Bid out of life by a nod, a glance, —
Stumbling, mute-mazed, at nature's chance, —
With a rapid finger circled round,
Fixed to the first poor inch of ground
To fight from, where his foot was found;
Whose ear but a minute since lay free
To the wide camp's buzz and gossipry —
Summoned, a solitary man,
To end his life where his life began,
From the safe glad rear, to the dreadful van!
Soul of mine, hadst thou caught and held
By the hem of the vesture! —

XXI.

       And I caught
At the flying robe, and unrepelled
Was lapped again in its folds full-fraught
With warmth and wonder and delight,
God's mercy being infinite.

For scarce had the words escaped my tongue,
When, at a passionate bound, I sprung
Out of the wandering world of rain,
Into the little chapel again.

XXII.

How else was I found there, bolt upright
On my bench, as if I had never left it?
— Never flung out on the common at night,
Nor met the storm and wedge-like cleft it,
Seen the raree-show of Peter's successor,
Or the laboratory of the Professor!
For the Vision, that was true, I wist,
True as that heaven and earth exist.
There sat my friend, the yellow and tall,
With his neck and its wen in the selfsame place;
Yet my nearest neighbor's cheek showed gall.
She had slid away a contemptuous space:
And the old fat woman, late so placable,
Eyed me with symptoms, hardly mistakable,
Of her milk of kindness turning rancid.
In short, a spectator might have fancied
That I had nodded, betrayed by slumber,
Yet kept my seat, a warning ghastly,
Through the heads of the sermon, nine in number,
And woke up now at the tenth and lastly.
But again, could such disgrace have happened?
Each friend at my elbow had surely nudged it:
And, as for the sermon, where did my nap end?
Unless I heard it, could I have judged it?
Could I report as I do at the close,
First, the preacher speaks through his nose:
Second, his gesture is too emphatic:
Thirdly, to waive what's pedagogic,
The subject-matter itself lacks logic:
Fourthly, the English is ungrammatic.
Great news! the preacher is found no Pascal,
Whom, if I pleased, I might to the task call
Of making square to a finite eye
The circle of infinity,
And find so all-but-just-succeeding!
Great news! the sermon proves no reading
Where bee-like in the flowers I bury me,
Like Taylor's, the immortal Jeremy!
And now that I know the very worst of him,
What was it I thought to obtain at first of him?

Ha! Is God mocked, as he asks?
Shall I take on me to change his tasks,
And dare, dispatched to a river-head
For a simple draught of the element,
Neglect the thing for which he sent,
And return with another thing instead? —
Saying, " Because the water found
Welling up from underground,
Is mingled with the taints of earth,
While thou, I know, dost laugh at dearth,
And couldst, at wink or word, convulse
The world with the leap of a river-pulse. —
Therefore I turned from the oozings muddy,
And bring thee a chalice I found, instead:
See the brave veins in the breccia ruddy!
One would suppose that the marble bled.
What matters the water? A hope I have nursed
The waterless cup will quench my thirst."
— Better have knelt at the poorest stream
That trickles in pain from the straitest rift!
For the less or the more is all God's gift,
Who blocks up or breaks wide the granite-seam.
And here, is there water or not, to drink?
I then, in ignorance and weakness,
Taking God's help, have attained to think
My heart does best to receive in meekness
That mode of worship, as most to his mind,
Where earthly aids being cast behind,
His All in All appears serene
With the thinnest human veil between,
Letting the mystic lamps, the seven,
The many motions of his spirit,
Pass, as they list, to earth from heaven.
For the preacher's merit or demerit,
It were to be wished the flaws were fewer
In the earthen vessel, holding treasure
Which lies as safe in a golden ewer;
But the main thing is, does it hold good measure?
Heaven soon sets right all other matters! —
Ask, else, these ruins of humanity,
This flesh worn out to rags and tatters,
This soul at struggle with insanity,
Who thence take comfort — can I doubt? —
Which an empire gained, were a loss without.
May it be mine! And let us hope
That no worse blessing befall the Pope.

Turn'd sick at last of to-day's buffoonery,
Of posturings and petticoatings,
Beside his Bourbon bully's gloatings
In the bloody orgies of drunk poltroonery!
Nor may the Professor forego its peace
At Göttingen presently, when, in the dusk
Of his life, if his cough, as I fear, should increase,
Prophesied of by that horrible husk —
When thicker and thicker the darkness fills
The world through his misty spectacles,
And he gropes for something more substantial
Than a fable, myth or personification, —
May Christ do for him what no mere man shall,
And stand confessed as the God of salvation!
Meantime, in the still recurring fear
Lest myself, at unawares, be found,
While attacking the choice of my neighbors round,
With none of my own made — I choose here!
The giving out of the hymn reclaims me;
I have done : and if any blames me,
Thinking that merely to touch in brevity
The topics I dwell on, were unlawful, —
Or worse, that I trench, with undue levity,
On the bounds of the holy and the awful, —
I praise the heart, and pity the head of him,
And refer myself to THEE, instead of him,
Who head and heart alike discernest,
Looking below light speech we utter,
When frothy spume and frequent sputter
Prove that the soul's depths boil in earnest!
May truth shine out, stand ever before us!
I put up pencil and join chorus
To Hepzibah Tune, without further apology,
The last five verses of the third section
Of the seventeenth hymn of Whitfield's Collection,
To conclude with the doxology.

EASTER-DAY.

I.

How very hard it is to be
A Christian! Hard for you and me,
— Not the mere task of making real
That duty up to its ideal,
Effecting thus, complete and whole,

A purpose of the human soul —
For that is always hard to do;
But hard, I mean, for me and you
To realize it, more or less,
With even the moderate success
Which commonly repays our strife
To carry out the aims of life.
"This aim is greater," you will say,
"And so more arduous every way."
— But the importance of their fruits
Still proves to man, in all pursuits,
Proportional encouragement.
"Then, what if it be God's intent
That labor to this one result
Should seem unduly difficult?"
Ah, that's a question in the dark —
And the sole thing that I remark
Upon the difficulty, this:
We do not see it where it is,
At the beginning of the race:
As we proceed, it shifts its place,
And where we looked for crowns to fall,
We find the tug's to come, — that's all.

II.

At first you say, "The whole, or chief
Of difficulties, is belief.
Could I believe once thoroughly,
The rest were simple. What? Am I
An idiot, do you think, — a beast?
Prove to me, only that the least
Command of God is God's indeed,
And what injunction shall I need
To pay obedience? Death so nigh,
When time must end, eternity
Begin, — and cannot I compute,
Weigh loss and gain together, suit
My actions to the balance drawn,
And give my body to be sawn
Asunder, hacked in pieces, tied
To horses, stoned, burned, crucified,
Like any martyr of the list?
How gladly! — if I make acquist,
Through the brief minute's fierce annoy,
Of God's eternity of joy."

III.

— And certainly you name the point
Whereon all turns : for could you joint
This flexile finite life once tight
Into the fixed and infinite,
You, safe inside, would spurn what's out,
With carelessness enough, no doubt —
Would spurn mere life : but when time brings
To their next stage your reasonings,
Your eyes, late wide, begin to wink
Nor see the path so well, I think.

IV.

You say, " Faith may be, one agrees,
A touchstone for God's purposes,
Even as ourselves conceive of them.
Could he acquit us or condemn
For holding what no hand can loose,
Rejecting when we can't but choose?
As well award the victor's wreath
To whosoever should take breath
Duly each minute while he lived —
Grant heaven, because a man contrived
To see its sunlight every day
He walked forth on the public way.
You must mix some uncertainty
With faith, if you would have faith be.
Why, what but faith, do we abhor
And idolize each other for —
Faith in our evil or our good,
Which is or is not understood
Aright by those we love or those
We hate, thence called our friends or foes?
Your mistress saw your spirit's grace,
When, turning from the ugly face,
I found belief in it too hard;
And she and I have our reward.
— Yet here a doubt peeps : well for us
Weak beings, to go using thus
A touchstone for our little ends,
Trying with faith the foes and friends;
— But God, bethink you! I would fain
Conceive of the Creator's reign
As based upon exacter laws
Than creatures build by with applause.

In all God's acts — (as Plato cries
He doth) — he should geometrize.
Whence, I desiderate" . . .

v.

I see!
You would grow as a natural tree,
Stand as a rock, soar up like fire.
The world's so perfect and entire,
Quite above faith, so right and fit!
Go there, walk up and down in it!
No. The creation travails, groans —
Contrive your music from its moans.
Without or let or hindrance, friend!
That's an old story, and its end
As old — you come back (be sincere)
With every question you put here
(Here where there once was, and is still,
We think, a living oracle,
Whose answers you stand carping at)
This time flung back unanswered flat, —
Beside, perhaps, as many more
As those that drove you out before,
Now added, where was little need.
Questions impossible, indeed,
To us who sat still, all and each
Persuaded that our earth had speech,
Of God's, writ down, no matter if
In cursive type or hieroglyph, —
Which one fact freed us from the yoke
Of guessing why He never spoke.
You come back in no better plight
Than when you left us, — am I right?

vi.

So, the old process, I conclude,
Goes on, the reasoning's pursued
Further. You own, " 'T is well averred,
A scientific faith's absurd.
— Frustrates the very end 't was meant
To serve. So, I would rest content
With a mere probability,
But, probable; the chance must lie
Clear on one side. — lie all in rough,
So long as there be just enough
To pin my faith to, though it hap

Only at points : from gap to gap
One hangs up a huge curtain so,
Grandly, nor seeks to have it go
Foldless and flat along the wall.
What care I if some interval
Of life less plainly may depend
On God ?   I 'd hang there to the end ;
And thus I should not find it hard
To be a Christian and debarred
From trailing on the earth, till furled
Away by death. — Renounce the world !
Were that a mighty hardship ?   Plan
A pleasant life, and straight some man
Beside you, with, if he thought fit,
Abundant means to compass it,
Shall turn deliberate aside
To try and live as, if you tried
You clearly might, yet most despise.
One friend of mine wears out his eyes,
Slighting the stupid joys of sense,
In patient hope that, ten years hence,
' Somewhat completer,' he may say,
' My list of *coleoptera !* '
While just the other who most laughs
At him, above all epitaphs
Aspires to have his tomb describe
Himself as sole among the tribe
Of snuffbox-fanciers, who possessed
A Grignon with the Regent's crest.
So that, subduing, as you want,
Whatever stands predominant
Among my earthly appetites
For tastes and smells and sounds and sights,
I shall be doing that alone,
To gain a palm-branch and a throne,
Which fifty people undertake
To do, and gladly, for the sake
Of giving a Semitic guess,
Or playing pawns at blindfold chess."

VII.

Good : and the next thing is, — look round
For evidence enough !   'T is found,
No doubt : as is your sort of mind,
So is your sort of search : you 'll find
What you desire, and that 's to be

A Christian. What says history?
How comforting a point it were
To find some mummy-scrap declare
There lived a Moses! Better still,
Prove Jonah's whale translatable
Into some quicksand of the seas,
Isle, cavern, rock, or what you please,
That faith might flap her wings and crow
From such an eminence! Or, no —
The human heart 's best; you prefer
Making that prove the minister
To truth ; you probe its wants and needs,
And hopes and fears, then try what creeds
Meet these most aptly, — resolute
That faith plucks such substantial fruit
Wherever these two correspond,
She little needs to look beyond,
And puzzle out who Orpheus was,
Or Dionysius Zagrias.
You 'll find sufficient, as I say,
To satisfy you either way ;
You wanted to believe; your pains
Are crowned — you do : and what remains ?
" Renounce the world ! " — Ah, were it done
By merely cutting one by one
Your limbs off, with your wise head last,
How easy were it ! — how soon past,
If once in the believing mood !
" Such is man's usual gratitude,
Such thanks to God do we return,
For not exacting that we spurn
A single gift of life, forego
One real gain, — only taste them so
With gravity and temperance,
That those mild virtues may enhance
Such pleasures, rather than abstract —
Last spice of which, will be the fact
Of love discerned in every gift ;
While, when the scene of life shall shift,
And the gay heart be taught to ache,
As sorrows and privations take
The place of joy, — the thing that seems
Mere misery, under human schemes,
Becomes, regarded by the light
Of love, as very near or quite
As good a gift as joy before.

So plain is it that, all the more
A dispensation's merciful,
More pettishly we try and cull
Briers, thistles, from our private plot,
To mar God's ground where thorns are not!"

VIII.

Do you say this, or I?— Oh, you!
Then, what, my friend?— (thus I pursue
Our parley) — you indeed opine
That the Eternal and Divine
Did, eighteen centuries ago,
In very truth . . . Enough! you know
The all-stupendous tale, — that Birth,
That Life, that Death! And all, the earth
Shuddered at, — all, the heavens grew black
Rather than see; all, nature's rack
And throe at dissolution's brink
Attested, — all took place, you think,
Only to give our joys a zest,
And prove our sorrows for the best?
We differ, then! Were I, still pale
And heartstruck at the dreadful tale,
Waiting to hear God's voice declare
What horror followed for my share,
As implicated in the deed,
Apart from other sins, — concede
That if He blacked out in a blot
My brief life's pleasantness, 't were not
So very disproportionate!
Or there might be another fate —
I certainly could understand
(If fancies were the thing in hand)
How God might save, at that day's price,
The impure in their impurities,
Give license formal and complete
To choose the fair and pick the sweet.
But there be certain words, broad, plain,
Uttered again and yet again,
Hard to mistake or overgloss —
Announcing this world's gain for loss,
And bidding us reject the same:
The whole world lieth (they proclaim)
In wickedness, — come out of it!
Turn a deaf ear, if you think fit,
But I who thrill through every nerve

At thought of what deaf ears deserve —
How do you counsel in the case?

IX.

"I'd take, by all means, in your place,
The safe side, since it so appears:
Deny myself, a few brief years,
The natural pleasure, leave the fruit
Or cut the plant up by the root.
Remember what a martyr said
On the rude tablet overhead!
'I was born sickly, poor and mean,
A slave: no misery could screen
The holders of the pearl of price
From Cæsar's envy; therefore twice
I fought with beasts, and three times saw
My children suffer by his law;
At last my own release was earned:
I was some time in being burned.
But at the close a Hand came through
The fire above my head, and drew
My soul to Christ, whom now I see.
Sergius, a brother, writes for me
This testimony on the wall —
For me, I have forgot it all.'
You say right; this were not so hard!
And since one nowise is debarred
From this, why not escape some sins
By such a method?"

X.

Then begins
To the old point revulsion new —
(For 't is just this I bring you to) —
If after all we should mistake,
And so renounce life for the sake
Of death and nothing else? You hear
Each friend we jeered at, send the jeer
Back to ourselves with good effect —
"There were my beetles to collect!
My box — a trifle, I confess,
But here I hold it, ne'ertheless!"
Poor idiots, (let us pluck up heart
And answer) we, the better part
Have chosen, though 't were only hope, —
Nor envy moles like you that grope

Amid your veritable muck,
More than the grasshoppers would truck,
For yours, their passionate life away,
That spends itself in leaps all day
To reach the sun, you want the eyes
To see, as they the wings to rise
And match the noble hearts of them!
Thus the contemner we contemn, —
And, when doubt strikes us, thus we ward
Its stroke off, caught upon our guard,
— Not struck enough to overturn
Our faith, but shake it — make us learn
What I began with, and, I wis,
End, having proved, — how hard it is
To be a Christian!

XI.

" Proved, or not,
Howe'er you wis, small thanks, I wot,
You get of mine, for taking pains
To make it hard to me. Who gains
By that, I wonder? Here I live
In trusting ease ; and here you drive
At causing me to lose what most
Yourself would mourn for had you lost!"

XII.

But, do you see, my friend, that thus
You leave St. Paul for Æschylus?
— Who made his Titan's arch-device
The giving men *blind hopes* to spice
The meal of life with, else devoured
In bitter haste, while lo, death loured
Before them at the platter's edge!
If faith should be, as I allege,
Quite other than a condiment
To heighten flavors with, or meant
(Like that brave curry of his Grace)
To take at need the victuals' place?
If, having dined, you would digest
Besides, and turning to your rest
Should find instead . . .

XIII.

Now, you shall see
And judge if a mere foppery

Pricks on my speaking! I resolve
To utter — yes, it shall devolve
On you to hear as solemn, strange
And dread a thing as in the range
Of facts, — or fancies, if God will —
E'er happened to our kind! I still
Stand in the cloud and, while it wraps
My face, ought not to speak perhaps;
Seeing that if I carry through
My purpose, if my words in you
Find a live actual listener,
My story, reason must aver
False after all — the happy chance!
While, if each human countenance
I meet in London day by day,
Be what I fear, — my warnings fray
No one, and no one they convert,
And no one helps me to assert
How hard it is to really be
A Christian, and in vacancy
I pour this story!

XIV.

I commence
By trying to inform you, whence
It comes that every Easter-night
As now, I sit up, watch, till light,
Upon those chimney-stacks and roofs,
Give, through my window-pane, gray proofs
That Easter-Day is breaking slow.
On such a night, three years ago,
It chanced that I had cause to cross
The common, where the chapel was,
Our friend spoke of, the other day —
You've not forgotten, I dare say.
I fell to musing of the time
So close, the blessed matin-prime
All hearts leap up at, in some guise —
One could not well do otherwise.
Insensibly my thoughts were bent
Toward the main point; I overwent
Much the same ground of reasoning
As you and I just now. One thing
Remained, however — one that tasked
My soul to answer; and I asked,
Fairly and frankly, what might be

That History, that Faith, to me
— Me there — not me in some domain
Built up and peopled by my brain,
Weighing its merits as one weighs
Mere theories for blame or praise,
— The kingcraft of the Lucumons,
Or Fourier's scheme, its pros and cons, —
But my faith there, or none at all.
" How were my case, now, did I fall
Dead here, this minute — should I lie
Faithful or faithless ? "   Note that I
Inclined thus ever ! — little prone
For instance, when I lay alone
In childhood, to go calm to sleep
And leave a closet where might keep
His watch perdue some murderer
Waiting till twelve o'clock to stir,
As good authentic legends tell:
" He might: but how improbable !
How little likely to deserve
The pains and trial to the nerve
Of thrusting head into the dark ! " —
Urged my old nurse, and bade me mark
Beside, that, should the dreadful scout
Really lie hid there, and leap out
At first turn of the rusty key,
Mine were small gain that she could see,
Killed not in bed but on the floor,
And losing one night's sleep the more.
I tell you, I would always burst
The door ope, know my fate at first.
This time, indeed, the closet penned
No such assassin : but a friend
Rather, peeped out to guard me, fit
For counsel, Common Sense, to wit,
Who said a good deal that might pass, —
Heartening, impartial too, it was,
Judge else : " For, soberly now, — who
Should be a Christian if not you ? "
(Hear how he smoothed me down.)   " One takes
A whole life, sees what course it makes
Mainly, and not by fits and starts —
In spite of stoppage which imparts
Fresh value to the general speed.
A life, with none, would fly indeed :
Your progressing is slower — right !

We deal with progress and not flight.
Through baffling senses passionate,
Fancies as restless,— with a freight
Of knowledge cumbersome enough
To sink your ship when waves grow rough,
Though meant for ballast in the hold,—
I find, 'mid dangers manifold,
The good bark answers to the helm
Where faith sits, easier to o'erwhelm
Than some stout peasant's heavenly guide,
Whose hard head could not, if it tried,
Conceive a doubt, nor understand
How senses hornier than his hand
Should 'tice the Christian off his guard.
More happy! But shall we award
Less honor to the hull which, dogged
By storms, a mere wreck, waterlogged,
Masts by the board, her bulwarks gone
And stanchions going, yet bears on,—
Than to mere lifeboats, built to save,
And triumph o'er the breaking wave?
Make perfect your good ship as these,
And what were her performances!"
I added — " Would the ship reach home!
I wish indeed ' God's kingdom come ' —
The day when I shall see appear
His bidding, as my duty, clear
From doubt! And it shall dawn, that day,
Some future season: Easter may
Prove, not impossibly, the time —
Yes, that were striking — fates would chime
So aptly! Easter-morn, to bring
The Judgment! — deeper in the spring
Than now, however, when there's snow
Capping the hills; for earth must show
All signs of meaning to pursue
Her tasks as she was wont to do
— The skylark, taken by surprise
As we ourselves, shall recognize
Sudden the end. For suddenly
It comes; the dreadfulness must be
In that; all warrants the belief —
'At night it cometh like a thief.'
I fancy why the trumpet blows;
— Plainly, to wake one. From repose
We shall start up, at last awake

From life, that insane dream we take
For waking now, because it seems.
And as, when now we wake from dreams,
We laugh, while we recall them, 'Fool,
To let the chance slip, linger cool
When such adventure offered! Just
A bridge to cross, a dwarf to thrust
Aside, a wicked mage to stab —
And, lo ye, I had kissed Queen Mab!'
So shall we marvel why we grudged
Our labor here, and idly judged
Of heaven, we might have gained, but lose!
Lose? Talk of loss, and I refuse
To plead at all! You speak no worse
Nor better than my ancient nurse
When she would tell me in my youth
I well deserved that shapes uncouth
Frighted and teased me in my sleep:
Why could I not in memory keep
Her precept for the evil's cure?
'Pinch your own arm, boy, and be sure
You 'll wake forthwith!'"

XV.

And as I said
This nonsense, throwing back my head
With light complacent laugh, I found
Suddenly all the midnight round
One fire. The dome of heaven had stood
As made up of a multitude
Of handbreadth cloudlets, one vast rack
Of ripples infinite and black,
From sky to sky. Sudden there went,
Like horror and astonishment,
A fierce vindictive scribble of red
Quick flame across, as if one said
(The angry scribe of Judgment) "There —
Burn it!" And straight I was aware
That the whole ribwork round, minute
Cloud touching cloud beyond compute,
Was tinted, each with its own spot
Of burning at the core, till clot
Jammed against clot, and spilt its fire
Over all heaven, which 'gan suspire
As fanned to measure equable, —
Just so great conflagrations kill

Night overhead, and rise and sink,
Reflected. Now the fire would shrink
And wither off the blasted face
Of heaven, and I distinct might trace
The sharp black ridgy outlines left
Unburned like network — then, each cleft
The fire had been sucked back into,
Regorged, and out it surging flew
Furiously, and night writhed inflamed,
Till, tolerating to be tamed
No longer, certain rays world-wide
Shot downwardly. On every side
Caught past escape, the earth was lit;
As if a dragon's nostril split
And all his famished ire o'erflowed;
Then as he winced at his lord's goad,
Back he inhaled: whereat I found
The clouds into vast pillars bound,
Based on the corners of the earth,
Propping the skies at top: a dearth
Of fire i' the violet intervals,
Leaving exposed the utmost walls
Of time, about to tumble in
And end the world.

XVI.

I felt begin
The Judgment-Day: to retrocede
Was too late now. "In very deed,"
(I uttered to myself) "that Day!"
The intuition burned away
All darkness from my spirit too:
There, stood I, found and fixed, I knew,
Choosing the world. The choice was made;
And naked and disguiseless stayed,
And unevadable, the fact.
My brain held all the same compact
Its senses, nor my heart declined
Its office; rather, both combined
To help me in this juncture. I
Lost not a second, — agony
Gave boldness: since my life had end
And my choice with it — best defend,
Applaud both! I resolved to say,
"So was I framed by thee, such way
I put to use thy senses here!

It was so beautiful, so near,
Thy world, — what could I then but choose
My part there? Nor did I refuse
To look above the transient boon
Of time ; but it was hard so soon
As in a short life, to give up
Such beauty: I could put the cup,
Undrained of half its fulness, by ;
But, to renounce it utterly,
— 'That was too hard! Nor did the cry
Which bade renounce it, touch my brain
Authentically deep and plain
Enough to make my lips let go.
But thou, who knowest all, dost know
Whether I was not, life's brief while,
Endeavoring to reconcile
Those lips (too tardily, alas!)
To letting the dear remnant pass,
One day, — some drops of earthly good
Untasted! Is it for this mood,
That Thou, whose earth delights so well,
Hast made its complement a hell?"

XVII.

A final belch of fire like blood,
Overbroke all heaven in one flood
Of doom. Then fire was sky, and sky
Fire, and both, one brief ecstasy,
Then ashes. But I heard no noise
(Whatever was) because a voice
Beside me spoke thus, "Life is done,
Time ends, Eternity's begun,
And thou art judged forevermore."

XVIII.

I looked up; all seemed as before;
Of that cloud-Tophet overhead
No trace was left: I saw instead
The common round me, and the sky
Above, stretched drear and emptily
Of life. 'T was the last watch of night,
Except what brings the morning quite;
When the armed angel, conscience-clear,
His task nigh done, leans o'er his spear
And gazes on the earth he guards,
Safe one night more through all its wards,

Till God relieve him at his post.
"A dream — a waking dream at most!"
(I spoke out quick, that I might shake
The horrid nightmare off, and wake.)
"The world gone, yet the world is here?
Are not all things as they appear?
Is Judgment past for me alone?
— And where had place the great white throne?
The rising of the quick and dead?
Where stood they, small and great? Who read
The sentence from the opened book?"
So, by degrees, the blood forsook
My heart, and let it beat afresh;
I knew I should break through the mesh
Of horror, and breathe presently:
When, lo, again, the voice by me!

XIX.

I saw . . . O brother, 'mid far sands
The palm-tree-cinctured city stands,
Bright-white beneath, as heaven, bright-blue,
Leans o'er it, while the years pursue
Their course, unable to abate
Its paradisal laugh at fate!
One morn, — the Arab staggers blind
O'er a new tract of death, calcined
To ashes, silence, nothingness, —
And strives, with dizzy wits, to guess
Whence fell the blow. What if, 'twixt skies
And prostrate earth, he should surprise
The imaged vapor, head to foot,
Surveying, motionless and mute,
Its work, ere, in a whirlwind rapt
It vanish up again? — So hapt
My chance. He stood there. Like the smoke
Pillared o'er Sodom, when day broke, —
I saw Him. One magnific pall
Mantled in massive fold and fall
His head, and coiled in snaky swathes
About His feet: night's black, that bathes
All else, broke, grizzled with despair,
Against the soul of blackness there.
A gesture told the mood within —
That wrapped right hand which based the chin,
That intense meditation fixed
On His procedure, — pity mixed

With the fulfilment of decree.
Motionless, thus, He spoke to me,
Who fell before His feet, a mass,
No man now.

XX.

"All is come to pass.
Such shows are over for each soul
They had respect to. In the roll
Of Judgment which convinced mankind
Of sin, stood many, bold and blind,
Terror must burn the truth into:
Their fate for them! — thou hadst to do
With absolute omnipotence,
Able its judgments to dispense
To the whole race, as every one
Were its sole object. Judgment done,
God is, thou art, — the rest is hurled
To nothingness for thee. This world,
This finite life, thou hast preferred,
In disbelief of God's plain word,
To heaven and to infinity.
Here the probation was for thee,
To show thy soul the earthly mixed
With heavenly, it must choose betwixt.
The earthly joys lay palpable, —
A taint, in each, distinct as well;
The heavenly flitted, faint and rare,
Above them, but as truly were
Taintless, so, in their nature, best.
Thy choice was earth: thou didst attest
'T was fitter spirit should subserve
The flesh, than flesh refine to nerve
Beneath the spirit's play. Advance
No claim to their inheritance
Who chose the spirit's fugitive
Brief gleams, and yearned, ' This were to live
Indeed, if rays, completely pure
From flesh that dulls them, could endure, —
Not shoot in meteor-light athwart
Our earth, to show how cold and swart
It lies beneath their fire, but stand
As stars do, destined to expand,
Prove veritable worlds, our home!'
Thou saidst, — ' Let spirit star the dome
Of sky, that flesh may miss no peak,

No nook of earth, — I shall not seek
Its service further!' Thou art shut
Out of the heaven of spirit; glut
Thy sense upon the world: 't is thine
Forever — take it!"

XXI.

"How? Is mine,
The world?" (I cried, while my soul broke
Out in a transport.) "Hast Thou spoke
Plainly in that? Earth's exquisite
Treasures of wonder and delight
For me?"

XXII.

The austere voice returned, —
"So soon made happy? Hadst thou learned
What God accounteth happiness,
Thou wouldst not find it hard to guess
What hell may be his punishment
For those who doubt if God invent
Better than they. Let such men rest
Content with what they judged the best.
Let the unjust usurp at will:
The filthy shall be filthy still:
Miser, there waits the gold for thee!
Hater, indulge thine enmity!
And thou, whose heaven self-ordained
Was, to enjoy earth unrestrained.
Do it! Take all the ancient show!
The woods shall wave, the rivers flow,
And men apparently pursue
Their works, as they were wont to do,
While living in probation yet.
I promise not thou shalt forget
The past, now gone to its account;
But leave thee with the old amount
Of faculties, nor less nor more,
Unvisited, as heretofore.
By God's free spirit, that makes an end.
So, once more, take thy world! Expend
Eternity upon its shows,
Flung thee as freely as one rose
Out of a summer's opulence,
Over the Eden-barrier whence
Thou art excluded. Knock in vain!"

EASTER-DAY

XXIII.

I sat up. All was still again.
I breathed free: to my heart, back fled
The warmth. "But, all the world!" — I said.
I stooped and picked a leaf of fern,
And recollected I might learn
From books, how many myriad sorts
Of fern exist, to trust reports,
Each as distinct and beautiful
As this, the very first I cull.
Think, from the first leaf to the last!
Conceive, then, earth's resources! Vast
Exhaustless beauty, endless change
Of wonder! And this foot shall range
Alps, Andes, — and this eye devour
The bee-bird and the aloe-flower?

XXIV.

Then the voice: "Welcome so to rate
The arras-folds that variegate
The earth, God's antechamber, well!
The wise, who waited there, could tell
By these, what royalties in store
Lay one step past the entrance-door.
For whom, was reckoned, not too much,
This life's munificence? For such
As thou, — a race, whereof scarce one
Was able, in a million,
To feel that any marvel lay
In objects round his feet all day;
Scarce one, in many millions more,
Willing, if able, to explore
The secreter, minuter charm!
— Brave souls, a fern-leaf could disarm
Of power to cope with God's intent, —
Or scared if the south firmament
With north-fire did its wings refledge!
All partial beauty was a pledge
Of beauty in its plenitude:
But since the pledge sufficed thy mood,
Retain it! plenitude be theirs
Who looked above!"

XXV.

                          Though sharp despairs
Shot through me, I held up, bore on.
"What matter though my trust were gone
From natural things?   Henceforth my part
Be less with nature than with art!
For art supplants, gives mainly worth
To nature; 't is man stamps the earth —
And I will seek his impress, seek
The statuary of the Greek,
Italy's painting — there my choice
Shall fix!"

XXVI.

                  "Obtain it!" said the voice,
" — The one form with its single act,
Which sculptors labored to abstract,
The one face, painters tried to draw,
With its one look, from throngs they saw.
And that perfection in their soul,
These only hinted at?   The whole,
They were but parts of?   What each laid
His claim to glory on? — afraid
His fellow-men should give him rank
By mere tentatives which he shrank
Smitten at heart from, all the more,
That gazers pressed in to adore!
'Shall I be judged by only these?'
If such his soul's capacities,
Even while he trod the earth, — think, now,
What pomp in Buonarroti's brow,
With its new palace-brain where dwells
Superb the soul, unvexed by cells
That crumbled with the transient clay!
What visions will his right hand's sway
Still turn to forms, as still they burst
Upon him?   How will he quench thirst,
Titanically infantine,
Laid at the breast of the Divine?
Does it confound thee, — this first page
Emblazoning man's heritage? —
Can this alone absorb thy sight,
As pages were not infinite, —
Like the omnipotence which tasks
Itself to furnish all that asks

The soul it means to satiate?
What was the world, the starry state
Of the broad skies, — what, all displays
Of power and beauty intermixed,
Which now thy soul is chained betwixt, —
What else than needful furniture
For life's first stage?   God's work, be sure,
No more spreads wasted, than falls scant!
He filled, did not exceed, man's want
Of beauty in this life.   But through
Life pierce, — and what has earth to do,
Its utmost beauty's appanage,
With the requirement of next stage?
Did God pronounce earth ' very good'?
Needs must it be, while understood
For man's preparatory state;
Nought here to heighten nor abate;
Transfer the same completeness here,
To serve a new state's use, — and drear
Deficiency gapes every side!
The good, tried once, were bad, retried.
See the enwrapping rocky niche,
Sufficient for the sleep in which
The lizard breathes for ages safe:
Split the mould — and as light would chafe
The creature's new world-widened sense,
Dazzled to death at evidence
Of all the sounds and sights that broke
Innumerous at the chisel's stroke, —
So, in God's eye, the earth's first stuff
Was, neither more nor less, enough
To house man's soul, man's need fulfil.
Man reckoned it immeasurable?
So thinks the lizard of his vault!
Could God be taken in default,
Short of contrivances, by you, —
Or reached, ere ready to pursue
His progress through eternity?
That chambered rock, the lizard's world,
Your easy mallet's blow has hurled
To nothingness forever; so,
Has God abolished at a blow
This world, wherein his saints were pent, —
Who, though found grateful and content,
With the provision there, as thou,
Yet knew he would not disallow

Their spirit's hunger, felt as well, —
Unsated, — not unsatable,
As paradise gives proof. Deride
Their choice now, thou who sit'st outside!"

XXVII.

I cried in anguish: " Mind, the mind,
So miserably cast behind,
To gain what had been wisely lost!
Oh, let me strive to make the most
Of the poor stinted soul, I nipped
Of budding wings, else now equipped
For voyage from summer isle to isle!
And though she needs must reconcile
Ambition to the life on ground,
Still, I can profit by late found
But precious knowledge. Mind is best —
I will seize mind, forego the rest,
And try how far my tethered strength
May crawl in this poor breadth and length.
Let me, since I can fly no more,
At least spin dervish-like about
(Till giddy rapture almost doubt
I fly) through circling sciences,
Philosophies and histories!
Should the whirl slacken there, then verse,
Fining to music, shall asperse
Fresh and fresh fire-dew, till I strain
Intoxicate, half-break my chain!
Not joyless, though more favored feet
Stand calm, where I want wings to beat
The floor. At least earth's bond is broke!"

XXVIII.

Then (sickening even while I spoke):
"Let me alone! No answer, pray,
To this! I know what thou wilt say!
All still is earth's, — to know, as much
As feel its truths, which if we touch
With sense, or apprehend in soul.
What matter? I have reached the goal —
'Whereto does knowledge serve!' will burn
My eyes, too sure, at every turn!
I cannot look back now, nor stake
Bliss on the race, for running's sake.
The goal 's a ruin like the rest! —

And so much worse thy latter quest,"
(Added the voice,) " that even on earth —
Whenever, in man's soul, had birth
Those intuitions, grasps of guess,
Which pull the more into the less,
Making the finite comprehend
Infinity, — the bard would spend
Such praise alone, upon his craft,
As, when wind-lyres obey the waft,
Goes to the craftsman who arranged
The seven strings, changed them and rechanged —
Knowing it was the South that harped.
He felt his song, in singing, warped ;
Distinguished his and God's part: whence
A world of spirit as of sense
Was plain to him, yet not too plain,
Which he could traverse, not remain
A guest in : — else were permanent
Heaven on the earth its gleams were meant
To sting with hunger for full light, —
Made visible in verse, despite
The veiling weakness, — truth by means
Of fable, showing while it screens, —
Since highest truth, man e'er supplied,
Was ever fable on outside.
Such gleams made bright the earth an age ;
Now the whole sun 's his heritage !
Take up thy world, it is allowed,
Thou who hast entered in the cloud !' "

XXIX.

Then I — " Behold, my spirit bleeds,
Catches no more at broken reeds, —
But lilies flower those reeds above :
I let the world go, and take love !
Love survives in me, albeit those
I love be henceforth masks and shows,
Not living men and women : still
I mind how love repaired all ill,
Cured wrong, soothed grief, made earth amends
With parents, brothers, children, friends !
Some semblance of a woman yet
With eyes to help me to forget,
Shall look on me ; and I will match
Departed love with love, attach
Old memories to new dreams, nor scorn

The poorest of the grains of corn
I save from shipwreck on this isle,
Trusting its barrenness may smile
With happy foodful green one day,
More precious for the pains. I pray, —
Leave to love, only ! "

XXX.

At the word,
The form, I looked to have been stirred
With pity and approval, rose
O'er me, as when the headsman throws
Axe over shoulder to make end —
I fell prone, letting Him expend
His wrath, while thus the inflicting voice
Smote me. " Is this thy final choice?
Love is the best? 'T is somewhat late !
And all thou dost enumerate
Of power and beauty in the world,
The mightiness of love was curled
Inextricably round about.
Love lay within it and without,
To clasp thee, — but in vain ! Thy soul
Still shrunk from Him who made the whole,
Still set deliberate aside
His love ! — Now take love ! Well betide
Thy tardy conscience ! Haste to take
The show of love for the name's sake,
Remembering every moment Who,
Beside creating thee unto
These ends, and these for thee, was said
To undergo death in thy stead
In flesh like thine : so ran the tale.
What doubt in thee could countervail
Belief in it ? Upon the ground
'That in the story had been found
Too much love ! How could God love so ? '
He who in all his works below
Adapted to the needs of man,
Made love the basis of the plan, —
Did love, as was demonstrated :
While man, who was so fit instead
To hate, as every day gave proof, —
Man thought man, for his kind's behoof,
Both could and did invent that scheme
Of perfect love : 't would well beseem

Cain's nature thou wast wont to praise,
Not tally with God's usual ways!"

XXXI.

And I cowered deprecatingly —
"Thou Love of God! Or let me die,
Or grant what shall seem heaven almost!
Let me not know that all is lost,
Though lost it be — leave me not tied
To this despair, this corpse-like bride!
Let that old life seem mine — no more —
With limitation as before,
With darkness, hunger, toil, distress:
Be all the earth a wilderness!
Only let me go on, go on,
Still hoping ever and anon
To reach one eve the Better Land!"

XXXII.

Then did the form expand, expand —
I knew Him through the dread disguise
As the whole God within His eyes
Embraced me.

XXXIII.

When I lived again,
The day was breaking, — the gray plain
I rose from, silvered thick with dew.
Was this a vision? False or true?
Since then, three varied years are spent,
And commonly my mind is bent
To think it was a dream — be sure
A mere dream and distemperature —
The last day's watching: then the night, —
The shock of that strange Northern Light
Set my head swimming, bred in me
A dream. And so I live, you see,
Go through the world, try, prove, reject,
Prefer, still struggling to effect
My warfare; happy that I can
Be crossed and thwarted as a man,
Not left in God's contempt apart,
With ghastly smooth life, dead at heart,
Tame in earth's paddock as her prize.
Thank God, she still each method tries
To catch me, who may yet escape,

She knows, — the fiend in angel's shape !
Thank God, no paradise stands barred
To entry, and I find it hard
To be a Christian, as I said !
Still every now and then my head
Raised glad, sinks mournful — all grows drear
Spite of the sunshine, while I fear
And think, " How dreadful to be grudged
No ease henceforth, as one that's judged,
Condemned to earth forever, shut
From heaven ! "
     But Easter-Day breaks ! But
Christ rises ! Mercy every way
Is infinite, — and who can say ?

MEN AND WOMEN

LONDON AND FLORENCE, 184- 185-.

"TRANSCENDENTALISM: A POEM IN TWELVE BOOKS."

STOP playing, poet! May a brother speak?
'T is you speak, that's your error. Song's our art:
Whereas you please to speak these naked thoughts
Instead of draping them in sights and sounds.
— True thoughts, good thoughts, thoughts fit to treasure up!
But why such long prolusion and display,
Such turning and adjustment of the harp,
And taking it upon your breast, at length,
Only to speak dry words across its strings?
Stark-naked thought is in request enough:
Speak prose and hollo it till Europe hears!
The six-foot Swiss tube, braced about with bark,
Which helps the hunter's voice from Alp to Alp —
Exchange our harp for that, — who hinders you?

But here's your fault; grown men want thought, you think;
Thought's what they mean by verse, and seek in verse:
Boys seek for images and melody,
Men must have reason — so, you aim at men.
Quite otherwise! Objects throng our youth, 't is true;
We see and hear and do not wonder much:
If you could tell us what they mean, indeed!
As German Boehme never cared for plants
Until it happed, a-walking in the fields,
He noticed all at once that plants could speak,
Nay, turned with loosened tongue to talk with him.
That day the daisy had an eye indeed —
Colloquized with the cowslip on such themes!
We find them extant yet in Jacob's prose.
But by the time youth slips a stage or two
While reading prose in that tough book he wrote
(Collating and emendating the same
And settling on the sense most to our mind),
We shut the clasps and find life's summer past.

Then, who helps more, pray, to repair our loss —
Another Boehme with a tougher book
And subtler meanings of what roses say, —
Or some stout Mage like him of Halberstadt,
John, who made things Boehme wrote thoughts about?
He with a " look you ! " vents a brace of rhymes,
And in there breaks the sudden rose herself,
Over us, under, round us every side,
Nay, in and out the tables and the chairs
And musty volumes, Boehme's book and all, —
Buries us with a glory, young once more,
Pouring heaven into this shut house of life.

So come, the harp back to your heart again!
You are a poem, though your poem's nought.
The best of all you showed before, believe,
Was your own boy-face o'er the finer chords
Bent, following the cherub at the top
That points to God with his paired half-moon wings.

HOW IT STRIKES A CONTEMPORARY.

I ONLY knew one poet in my life:
And this, or something like it, was his way.

You saw go up and down Valladolid,
A man of mark, to know next time you saw.
His very serviceable suit of black
Was courtly once and conscientious still,
And many might have worn it, though none did :
The cloak, that somewhat shone and showed the threads,
Had purpose, and the ruff, significance.
He walked and tapped the pavement with his cane,
Scenting the world, looking it full in face,
An old dog, bald and blindish, at his heels.
They turned up, now, the alley by the church,
That leads no whither; now, they breathed themselves
On the main promenade just at the wrong time :
You'd come upon his scrutinizing hat,
Making a peaked shade blacker than itself
Against the single window spared some house
Intact yet with its mouldered Moorish work,—
Or else surprise the ferrel of his stick
Trying the mortar's temper 'tween the chinks

Of some new shop a-building, French and fine.
He stood and watched the cobbler at his trade,
The man who slices lemons into drink,
The coffee-roaster's brazier, and the boys
That volunteer to help him turn its winch.
He glanced o'er books on stalls with half an eye,
And fly-leaf ballads on the vender's string,
And broad-edge bold-print posters by the wall.
He took such cognizance of men and things,
If any beat a horse, you felt he saw;
If any cursed a woman, he took note;
Yet stared at nobody, — you stared at him,
And found, less to your pleasure than surprise,
He seemed to know you and expect as much.
So, next time that a neighbor's tongue was loosed,
It marked the shameful and notorious fact,
We had among us, not so much a spy,
As a recording chief-inquisitor,
The town's true master if the town but knew!
We merely kept a governor for form,
While this man walked about and took account
Of all thought, said and acted, then went home,
And wrote it fully to our Lord the King
Who has an itch to know things, he knows why,
And reads them in his bedroom of a night.
Oh, you might smile! there wanted not a touch,
A tang of . . . well, it was not wholly ease
As back into your mind the man's look came.
Stricken in years a little, — such a brow
His eyes had to live under! — clear as flint
On either side the formidable nose
Curved, cut and colored like an eagle's claw.
Had he to do with A's surprising fate?
When altogether old B disappeared
And young C got his mistress, — was 't our friend,
His letter to the King, that did it all?
What paid the bloodless man for so much pains?
Our Lord the King has favorites manifold,
And shifts his ministry some once a month;
Our city gets new governors at whiles, —
But never word or sign, that I could hear,
Notified to this man about the streets
The King's approval of those letters conned
The last thing duly at the dead of night.
Did the man love his office? Frowned our Lord,
Exhorting when none heard — " Beseech me not!

Too far above my people, — beneath me!
I set the watch, — how should the people know?
Forget them, keep me all the more in mind!"
Was some such understanding 'twixt the two?

I found no truth in one report at least —
That if you tracked him to his home, down lanes
Beyond the Jewry, and as clean to pace,
You found he ate his supper in a room
Blazing with lights, four Titians on the wall,
And twenty naked girls to change his plate!
Poor man, he lived another kind of life
In that new stuccoed third house by the bridge,
Fresh-painted, rather smart than otherwise!
The whole street might o'erlook him as he sat,
Leg crossing leg, one foot on the dog's back,
Playing a decent cribbage with his maid
(Jacynth, you're sure her name was) o'er the cheese
And fruit, three red halves of starved winter-pears,
Or treat of radishes in April. Nine,
Ten, struck the church clock, straight to bed went he.

My father, like the man of sense he was,
Would point him out to me a dozen times;
"'St — 'st," he'd whisper, "the Corregidor!"
I had been used to think that personage
Was one with lacquered breeches, lustrous belt,
And feathers like a forest in his hat,
Who blew a trumpet and proclaimed the news,
Announced the bull-fights, gave each church its turn,
And memorized the miracle in vogue!
He had a great observance from us boys;
We were in error; that was not the man.

I'd like now, yet had haply been afraid,
To have just looked, when this man came to die,
And seen who lined the clean gay garret-sides
And stood about the neat low truckle-bed,
With the heavenly manner of relieving guard.
Here had been, mark, the general-in-chief,
Through a whole campaign of the world's life and death,
Doing the King's work all the dim day long,
In his old coat and up to knees in mud,
Smoked liked a herring, dining on a crust, —
And, now the day was won, relieved at once!
No further show or need for that old coat,

You are sure, for one thing! Bless us, all the while
How sprucely we are dressed out, you and I!
A second, and the angels alter that.
Well, I could never write a verse, — could you?
Let's to the Prado and make the most of time.

ARTEMIS PROLOGIZES.

I AM a goddess of the ambrosial courts,
And save by Here, Queen of Pride, surpassed
By none whose temples whiten this the world.
Through heaven I roll my lucid moon along;
I shed in hell o'er my pale people peace;
On earth I, caring for the creatures, guard
Each pregnant yellow wolf and fox-bitch sleek,
And every feathered mother's callow brood,
And all that love green haunts and loneliness.
Of men, the chaste adore me, hanging crowns
Of poppies red to blackness, bell and stem,
Upon my image at Athenai here;
And this dead Youth, Asclepios bends above,
Was dearest to me. He, my buskined step
To follow through the wild-wood leafy ways,
And chase the panting stag, or swift with darts
Stop the swift ounce, or lay the leopard low,
Neglected homage to another god:
Whence Aphrodite, by no midnight smoke
Of tapers lulled, in jealousy dispatched
A noisome lust that, as the gadbee stings,
Possessed his stepdame Phaidra for himself
The son of Theseus her great absent spouse.
Hippolutos exclaiming in his rage
Against the fury of the Queen, she judged
Life insupportable; and, pricked at heart
An Amazonian stranger's race should dare
To scorn her, perished by the murderous cord:
Yet, ere she perished, blasted in a scroll
The fame of him her swerving made not swerve.
And Theseus, read, returning, and believed,
And exiled, in the blindness of his wrath,
The man without a crime who, last as first,
Loyal, divulged not to his sire the truth.
Now Theseus from Poseidon had obtained
That of his wishes should be granted three,

And one he imprecated straight — "Alive
May ne'er Hippolutos reach other lands!"
Poseidon heard, ai ai! And scarce the prince
Had stepped into the fixed boots of the car
That give the feet a stay against the strength
Of the Henetian horses, and around
His body flung the rein, and urged their speed
Along the rocks and shingles of the shore,
When from the gaping wave a monster flung
His obscene body in the coursers' path.
These, mad with terror, as the sea-bull sprawled
Wallowing about their feet, lost care of him
That reared them; and the master-chariot-pole
Snapping beneath their plunges like a reed,
Hippolutos, whose feet were trammelled fast,
Was yet dragged forward by the circling rein
Which either hand directed; nor they quenched
The frenzy of their flight before each trace,
Wheel-spoke and splinter of the woful car,
Each boulder-stone, sharp stub and spiny shell,
Huge fishbone wrecked and wreathed amid the sands
On that detested beach, was bright with blood
And morsels of his flesh: then fell the steeds
Head-foremost, crashing in their mooned fronts,
Shivering with sweat, each white eye horror-fixed.
His people, who had witnessed all afar,
Bore back the ruins of Hippolutos.
But when his sire, too swoln with pride, rejoiced
(Indomitable as a man foredoomed)
That vast Poseidon had fulfilled his prayer,
I, in a flood of glory visible,
Stood o'er my dying votary and, deed
By deed, revealed, as all took place, the truth.
Then Theseus lay the wofullest of men,
And worthily; but ere the death-veils hid
His face, the murdered prince full pardon breathed
To his rash sire. Whereat Athenai wails.

So I, who ne'er forsake my votaries,
Lest in the crossway none the honey-cake
Should tender, nor pour out the dog's hot life;
Lest at my fane the priests disconsolate
Should dress my image with some faded poor
Few crowns, made favors of, nor dare object
Such slackness to my worshippers who turn
Elsewhere the trusting heart and loaded hand,

As they had climbed Olumpos to report
Of Artemis and nowhere found her throne —
I interposed : and, this eventful night, —
(While round the funeral pyre the populace
Stood with fierce light on their black robes which bound
Each sobbing head, while yet their hair they clipped
O'er the dead body of their withered prince,
And, in his palace, Theseus prostrated
On the cold hearth, his brow cold as the slab
'T was bruised on, groaned away the heavy grief —
As the pyre fell, and down the cross logs crashed
Sending a crowd of sparkles through the night,
And the gay fire, elate with mastery,
Towered like a serpent o'er the clotted jars
Of wine, dissolving oils and frankincense,
And splendid gums like gold,) — my potency
Conveyed the perished man to my retreat
In the thrice-venerable forest here.
And this white-bearded sage who squeezes now
The berried plant, is Phoibos' son of fame,
Asclepios, whom my radiant brother taught
The doctrine of each herb and flower and root,
To know their secret'st virtue and express
The saving soul of all : who so has soothed
With lavers the torn brow and murdered cheeks,
Composed the hair and brought its gloss again,
And called the red bloom to the pale skin back,
And laid the strips and jagged ends of flesh
Even once more, and slacked the sinew's knot
Of every tortured limb — that now he lies
As if mere sleep possessed him underneath
These interwoven oaks and pines. Oh cheer,
Divine presenter of the healing rod,
Thy snake, with ardent throat and lulling eye,
Twines his lithe spires around ! I say, much cheer !
Proceed thou with thy wisest pharmacies !
And ye, white crowd of woodland sister-nymphs,
Ply, as the sage directs, these buds and leaves
That strew the turf around the twain ! While I
Await, in fitting silence, the event.

AN EPISTLE

CONTAINING THE

STRANGE MEDICAL EXPERIENCE OF KARSHISH, THE ARAB PHYSICIAN.

KARSHISH, the picker-up of learning's crumbs,
The not-incurious in God's handiwork
('This man's-flesh he hath admirably made,
Blown like a bubble, kneaded like a paste,
To coop up and keep down on earth a space
That puff of vapor from his mouth, man's soul)
— To Abib, all-sagacious in our art,
Breeder in me of what poor skill I boast,
Like me inquisitive how pricks and cracks
Befall the flesh through too much stress and strain,
Whereby the wily vapor fain would slip
Back and rejoin its source before the term, —
And aptest in contrivance (under God)
To baffle it by deftly stopping such : —
The vagrant Scholar to his Sage at home
Sends greeting (health and knowledge, fame with peace)
Three samples of true snake-stone — rarer still,
One of the other sort, the melon-shaped,
(But fitter, pounded fine, for charms than drugs)
And writeth now the twenty-second time.

My journeyings were brought to Jericho :
Thus I resume.   Who studious in our art
Shall count a little labor unrepaid ?
I have shed sweat enough, left flesh and bone
On many a flinty furlong of this land.
Also, the country-side is all on fire
With rumors of a marching hitherward :
Some say Vespasian cometh, some, his son.
A black lynx snarled and pricked a tufted ear ;
Lust of my blood inflamed his yellow balls :
I cried and threw my staff and he was gone.
Twice have the robbers stripped and beaten me,
And once a town declared me for a spy ;
But at the end, I reach Jerusalem,
Since this poor covert where I pass the night,
This Bethany, lies scarce the distance thence
A man with plague-sores at the third degree

Runs till he drops down dead. Thou laughest here!
'Sooth, it elates me, thus reposed and safe,
To void the stuffing of my travel-scrip
And share with thee whatever Jewry yields.
A viscid choler is observable
In tertians, I was nearly bold to say;
And falling-sickness hath a happier cure
Than our school wots of: there's a spider here
Weaves no web, watches on the ledge of tombs,
Sprinkled with mottles on an ash-gray back;
Take five and drop them . . . but who knows his mind,
The Syrian runagate I trust this to?
His service payeth me a sublimate
Blown up his nose to help the ailing eye.
Best wait: I reach Jerusalem at morn,
There set in order my experiences,
Gather what most deserves, and give thee all —
Or I might add, Judæa's gum-tragacanth
Scales off in purer flakes, shines clearer-grained,
Cracks 'twixt the pestle and the porphyry,
In fine exceeds our produce. Scalp-disease
Confounds me, crossing so with leprosy —
Thou hadst admired one sort I gained at Zoar —
But zeal outruns discretion. Here I end.

   Yet stay: my Syrian blinketh gratefully,
Protesteth his devotion is my price —
Suppose I write what harms not, though he steal?
I half resolve to tell thee, yet I blush,
What set me off a-writing first of all.
An itch I had, a sting to write, a tang!
For, be it this town's barrenness — or else
The Man had something in the look of him —
His case has struck me far more than 't is worth.
So, pardon if — (lest presently I lose
In the great press of novelty at hand
The care and pains this somehow stole from me)
I bid thee take the thing while fresh in mind,
Almost in sight — for, wilt thou have the truth?
The very man is gone from me but now,
Whose ailment is the subject of discourse.
Thus then, and let thy better wit help all!

   'T is but a case of mania — subinduced
By epilepsy, at the turning-point
Of trance prolonged unduly some three days:

When, by the exhibition of some drug
Or spell, exorcization, stroke of art
Unknown to me and which 't were well to know,
The evil thing out-breaking all at once
Left the man whole and sound of body indeed, —
But, flinging (so to speak) life's gates too wide,
Making a clear house of it too suddenly,
The first conceit that entered might inscribe
Whatever it was minded on the wall
So plainly at that vantage, as it were,
(First come, first served) that nothing subsequent
Attaineth to erase those fancy-scrawls
The just-returned and new-established soul
Hath gotten now so thoroughly by heart
That henceforth she will read or these or none.
And first — the man's own firm conviction rests
That he was dead (in fact they buried him)
— That he was dead and then restored to life
By a Nazarene physician of his tribe:
— 'Sayeth, the same bade " Rise," and he did rise.
" Such cases are diurnal," thou wilt cry.
Not so this figment! — not, that such a fume,
Instead of giving way to time and health,
Should eat itself into the life of life,
As saffron tingeth flesh, blood, bones and all!
For see, how he takes up the after-life.
The man — it is one Lazarus a Jew,
Sanguine, proportioned, fifty years of age,
The body's habit wholly laudable,
As much, indeed, beyond the common health
As he were made and put aside to show.
Think, could we penetrate by any drug
And bathe the wearied soul and worried flesh,
And bring it clear and fair, by three days' sleep!
Whence has the man the balm that brightens all?
This grown man eyes the world now like a child.
Some elders of his tribe, I should premise,
Led in their friend, obedient as a sheep,
To bear my inquisition. While they spoke,
Now sharply, now with sorrow, — told the case, —
He listened not except I spoke to him,
But folded his two hands and let them talk,
Watching the flies that buzzed: and yet no fool.
And that's a sample how his years must go.
Look, if a beggar, in fixed middle-life,
Should find a treasure, — can he use the same

With straitened habits and with tastes starved small,
And take at once to his impoverished brain
The sudden element that changes things,
That sets the undreamed-of rapture at his hand
And puts the cheap old joy in the scorned dust?
Is he not such an one as moves to mirth —
Warily parsimonious, when no need,
Wasteful as drunkenness at undue times?
All prudent counsel as to what befits
The golden mean, is lost on such an one:
The man's fantastic will is the man's law.
So here — we call the treasure knowledge, say,
Increased beyond the fleshly faculty —
Heaven opened to a soul while yet on earth,
Earth forced on a soul's use while seeing heaven:
The man is witless of the size, the sum,
The value in proportion of all things,
Or whether it be little or be much.
Discourse to him of prodigious armaments
Assembled to besiege his city now,
And of the passing of a mule with gourds —
'T is one! Then take it on the other side,
Speak of some trifling fact, — he will gaze rapt
With stupor at its very littleness,
(Far as I see) as if in that indeed
He caught prodigious import, whole results;
And so will turn to us the bystanders
In ever the same stupor (note this point)
That we too see not with his opened eyes.
Wonder and doubt come wrongly into play,
Preposterously, at cross purposes.
Should his child sicken unto death, — why, look
For scarce abatement of his cheerfulness,
Or pretermission of the daily craft!
While a word, gesture, glance from that same child
At play or in the school or laid asleep,
Will startle him to an agony of fear,
Exasperation, just as like. Demand
The reason why — "'t is but a word," object —
"A gesture" — he regards thee as our lord
Who lived there in the pyramid alone,
Looked at us (dost thou mind?) when, being young,
We both would unadvisedly recite
Some charm's beginning, from that book of his,
Able to bid the sun throb wide and burst
All into stars, as suns grown old are wont.

Thou and the child have each a veil alike
Thrown o'er your heads, from under which ye both
Stretch your blind hands and trifle with a match
Over a mine of Greek fire, did ye know!
He holds on firmly to some thread of life —
(It is the life to lead perforcedly)
Which runs across some vast distracting orb
Of glory on either side that meagre thread,
Which, conscious of, he must not enter yet —
The spiritual life around the earthly life:
The law of that is known to him as this,
His heart and brain move there, his feet stay here.
So is the man perplext with impulses
Sudden to start off crosswise, not straight on,
Proclaiming what is right and wrong across,
And not along, this black thread through the blaze —
"It should be" balked by "here it cannot be."
And oft the man's soul springs into his face
As if he saw again and heard again
His sage that bade him "Rise" and he did rise.
Something, a word, a tick o' the blood within
Admonishes: then back he sinks at once
To ashes, who was very fire before,
In sedulous recurrence to his trade
Whereby he earneth him the daily bread;
And studiously the humbler for that pride,
Professedly the faultier that he knows
God's secret, while he holds the thread of life.
Indeed the especial marking of the man
Is prone submission to the heavenly will —
Seeing it, what it is, and why it is.
'Sayeth, he will wait patient to the last
For that same death which must restore his being
To equilibrium, body loosening soul
Divorced even now by premature full growth:
He will live, nay, it pleaseth him to live
So long as God please, and just how God please.
He even seeketh not to please God more
(Which meaneth, otherwise) than as God please.
Hence, I perceive not he affects to preach
The doctrine of his sect whate'er it be,
Make proselytes as madmen thirst to do:
How can he give his neighbor the real ground,
His own conviction? Ardent as he is —
Call his great truth a lie, why, still the old
"Be it as God please" reassureth him.

I probed the sore as thy disciple should:
"How, beast," said I, "this stolid carelessness
Sufficeth thee, when Rome is on her march
To stamp out like a little spark thy town,
Thy tribe, thy crazy tale and thee at once?"
He merely looked with his large eyes on me.
The man is apathetic, you deduce?
Contrariwise, he loves both old and young,
Able and weak, affects the very brutes
And birds — how say I? flowers of the field —
As a wise workman recognizes tools
In a master's workshop, loving what they make.
Thus is the man as harmless as a lamb:
Only impatient, let him do his best,
At ignorance and carelessness and sin —
An indignation which is promptly curbed:
As when in certain travel I have feigned
To be an ignoramus in our art
According to some preconceived design,
And happed to hear the land's practitioners,
Steeped in conceit sublimed by ignorance,
Prattle fantastically on disease,
Its cause and cure — and I must hold my peace!

Thou wilt object — Why have I not ere this
Sought out the sage himself, the Nazarene
Who wrought this cure, inquiring at the source,
Conferring with the frankness that befits?
Alas! it grieveth me, the learned leech
Perished in a tumult many years ago,
Accused — our learning's fate — of wizardry,
Rebellion, to the setting up a rule
And creed prodigious as described to me.
His death, which happened when the earthquake fell
(Prefiguring, as soon appeared, the loss
To occult learning in our lord the sage
Who lived there in the pyramid alone)
Was wrought by the mad people — that's their wont!
On vain recourse, as I conjecture it,
To his tried virtue, for miraculous help —
How could he stop the earthquake? That's their way!
The other imputations must be lies:
But take one, though I loathe to give it thee,
In mere respect for any good man's fame.
(And after all, our patient Lazarus
Is stark mad; should we count on what he says?

Perhaps not : though in writing to a leech
'T is well to keep back nothing of a case.)
This man so cured regards the curer, then,
As — God forgive me ! who but God himself,
Creator and sustainer of the world,
That came and dwelt in flesh on it awhile !
— 'Sayeth that such an one was born and lived,
Taught, healed the sick, broke bread at his own house,
Then died, with Lazarus by, for aught I know,
And yet was . . . what I said nor choose repeat,
And must have so avouched himself, in fact,
In hearing of this very Lazarus
Who saith — but why all this of what he saith ?
Why write of trivial matters, things of price
Calling at every moment for remark ?
I noticed on the margin of a pool
Blue-flowering borage, the Aleppo sort,
Aboundeth, very nitrous. It is strange !

   Thy pardon for this long and tedious case,
Which, now that I review it, needs must seem
Unduly dwelt on, prolixly set forth !
Nor I myself discern in what is writ
Good cause for the peculiar interest
And awe indeed this man has touched me with.
Perhaps the journey's end, the weariness
Had wrought upon me first. I met him thus :
I crossed a ridge of short sharp broken hills
Like an old lion's cheek teeth. Out there came
A moon made like a face with certain spots
Multiform, manifold, and menacing :
Then a wind rose behind me. So we met
In this old sleepy town at unaware,
The man and I. I send thee what is writ.
Regard it as a chance, a matter risked
To this ambiguous Syrian — he may lose,
Or steal, or give it thee with equal good.
Jerusalem's repose shall make amends
For time this letter wastes, thy time and mine ;
Till when, once more thy pardon and farewell !

   The very God ! think, Abib ; dost thou think ?
So, the All-Great, were the All-Loving too —
So, through the thunder comes a human voice
Saying, " O heart I made, a heart beats here !
Face, my hands fashioned, see it in myself !

Thou hast no power nor may'st conceive of mine,
But love I gave thee, with myself to love,
And thou must love me who have died for thee!"
The madman saith He said so: it is strange.

JOHANNES AGRICOLA IN MEDITATION.

THERE's heaven above, and night by night
   I look right through its gorgeous roof;
No suns and moons though e'er so bright
    Avail to stop me; splendor-proof
    I keep the broods of stars aloof:
For I intend to get to God,
   For 't is to God I speed so fast,
For in God's breast, my own abode,
    Those shoals of dazzling glory, passed,
    I lay my spirit down at last.
I lie where I have always lain,
   God smiles as he has always smiled;
Ere suns and moons could wax and wane,
    Ere stars were thundergirt, or piled
    The heavens, God thought on me his child;
Ordained a life for me, arrayed
   Its circumstances every one
To the minutest; ay, God said
    This head this hand should rest upon
    Thus, ere he fashioned star or sun.
And having thus created me,
   Thus rooted me, he bade me grow,
Guiltless forever, like a tree
    That buds and blooms, nor seeks to know
    The law by which it prospers so:
But sure that thought and word and deed
   All go to swell his love for me,
Me, made because that love had need
    Of something irreversibly
    Pledged solely its content to be.
Yes, yes, a tree which must ascend,
   No poison-gourd foredoomed to stoop!
I have God's warrant, could I blend
    All hideous sins, as in a cup,
    To drink the mingled venoms up;
Secure my nature will convert
   The draught to blossoming gladness fast:
While sweet dews turn to the gourd's hurt,

And bloat, and while they bloat it, blast,
 As from the first its lot was cast.
For as I lie, smiled on, full-fed
 By unexhausted power to bless,
I gaze below on hell's fierce bed,
 And those its waves of flame oppress,
Swarming in ghastly wretchedness;
Whose life on earth aspired to be
 One altar-smoke, so pure! — to win
If not love like God's love for me,
 At least to keep his anger in;
 And all their striving turned to sin.
Priest, doctor, hermit, monk grown white
 With prayer, the broken-hearted nun,
The martyr, the wan acolyte,
 The incense-swinging child, — undone
Before God fashioned star or sun!
God, whom I praise; how could I praise,
 If such as I might understand,
Make out and reckon on his ways,
 And bargain for his love, and stand,
 Paying a price, at his right hand?

PICTOR IGNOTUS.

Florence, 15—.

I could have painted pictures like that youth's
 Ye praise so. How my soul springs up! No bar
Stayed me — ah, thought which saddens while it soothes!
 — Never did fate forbid me, star by star,
To outburst on your night with all my gift
 Of fires from God: nor would my flesh have shrunk
From seconding my soul, with eyes uplift
 And wide to heaven, or, straight like thunder, sunk
To the centre, of an instant; or around
 Turned calmly and inquisitive, to scan
The license and the limit, space and bound,
 Allowed to truth made visible in man.
And, like that youth ye praise so, all I saw,
 Over the canvas could my hand have flung,
Each face obedient to its passion's law,
 Each passion clear proclaimed without a tongue;
Whether Hope rose at once in all the blood,
 A-tiptoe for the blessing of embrace,

Or Rapture drooped the eyes, as when her brood
  Pull down the nesting dove's heart to its place;
Or Confidence lit swift the forehead up,
  And locked the mouth fast, like a castle braved, —
O human faces, hath it spilt, my cup?
What did ye give me that I have not saved?
Nor will I say I have not dreamed (how well!)
  Of going — I, in each new picture, — forth,
As, making new hearts beat and bosoms swell,
  To Pope or Kaiser, East, West, South, or North,
Bound for the calmly satisfied great State,
  Or glad aspiring little burgh, it went,
Flowers cast upon the car which bore the freight,
Through old streets named afresh from the event,
Till it reached home, where learned age should greet
  My face, and youth, the star not yet distinct
Above his hair, lie learning at my feet! —
  Oh, thus to live, I and my picture, linked
With love about, and praise, till life should end,
  And then not go to heaven, but linger here,
Here on my earth, earth's every man my friend, —
  The thought grew frightful, 't was so wildly dear!
But a voice changed it. Glimpses of such sights
  Have scared me, like the revels through a door
Of some strange house of idols at its rites!
This world seemed not the world it was before:
Mixed with my loving trusting ones, there trooped
  . . . Who summoned those cold faces that begun
To press on me and judge me? Though I stooped
  Shrinking, as from the soldiery a nun,
They drew me forth, and spite of me . . . enough!
  These buy and sell our pictures, take and give,
Count them for garniture and household-stuff,
  And where they live needs must our pictures live
And see their faces, listen to their prate,
  Partakers of their daily pettiness,
Discussed of, — " This I love, or this I hate,
  This likes me more, and this affects me less!"
Wherefore I chose my portion. If at whiles
  My heart sinks, as monotonous I paint
These endless cloisters and eternal aisles
  With the same series, Virgin, Babe and Saint,
With the same cold calm beautiful regard, —
  At least no merchant traffics in my heart;
The sanctuary's gloom at least shall ward
  Vain tongues from where my pictures stand apart:

Only prayer breaks the silence of the shrine
   While, blackening in the daily candle-smoke,
They moulder on the damp wall's travertine,
   'Mid echoes the light footstep never woke.
So, die my pictures! surely, gently die!
   O youth, men praise so, — holds their praise its worth?
Blown harshly, keeps the trump its golden cry?
   Tastes sweet the water with such specks of earth?

FRA LIPPO LIPPI.

I AM poor brother Lippo, by your leave!
You need not clap your torches to my face.
Zooks, what's to blame? you think you see a monk!
What, 't is past midnight, and you go the rounds,
And here you catch me at an alley's end
Where sportive ladies leave their doors ajar?
The Carmine's my cloister: hunt it up,
Do, — harry out, if you must show your zeal,
Whatever rat, there, haps on his wrong hole,
And nip each softling of a wee white mouse,
Weke, weke, that's crept to keep him company!
Aha, you know your betters! Then, you'll take
Your hand away that's fiddling on my throat,
And please to know me likewise. Who am I?
Why, one, sir, who is lodging with a friend
Three streets off — he's a certain . . . how d' ye call?
Master — a . . . Cosimo of the Medici,
I' the house that caps the corner. Boh! you were best!
Remember and tell me, the day you're hanged,
How you affected such a gullet's-gripe!
But you, sir, it concerns you that your knaves
Pick up a manner nor discredit you:
Zooks, are we pilchards, that they sweep the streets
And count fair prize what comes into their net?
He's Judas to a tittle, that man is!
Just such a face! Why, sir, you make amends.
Lord, I'm not angry! Bid your hangdogs go
Drink out this quarter-florin to the health
Of the munificent House that harbors me
(And many more beside, lads! more beside!)
And all's come square again. I'd like his face —
His, elbowing on his comrade in the door
With the pike and lantern, — for the slave that holds
John Baptist's head a-dangle by the hair

With one hand ("Look you, now," as who should say)
And his weapon in the other, yet unwiped!
It's not your chance to have a bit of chalk,
A wood-coal or the like? or you should see!
Yes, I'm the painter, since you style me so.
What, brother Lippo's doings, up and down,
You know them and they take you? like enough!
I saw the proper twinkle in your eye —
'Tell you, I liked your looks at very first.
Let 's sit and set things straight now, hip to haunch.
Here 's spring come, and the nights one makes up bands
To roam the town and sing out carnival,
And I 've been three weeks shut within my mew,
A-painting for the great man, saints and saints
And saints again. I could not paint all night —
Ouf! I leaned out of window for fresh air.
There came a hurry of feet and little feet,
A sweep of lute-strings, laughs, and whiffs of song, —
Flower o' the broom,
Take away love, and our earth is a tomb!
Flower o' the quince,
I let Lisa go, and what good in life since?
Flower o' the thyme — and so on. Round they went.
Scarce had they turned the corner when a titter
Like the skipping of rabbits by moonlight, — three slim shapes,
And a face that looked up . . . zooks, sir, flesh and blood,
That 's all I 'm made of! Into shreds it went,
Curtain and counterpane and coverlet,
All the bed-furniture — a dozen knots,
There was a ladder! Down I let myself,
Hands and feet, scrambling somehow, and so dropped,
And after them. I came up with the fun
Hard by Saint Laurence, hail fellow, well met, —
Flower o' the rose,
If I 've been merry, what matter who knows?
And so as I was stealing back again
To get to bed and have a bit of sleep
Ere I rise up to-morrow and go work
On Jerome knocking at his poor old breast
With his great round stone to subdue the flesh,
You snap me of the sudden. Ah, I see!
Though your eye twinkles still, you shake your head —
Mine 's shaved — a monk, you say — the sting 's in that!
If Master Cosimo announced himself,
Mum 's the word naturally; but a monk!
Come, what am I a beast for? tell us, now!

I was a baby when my mother died
And father died and left me in the street.
I starved there, God knows how, a year or two
On fig-skins, melon-parings, rinds and shucks,
Refuse and rubbish. One fine frosty day,
My stomach being empty as your hat,
The wind doubled me up and down I went.
Old Aunt Lapaccia trussed me with one hand,
(Its fellow was a stinger as I knew)
And so along the wall, over the bridge,
By the straight cut to the convent. Six words there,
While I stood munching my first bread that month:
" So, boy, you 're minded," quoth the good fat father,
Wiping his own mouth, 't was refection-time, —
" To quit this very miserable world?
Will you renounce " . . . " the mouthful of bread ? " thought
By no means ! Brief, they made a monk of me ;
I did renounce the world, its pride and greed,
Palace, farm, villa, shop, and banking-house,
Trash, such as these poor devils of Medici
Have given their hearts to — all at eight years old.
Well, sir, I found in time, you may be sure,
'T was not for nothing — the good bellyful,
The warm serge and the rope that goes all round,
And day-long blessed idleness beside!
" Let 's see what the urchin 's fit for " — that came next.
Not overmuch their way, I must confess.
Such a to-do ! They tried me with their books :
Lord, they 'd have taught me Latin in pure waste !
Flower o' the clove,
All the Latin I construe is, " amo " I love !
But, mind you, when a boy starves in the streets
Eight years together, as my fortune was,
Watching folk's faces to know who will fling
The bit of half-stripped grape-bunch he desires,
And who will curse or kick him for his pains, —
Which gentleman processional and fine,
Holding a candle to the Sacrament,
Will wink and let him lift a plate and catch
The droppings of the wax to sell again,
Or holla for the Eight and have him whipped, —
How say I ? — nay, which dog bites, which lets drop
His bone from the heap of offal in the street, —
Why, soul and sense of him grow sharp alike,
He learns the look of things, and none the less
For admonition from the hunger-pinch.

I had a store of such remarks, be sure,
Which, after I found leisure, turned to use.
I drew men's faces on my copy-books,
Scrawled them within the antiphonary's marge,
Joined legs and arms to the long music-notes,
Found eyes and nose and chin for A's and B's,
And made a string of pictures of the world
Betwixt the ins and outs of verb and noun,
On the wall, the bench, the door. The monks looked black.
"Nay," quoth the Prior, "turn him out, d' ye say?
In no wise. Lose a crow and catch a lark.
What if at last we get our man of parts,
We Carmelites, like those Camaldolese
And Preaching Friars, to do our church up fine
And put the front on it that ought to be!"
And hereupon he bade me daub away.
Thank you! my head being crammed, the walls a blank,
Never was such prompt disemburdening.
First, every sort of monk, the black and white,
I drew them, fat and lean: then, folk at church,
From good old gossips waiting to confess
Their cribs of barrel-droppings, candle-ends, —
To the breathless fellow at the altar-foot,
Fresh from his murder, safe and sitting there
With the little children round him in a row
Of admiration, half for his beard and half
For that white anger of his victim's son
Shaking a fist at him with one fierce arm,
Signing himself with the other because of Christ
(Whose sad face on the cross sees only this
After the passion of a thousand years)
Till some poor girl, her apron o'er her head,
(Which the intense eyes looked through) came at eve
On tiptoe, said a word, dropped in a loaf,
Her pair of earrings and a bunch of flowers
(The brute took growling), prayed, and so was gone.
I painted all, then cried "'T is ask and have;
Choose, for more's ready!" — laid the ladder flat,
And showed my covered bit of cloister-wall.
The monks closed in a circle and praised loud
Till checked, taught what to see and not to see,
Being simple bodies, — "That's the very man!
Look at the boy who stoops to pat the dog!
That woman's like the Prior's niece who comes
To care about his asthma: it's the life!"
But there my triumph's straw-fire flared and funked;

Their betters took their turn to see and say:
The Prior and the learned pulled a face
And stopped all that in no time. "How? what's here?
Quite from the mark of painting, bless us all!
Faces, arms, legs, and bodies like the true
As much as pea and pea! it's devil's-game!
Your business is not to catch men with show,
With homage to the perishable clay,
But lift them over it, ignore it all,
Make them forget there's such a thing as flesh.
Your business is to paint the souls of men —
Man's soul, and it's a fire, smoke . . . no, it's not . . .
It's vapor done up like a new-born babe —
(In that shape when you die it leaves your mouth)
It's . . . well, what matters talking, it's the soul!
Give us no more of body than shows soul!
Here's Giotto, with his Saint a-praising God,
That sets us praising, — why not stop with him?
Why put all thoughts of praise out of our head
With wonder at lines, colors, and what not?
Paint the soul, never mind the legs and arms!
Rub all out, try at it a second time.
Oh, that white smallish female with the breasts,
She's just my niece . . . Herodias, I would say, —
Who went and danced and got men's heads cut off!
Have it all out!" Now, is this sense, I ask?
A fine way to paint soul, by painting body
So ill, the eye can't stop there, must go further
And can't fare worse! Thus, yellow does for white
When what you put for yellow's simply black,
And any sort of meaning looks intense
When all beside itself means and looks nought.
Why can't a painter lift each foot in turn,
Left foot and right foot, go a double step,
Make his flesh liker and his soul more like,
Both in their order? Take the prettiest face,
The Prior's niece . . . patron-saint — is it so pretty
You can't discover if it means hope, fear,
Sorrow or joy? won't beauty go with these?
Suppose I've made her eyes all right and blue,
Can't I take breath and try to add life's flash,
And then add soul and heighten them threefold?
Or say there's beauty with no soul at all —
(I never saw it — put the case the same —)
If you get simple beauty and nought else,
You get about the best thing God invents:

That's somewhat: and you'll find the soul you have
    missed,
Within yourself, when you return him thanks.
"Rub all out!" Well, well, there's my life, in short,
And so the thing has gone on ever since.
I'm grown a man no doubt, I've broken bounds:
You should not take a fellow eight years old
And make him swear to never kiss the girls.
I'm my own master, paint now as I please —
Having a friend, you see, in the Corner-house!
Lord, it's fast holding by the rings in front —
Those great rings serve more purposes than just
To plant a flag in, or tie up a horse!
And yet the old schooling sticks, the old grave eyes
Are peeping o'er my shoulder as I work,
The heads shake still — "It's art's decline, my son!
You're not of the true painters, great and old;
Brother Angelico's the man, you'll find;
Brother Lorenzo stands his single peer:
Fag on at flesh, you'll never make the third!"
Flower o' the pine,
You keep your mistr . . . manners, and I'll stick to mine!
I'm not the third, then: bless us, they must know!
Don't you think they're the likeliest to know,
They with their Latin? So, I swallow my rage,
Clench my teeth, suck my lips in tight, and paint
To please them — sometimes do and sometimes don't;
For, doing most, there's pretty sure to come
A turn, some warm eve finds me at my saints —
A laugh, a cry, the business of the world —
(*Flower o' the peach,*
Death for us all, and his own life for each!)
And my whole soul revolves, the cup runs over,
The world and life's too big to pass for a dream,
And I do these wild things in sheer despite,
And play the fooleries you catch me at,
In pure rage! The old mill-horse, out at grass
After hard years, throws up his stiff heels so,
Although the miller does not preach to him
The only good of grass is to make chaff.
What would men have? Do they like grass or no —
May they or may n't they? all I want's the thing
Settled forever one way. As it is,
You tell too many lies and hurt yourself:
You don't like what you only like too much,
You do like what, if given you at your word,

You find abundantly detestable.
For me, I think I speak as I was taught;
I always see the garden and God there
A-making man's wife: and, my lesson learned,
The value and significance of flesh,
I can't unlearn ten minutes afterwards.

You understand me: I'm a beast, I know.
But see, now — why, I see as certainly
As that the morning-star's about to shine,
What will hap some day. We've a youngster here
Comes to our convent, studies what I do,
Slouches and stares and lets no atom drop:
His name is Guidi — he'll not mind the monks —
They call him Hulking Tom, he lets them talk —
He picks my practice up — he'll paint apace,
I hope so — though I never live so long,
I know what's sure to follow. You be judge!
You speak no Latin more than I, belike;
However, you're my man, you've seen the world
— The beauty and the wonder and the power,
The shapes of things, their colors, lights and shades,
Changes, surprises, — and God made it all!
— For what? Do you feel thankful, ay or no,
For this fair town's face, yonder river's line,
The mountain round it and the sky above,
Much more the figures of man, woman, child,
These are the frame to? What's it all about?
To be passed over, despised? or dwelt upon,
Wondered at? oh, this last of course! — you say.
But why not do as well as say, — paint these
Just as they are, careless what comes of it?
God's works — paint any one, and count it crime
To let a truth slip. Don't object, "His works
Are here already; nature is complete:
Suppose you reproduce her — (which you can't)
There's no advantage! you must beat her, then."
For, don't you mark? we're made so that we love
First when we see them painted, things we have passed
Perhaps a hundred times nor cared to see;
And so they are better, painted — better to us,
Which is the same thing. Art was given for that;
God uses us to help each other so,
Lending our minds out. Have you noticed, now,
Your cullion's hanging face? A bit of chalk,
And trust me but you should, though! How much more,

If I drew higher things with the same truth!
That were to take the Prior's pulpit-place,
Interpret God to all of you! Oh, oh,
It makes me mad to see what men shall do
And we in our graves! This world's no blot for us,
Nor blank; it means intensely, and means good:
To find its meaning is my meat and drink.
"Ay, but you don't so instigate to prayer!"
Strikes in the Prior: "when your meaning's plain
It does not say to folk — remember matins,
Or, mind you fast next Friday!" Why, for this
What need of art at all? A skull and bones,
Two bits of stick nailed crosswise, or, what's best,
A bell to chime the hour with, does as well.
I painted a Saint Laurence six months since
At Prato, splashed the fresco in fine style:
"How looks my painting, now the scaffold's down?"
I ask a brother: "Hugely," he returns —
"Already not one phiz of your three slaves
Who turn the Deacon off his toasted side,
But's scratched and prodded to our heart's content,
The pious people have so eased their own
With coming to say prayers there in a rage:
We get on fast to see the bricks beneath.
Expect another job this time next year,
For pity and religion grow i' the crowd —
Your painting serves its purpose!" Hang the fools!

— That is — you'll not mistake an idle word
Spoke in a huff by a poor monk, God wot,
Tasting the air this spicy night which turns
The unaccustomed head like Chianti wine!
Oh, the church knows! don't misreport me, now!
It's natural a poor monk out of bounds
Should have his apt word to excuse himself:
And hearken how I plot to make amends.
I have bethought me: I shall paint a piece
. . . There's for you! Give me six months, then go, see
Something in Sant' Ambrogio's! Bless the nuns!
They want a cast o' my office. I shall paint
God in the midst, Madonna and her babe,
Ringed by a bowery, flowery angel-brood,
Lilies and vestments and white faces, sweet
As puff on puff of grated orris-root
When ladies crowd to church at midsummer.
And then i' the front, of course a saint or two —

Saint John, because he saves the Florentines,
Saint Ambrose, who puts down in black and white
The convent's friends and gives them a long day,
And Job, I must have him there past mistake,
The man of Uz (and Us without the z,
Painters who need his patience). Well, all these
Secured at their devotion, up shall come
Out of a corner when you least expect,
As one by a dark stair into a great light,
Music and talking, who but Lippo! I! —
Mazed, motionless, and moonstruck — I 'm the man!
Back I shrink — what is this I see and hear?
I, caught up with my monk's-things by mistake,
My old serge gown and rope that goes all round,
I, in this presence, this pure company!
Where 's a hole, where 's a corner for escape?
Then steps a sweet angelic slip of a thing
Forward, puts out a soft palm — " Not so fast!"
— Addresses the celestial presence, "nay —
He made you and devised you, after all,
Though he 's none of you! Could Saint John there draw —
His camel-hair make up a painting-brush?
We come to brother Lippo for all that,
Iste perfecit opus!" So, all smile —
I shuffle sideways with my blushing face
Under the cover of a hundred wings
Thrown like a spread of kirtles when you 're gay
And play hot cockles, all the doors being shut,
Till, wholly unexpected, in there pops
The hothead husband! Thus I scuttle off
To some safe bench behind, not letting go
The palm of her, the little lily thing
That spoke the good word for me in the nick,
Like the Prior's niece . . . Saint Lucy, I would say.
And so all 's saved for me, and for the church
A pretty picture gained. Go, six months hence!
Your hand, sir, and good-bye: no lights, no lights!
The street 's hushed, and I know my own way back,
Don't fear me! There 's the gray beginning. Zooks!

ANDREA DEL SARTO.

CALLED "THE FAULTLESS PAINTER."

BUT do not let us quarrel any more,
No, my Lucrezia; bear with me for once:
Sit down and all shall happen as you wish.
You turn your face, but does it bring your heart?
I'll work then for your friend's friend, never fear,
Treat his own subject after his own way,
Fix his own time, accept too his own price,
And shut the money into this small hand
When next it takes mine. Will it? tenderly?
Oh, I'll content him, — but to-morrow, Love!
I often am much wearier than you think,
This evening more than usual, and it seems
As if — forgive now — should you let me sit
Here by the window with your hand in mine
And look a half-hour forth on Fiesole,
Both of one mind, as married people use,
Quietly, quietly the evening through,
I might get up to-morrow to my work
Cheerful and fresh as ever. Let us try.
To-morrow, how you shall be glad for this!
Your soft hand is a woman of itself,
And mine the man's bared breast she curls inside.
Don't count the time lost, neither; you must serve
For each of the five pictures we require:
It saves a model. So! keep looking so —
My serpentining beauty, rounds on rounds!
— How could you ever prick those perfect ears,
Even to put the pearl there! oh, so sweet —
My face, my moon, my everybody's moon,
Which everybody looks on and calls his,
And, I suppose, is looked on by in turn,
While she looks — no one's: very dear, no less.
You smile? why, there's my picture ready made,
There's what we painters call our harmony!
A common grayness silvers everything, —
All in a twilight, you and I alike
— You, at the point of your first pride in me
(That's gone you know), — but I, at every point;
My youth, my hope, my art, being all toned down
To yonder sober pleasant Fiesole.
There's the bell clinking from the chapel-top;

That length of convent-wall across the way
Holds the trees safer, huddled more inside ;
The last monk leaves the garden ; days decrease,
And autumn grows, autumn in everything.
Eh ? the whole seems to fall into a shape
As if I saw alike my work and self
And all that I was born to be and do,
A twilight-piece. Love, we are in God's hand.
How strange now looks the life he makes us lead ;
So free we seem, so fettered fast we are !
I feel he laid the fetter : let it lie !
This chamber for example — turn your head —
All that 's behind us ! You don't understand
Nor care to understand about my art,
But you can hear at least when people speak :
And that cartoon, the second from the door
— It is the thing, Love ! so such things should be —
Behold Madonna ! — I am bold to say.
I can do with my pencil what I know,
What I see, what at bottom of my heart
I wish for, if I ever wish so deep —
Do easily, too — when I say, perfectly,
I do not boast, perhaps : yourself are judge,
Who listened to the Legate's talk last week,
And just as much they used to say in France.
At any rate 't is easy, all of it !
No sketches first, no studies, that 's long past :
I do what many dream of all their lives,
— Dream ? strive to do, and agonize to do,
And fail in doing. I could count twenty such
On twice your fingers, and not leave this town,
Who strive — you don't know how the others strive
To paint a little thing like that you smeared
Carelessly passing with your robes afloat, —
Yet do much less, so much less, Someone says,
(I know his name, no matter) — so much less !
Well, less is more, Lucrezia : I am judged.
There burns a truer light of God in them,
In their vexed beating stuffed and stopped-up brain,
Heart, or whate'er else, than goes on to prompt
This low-pulsed forthright craftsman's hand of mine.
Their works drop groundward, but themselves, I know,
Reach many a time a heaven that 's shut to me,
Enter and take their place there sure enough,
Though they come back and cannot tell the world.
My works are nearer heaven, but I sit here.

The sudden blood of these men! at a word —
Praise them, it boils, or blame them, it boils too.
I, painting from myself and to myself,
Know what I do, am unmoved by men's blame
Or their praise either. Somebody remarks
Morello's outline there is wrongly traced,
His hue mistaken; what of that? or else,
Rightly traced and well ordered; what of that?
Speak as they please, what does the mountain care?
Ah, but a man's reach should exceed his grasp,
Or what's a heaven for? All is silver-gray
Placid and perfect with my art: the worse!
I know both what I want and what might gain,
And yet how profitless to know, to sigh
"Had I been two, another and myself,
Our head would have o'erlooked the world!" No doubt.
Yonder's a work now, of that famous youth
The Urbinate who died five years ago.
('T is copied, George Vasari sent it me.)
Well, I can fancy how he did it all,
Pouring his soul, with kings and popes to see,
Reaching, that heaven might so replenish him,
Above and through his art — for it gives way;
That arm is wrongly put — and there again —
A fault to pardon in the drawing's lines,
Its body, so to speak: its soul is right,
He means right — that, a child may understand.
Still, what an arm! and I could alter it:
But all the play, the insight and the stretch —
Out of me, out of me! And wherefore out?
Had you enjoined them on me, given me soul,
We might have risen to Rafael, I and you!
Nay, Love, you did give all I asked, I think —
More than I merit, yes, by many times.
But had you — oh, with the same perfect brow,
And perfect eyes, and more than perfect mouth,
And the low voice my soul hears, as a bird
The fowler's pipe, and follows to the snare —
Had you, with these the same, but brought a mind!
Some women do so. Had the mouth there urged,
"God and the glory! never care for gain.
The present by the future, what is that?
Live for fame, side by side with Agnolo!
Rafael is waiting: up to God, all three!"
I might have done it for you. So it seems:
Perhaps not. All is as God overrules.

Beside, incentives come from the soul's self;
The rest avail not. Why do I need you?
What wife had Rafael, or has Agnolo?
In this world, who can do a thing, will not;
And who would do it, cannot, I perceive:
Yet the will 's somewhat — somewhat, too, the power —
And thus we half-men struggle. At the end,
God, I conclude, compensates, punishes.
'T is safer for me, if the award be strict,
That I am something underrated here,
Poor this long while, despised, to speak the truth.
I dared not, do you know, leave home all day,
For fear of chancing on the Paris lords.
The best is when they pass and look aside;
But they speak sometimes; I must bear it all.
Well may they speak! That Francis, that first time,
And that long festal year at Fontainebleau!
I surely then could sometimes leave the ground,
Put on the glory, Rafael's daily wear,
In that humane great monarch's golden look, —
One finger in his beard or twisted curl
Over his mouth's good mark that made the smile,
One arm about my shoulder, round my neck,
The jingle of his gold chain in my ear,
I painting proudly with his breath on me,
All his court round him, seeing with his eyes,
Such frank French eyes, and such a fire of souls
Profuse, my hand kept plying by those hearts, —
And, best of all, this, this, this face beyond,
This in the background, waiting on my work,
To crown the issue with a last reward!
A good time, was it not, my kingly days?
And had you not grown restless . . . but I know —
'T is done and past; 't was right, my instinct said;
Too live the life grow, golden and not gray,
And I 'm the weak-eyed bat no sun should tempt
Out of the grange whose four walls make his world.
How could it end in any other way?
You called me, and I came home to your heart.
The triumph was — to reach and stay there; since
I reached it ere the triumph, what is lost?
Let my hands frame your face in your hair's gold,
You beautiful Lucrezia that are mine!
" Rafael did this, Andrea painted that;
The Roman's is the better when you pray,
But still the other's Virgin was his wife " —

Men will excuse me. I am glad to judge
Both pictures in your presence; clearer grows
My better fortune, I resolve to think.
For, do you know, Lucrezia, as God lives,
Said one day Agnolo, his very self,
To Rafael . . . I have known it all these years . . .
(When the young man was flaming out his thoughts
Upon a palace-wall for Rome to see,
Too lifted up in heart because of it)
"Friend, there's a certain sorry little scrub
Goes up and down our Florence, none cares how,
Who, were he set to plan and execute
As you are, pricked on by your popes and kings,
Would bring the sweat into that brow of yours!"
To Rafael's! — And indeed the arm is wrong.
I hardly dare . . . yet, only you to see,
Give the chalk here — quick, thus the line should go!
Ay, but the soul! he's Rafael! rub it out!
Still, all I care for, if he spoke the truth,
(What he? why, who but Michel Agnolo?
Do you forget already words like those?)
If really there was such a chance, so lost, —
Is, whether you're — not grateful — but more pleased.
Well, let me think so. And you smile indeed!
This hour has been an hour! Another smile?
If you would sit thus by me every night
I should work better, do you comprehend?
I mean that I should earn more, give you more.
See, it is settled dusk now; there's a star;
Morello's gone, the watch-lights show the wall,
The cue-owls speak the name we call them by.
Come from the window, love, — come in, at last,
Inside the melancholy little house
We built to be so gay with. God is just.
King Francis may forgive me: oft at nights
When I look up from painting, eyes tired out,
The walls become illumined, brick from brick
Distinct, instead of mortar, fierce bright gold,
That gold of his I did cement them with!
Let us but love each other. Must you go?
That Cousin here again? he waits outside?
Must see you — you, and not with me? Those loans?
More gaming debts to pay? you smiled for that?
Well, let smiles buy me! have you more to spend?
While hand and eye and something of a heart
Are left me, work's my ware, and what's it worth?

I 'll pay my fancy. Only let me sit
The gray remainder of the evening out,
Idle, you call it, and muse perfectly
How I could paint, were I but back in France,
One picture, just one more — the Virgin's face,
Not yours this time! I want you at my side
To hear them — that is, Michel Agnolo —
Judge all I do and tell you of its worth.
Will you? To-morrow, satisfy your friend.
I take the subjects for his corridor,
Finish the portrait out of hand — there, there,
And throw him in another thing or two
If he demurs; the whole should prove enough
To pay for this same Cousin's freak. Beside,
What 's better and what 's all I care about,
Get you the thirteen scudi for the ruff!
Love, does that please you? Ah, but what does he,
The Cousin! what does he to please you more?

  I am grown peaceful as old age to-night.
I regret little, I would change still less.
Since there my past life lies, why alter it?
The very wrong to Francis! — it is true
I took his coin, was tempted and complied,
And built this house and sinned, and all is said.
My father and my mother died of want.
Well, had I riches of my own? you see
How one gets rich! Let each one bear his lot.
They were born poor, lived poor, and poor they died:
And I have labored somewhat in my time
And not been paid profusely. Some good son
Paint my two hundred pictures — let him try!
No doubt, there 's something strikes a balance. Yes,
You loved me quite enough, it seems to-night.
This must suffice me here. What would one have?
In heaven, perhaps, new chances, one more chance —
Four great walls in the New Jerusalem,
Meted on each side by the angel's reed,
For Leonard, Rafael, Agnolo and me
To cover — the three first without a wife,
While I have mine! So — still they overcome
Because there 's still Lucrezia, — as I choose.

  Again the Cousin's whistle! Go, my Love.

THE BISHOP ORDERS HIS TOMB AT SAINT PRAXED'S CHURCH.

ROME, 15—.

VANITY, saith the preacher, vanity!
Draw round my bed: is Anselm keeping back?
Nephews — sons mine . . . ah God, I know not! Well —
She, men would have to be your mother once,
Old Gandolf envied me, so fair she was!
What's done is done, and she is dead beside,
Dead long ago, and I am Bishop since,
And as she died so must we die ourselves,
And thence ye may perceive the world's a dream.
Life, how and what is it? As here I lie
In this state-chamber, dying by degrees,
Hours and long hours in the dead night, I ask
" Do I live, am I dead?" Peace, peace seems all.
Saint Praxed's ever was the church for peace;
And so, about this tomb of mine. I fought
With tooth and nail to save my niche, ye know:
— Old Gandolf cozened me, despite my care;
Shrewd was that snatch from out the corner South
He graced his carrion with, God curse the same!
Yet still my niche is not so cramped but thence
One sees the pulpit o' the epistle-side,
And somewhat of the choir, those silent seats,
And up into the aery dome where live
The angels, and a sunbeam's sure to lurk:
And I shall fill my slab of basalt there,
And 'neath my tabernacle take my rest,
With those nine columns round me, two and two,
The odd one at my feet where Anselm stands:
Peach-blossom marble all, the rare, the ripe
As fresh-poured red wine of a mighty pulse.
— Old Gandolf with his paltry onion-stone,
Put me where I may look at him! True peach,
Rosy and flawless: how I earned the prize!
Draw close: that conflagration of my church
— What then? So much was saved if aught were missed!
My sons, ye would not be my death? Go dig
The white-grape vineyard where the oil-press stood,
Drop water gently till the surface sink,
And if ye find . . . Ah God, I know not, I ! . . .
Bedded in store of rotten fig-leaves soft,

And corded up in a tight olive-frail,
Some lump, ah God, of *lapis lazuli*,
Big as a Jew's head cut off at the nape,
Blue as a vein o'er the Madonna's breast . . .
Sons, all have I bequeathed you, villas, all,
That brave Frascati villa with its bath,
So, let the blue lump poise between my knees,
Like God the Father's globe on both his hands
Ye worship in the Jesu Church so gay,
For Gandolf shall not choose but see and burst!
Swift as a weaver's shuttle fleet our years:
Man goeth to the grave, and where is he?
Did I say basalt for my slab, sons? Black —
'T was ever antique-black I meant! How else
Shall ye contrast my frieze to come beneath?
The bas-relief in bronze ye promised me,
Those Pans and Nymphs ye wot of, and perchance
Some tripod, thyrsus, with a vase or so,
The Saviour at his sermon on the mount,
Saint Praxed in a glory, and one Pan
Ready to twitch the Nymph's last garment off,
And Moses with the tables . . . but I know
Ye mark me not! What do they whisper thee,
Child of my bowels, Anselm? Ah, ye hope
To revel down my villas while I gasp
Bricked o'er with beggar's mouldy travertine
Which Gandolf from his tomb-top chuckles at!
Nay, boys, ye love me — all of jasper, then!
'T is jasper ye stand pledged to, lest I grieve
My bath must needs be left behind, alas!
One block, pure green as a pistachio-nut,
There's plenty jasper somewhere in the world —
And have I not Saint Praxed's ear to pray
Horses for ye, and brown Greek manuscripts,
And mistresses with great smooth marbly limbs?
— That's if ye carve my epitaph aright,
Choice Latin, picked phrase, Tully's every word,
No gaudy ware like Gandolf's second line —
Tully, my masters? Ulpian serves his need!
And then how I shall lie through centuries,
And hear the blessed mutter of the mass,
And see God made and eaten all day long,
And feel the steady candle-flame, and taste
Good strong thick stupefying incense-smoke!
For as I lie here, hours of the dead night,
Dying in state and by such slow degrees,

I fold my arms as if they clasped a crook,
And stretch my feet forth straight as stone can point,
And let the bedclothes, for a mortcloth, drop
Into great laps and folds of sculptor's-work:
And as yon tapers dwindle, and strange thoughts
Grow, with a certain humming in my ears,
About the life before I lived this life,
And this life too, popes, cardinals and priests,
Saint Praxed at his sermon on the mount,
Your tall pale mother with her talking eyes,
And new-found agate urns as fresh as day,
And marble's language, Latin pure, discreet,
— Aha, ELUCESCEBAT quoth our friend?
No Tully, said I, Ulpian at the best!
Evil and brief hath been my pilgrimage.
All *lapis*, all, sons! Else I give the Pope
My villas! Will ye ever eat my heart?
Ever your eyes were as a lizard's quick,
They glitter like your mother's for my soul,
Or ye would heighten my impoverished frieze,
Piece out its starved design, and fill my vase
With grapes, and add a visor and a Term,
And to the tripod ye would tie a lynx
That in his struggle throws the thyrsus down,
To comfort me on my entablature
Whereon I am to lie till I must ask
" Do I live, am I dead?" There, leave me, there!
For ye have stabbed me with ingratitude
To death — ye wish it — God, ye wish it! Stone —
Gritstone, a-crumble! Clammy squares which sweat
As if the corpse they keep were oozing through —
And no more *lapis* to delight the world!
Well, go! I bless ye. Fewer tapers there,
But in a row: and, going, turn your backs
— Ay, like departing altar-ministrants,
And leave me in my church, the church for peace,
That I may watch at leisure if he leers —
Old Gandolf, at me, from his onion-stone,
As still he envied me, so fair she was!

BISHOP BLOUGRAM'S APOLOGY.

No more wine? then we'll push back chairs and talk.
A final glass for me, though: cool, i' faith!
We ought to have our Abbey back, you see.

It 's different, preaching in basilicas,
And doing duty in some masterpiece
Like this of brother Pugin's, bless his heart!
I doubt if they 're half baked, those chalk rosettes,
Ciphers and stucco-twiddlings everywhere;
It 's just like breathing in a lime-kiln: eh?
These hot long ceremonies of our church
Cost us a little — oh, they pay the price,
You take me — amply pay it! Now, we 'll talk.

So, you despise me, Mr. Gigadibs.
No deprecation, — nay, I beg you, sir!
Beside 't is our engagement : don't you know,
I promised, if you 'd watch a dinner out,
We 'd see truth dawn together? — truth that peeps
Over the glasses' edge when dinner 's done,
And body gets its sop and holds its noise
And leaves soul free a little. Now 's the time:
Truth's break of day! You do despise me then.
And if I say, " despise me," — never fear!
I know you do not in a certain sense —
Not in my arm-chair, for example : here,
I well imagine you respect my place
(*Status, entourage,* worldly circumstance)
Quite to its value — very much indeed :
— Are up to the protesting eyes of you
In pride at being seated here for once —
You 'll turn it to such capital account!
When somebody, through years and years to come,
Hints of the bishop, — names me — that 's enough :
" Blougram? I knew him " — (into it you slide)
" Dined with him once, a Corpus Christi Day,
All alone, we two ; he 's a clever man :
And after dinner, — why, the wine you know, —
Oh, there was wine, and good! — what with the wine . .
'Faith, we began upon all sorts of talk!
He 's no bad fellow, Blougram ; he had seen
Something of mine he relished, some review :
He 's quite above their humbug in his heart.
Half-said as much, indeed — the thing 's his trade.
I warrant, Blougram 's sceptical at times :
How otherwise? I liked him, I confess ! "
Che che, my dear sir, as we say at Rome,
Don't you protest now! It 's fair give and take ;
You have had your turn and spoken your home-truths :
The hand 's mine now, and here you follow suit.

Thus much conceded, still the first fact stays —
You do despise me; your ideal of life
Is not the bishop's: you would not be I.
You would like better to be Goethe, now,
Or Buonaparte, or, bless me, lower still,
Count D'Orsay, — so you did what you preferred,
Spoke as you thought, and, as you cannot help,
Believed or disbelieved, no matter what,
So long as on that point, whate'er it was,
You loosed your mind, were whole and sole yourself.
— That, my ideal never can include,
Upon that element of truth and worth
Never be based! for say they make me Pope —
(They can't — suppose it for our argument!)
Why, there I'm at my tether's end, I've reached
My height, and not a height which pleases you:
An unbelieving Pope won't do, you say.
It's like those eerie stories nurses tell,
Of how some actor on a stage played Death,
With pasteboard crown, sham orb and tinselled dart,
And called himself the monarch of the world;
Then, going in the tire-room afterward,
Because the play was done, to shift himself,
Got touched upon the sleeve familiarly,
The moment he had shut the closet door,
By Death himself. Thus God might touch a Pope
At unawares, ask what his baubles mean,
And whose part he presumed to play just now?
Best be yourself, imperial, plain and true!

So, drawing comfortable breath again,
You weigh and find, whatever more or less
I boast of my ideal realized,
Is nothing in the balance when opposed
To your ideal, your grand simple life,
Of which you will not realize one jot.
I am much, you are nothing; you would be all,
I would be merely much: you beat me there.

No, friend, you do not beat me: hearken why!
The common problem, yours, mine, every one's,
Is — not to fancy what were fair in life
Provided it could be, — but, finding first
What may be, then find how to make it fair
Up to our means: a very different thing!
No abstract intellectual plan of life

Quite irrespective of life's plainest laws,
But one, a man, who is man and nothing more,
May lead within a world which (by your leave)
Is Rome or London, not Fool's-paradise.
Embellish Rome, idealize away,
Make paradise of London if you can,
You 're welcome, nay, you 're wise.

         A simile!
We mortals cross the ocean of this world
Each in his average cabin of a life ;
The best 's not big, the worst yields elbow-room.
Now for our six months' voyage — how prepare?
You come on shipboard with a landsman's list
Of things he calls convenient : so they are !
An India screen is pretty furniture,
A piano-forte is a fine resource,
All Balzac's novels occupy one shelf,
The new edition fifty volumes long ;
And little Greek books, with the funny type
They get up well at Leipsic, fill the next :
Go on! slabbed marble, what a bath it makes !
And Parma's pride, the Jerome, let us add!
'T were pleasant could Correggio's fleeting glow
Hang full in face of one where'er one roams.
Since he more than the others brings with him
Italy's self, — the marvellous Modenese ! —
Yet was not on your list before, perhaps.
 — Alas, friend, here 's the agent . . . is 't the name?
The captain, or whoever 's master here —
You see him screw his face up ; what 's his cry
Ere you set foot on shipboard ? "Six feet square!"
If you won't understand what six feet mean,
Compute and purchase stores accordingly —
And if, in pique because he overhauls
Your Jerome, piano, bath, you come on board
Bare — why, you cut a figure at the first
While sympathetic landsmen see you off ;
Not afterward, when long ere half seas over,
You peep up from your utterly naked boards
Into some snug and well-appointed berth,
Like mine for instance (try the cooler jug —
Put back the other, but don't jog the ice!)
And mortified you mutter, "Well and good ;
He sits enjoying his sea-furniture ;
'T is stout and proper, and there 's store of it :

Though I 've the better notion, all agree,
Of fitting rooms up. Hang the carpenter,
Neat ship-shape fixings and contrivances —
I would have brought my Jerome, frame and all!"
And meantime you bring nothing: never mind —
You 've proved your artist-nature: what you don't
You might bring, so despise me, as I say.

Now come, let 's backward to the starting-place.
See my way: we 're two college friends, suppose.
Prepare together for our voyage, then;
Each note and check the other in his work, —
Here 's mine, a bishop's outfit; criticise!
What 's wrong? why won't you be a bishop too?

Why first, you don't believe, you don't and can't,
(Not statedly, that is, and fixedly
And absolutely and exclusively)
In any revelation called divine.
No dogmas nail your faith; and what remains
But say so, like the honest man you are?
First, therefore, overhaul theology!
Nay, I too, not a fool, you please to think,
Must find believing every whit as hard:
And if I do not frankly say as much,
The ugly consequence is clear enough.

Now wait, my friend: well, I do not believe —
If you 'll accept no faith that is not fixed,
Absolute and exclusive, as you say.
You 're wrong — I mean to prove it in due time.
Meanwhile, I know where difficulties lie
I could not, cannot solve, nor ever shall,
So give up hope accordingly to solve —
(To you, and over the wine). Our dogmas then
With both of us, though in unlike degree,
Missing full credence — overboard with them!
I mean to meet you on your own premise:
Good, there go mine in company with yours!

And now what are we? unbelievers both,
Calm and complete, determinately fixed
To-day, to-morrow, and forever, pray?
You 'll guarantee me that? Not so, I think!
In no wise! all we 've gained is, that belief,
As unbelief before, shakes us by fits,

Confounds us like its predecessor. Where's
The gain? how can we guard our unbelief,
Make it bear fruit to us?— the problem here.
Just when we are safest, there's a sunset-touch,
A fancy from a flower-bell, some one's death,
A chorus-ending from Euripides, —
And that's enough for fifty hopes and fears
As old and new at once as nature's self,
To rap and knock and enter in our soul,
Take hands and dance there, a fantastic ring,
Round the ancient idol, on his base again, —
The grand Perhaps! We look on helplessly.
There the old misgivings, crooked questions are —
This good God, — what he could do, if he would,
Would, if he could — then must have done long since :
If so, when, where and how? some way must be, —
Once feel about, and soon or late you hit
Some sense, in which it might be, after all.
Why not, "The Way, the Truth, the Life?"

— That way
Over the mountain, which who stands upon
Is apt to doubt if it be meant for a road ;
While, if he views it from the waste itself,
Up goes the line there, plain from base to brow,
Not vague, mistakable! what's a break or two
Seen from the unbroken desert either side?
And then (to bring in fresh philosophy)
What if the breaks themselves should prove at last
The most consummate of contrivances
To train a man's eye, teach him what is faith?
And so we stumble at truth's very test!
All we have gained then by our unbelief
Is a life of doubt diversified by faith,
For one of faith diversified by doubt :
We called the chess-board white, — we call it black.

"Well," you rejoin, "the end's no worse, at least;
We've reason for both colors on the board :
Why not confess then, where I drop the faith
And you the doubt, that I'm as right as you?"

Because, friend, in the next place, this being so,
And both things even, — faith and unbelief
Left to a man's choice, — we'll proceed a step,
Returning to our image, which I like.

A man's choice, yes — but a cabin-passenger's —
The man made for the special life o' the world —
Do you forget him? I remember though!
Consult our ship's conditions and you find
One and but one choice suitable to all;
The choice, that you unluckily prefer,
Turning things topsy-turvy — they or it
Going to the ground. Belief or unbelief
Bears upon life, determines its whole course,
Begins at its beginning. See the world
Such as it is, — you made it not, nor I;
I mean to take it as it is, — and you,
Not so you 'll take it, — though you get nought else.
I know the special kind of life I like,
What suits the most my idiosyncrasy,
Brings out the best of me and bears me fruit
In power, peace, pleasantness and length of days.
I find that positive belief does this
For me, and unbelief, no whit of this.
— For you, it does, however? — that, we'll try!
'T is clear, I cannot lead my life, at least,
Induce the world to let me peaceably,
Without declaring at the outset, "Friends,
I absolutely and peremptorily
Believe!" — I say, faith is my waking life:
One sleeps, indeed, and dreams at intervals,
We know, but waking 's the main point with us,
And my provision 's for life's waking part.
Accordingly, I use heart, head and hand
All day, I build, scheme, study, and make friends;
And when night overtakes me, down I lie,
Sleep, dream a little, and get done with it,
The sooner the better, to begin afresh.
What 's midnight doubt before the dayspring's faith?
You, the philosopher, that disbelieve,
That recognize the night, give dreams their weight —
To be consistent you should keep your bed,
Abstain from healthy acts that prove you man,
For fear you drowse perhaps at unawares!
And certainly at night you 'll sleep and dream,
Live through the day and bustle as you please.
And so you live to sleep as I to wake,
To unbelieve as I to still believe?
Well, and the common sense o' the world calls you
Bed-ridden, — and its good things come to me.
Its estimation, which is half the fight,

That's the first-cabin comfort I secure :
The next . . . but you perceive with half an eye!
Come, come, it's best believing, if we may ;
You can't but own that !

       Next, concede again,
If once we choose belief, on all accounts
We can't be too decisive in our faith,
Conclusive and exclusive in its terms,
To suit the world which gives us the good things.
In every man's career are certain points
Whereon he dares not be indifferent ;
The world detects him clearly, if he dare,
As baffled at the game, and losing life.
He may care little or he may care much
For riches, honor, pleasure, work, repose,
Since various theories of life and life's
Success are extant which might easily
Comport with either estimate of these ;
And whoso chooses wealth or poverty,
Labor or quiet, is not judged a fool
Because his fellow would choose otherwise :
We let him choose upon his own account
So long as he's consistent with his choice.
But certain points, left wholly to himself,
When once a man has arbitrated on,
We say he must succeed there or go hang.
Thus, he should wed the woman he loves most
Or needs most, whatsoe'er the love or need —
For he can't wed twice. Then, he must avouch,
Or follow, at the least, sufficiently,
The form of faith his conscience holds the best,
Whate'er the process of conviction was :
For nothing can compensate his mistake
On such a point, the man himself being judge :
He cannot wed twice, nor twice lose his soul.

  Well now, there's one great form of Christian faith
I happened to be born in — which to teach
Was given me as I grew up, on all hands,
As best and readiest means of living by ;
The same on examination being proved
The most pronounced moreover, fixed, precise
And absolute form of faith in the whole world —
Accordingly, most potent of all forms
For working on the world. Observe, my friend !

BISHOP BLOUGRAM'S APOLOGY

Such as you know me, I am free to say,
In these hard latter days which hamper one,
Myself — by no immoderate exercise
Of intellect and learning, but the tact
To let external forces work for me,
— Bid the street's stones be bread and they are bread;
Bid Peter's creed, or rather, Hildebrand's,
Exalt me o'er my fellows in the world
And make my life an ease and joy and pride;
It does so, — which for me 's a great point gained,
Who have a soul and body that exact
A comfortable care in many ways.
There 's power in me and will to dominate
Which I must exercise, they hurt me else:
In many ways I need mankind's respect,
Obedience, and the love that 's born of fear:
While at the same time, there 's a taste I have,
A toy of soul, a titillating thing,
Refuses to digest these dainties crude.
The naked life is gross till clothed upon:
I must take what men offer, with a grace
As though I would not, could I help it, take!
An uniform I wear though over-rich —
Something imposed on me, no choice of mine;
No fancy-dress worn for pure fancy's sake
And despicable therefore! now folk kneel
And kiss my hand — of course the Church's hand.
Thus I am made, thus life is best for me,
And thus that it should be I have procured;
And thus it could not be another way,
I venture to imagine.

     You'll reply,
So far my choice, no doubt, is a success;
But were I made of better elements,
With nobler instincts, purer tastes, like you,
I hardly would account the thing success
Though it did all for me I say.

       But, friend,
We speak of what is; not of what might be,
And how 't were better if 't were otherwise.
I am the man you see here plain enough:
Grant I 'm a beast, why, beasts must lead beasts' lives!
Suppose I own at once to tail and claws;
The tailless man exceeds me: but being tailed

I 'll lash out lion fashion, and leave apes
To dock their stump and dress their haunches up.
My business is not to remake myself,
But make the absolute best of what God made.
Or — our first simile — though you prove me doomed
To a viler berth still, to the steerage-hole,
The sheep-pen or the pig-sty, I should strive
To make what use of each were possible ;
And as this cabin gets upholstery,
That hutch should rustle with sufficient straw.

But, friend, I don't acknowledge quite so fast
I fail of all your manhood's lofty tastes
Enumerated so complacently,
On the mere ground that you forsooth can find
In this particular life I choose to lead
No fit provision for them.   Can you not?
Say you, my fault is I address myself
To grosser estimators than should judge ?
And that 's no way of holding up the soul,
Which, nobler, needs men's praise perhaps, yet knows
One wise man's verdict outweighs all the fools' —
Would like the two, but, forced to choose, takes that.
I pine among my million imbeciles
(You think) aware some dozen men of sense
Eye me and know me, whether I believe
In the last winking Virgin, as I vow,
And am a fool, or disbelieve in her
And am a knave, — approve in neither case,
Withhold their voices though I look their way :
Like Verdi when, at his worst opera's end
(The thing they gave at Florence, — what 's its name ?)
While the mad houseful's plaudits near out-bang
His orchestra of salt-box, tongs, and bones,
He looks through all the roaring and the wreaths
Where sits Rossini patient in his stall.

Nay, friend, I meet you with an answer here —
That even your prime men who appraise their kind
Are men still, catch a wheel within a wheel,
See more in a truth than the truth's simple self,
Confuse themselves.   You see lads walk the street
Sixty the minute ; what 's to note in that ?
You see one lad o'erstride a chimney-stack ;
Him you must watch — he 's sure to fall, yet stands !
Our interest 's on the dangerous edge of things.

The honest thief, the tender murderer,
The superstitious atheist, demirep
That loves and saves her soul in new French books —
We watch while these in equilibrium keep
The giddy line midway : one step aside,
They 're classed and done with. I, then, keep the line
Before your sages, — just the men to shrink
From the gross weights, coarse scales and labels broad
You offer their refinement. Fool or knave?
Why needs a bishop be a fool or knave
When there 's a thousand diamond weights between?
So, I enlist them. Your picked twelve, you 'll find,
Profess themselves indignant, scandalized
At thus being held unable to explain
How a superior man who disbelieves
May not believe as well : that 's Schelling's way!
It 's through my coming in the tail of time,
Nicking the minute with a happy tact.
Had I been born three hundred years ago
They 'd say, " What 's strange? Blougram of course believes ; "
And, seventy years since, " disbelieves of course."
But now, " He may believe ; and yet, and yet
How can he ? " All eyes turn with interest.
Whereas, step off the line on either side —
You, for example, clever to a fault,
The rough and ready man who write apace,
Read somewhat seldomer, think perhaps even less —
You disbelieve ! Who wonders and who cares?
Lord So-and-so — his coat bedropped with wax,
All Peter's chains about his waist, his back
Brave with the needlework of Noodledom —
Believes ! Again, who wonders and who cares?
But I, the man of sense and learning too,
The able to think yet act, the this, the that,
I, to believe at this late time of day !
Enough ; you see, I need not fear contempt.

— Except it 's yours ! Admire me as these may,
You don't. But whom at least do you admire?
Present your own perfection, your ideal,
Your pattern man for a minute — oh, make haste!
Is it Napoleon you would have us grow?
Concede the means ; allow his head and hand,
(A large concession, clever as you are)
Good ! In our common primal element

Of unbelief (we can't believe, you know —
We 're still at that admission, recollect !)
Where do you find — apart from, towering o'er
The secondary temporary aims
Which satisfy the gross taste you despise —
Where do you find his star ? — his crazy trust
God knows through what or in what ? it 's alive
And shines and leads him, and that 's all we want.
Have we aught in our sober night shall point
Such ends as his were, and direct the means
Of working out our purpose straight as his,
Nor bring a moment's trouble on success
With after-care to justify the same ?
— Be a Napoleon, and yet disbelieve —
Why, the man 's mad, friend, take his light away !
What 's the vague good o' the world, for which you dare
With comfort to yourself blow millions up ?
We neither of us see it ! we do see
The blown-up millions — spatter of their brains
And writhing of their bowels and so forth,
In that bewildering entanglement
Of horrible eventualities
Past calculation to the end of time !
Can I mistake for some clear word of God
(Which were my ample warrant for it all)
His puff of hazy instinct, idle talk,
"The State, that 's I." quack-nonsense about crowns,
And (when one beats the man to his last hold)
A vague idea of setting things to rights,
Policing people efficaciously,
More to their profit, most of all to his own ;
The whole to end that dismallest of ends
By an Austrian marriage, cant to us the Church,
And resurrection of the old régime ?
Would I, who hope to live a dozen years,
Fight Austerlitz for reasons such and such ?
No : for, concede me but the merest chance
Doubt may be wrong — there 's judgment, life to come !
With just that chance, I dare not. Doubt proves right ?
This present life is all ? — you offer me
Its dozen noisy years, without a chance
That wedding an archduchess, wearing lace,
And getting called by divers new-coined names,
Will drive off ugly thoughts and let me dine,
Sleep, read and chat in quiet as I like !
Therefore I will not.

					Take another case;
Fit up the cabin yet another way.
What say you to the poets? shall we write
Hamlet, Othello — make the world our own,
Without a risk to run of either sort?
I can't! — to put the strongest reason first.
" But try," you urge, " the trying shall suffice;
The aim, if reached or not, makes great the life:
Try to be Shakespeare, leave the rest to fate!"
Spare my self-knowledge — there's no fooling me!
If I prefer remaining my poor self,
I say so not in self-dispraise but praise.
If I'm a Shakespeare, let the well alone;
Why should I try to be what now I am?
If I'm no Shakespeare, as too probable, —
His power and consciousness and self-delight
And all we want in common, shall I find —
Trying forever? while on points of taste
Wherewith, to speak it humbly, he and I
Are dowered alike — I'll ask you, I or he,
Which in our two lives realizes most?
Much, he imagined — somewhat, I possess.
He had the imagination; stick to that!
Let him say, " In the face of my soul's works
Your world is worthless and I touch it not
Lest I should wrong them " — I'll withdraw my plea.
But does he say so? look upon his life!
Himself, who only can, gives judgment there.
He leaves his towers and gorgeous palaces
To build the trimmest house in Stratford town;
Saves money, spends it, owns the worth of things,
Giulio Romano's pictures, Dowland's lute;
Enjoys a show, respects the puppets, too,
And none more, had he seen its entry once,
Than " Pandulph, of fair Milan cardinal."
Why then should I who play that personage,
The very Pandulph Shakespeare's fancy made,
Be told that had the poet chanced to start
From where I stand now (some degree like mine
Being just the goal he ran his race to reach)
He would have run the whole race back, forsooth,
And left being Pandulph, to begin write plays?
Ah, the earth's best can be but the earth's best!
Did Shakespeare live, he could but sit at home
And get himself in dreams the Vatican,
Greek busts, Venetian paintings, Roman walls,

And English books, none equal to his own,
Which I read, bound in gold (he never did).
— Terni's fall, Naples' bay, and Gothard's top —
Eh, friend? I could not fancy one of these;
But, as I pour this claret, there they are:
I've gained them — crossed St. Gothard last July
With ten mules to the carriage and a bed
Slung inside; is my hap the worse for that?
We want the same things, Shakespeare and myself,
And what I want, I have: he, gifted more,
Could fancy he too had them when he liked,
But not so thoroughly that, if fate allowed,
He would not have them also in my sense.
We play one game; I send the ball aloft
No less adroitly that of fifty strokes
Scarce five go o'er the wall so wide and high
Which sends them back to me: I wish and get.
He struck balls higher and with better skill,
But at a poor fence level with his head,
And hit — his Stratford house, a coat of arms,
Successful dealings in his grain and wool, —
While I receive heaven's incense in my nose
And style myself the cousin of Queen Bess.
Ask him, if this life's all, who wins the game?

  Believe — and our whole argument breaks up.
Enthusiasm's the best thing, I repeat;
Only, we can't command it; fire and life
Are all, dead matter's nothing, we agree:
And be it a mad dream or God's very breath,
The fact's the same, — belief's fire, once in us,
Makes of all else mere stuff to show itself:
We penetrate our life with such a glow
As fire lends wood and iron — this turns steel,
That burns to ash — all's one, fire proves its power
For good or ill, since men call flare success.
But paint a fire, it will not therefore burn.
Light one in me, I'll find it food enough!
Why, to be Luther — that's a life to lead,
Incomparably better than my own.
He comes, reclaims God's earth for God, he says,
Sets up God's rule again by simple means,
Reopens a shut book, and all is done.
He flared out in the flaring of mankind;
Such Luther's luck was: how shall such be mine?
If he succeeded, nothing's left to do:

And if he did not altogether — well,
Strauss is the next advance. All Strauss should be
I might be also. But to what result?
He looks upon no future: Luther did.
What can I gain on the denying side?
Ice makes no conflagration. State the facts,
Read the text right, emancipate the world —
The emancipated world enjoys itself
With scarce a thank-you: Blougram told it first
It could not owe a farthing, — not to him
More than Saint Paul! 't would press its pay, you think?
Then add there's still that plaguy hundredth chance
Strauss may be wrong. And so a risk is run —
For what gain? not for Luther's, who secured
A real heaven in his heart throughout his life,
Supposing death a little altered things.

" Ay, but since really you lack faith," you cry,
" You run the same risk really on all sides,
In cool indifference as bold unbelief.
As well be Strauss as swing 'twixt Paul and him.
It's not worth having, such imperfect faith,
No more available to do faith's work
Than unbelief like mine. Whole faith, or none! "

Softly, my friend! I must dispute that point.
Once own the use of faith, I'll find you faith.
We're back on Christian ground. You call for faith:
I show you doubt, to prove that faith exists.
The more of doubt, the stronger faith, I say,
If faith o'ercomes doubt. How I know it does?
By life and man's free will, God gave for that!
To mould life as we choose it, shows our choice:
That's our one act, the previous work's his own.
You criticise the soul? it reared this tree —
This broad life and whatever fruit it bears!
What matter though I doubt at every pore,
Head-doubts, heart-doubts, doubts at my fingers' ends,
Doubts in the trivial work of every day,
Doubts at the very bases of my soul
In the grand moments when she probes herself —
If finally I have a life to show,
The thing I did, brought out in evidence
Against the thing done to me underground
By hell and all its brood, for aught I know?
I say, whence sprang this? shows it faith or doubt?

All's doubt in me; where's break of faith in this?
It is the idea, the feeling and the love,
God means mankind should strive for and show forth
Whatever be the process to that end, —
And not historic knowledge, logic sound,
And metaphysical acumen, sure!
" What think ye of Christ." friend? when all's done and said,
Like you this Christianity or not?
It may be false, but will you wish it true?
Has it your vote to be so if it can?
Trust you an instinct silenced long ago
That will break silence and enjoin you love
What mortified philosophy is hoarse,
And all in vain, with bidding you despise?
If you desire faith — then you've faith enough:
What else seeks God — nay, what else seek ourselves?
You form a notion of me, we'll suppose,
On hearsay; it's a favorable one:
" But still " (you add), " there was no such good man,
Because of contradiction in the facts.
One proves, for instance, he was born in Rome,
This Blougram; yet throughout the tales of him
I see he figures as an Englishman."
Well, the two things are reconcilable.
But would I rather you discovered that,
Subjoining — " Still, what matter though they be?
Blougram concerns me nought, born here or there."

Pure faith indeed — you know not what you ask!
Naked belief in God the Omnipotent,
Omniscient, Omnipresent, sears too much
The sense of conscious creatures to be borne.
It were the seeing him, no flesh shall dare.
Some think, Creation's meant to show him forth:
I say it's meant to hide him all it can,
And that's what all the blessed evil's for.
Its use in Time is to environ us,
Our breath, our drop of dew, with shield enough
Against that sight till we can bear its stress.
Under a vertical sun, the exposed brain
And lidless eye and disemprisoned heart
Less certainly would wither up at once
Than mind, confronted with the truth of him.
But time and earth case-harden us to live;
The feeblest sense is trusted most: the child
Feels God a moment, ichors o'er the place,

Plays on and grows to be a man like us.
With me, faith means perpetual unbelief
Kept quiet like the snake 'neath Michael's foot
Who stands calm just because he feels it writhe.
Or, if that's too ambitious, — here's my box —
I need the excitation of a pinch
Threatening the torpor of the inside-nose
Nigh on the imminent sneeze that never comes.
Leave it in peace," advise the simple folk:
Make it aware of peace by itching-fits,
Say I — let doubt occasion still more faith!

You'll say, once all believed, man, woman, child,
In that dear middle-age these noodles praise.
How you'd exult if I could put you back
Six hundred years, blot out cosmogony,
Geology, ethnology, what not
(Greek endings, each the little passing-bell
That signifies some faith's about to die),
And set you square with Genesis again, —
When such a traveller told you his last news,
He saw the ark a-top of Ararat
But did not climb there since 't was getting dusk
And robber-bands infest the mountain's foot!
How should you feel, I ask, in such an age,
How act? As other people felt and did;
With soul more blank than this decanter's knob,
Believe — and yet lie, kill, rob, fornicate,
Full in belief's face, like the beast you'd be!

No, when the fight begins within himself,
A man's worth something. God stoops o'er his head,
Satan looks up between his feet — both tug —
He's left, himself, i' the middle: the soul wakes
And grows. Prolong that battle through his life!
Never leave growing till the life to come!
Here, we've got callous to the Virgin's winks
That used to puzzle people wholesomely:
Men have outgrown the shame of being fools.
What are the laws of nature, not to bend
If the Church bid them? — brother Newman asks.
Up with the Immaculate Conception, then —
On to the rack with faith! — is my advice.
Will not that hurry us upon our knees,
Knocking our breasts, "It can't be — yet it shall!
Who am I, the worm, to argue with my Pope?

Low things confound the high things!" and so forth.
That's better than acquitting God with grace
As some folk do. He's tried — no case is proved,
Philosophy is lenient — he may go!

You'll say, the old system's not so obsolete
But men believe still: ay, but who and where?
King Bomba's lazzaroni foster yet
The sacred flame, so Antonelli writes;
But even of these, what ragamuffin-saint
Believes God watches him continually,
As he believes in fire that it will burn,
Or rain that it will drench him? Break fire's law,
Sin against rain, although the penalty
Be just a singe or soaking? "No," he smiles;
"Those laws are laws that can enforce themselves."

The sum of all is — yes, my doubt is great,
My faith's still greater, then my faith's enough.
I have read much, thought much, experienced much,
Yet would die rather than avow my fear
The Naples' liquefaction may be false,
When set to happen by the palace-clock
According to the clouds or dinner-time.
I hear you recommend, I might at least
Eliminate, decrassify my faith
Since I adopt it; keeping what I must
And leaving what I can — such points as this.
I won't — that is, I can't throw one away.
Supposing there's no truth in what I hold
About the need of trial to man's faith,
Still, when you bid me purify the same,
To such a process I discern no end.
Clearing off one excrescence to see two,
There's ever a next in size, now grown as big,
That meets the knife: I cut and cut again!
First cut the Liquefaction, what comes last
But Fichte's clever cut at God himself?
Experimentalize on sacred things!
I trust nor hand nor eye nor heart nor brain
To stop betimes: they all get drunk alike.
The first step, I am master not to take.

You'd find the cutting-process to your taste
As much as leaving growths of lies unpruned,
Nor see more danger in it, — you retort.

Your taste 's worth mine ; but my taste proves more wise
When we consider that the steadfast hold
On the extreme end of the chain of faith
Gives all the advantage, makes the difference
With the rough purblind mass we seek to rule :
We are their lords, or they are free of us,
Just as we tighten or relax our hold.
So, other matters equal, we 'll revert
To the first problem — which, if solved my way
And thrown into the balance, turns the scale —
How we may lead a comfortable life,
How suit our luggage to the cabin's size.

Of course you are remarking all this time
How narrowly and grossly I view life,
Respect the creature-comforts, care to rule
The masses, and regard complacently
" The cabin," in our old phrase. Well, I do.
I act for, talk for, live for this world now,
As this world prizes action, life and talk :
No prejudice to what next world may prove,
Whose new laws and requirements, my best pledge
To observe then, is that I observe these now,
Shall do hereafter what I do meanwhile.
Let us concede (gratuitously though)
Next life relieves the soul of body, yields
Pure spiritual enjoyment: well, my friend,
Why lose this life i' the meantime, since its use
May be to make the next life more intense ?

Do you know, I have often had a dream
(Work it up in your next month's article)
Of man's poor spirit in its progress, still
Losing true life forever and a day
Through ever trying to be and ever being —
In the evolution of successive spheres —
Before its actual sphere and place of life,
Halfway into the next, which having reached,
It shoots with corresponding foolery
Halfway into the next still, on and off !
As when a traveller, bound from North to South,
Scouts fur in Russia : what 's its use in France ?
In France spurns flannel : where 's its need in Spain ?
In Spain drops cloth, too cumbrous for Algiers !
Linen goes next, and last the skin itself,
A superfluity at Timbuctoo.

When, through his journey, was the fool at ease?
I'm at ease now, friend; worldly in this world,
I take and like its way of life; I think
My brothers, who administer the means,
Live better for my comfort — that's good too;
And God, if he pronounce upon such life,
Approves my service, which is better still.
If he keep silence, — why, for you or me
Or that brute beast pulled-up in to-day's "Times,"
What odds is 't, save to ourselves, what life we lead?

You meet me at this issue: you declare, —
All special-pleading done with — truth is truth,
And justifies itself by undreamed ways.
You don't fear but it's better, if we doubt,
To say so, act up to our truth perceived
However feebly. Do then, — act away!
'T is there I'm on the watch for you. How one acts
Is, both of us agree, our chief concern:
And how you'll act is what I fain would see
If, like the candid person you appear,
You dare to make the most of your life's scheme
As I of mine, live up to its full law
Since there's no higher law that counterchecks.
Put natural religion to the test
You've just demolished the revealed with — quick,
Down to the root of all that checks your will,
All prohibition to lie, kill and thieve,
Or even to be an atheistic priest!
Suppose a pricking to incontinence —
Philosophers deduce you chastity
Or shame, from just the fact that at the first
Whoso embraced a woman in the field,
Threw club down and forewent his brains beside,
So, stood a ready victim in the reach
Of any brother savage, club in hand;
Hence saw the use of going out of sight
In wood or cave to prosecute his loves:
I read this in a French book t' other day.
Does law so analyzed coerce you much?
Oh, men spin clouds of fuzz where matters end,
But you who reach where the first thread begins,
You'll soon cut that! — which means you can, but won't,
Through certain instincts, blind, unreasoned-out,
You dare not set aside, you can't tell why,
But there they are, and so you let them rule.

Then, friend, you seem as much a slave as I,
A liar, conscious coward and hypocrite,
Without the good the slave expects to get,
In case he has a master after all!
You own your instincts? why, what else do I,
Who want, am made for, and must have a God
Ere I can be aught, do aught? — no mere name
Want, but the true thing with what proves its truth,
To wit, a relation from that thing to me,
Touching from head to foot — which touch I feel,
And with it take the rest, this life of ours!
I live my life here; yours you dare not live.

— Not as I state it, who (you please subjoin)
Disfigure such a life and call it names,
While, to your mind, remains another way
For simple men: knowledge and power have rights,
But ignorance and weakness have rights too.
There needs no crucial effort to find truth
If here or there or anywhere about:
We ought to turn each side, try hard and see,
And if we can't, be glad we 've earned at least
The right, by one laborious proof the more,
To graze in peace earth's pleasant pasturage.
Men are not angels, neither are they brutes:
Something we may see, all we cannot see.
What need of lying? I say, I see all,
And swear to each detail the most minute
In what I think a Pan's face — you, mere cloud:
I swear I hear him speak and see him wink,
For fear, if once I drop the emphasis,
Mankind may doubt there's any cloud at all.
You take the simple life — ready to see,
Willing to see (for no cloud's worth a face) —
And leaving quiet what no strength can move,
And which, who bids you move? who has the right?
I bid you; but you are God's sheep, not mine:
Pastor est tui Dominus." You find
In this the pleasant pasture of our life
Much you may eat without the least offence,
Much you don't eat because your maw objects,
Much you would eat but that your fellow-flock
Open great eyes at you and even butt,
And thereupon you like your mates so well
You cannot please yourself, offending them;
Though when they seem exorbitantly sheep,

You weigh your pleasure with their butts and bleats
And strike the balance. Sometimes certain fears
Restrain you, real checks since you find them so;
Sometimes you please yourself and nothing checks:
And thus you graze through life with not one lie,
And like it best.
     But do you, in truth's name?
If so, you beat — which means you are not I —
Who needs must make earth mine and feed my fill
Not simply unbutted at, unbickered with,
But motioned to the velvet of the sward
By those obsequious wethers' very selves.
Look at me, sir; my age is double yours:
At yours, I knew beforehand, so enjoyed,
What now I should be — as, permit the word,
I pretty well imagine your whole range
And stretch of tether twenty years to come.
We both have minds and bodies much alike:
In truth's name, don't you want my bishopric,
My daily bread, my influence, and my state?
You're young. I'm old; you must be old one day;
Will you find then, as I do hour by hour,
Women their lovers kneel to, who cut curls
From your fat lap-dog's ear to grace a brooch —
Dukes, who petition just to kiss your ring —
With much beside you know or may conceive?
Suppose we die to-night: well, here am I,
Such were my gains, life bore this fruit to me,
While writing all the same my articles
On music, poetry, the fictile vase
Found at Albano, chess, Anacreon's Greek.
But you — the highest honor in your life,
The thing you'll crown yourself with, all your days,
Is — dining here and drinking this last glass
I pour you out in sign of amity
Before we part forever. Of your power
And social influence, worldly worth in short,
Judge what's my estimation by the fact,
I do not condescend to enjoin, beseech,
Hint secrecy on one of all these words!
You're shrewd and know that should you publish one
The world would brand the lie — my enemies first,
Who'd sneer — "the bishop's an arch-hypocrite
And knave perhaps, but not so frank a fool."
Whereas I should not dare for both my ears

Breathe one such syllable, smile one such smile,
Before the chaplain who reflects myself —
My shade's so much more potent than your flesh.
What's your reward, self-abnegating friend?
Stood you confessed of those exceptional
And privileged great natures that dwarf mine —
A zealot with a mad ideal in reach,
A poet just about to print his ode,
A statesman with a scheme to stop this war,
An artist whose religion is his art —
I should have nothing to object: such men
Carry the fire, all things grow warm to them,
Their drugget's worth my purple, they beat me.
But you, — you're just as little those as I —
You, Gigadibs, who, thirty years of age,
Write statedly for Blackwood's Magazine,
Believe you see two points in Hamlet's soul
Unseized by the Germans yet — which view you'll print —
Meantime the best you have to show being still
That lively lightsome article we took
Almost for the true Dickens, — what's its name?
" The Slum and Cellar, or Whitechapel life
Limned after dark!" it made me laugh, I know,
And pleased a month, and brought you in ten pounds.
— Success I recognize and compliment,
And therefore give you, if you choose, three words
(The card and pencil-scratch is quite enough)
Which whether here, in Dublin or New York,
Will get you, prompt as at my eyebrow's wink,
Such terms as never you aspired to get
In all our own reviews and some not ours.
Go write your lively sketches! be the first
" Blougram, or The Eccentric Confidence " —
Or better simply say, " The Outward-bound."
Why, men as soon would throw it in my teeth
As copy and quote the infamy chalked broad
About me on the church-door opposite.
You will not wait for that experience though,
I fancy, howsoever you decide,
To discontinue — not detesting, not
Defaming, but at least — despising me!

    Over his wine so smiled and talked his hour
Sylvester Blougram, styled *in partibus*
Episcopus, nec non — (the deuce knows what

It's changed to by our novel hierarchy)
With Gigadibs the literary man,
Who played with spoons, explored his plate's design,
And ranged the olive-stones about its edge,
While the great bishop rolled him out a mind
Long crumpled, till creased consciousness lay smooth.

For Blougram, he believed, say, half he spoke.
The other portion, as he shaped it thus
For argumentatory purposes,
He felt his foe was foolish to dispute.
Some arbitrary accidental thoughts
That crossed his mind, amusing because new,
He chose to represent as fixtures there,
Invariable convictions (such they seemed
Beside his interlocutor's loose cards
Flung daily down, and not the same way twice),
While certain hell-deep instincts, man's weak tongue
Is never bold to utter in their truth
Because styled hell-deep ('t is an old mistake
To place hell at the bottom of the earth),
He ignored these, — not having in readiness
Their nomenclature and philosophy :
He said true things, but called them by wrong names.
" On the whole," he thought, " I justify myself
On every point where cavillers like this
Oppugn my life : he tries one kind of fence,
I close, he 's worsted, that 's enough for him.
He 's on the ground : if ground should break away
I take my stand on, there 's a firmer yet
Beneath it, both of us may sink and reach.
His ground was over mine and broke the first :
So, let him sit with me this many a year ! "

He did not sit five minutes. Just a week
Sufficed his sudden healthy vehemence.
Something had struck him in the " Outward-bound "
Another way than Blougram's purpose was :
And having bought, not cabin-furniture
But settler's-implements (enough for three)
And started for Australia — there, I hope,
By this time he has tested his first plough,
And studied his last chapter of St. John.

CLEON.

"As certain also of your own poets have said" —

CLEON the poet (from the sprinkled isles,
Lily on lily, that o'erlace the sea,
And laugh their pride when the light wave lisps "Greece")—
To Protus in his Tyranny: much health!

   They give thy letter to me, even now:
I read and seem as if I heard thee speak.
The master of thy galley still unlades
Gift after gift; they block my court at last
And pile themselves along its portico
Royal with sunset, like a thought of thee:
And one white she-slave from the group dispersed
Of black and white slaves (like the chequer-work
Pavement, at once my nation's work and gift,
Now covered with this settle-down of doves),
One lyric woman, in her crocus vest
Woven of sea-wools, with her two white hands
Commends to me the strainer and the cup
Thy lip hath bettered ere it blesses mine.

   Well-counselled, king, in thy munificence!
For so shall men remark, in such an act
Of love for him whose song gives life its joy,
Thy recognition of the use of life;
Nor call thy spirit barely adequate
To help on life in straight ways, broad enough
For vulgar souls, by ruling and the rest.
Thou, in the daily building of thy tower, —
Whether in fierce and sudden spasms of toil,
Or through dim lulls of unapparent growth,
Or when the general work 'mid good acclaim
Climbed with the eye to cheer the architect, —
Didst ne'er engage in work for mere work's sake —
Hadst ever in thy heart the luring hope
Of some eventual rest a-top of it,
Whence, all the tumult of the building hushed,
Thou first of men might'st look out to the East:
The vulgar saw thy tower, thou sawest the sun.
For this, I promise on thy festival
To pour libation, looking o'er the sea,
Making this slave narrate thy fortunes, speak

Thy great words, and describe thy royal face —
Wishing thee wholly where Zeus lives the most,
Within the eventual element of calm.

   Thy letter's first requirement meets me here.
It is as thou hast heard : in one short life
I, Cleon, have effected all those things
Thou wonderingly dost enumerate.
That epos on thy hundred plates of gold
Is mine, — and also mine the little chant,
So sure to rise from every fishing-bark
When, lights at prow, the seamen haul their net.
The image of the sun-god on the phare,
Men turn from the sun's self to see, is mine;
The Pœcile, o'er-storied its whole length,
As thou didst hear, with painting, is mine too.
I know the true proportions of a man
And woman also, not observed before ;
And I have written three books on the soul,
Proving absurd all written hitherto,
And putting us to ignorance again.
For music, — why, I have combined the moods,
Inventing one. In brief, all arts are mine;
Thus much the people know and recognize,
Throughout our seventeen islands. Marvel not.
We of these latter days, with greater mind
Than our forerunners, since more composite,
Look not so great, beside their simple way,
To a judge who only sees one way at once,
One mind-point and no other at a time, —
Compares the small part of a man of us
With some whole man of the heroic age,
Great in his way — not ours, nor meant for ours.
And ours is greater, had we skill to know :
For, what we call this life of men on earth,
This sequence of the soul's achievements here
Being, as I find much reason to conceive,
Intended to be viewed eventually
As a great whole, not analyzed to parts,
But each part having reference to all, —
How shall a certain part, pronounced complete,
Endure effacement by another part?
Was the thing done ? — then, what's to do again ?
See, in the chequered pavement opposite,
Suppose the artist made a perfect rhomb,
And next a lozenge, then a trapezoid —

He did not overlay them, superimpose
The new upon the old and blot it out,
But laid them on a level in his work,
Making at last a picture; there it lies.
So, first the perfect separate forms were made,
The portions of mankind; and after, so,
Occurred the combination of the same.
For where had been a progress, otherwise?
Mankind, made up of all the single men, —
In such a synthesis the labor ends.
Now mark me! those divine men of old time
Have reached, thou sayest well, each at one point
The outside verge that rounds our faculty;
And where they reached, who can do more than reach?
It takes but little water just to touch
At some one point the inside of a sphere,
And, as we turn the sphere, touch all the rest
In due succession: but the finer air
Which not so palpably nor obviously,
Though no less universally, can touch
The whole circumference of that emptied sphere,
Fills it more fully than the water did;
Holds thrice the weight of water in itself
Resolved into a subtler element.
And yet the vulgar call the sphere first full
Up to the visible height — and after, void;
Not knowing air's more hidden properties.
And thus our soul, misknown, cries out to Zeus
To vindicate his purpose in our life:
Why stay we on the earth unless to grow?
Long since, I imaged, wrote the fiction out,
That he or other god descended here
And, once for all, showed simultaneously
What, in its nature, never can be shown,
Piecemeal or in succession; — showed, I say,
The worth both absolute and relative
Of all his children from the birth of time,
His instruments for all appointed work.
I now go on to image, — might we hear
The judgment which should give the due to each,
Show where the labor lay and where the ease,
And prove Zeus' self, the latent everywhere!
This is a dream: — but no dream, let us hope,
That years and days, the summers and the springs,
Follow each other with unwaning powers.
The grapes which dye thy wine are richer far,

Through culture, than the wild wealth of the rock ;
The suave plum than the savage-tasted drupe ;
The pastured honey-bee drops choicer sweet ;
The flowers turn double, and the leaves turn flowers ;
That young and tender crescent-moon, thy slave,
Sleeping above her robe as buoyed by clouds,
Refines upon the women of my youth.
What, and the soul alone deteriorates ?
I have not chanted verse like Homer, no —
Nor swept string like Terpander, no — nor carved
And painted men like Phidias and his friend :
I am not great as they are, point by point.
But I have entered into sympathy
With these four, running these into one soul,
Who, separate, ignored each other's art.
Say, is it nothing that I know them all ?
The wild flower was the larger ; I have dashed
Rose-blood upon its petals, pricked its cup's
Honey with wine, and driven its seed to fruit,
And show a better flower if not so large :
I stand myself. Refer this to the gods
Whose gift alone it is ! which, shall I dare
(All pride apart) upon the absurd pretext
That such a gift by chance lay in my hand,
Discourse of lightly or depreciate ?
It might have fallen to another's hand : what then ?
I pass too surely : let at least truth stay !

And next, of what thou followest on to ask.
This being with me as I declare, O king,
My works, in all these varicolored kinds,
So done by me, accepted so by men —
Thou askest, if (my soul thus in men's hearts)
I must not be accounted to attain
The very crown and proper end of life ?
Inquiring thence how, now life closeth up,
I face death with success in my right hand :
Whether I fear death less than dost thyself
The fortunate of men ? " For " (writest thou)
" Thou leavest much behind, while I leave nought.
Thy life stays in the poems men shall sing,
The pictures men shall study ; while my life,
Complete and whole now in its power and joy,
Dies altogether with my brain and arm,
Is lost indeed ; since, what survives myself ?
The brazen statue to o'erlook my grave,

Set on the promontory which I named.
And that — some supple courtier of my heir
Shall use its robed and sceptred arm, perhaps,
To fix the rope to, which best drags it down.
I go then: triumph thou, who dost not go!"

   Nay, thou art worthy of hearing my whole mind.
Is this apparent, when thou turn'st to muse
Upon the scheme of earth and man in chief,
That admiration grows as knowledge grows?
That imperfection means perfection hid,
Reserved in part, to grace the after-time?
If, in the morning of philosophy,
Ere aught had been recorded, nay perceived,
Thou, with the light now in thee, couldst have looked
On all earth's tenantry, from worm to bird,
Ere man, her last, appeared upon the stage —
Thou wouldst have seen them perfect, and deduced
The perfectness of others yet unseen.
Conceding which, — had Zeus then questioned thee,
"Shall I go on a step, improve on this,
Do more for visible creatures than is done?"
Thou wouldst have answered, "Ay, by making each
Grow conscious in himself — by that alone.
All's perfect else: the shell sucks fast the rock,
The fish strikes through the sea, the snake both swims
And slides, forth range the beasts, the birds take flight,
Till life's mechanics can no further go —
And all this joy in natural life is put
Like fire from off thy finger into each,
So exquisitely perfect is the same.
But 't is pure fire, and they mere matter are;
It has them, not they it: and so I choose
For man, thy last premeditated work
(If I might add a glory to the scheme),
That a third thing should stand apart from both,
A quality arise within his soul,
Which, intro-active, made to supervise
And feel the force it has, may view itself,
And so be happy." Man might live at first
The animal life: but is there nothing more?
In due time, let him critically learn
How he lives; and, the more he gets to know
Of his own life's adaptabilities,
The more joy-giving will his life become.
Thus man, who hath this quality, is best.

But thou, king, hadst more reasonably said:
" Let progress end at once, — man make no step
Beyond the natural man, the better beast,
Using his senses, not the sense of sense."
In man there 's failure, only since he left
The lower and inconscious forms of life.
We called it an advance, the rendering plain
Man's spirit might grow conscious of man's life,
And, by new lore so added to the old,
Take each step higher over the brute's head.
This grew the only life, the pleasure-house,
Watch-tower and treasure-fortress of the soul,
Which whole surrounding flats of natural life
Seemed only fit to yield subsistence to;
A tower that crowns a country. But alas,
The soul now climbs it just to perish there!
For thence we have discovered ('t is no dream
We know this, which we had not else perceived)
That there 's a world of capability
For joy, spread round about us, meant for us,
Inviting us; and still the soul craves all,
And still the flesh replies, " Take no jot more
Than ere thou clombst the tower to look abroad!
Nay, so much less as that fatigue has brought
Deduction to it." We struggle, fain to enlarge
Our bounded physical recipiency,
Increase our power, supply fresh oil to life,
Repair the waste of age and sickness: no,
It skills not! life 's inadequate to joy,
As the soul sees joy, tempting life to take.
They praise a fountain in my garden here
Wherein a Naiad sends the water-bow
Thin from her tube; she smiles to see it rise.
What if I told her, it is just a thread
From that great river which the hills shut up,
And mock her with my leave to take the same?
The artificer has given her one small tube
Past power to widen or exchange — what boots
To know she might spout oceans if she could?
She cannot lift beyond her first thin thread:
And so a man can use but a man's joy
While he sees God's. Is it for Zeus to boast,
" See, man, how happy I live, and despair —
That I may be still happier — for thy use!"
If this were so, we could not thank our lord,
As hearts beat on to doing; 't is not so —

Malice it is not. Is it carelessness?
Still, no. If care — where is the sign? I ask,
And get no answer, and agree in sum,
O king, with thy profound discouragement,
Who seest the wider but to sigh the more.
Most progress is most failure : thou sayest well.

The last point now : — thou dost except a case —
Holding joy not impossible to one
With artist-gifts — to such a man as I
Who leave behind me living works indeed ;
For, such a poem, such a painting lives.
What? dost thou verily trip upon a word,
Confound the accurate view of what joy is
(Caught somewhat clearer by my eyes than thine)
With feeling joy? confound the knowing how
And showing how to live (my faculty)
With actually living? — Otherwise
Where is the artist's vantage o'er the king?
Because in my great epos I display
How divers men young, strong, fair, wise, can act —
Is this as though I acted? if I paint,
Carve the young Phœbus, am I therefore young?
Methinks I'm older that I bowed myself
The many years of pain that taught me art!
Indeed, to know is something, and to prove
How all this beauty might be enjoyed, is more :
But, knowing nought, to enjoy is something too.
Yon rower, with the moulded muscles there,
Lowering the sail, is nearer it than I.
I can write love-odes : thy fair slave's an ode.
I get to sing of love, when grown too gray
For being beloved : she turns to that young man,
The muscles all a-ripple on his back.
I know the joy of kingship : well, thou art king !

"But," sayest thou — (and I marvel, I repeat,
To find thee trip on such a mere word) "what
Thou writest, paintest, stays ; that does not die :
Sappho survives, because we sing her songs,
And Æschylus, because we read his plays!"
Why, if they live still, let them come and take
Thy slave in my despite, drink from thy cup,
Speak in my place. Thou diest while I survive?
Say rather that my fate is deadlier still,
In this, that every day my sense of joy

Grows more acute, my soul (intensified
By power and insight) more enlarged, more keen;
While every day my hairs fall more and more,
My hand shakes, and the heavy years increase —
The horror quickening still from year to year,
The consummation coming past escape,
When I shall know most, and yet least enjoy —
When all my works wherein I prove my worth,
Being present still to mock me in men's mouths,
Alive still, in the praise of such as thou,
I, I the feeling, thinking, acting man,
The man who loved his life so over-much,
Sleep in my urn. It is so horrible,
I dare at times imagine to my need
Some future state revealed to us by Zeus,
Unlimited in capability
For joy, as this is in desire for joy,
— To seek which, the joy-hunger forces us:
That, stung by straitness of our life, made strait
On purpose to make prized the life at large —
Freed by the throbbing impulse we call death,
We burst there as the worm into the fly,
Who, while a worm still, wants his wings. But no!
Zeus has not yet revealed it; and alas,
He must have done so, were it possible!

Live long and happy, and in that thought die:
Glad for what was! Farewell. And for the rest,
I cannot tell thy messenger aright
Where to deliver what he bears of thine
To one called Paulus; we have heard his fame
Indeed, if Christus be not one with him —
I know not, nor am troubled much to know.
Thou canst not think a mere barbarian Jew,
As Paulus proves to be, one circumcised,
Hath access to a secret shut from us?
Thou wrongest our philosophy, O king,
In stooping to inquire of such an one,
As if his answer could impose at all!
He writeth, doth he? well, and he may write.
Oh, the Jew findeth scholars! certain slaves
Who touched on this same isle, preached him and Christ;
And (as I gathered from a bystander)
Their doctrine could be held by no sane man.

RUDEL TO THE LADY OF TRIPOLI.

I.

I KNOW a Mount, the gracious Sun perceives
First, when he visits, last, too, when he leaves
The world; and, vainly favored, it repays
The day-long glory of his steadfast gaze
By no change of its large calm front of snow.
And underneath the Mount, a Flower I know,
He cannot have perceived, that changes ever
At his approach; and, in the lost endeavor
To live his life, has parted, one by one,
With all a flower's true graces, for the grace
Of being but a foolish mimic sun,
With ray-like florets round a disk-like face.
Men nobly call by many a name the Mount
As over many a land of theirs its large
Calm front of snow like a triumphal targe
Is reared, and still with old names, fresh names vie,
Each to its proper praise and own account:
Men call the Flower, the Sunflower, sportively.

II.

Oh, Angel of the East, one, one gold look
Across the waters to this twilight nook,
— The far sad waters, Angel, to this nook!

III.

Dear Pilgrim, art thou for the East indeed?
Go! — saying ever as thou dost proceed,
That I, French Rudel, choose for my device
A sunflower outspread like a sacrifice
Before its idol. See! These inexpert
And hurried fingers could not fail to hurt
The woven picture; 't is a woman's skill
Indeed; but nothing baffled me, so, ill
Or well, the work is finished. Say, men feed
On songs I sing, and therefore bask the bees
On my flower's breast as on a platform broad:
But, as the flower's concern is not for these
But solely for the sun, so men applaud
In vain this Rudel, he not looking here
But to the East — the East! Go, say this, Pilgrim dear!

ONE WORD MORE.*

TO E. B. B.

LONDON, September, 1855.

I.

THERE they are, my fifty men and women
Naming me the fifty poems finished!
Take them, Love, the book and me together:
Where the heart lies, let the brain lie also.

II.

Rafael made a century of sonnets,
Made and wrote them in a certain volume
Dinted with the silver-pointed pencil
Else he only used to draw Madonnas:
These, the world might view — but one, the volume.
Who that one, you ask? Your heart instructs you.
Did she live and love it all her lifetime?
Did she drop, his lady of the sonnets,
Die, and let it drop beside her pillow
Where it lay in place of Rafael's glory,
Rafael's cheek so duteous and so loving —
Cheek, the world was wont to hail a painter's,
Rafael's cheek, her love had turned a poet's?

III.

You and I would rather read that volume,
(Taken to his beating bosom by it)
Lean and list the bosom-beats of Rafael,
Would we not? than wonder at Madonnas —
Her, San Sisto named, and Her, Foligno,
Her, that visits Florence in a vision,
Her, that's left with lilies in the Louvre —
Seen by us and all the world in circle.

IV.

You and I will never read that volume.
Guido Reni, like his own eye's apple
Guarded long the treasure-book and loved it.
Guido Reni dying, all Bologna

---

* Originally appended to the collection of Poems called "Men and Women," the greater portion of which has now been, more correctly, distributed under the other titles of this edition.

Cried, and the world cried too, "Ours, the treasure!"
Suddenly, as rare things will, it vanished.

V.

Dante once prepared to paint an angel:
Whom to please? You whisper "Beatrice."
While he mused and traced it and retraced it,
(Peradventure with a pen corroded
Still by drops of that hot ink he dipped for,
When, his left-hand i' the hair o' the wicked,
Back he held the brow and pricked its stigma,
Bit into the live man's flesh for parchment,
Loosed him, laughed to see the writing rankle,
Let the wretch go festering through Florence) —
Dante, who loved well because he hated,
Hated wickedness that hinders loving,
Dante standing, studying his angel, —
In there broke the folk of his Inferno.
Says he — "Certain people of importance"
(Such he gave his daily dreadful line to)
"Entered and would seize, forsooth, the poet."
Says the poet — "Then I stopped my painting."

VI.

You and I would rather see that angel,
Painted by the tenderness of Dante,
Would we not? — than read a fresh Inferno.

VII.

You and I will never see that picture.
While he mused on love and Beatrice,
While he softened o'er his outlined angel,
In they broke, those "people of importance:"
We and Bice bear the loss forever.

VIII.

What of Rafael's sonnets, Dante's picture?
This: no artist lives and loves, that longs not
Once, and only once, and for one only,
(Ah, the prize!) to find his love a language
Fit and fair and simple and sufficient —
Using nature that's an art to others,
Not, this one time, art that's turned his nature.
Ay, of all the artists living, loving,
None but would forego his proper dowry, —
Does he paint? he fain would write a poem, —

Does he write? he fain would paint a picture,
Put to proof art alien to the artist's,
Once, and only once, and for one only,
So to be the man and leave the artist,
Gain the man's joy, miss the artist's sorrow.

IX.

Wherefore? Heaven's gift takes earth's abatement!
He who smites the rock and spreads the water,
Bidding drink and live a crowd beneath him,
Even he, the minute makes immortal,
Proves, perchance, but mortal in the minute,
Desecrates, belike, the deed in doing.
While he smites, how can he but remember,
So he smote before, in such a peril,
When they stood and mocked — " Shall smiting help us?
When they drank and sneered — " A stroke is easy!"
When they wiped their mouths and went their journey,
Throwing him for thanks — " But drought was pleasant."
Thus old memories mar the actual triumph;
Thus the doing savors of disrelish;
Thus achievement lacks a gracious somewhat;
O'er-importuned brows becloud the mandate,
Carelessness or consciousness — the gesture.
For he bears an ancient wrong about him,
Sees and knows again those phalanxed faces,
Hears, yet one time more, the 'customed prelude —
" How shouldst thou, of all men, smite, and save us?"
Guesses what is like to prove the sequel —
" Egypt's flesh-pots — nay, the drought was better."

X.

Oh, the crowd must have emphatic warrant!
Theirs, the Sinai-forehead's cloven brilliance,
Right-arm's rod-sweep, tongue's imperial fiat.
Never dares the man put off the prophet.

XI.

Did he love one face from out the thousands,
(Were she Jethro's daughter, white and wifely,
Were she but the Æthiopian bondslave,)
He would envy yon dumb patient camel,
Keeping a reserve of scanty water
Meant to save his own life in the desert;
Ready in the desert to deliver
(Kneeling down to let his breast be opened)
Hoard and life together for his mistress.

XII.

I shall never, in the years remaining,
Paint you pictures, no, nor carve you statues,
Make you music that should all-express me;
So it seems: I stand on my attainment.
This of verse alone, one life allows me;
Verse and nothing else have I to give you.
Other heights in other lives, God willing:
All the gifts from all the heights, your own, Love!

XIII.

Yet a semblance of resource avails us —
Shade so finely touched, love's sense must seize it.
Take these lines, look lovingly and nearly,
Lines I write the first time and the last time.
He who works in fresco, steals a hairbrush,
Curbs the liberal hand, subservient proudly,
Cramps his spirit, crowds its all in little,
Makes a strange art of an art familiar,
Fills his lady's missal-marge with flowerets.
He who blows through bronze, may breathe through silver,
Fitly serenade a slumbrous princess.
He who writes, may write for once as I do.

XIV.

Love, you saw me gather men and women,
Live or dead or fashioned by my fancy,
Enter each and all, and use their service,
Speak from every mouth, — the speech, a poem.
Hardly shall I tell my joys and sorrows,
Hopes and fears, belief and disbelieving:
I am mine and yours — the rest be all men's,
Karshish, Cleon, Norbert, and the fifty.
Let me speak this once in my true person,
Not as Lippo, Roland, or Andrea,
Though the fruit of speech be just this sentence —
Pray you, look on these my men and women,
Take and keep my fifty poems finished;
Where my heart lies, let my brain lie also!
Poor the speech; be how I speak, for all things.

XV.

Not but that you know me! Lo, the moon's self!
Here in London, yonder late in Florence,
Still we find her face, the thrice-transfigured.

Curving on a sky imbrued with color,
Drifted over Fiesole by twilight,
Came she, our new crescent of a hair's-breadth.
Full she flared it, lamping Samminiato,
Rounder 'twixt the cypresses and rounder,
Perfect till the nightingales applauded.
Now, a piece of her old self, impoverished,
Hard to greet, she traverses the house-roofs,
Hurries with unhandsome thrift of silver,
Goes dispiritedly, glad to finish.

XVI.

What, there's nothing in the moon noteworthy?
Nay: for if that moon could love a mortal,
Use, to charm him (so to fit a fancy),
All her magic ('t is the old sweet mythos),
She would turn a new side to her mortal,
Side unseen of herdsman, huntsman, steersman —
Blank to Zoroaster on his terrace,
Blind to Galileo on his turret,
Dumb to Homer, dumb to Keats — him, even!
Think, the wonder of the moonstruck mortal —
When she turns round, comes again in heaven,
Opens out anew for worse or better!
Proves she like some portent of an iceberg
Swimming full upon the ship it founders,
Hungry with huge teeth of splintered crystals?
Proves she as the paved work of a sapphire
Seen by Moses when he climbed the mountain?
Moses, Aaron, Nadab and Abihu
Climbed and saw the very God, the Highest,
Stand upon the paved work of a sapphire.
Like the bodied heaven in his clearness
Shone the stone, the sapphire of that paved work,
When they ate and drank and saw God also!

XVII.

What were seen? None knows, none ever shall know.
Only this is sure — the sight were other,
Not the moon's same side, born late in Florence,
Dying now impoverished here in London.
God be thanked, the meanest of his creatures
Boasts two soul-sides, one to face the world with,
One to show a woman when he loves her!

XVIII.

This I say of me, but think of you, Love!
This to you — yourself my moon of poets!
Ah, but that's the world's side, there's the wonder,
Thus they see you, praise you, think they know you!
There, in turn I stand with them and praise you —
Out of my own self, I dare to phrase it.
But the best is when I glide from out them,
Cross a step or two of dubious twilight,
Come out on the other side, the novel
Silent silver lights and darks undreamed of,
Where I hush and bless myself with silence.

XIX.

Oh, their Rafael of the dear Madonnas,
Oh, their Dante of the dread Inferno,
Wrote one song — and in my brain I sing it,
Drew one angel — borne, see, on my bosom!

IN A BALCONY

1853

CONSTANCE and NORBERT.

Nor. Now!
Con.   Not now!
Nor.   Give me them again, those hands:
Put them upon my forehead, how it throbs!
Press them before my eyes, the fire comes through!
You cruellest, you dearest in the world,
Let me! The Queen must grant whate'er I ask —
How can I gain you and not ask the Queen?
There she stays waiting for me, here stand you;
Some time or other this was to be asked;
Now is the one time — what I ask, I gain:
Let me ask now, Love!
Con.   Do, and ruin us!
Nor. Let it be now, Love! All my soul breaks forth.
How I do love you! Give my love its way!
A man can have but one life and one death,
One heaven, one hell. Let me fulfil my fate —
Grant me my heaven now! Let me know you mine,
Prove you mine, write my name upon your brow,
Hold you and have you, and then die away,
If God please, with completion in my soul!
Con. I am not yours then? How content this man!
I am not his — who change into himself,
Have passed into his heart and beat its beats,
Who give my hands to him, my eyes, my hair,
Give all that was of me away to him —
So well, that now, my spirit turned his own,
Takes part with him against the woman here,
Bids him not stumble at so mere a straw
As caring that the world be cognizant
How he loves her and how she worships him.
You have this woman, not as yet that world.
Go on, I bid, nor stop to care for me
By saving what I cease to care about,

The courtly name and pride of circumstance —
The name you'll pick up and be cumbered with
Just for the poor parade's sake, nothing more ;
Just that the world may slip from under you —
Just that the world may cry, "So much for him —
The man predestined to the heap of crowns :
There goes his chance of winning one, at least!"
 Nor. The world!
 Con.   You love it! Love me quite as well,
And see if I shall pray for this in vain!
Why must you ponder what it knows or thinks?
 Nor. You pray for — what, in vain?
 Con.   Oh my heart's heart,
How I do love you, Norbert! That is right :
But listen, or I take my hands away!
You say, "let it be now :" you would go now
And tell the Queen, perhaps six steps from us,
You love me — so you do, thank God!
 Nor.   Thank God!
 Con. Yes, Norbert, — but you fain would tell your love,
And, what succeeds the telling, ask of her
My hand. Now take this rose and look at it,
Listening to me. You are the minister,
The Queen's first favorite, nor without a cause.
To-night completes your wonderful year's-work
(This palace-feast is held to celebrate)
Made memorable by her life's success,
The junction of two crowns, on her sole head,
Her house had only dreamed of anciently :
That this mere dream is grown a stable truth,
To-night's feast makes authentic. Whose the praise?
Whose genius, patience, energy, achieved
What turned the many heads and broke the hearts?
You are the fate, your minute's in the heaven.
Next comes the Queen's turn. "Name your own reward!"
With leave to clench the past, chain the to-come,
Put out an arm and touch and take the sun
And fix it ever full-faced on your earth,
Possess yourself supremely of her life, —
You choose the single thing she will not grant;
Nay, very declaration of which choice
Will turn the scale and neutralize your work :
At best she will forgive you, if she can.
You think I'll let you choose — her cousin's hand?
 Nor. Wait. First, do you retain your old belief
The Queen is generous, — nay, is just?

Con.   There, there!
So men make women love them, while they know
No more of women's hearts than . . . look you here,
You that are just and generous beside,
Make it your own case! For example now,
I 'll say — I let you kiss me, hold my hands —
Why? do you know why? I 'll instruct you, then —
The kiss, because you have a name at court;
This hand and this, that you may shut in each
A jewel, if you please to pick up such.
That's horrible? Apply it to the Queen —
Suppose I am the Queen to whom you speak.
"I was a nameless man; you needed me:
Why did I proffer you my aid? there stood
A certain pretty cousin at your side.
Why did I make such common cause with you?
Access to her had not been easy else.
You give my labor here abundant praise?
'Faith, labor, which she overlooked, grew play.
How shall your gratitude discharge itself?
Give me her hand!"
        Nor.   And still I urge the same.
Is the Queen just? just — generous or no!
    Con. Yes, just. You love a rose; no harm in that:
But was it for the rose's sake or mine
You put it in your bosom? mine, you said —
Then, mine you still must say or else be false.
You told the Queen you served her for herself;
If so, to serve her was to serve yourself,
She thinks, for all your unbelieving face!
I know her. In the hall, six steps from us,
One sees the twenty pictures; there's a life
Better than life, and yet no life at all.
Conceive her born in such a magic dome,
Pictures all round her! why, she sees the world,
Can recognize its given things and facts,
The fight of giants or the feast of gods,
Sages in senate, beauties at the bath,
Chases and battles, the whole earth's display,
Landscape and sea-piece, down to flowers and fruit —
And who shall question that she knows them all,
In better semblance than the things outside?
Yet bring into the silent gallery
Some live thing to contrast in breath and blood,
Some lion, with the painted lion there —
You think she 'll understand composedly?

—Say, "that's his fellow in the hunting-piece
Yonder, I've turned to praise a hundred times?"
Not so. Her knowledge of our actual earth,
Its hopes and fears, concerns and sympathies,
Must be too far, too mediate, too unreal.
The real exists for us outside, not her :
How should it, with that life in these four walls,
That father and that mother, first to last
No father and no mother — friends, a heap,
Lovers, no lack — a husband in due time,
And every one of them alike a lie!
Things painted by a Rubens out of nought
Into what kindness, friendship, love should be ;
All better, all more grandiose than the life,
Only no life ; mere cloth and surface-paint,
You feel, while you admire. How should she feel?
Yet now that she has stood thus fifty years
The sole spectator in that gallery,
You think to bring this warm real struggling love
In to her of a sudden, and suppose
She'll keep her state untroubled ? Here's the truth—
She'll apprehend truth's value at a glance,
Prefer it to the pictured loyalty ?
You only have to say, "So men are made,
For this they act ; the thing has many names,
But this the right one: and now, Queen, be just!"
Your life slips back ; you lose her at the word :
You do not even for amends gain me.
He will not understand! oh, Norbert, Norbert,
Do you not understand?
 Nor.   The Queen's the Queen,
I am myself — no picture, but alive
In every nerve and every muscle, here
At the palace-window o'er the people's street,
As she in the gallery where the pictures glow :
The good of life is precious to us both.
She cannot love ; what do I want with rule?
When first I saw your face a year ago
I knew my life's good, my soul heard one voice —
"The woman yonder, there's no use of life
 But just to obtain her ! heap earth's woes in one
And bear them — make a pile of all earth's joys
And spurn them, as they help or help not this ;
Only, obtain her !" How was it to be?
I found you were the cousin of the Queen ;
I must then serve the Queen to get to you.

No other way. Suppose there had been one,
And I, by saying prayers to some white star
With promise of my body and my soul,
Might gain you, — should I pray the star or no?
Instead, there was the Queen to serve! I served,
Helped, did what other servants failed to do.
Neither she sought nor I declared my end.
Her good is hers, my recompense be mine, —
I therefore name you as that recompense.
She dreamed that such a thing could never be?
Let her wake now. She thinks there was more cause
In love of power, high fame, pure loyalty?
Perhaps she fancies men wear out their lives
Chasing such shades. Then, I 've a fancy too;
I worked because I want you with my soul:
I therefore ask your hand. Let it be now!

   Con. Had I not loved you from the very first,
Were I not yours, could we not steal out thus
So wickedly, so wildly, and so well,
You might become impatient. What 's conceived
Of us without here, by the folk within?
Where are you now? immersed in cares of state —
Where am I now? intent on festal robes —
We two, embracing under death's spread hand!
What was this thought for, what that scruple of yours
Which broke the council up? — to bring about
One minute's meeting in the corridor!
And then the sudden sleights, strange secrecies,
Complots inscrutable, deep telegraphs,
Long-planned chance-meetings, hazards of a look,
"Does she know? does she not know? saved or lost?"
A year of this compression's ecstasy
All goes for nothing! you would give this up
For the old way, the open way, the world's,
His way who beats, and his who sells his wife!
What tempts you? — their notorious happiness
Makes you ashamed of ours? The best you 'll gain
Will be — the Queen grants all that you require,
Concedes the cousin, rids herself of you
And me at once, and gives us ample leave
To live like our five hundred happy friends.
The world will show us with officious hand
Our chamber-entry, and stand sentinel
Where we so oft have stolen across its traps!
Get the world's warrant, ring the falcons' feet,
And make it duty to be bold and swift,

Which long ago was nature. Have it so!
We never hawked by rights till flung from fist?
Oh, the man's thought! no woman's such a fool.
   Nor. Yes, the man's thought and my thought, which is
      more —
One made to love you, let the world take note!
Have I done worthy work? be love's the praise,
Though hampered by restrictions, barred against
By set forms, blinded by forced secrecies!
Set free my love, and see what love can do
Shown in my life — what work will spring from that!
The world is used to have its business done
On other grounds, find great effects produced
For power's sake, fame's sake, motives in men's mouth.
So, good : but let my low ground shame their high!
Truth is the strong thing. Let man's life be true!
And love's the truth of mine. Time prove the rest!
I choose to wear you stamped all over me,
Your name upon my forehead and my breast,
You, from the sword's blade to the ribbon's edge,
That men may see, all over, you in me —
That pale loves may die out of their pretence
In face of mine, shames thrown on love fall off.
Permit this, Constance! Love has been so long
Subdued in me, eating me through and through,
That now 't is all of me and must have way.
Think of my work, that chaos of intrigues,
Those hopes and fears, surprises and delays,
That long endeavor, earnest, patient, slow,
Trembling at last to its assured result :
Then think of this revulsion! I resume
Life after death, (it is no less than life,
After such long unlovely laboring days,)
And liberate to beauty life's great need
O' the beautiful, which, while it prompted work,
Suppressed itself erewhile. This eve 's the time,
This eve intense with yon first trembling star
We seem to pant and reach; scarce aught between
The earth that rises and the heaven that bends;
All nature self-abandoned, every tree
Flung as it will, pursuing its own thoughts
And fixed so, every flower and every weed,
No pride, no shame, no victory, no defeat;
All under God, each measured by itself.
These statues round us stand abrupt, distinct,
The strong in strength, the weak in weakness fixed,

The Muse forever wedded to her lyre,
Nymph to her fawn, and Silence to her rose:
See God's approval on his universe!
Let us do so — aspire to live as these
In harmony with truth, ourselves being true!
Take the first way, and let the second come!
My first is to possess myself of you;
The music sets the march-step — forward, then!
And there's the Queen, I go to claim you of,
The world to witness, wonder and applaud.
Our flower of life breaks open. No delay!
   Con. And so shall we be ruined, both of us.
Norbert, I know her to the skin and bone:
You do not know her, were not born to it,
To feel what she can see or cannot see.
Love, she is generous, — ay, despite your smile,
Generous as you are: for, in that thin frame
Pain-twisted, punctured through and through with cares,
There lived a lavish soul until it starved,
Debarred of healthy food. Look to the soul —
Pity that, stoop to that, ere you begin
(The true man's-way) on justice and your rights,
Exactions and acquittance of the past!
Begin so — see what justice she will deal!
We women hate a debt as men a gift.
Suppose her some poor keeper of a school
Whose business is to sit through summer months
And dole out children leave to go and play,
Herself superior to such lightness — she
In the arm-chair's state and pædagogic pomp —
To the life, the laughter, sun and youth outside:
We wonder such a face looks black on us?
I do not bid you wake her tenderness,
(That were vain truly — none is left to wake,)
But, let her think her justice is engaged
To take the shape of tenderness, and mark
If she 'll not coldly pay its warmest debt!
Does she love me, I ask you? not a whit:
Yet, thinking that her justice was engaged
To help a kinswoman, she took me up —
Did more on that bare ground than other loves
Would do on greater argument. For me,
I have no equivalent of such cold kind
To pay her with, but love alone to give
If I give anything. I give her love:
I feel I ought to help her, and I will.

So, for her sake, as yours, I tell you twice
That women hate a debt as men a gift.
If I were you, I could obtain this grace —
Could lay the whole I did to love's account,
Nor yet be very false as courtiers go —
Declaring my success was recompense ;
It would be so, in fact : what were it else ?
And then, once loose her generosity, —
Oh, how I see it ! then, were I but you
To turn it, let it seem to move itself,
And make it offer what I really take,
Accepting just, in the poor cousin's hand,
Her value as the next thing to the Queen's —
Since none love Queens directly, none dare that,
And a thing's shadow or a name's mere echo
Suffices those who miss the name and thing !
You pick up just a ribbon she has worn,
To keep in proof how near her breath you came.
Say, I'm so near I seem a piece of her —
Ask for me that way — (oh, you understand,)
You'd find the same gift yielded with a grace,
Which, if you make the least show to extort . . .
— You'll see ! and when you have ruined both of us,
Dissertate on the Queen's ingratitude !
   Nor. Then, if I turn it that way, you consent ?
'T is not my way ; I have more hope in truth :
Still, if you won't have truth — why, this indeed,
Were scarcely false, as I'd express the sense.
Will you remain here ?
   Con.   O best heart of mine,
How I have loved you ! then, you take my way ?
Are mine as you have been her minister,
Work out my thought, give it effect for me,
Paint plain my poor conceit and make it serve ?
I owe that withered woman everything —
Life, fortune, you, remember ! Take my part —
Help me to pay her ! Stand upon your rights ?
You, with my rose, my hands, my heart on you ?
Your rights are mine — you have no rights but mine.
   Nor. Remain here. How you know me !
   Con.   Ah, but still —

     [*He breaks from her ; she remains. Dance-music
      from within.*

Enter the QUEEN.

Queen. Constance? She is here as he said. Speak quick!
Is it so? Is it true or false? One word!
   Con. True.
   Queen. Mercifullest Mother, thanks to thee!
   Con. Madam?
   Queen. I love you, Constance, from my soul.
Now say once more, with any words you will,
'T is true, all true, as true as that I speak.
   Con. Why should you doubt it?
   Queen. Ah, why doubt? why doubt?
Dear, make me see it! Do you see it so?
None see themselves; another sees them best.
You say "why doubt it?"—you see him and me.
It is because the Mother has such grace
That if we had but faith — wherein we fail —
Whate'er we yearn for would be granted us;
Yet still we let our whims prescribe despair,
Our fancies thwart and cramp our will and power,
And while accepting life, abjure its use.
Constance, I had abjured the hope of love
And being loved, as truly as yon palm
The hope of seeing Egypt from that plot.
   Con. Heaven!
   Queen. But it was so, Constance, it was so!
Men say — or do men say it? fancies say —
"Stop here, your life is set, you are grown old.
Too late — no love for you, too late for love —
Leave love to girls. Be queen: let Constance love!"
One takes the hint — half meets it like a child,
Ashamed at any feelings that oppose.
"Oh love, true, never think of love again!
I am a queen: I rule, not love, forsooth."
So it goes on; so a face grows like this,
Hair like this hair, poor arms as lean as these,
Till, — nay, it does not end so, I thank God!
   Con. I cannot understand —
   Queen. The happier you!
Constance, I know not how it is with men:
For women (I am a woman now like you)
There is no good of life but love — but love!
What else looks good, is some shade flung from love;
Love gilds it, gives it worth. Be warned by me,
Never you cheat yourself one instant! Love,
Give love, ask only love, and leave the rest!
O Constance, how I love you!

Con.   I love you.
  Queen. I do believe that all is come through you.
I took you to my heart to keep it warm
When the last chance of love seemed dead in me;
I thought your fresh youth warmed my withered heart.
Oh, I am very old now, am I not?
Not so! it is true and it shall be true!
  Con. Tell it me: let me judge if true or false.
  Queen. Ah, but I fear you! you will look at me
And say, "she's old, she's grown unlovely quite
Who ne'er was beauteous: men want beauty still."
Well, so I feared — the curse! so I felt sure!
  Con. Be calm. And now you feel not sure, you say?
  Queen. Constance, he came, — the coming was not
    strange —
Do not I stand and see men come and go?
I turned a half-look from my pedestal
Where I grow marble — "one young man the more!
He will love some one; that is nought to me:
What would he with my marble stateliness?"
Yet this seemed somewhat worse than heretofore;
The man more gracious, youthful, like a god,
And I still older, with less flesh to change —
We two those dear extremes that long to touch.
It seemed still harder when he first began
To labor at those state-affairs, absorbed
The old way for the old end — interest.
Oh, to live with a thousand beating hearts
Around you, swift eyes, serviceable hands,
Professing they've no care but for your cause,
Thought but to help you, love but for yourself, —
And you the marble statue all the time
They praise and point at as preferred to life,
Yet leave for the first breathing woman's smile,
First dancer's, gypsy's, or street baladine's!
Why, how I have ground my teeth to hear men's speech
Stifled for fear it should alarm my ear,
Their gait subdued lest step should startle me,
Their eyes declined, such queendom to respect,
Their hands alert, such treasure to preserve,
While not a man of them broke rank and spoke,
Wrote me a vulgar letter all of love,
Or caught my hand and pressed it like a hand!
There have been moments, if the sentinel
Lowering his halbert to salute the queen,
Had flung it brutally and clasped my knees,
I would have stooped and kissed him with my soul.

IN A BALCONY

Con. Who could have comprehended?
Queen.   Ay, who — who?
Why, no one, Constance, but this one who did.
Not they, not you, not I. Even now perhaps
It comes too late — would you but tell the truth.
 Con. I wait to tell it.
 Queen.   Well, you see, he came,
Outfaced the others, did a work this year
Exceeds in value all was ever done,
You know — it is not I who say it — all
Say it. And so (a second pang and worse)
I grew aware not only of what he did,
But why so wondrously. Oh, never work
Like his was done for work's ignoble sake —
Souls need a finer aim to light and lure!
I felt, I saw, he loved — loved somebody.
And Constance, my dear Constance, do you know,
I did believe this while 't was you he loved.
 Con. Me, madam?
 Queen.   It did seem to me, your face
Met him where'er he looked: and whom but you
Was such a man to love? It seemed to me,
You saw he loved you, and approved his love,
And both of you were in intelligence.
You could not loiter in that garden, step
Into this balcony, but I straight was stung
And forced to understand. It seemed so true,
So right, so beautiful, so like you both,
That all this work should have been done by him
Not for the vulgar hope of recompense,
But that at last — suppose, some night like this —
Borne on to claim his due reward of me,
He might say, "Give her hand and pay me so."
And I (O Constance, you shall love me now!)
I thought, surmounting all the bitterness,
— " And he shall have it. I will make her blest,
My flower of youth, my woman's self that was,
My happiest woman's self that might have been!
These two shall have their joy and leave me here."
Yes — yes!
 Con. Thanks!
 Queen.   And the word was on my lips
When he burst in upon me. I looked to hear
A mere calm statement of his just desire
For payment of his labor. When — O heaven,
How can I tell you? lightning on my eyes

And thunder in my ears proved that first word
Which told 't was love of me, of me, did all —
He loved me — from the first step to the last,
Loved me!
    Con.   You hardly saw, scarce heard him speak
Of love: what if you should mistake?
    Queen.   No, no —
No mistake! Ha, there shall be no mistake!
He had not dared to hint the love he felt —
You were my reflex — (how I understood!)
He said you were the ribbon I had worn,
He kissed my hand, he looked into my eyes,
And love, love came at end of every phrase.
Love is begun; this much is come to pass:
The rest is easy. Constance, I am yours!
I will learn, I will place my life on you,
Teach me but how to keep what I have won!
Am I so old? This hair was early gray;
But joy ere now has brought hair brown again,
And joy will bring the cheek's red back, I feel.
I could sing once too; that was in my youth.
Still, when men paint me, they declare me . . . yes,
Beautiful — for the last French painter did!
I know they flatter somewhat; you are frank —
I trust you. How I loved you from the first!
Some queens would hardly seek a cousin out
And set her by their side to take the eye:
I must have felt that good would come from you.
I am not generous — like him — like you!
But he is not your lover after all:
It was not you he looked at. Saw you him?
You have not been mistaking words or looks?
He said you were the reflex of myself.
And yet he is not such a paragon
To you, to younger women who may choose
Among a thousand Norberts. Speak the truth!
You know you never named his name to me:
You know, I cannot give him up — ah God,
Not up now, even to you!
    Con.   Then calm yourself.
    Queen. See, I am old — look here, you happy girl!
I will not play the fool, deceive — ah, whom?
'T is all gone: put your cheek beside my cheek
And what a contrast does the moon behold!
But then I set my life upon one chance,
The last chance and the best — am *I* not left,

My soul, myself? All women love great men
If young or old; it is in all the tales:
Young beauties love old poets who can love —
Why should not he, the poems in my soul,
The passionate faith, the pride of sacrifice,
Life-long, death-long? I throw them at his feet.
Who cares to see the fountain's very shape,
Whether it be a Triton's or a Nymph's
That pours the foam, makes rainbows all around?
You could not praise indeed the empty conch;
But I'll pour floods of love and hide myself.
How I will love him! Cannot men love love?
Who was a queen and loved a poet once
Humpbacked, a dwarf? ah, women can do that!
Well, but men too; at least, they tell you so.
They love so many women in their youth,
And even in age they all love whom they please;
And yet the best of them confide to friends
That 't is not beauty makes the lasting love —
They spend a day with such and tire the next:
They like soul, — well then, they like phantasy,
Novelty even. Let us confess the truth,
Horrible though it be, that prejudice,
Prescription . . . curses! they will love a queen.
They will, they do: and will not, does not — he?
   Con. How can he? You are wedded: 't is a name
We know, but still a bond. Your rank remains,
His rank remains. How can he, nobly souled
As you believe and I incline to think,
Aspire to be your favorite, shame and all?
   Queen. Hear her! There, there now — could she love like
     me?
What did I say of smooth-cheeked youth and grace?
See all it does or could do! so youth loves!
Oh, tell him, Constance, you could never do
What I will — you, it was not born in! I
Will drive these difficulties far and fast
As yonder mists curdling before the moon.
I'll use my light too, gloriously retrieve
My youth from its enforced calamity,
Dissolve that hateful marriage, and be his,
His own in the eyes alike of God and man.
   Con. You will do — dare do . . . pause on what you say!
   Queen. Hear her! I thank you, sweet, for that surprise.
You have the fair face: for the soul, see mine!
I have the strong soul: let me teach you, here.

I think I have borne enough and long enough,
And patiently enough, the world remarks,
To have my own way now, unblamed by all.
It does so happen (I rejoice for it)
This most unhoped-for issue cuts the knot.
There's not a better way of settling claims
Than this; God sends the accident express:
And were it for my subjects' good, no more,
'T were best thus ordered. I am thankful now,
Mute, passive, acquiescent. I receive,
And bless God simply, or should almost fear
To walk so smoothly to my ends at last.
Why, how I baffle obstacles, spurn fate!
How strong I am! Could Norbert see me now!
   Con. Let me consider. It is all too strange.
   Queen. You, Constance, learn of me; do you, like me!
You are young, beautiful: my own, best girl,
You will have many lovers, and love one —
Light hair, not hair like Norbert's, to suit yours,
Taller than he is, since yourself are tall.
Love him, like me! Give all away to him;
Think never of yourself; throw by your pride,
Hope, fear, — your own good as you saw it once,
And love him simply for his very self.
Remember, I (and what am I to you?)
Would give up all for one, leave throne, lose life,
Do all but just unlove him! He loves me.
   Con. He shall.
   Queen.   You, step inside my inmost heart!
Give me your own heart: let us have one heart!
I'll come to you for counsel; "this he says,
This he does; what should this amount to, pray?
Beseech you, change it into current coin!
Is that worth kisses? Shall I please him there?"
And then we'll speak in turn of you — what else?
Your love, according to your beauty's worth,
For you shall have some noble love, all gold:
Whom choose you? we will get him at your choice.
— Constance, I leave you. Just a minute since,
I felt as I must die or be alone
Breathing my soul into an ear like yours:
Now, I would face the world with my new life,
Wear my new crown. I'll walk around the rooms,
And then come back and tell you how it feels.
How soon a smile of God can change the world!
How we are made for happiness — how work

IN A BALCONY 145

Grows play, adversity a winning fight!
True, I have lost so many years: what then?
Many remain: God has been very good.
You, stay here! 'T is as different from dreams,
From the mind's cold calm estimate of bliss,
As these stone statues from the flesh and blood.
The comfort thou hast caused mankind, God's moon!
 [*She goes out, leaving* CONSTANCE. *Dance-music from within.*

NORBERT *enters.*
Nor. Well? we have but one minute and one word!
Con. I am yours, Norbert!
Nor. Yes, mine.
Con. Not till now!
You were mine. Now I give myself to you.
Nor. Constance?
Con. Your own! I know the thriftier way
Of giving — haply, 't is the wiser way.
Meaning to give a treasure, I might dole
Coin after coin out (each, as that were all,
With a new largess still at each despair)
And force you keep in sight the deed, preserve
Exhaustless till the end my part and yours,
My giving and your taking; both our joys
Dying together. Is it the wiser way?
I choose the simpler; I give all at once.
Know what you have to trust to, trade upon!
Use it, abuse it, — anything but think
Hereafter, "Had I known she loved me so,
And what my means, I might have thriven with it."
This is your means. I give you all myself.
Nor. I take you and thank God.
Con. Look on through years!
We cannot kiss, a second day like this;
Else were this earth no earth.
Nor. With this day's heat
We shall go on through years of cold.
Con. So, best!
— I try to see those years — I think I see.
You walk quick and new warmth comes; you look back
And lay all to the first glow — not sit down
Forever brooding on a day like this
While seeing embers whiten and love die.
Yes, love lives best in its effect; and mine,
Full in its own life, yearns to live in yours.
Nor. Just so. I take and know you all at once.
Your soul is disengaged so easily,

Your face is there, I know you; give me time,
Let me be proud and think you shall know me.
My soul is slower: in a life I roll
The minute out whereto you condense yours —
The whole slow circle round you I must move,
To be just you. I look to a long life
To decompose this minute, prove its worth.
'T is the sparks' long succession one by one
Shall show you, in the end. what fire was crammed
In that mere stone you struck : how could you know,
If it lay ever unproved in your sight.
As now my heart lies? your own warmth would hide
Its coldness, were it cold.
  Con.   But how prove, how?
 Nor. Prove in my life, you ask?
  Con.   Quick, Norbert — how?
 Nor. That's easy told. I count life just a stuff
To try the soul's strength on, educe the man.
Who keeps one end in view makes all things serve.
As with the body — he who hurls a lance
Or heaps up stone on stone, shows strength alike :
So must I seize and task all means to prove
And show this soul of mine, you crown as yours,
And justify us both.
  Con.   Could you write books,
Paint pictures ! One sits down in poverty
And writes or paints, with pity for the rich.
 Nor. And loves one's painting and one's writing, then,
And not one's mistress ! All is best, believe,
And we best as no other than we are.
We live, and they experiment on life —
Those poets, painters, all who stand aloof
To overlook the farther. Let us be
The thing they look at ! I might take your face
And write of it and paint it — to what end ?
For whom ? what pale dictatress in the air
Feeds, smiling sadly. her fine ghost-like form
With earth's real blood and breath, the beauteous life
She makes despised forever ? You are mine,
Made for me, not for others in the world.
Nor yet for that which I should call my art,
The cold calm power to see how fair you look.
I come to you ; I leave you not, to write
Or paint. You are, I am : let Rubens there
Paint us !
  Con. So, best!

Nor.   I understand your soul.
You live, and rightly sympathize with life,
With action, power, success. This way is straight;
And time were short beside, to let me change
The craft my childhood learnt: my craft shall serve.
Men set me here to subjugate, enclose,
Manure their barren lives, and force thence fruit
First for themselves, and afterward for me
In the due tithe; the task of some one soul,
Through ways of work appointed by the world.
I am not bid create — men see no star
Transfiguring my brow to warrant that —
But find and bind and bring to bear their wills.
So I began: to-night sees how I end.
What if it see, too, power's first outbreak here
Amid the warmth, surprise and sympathy,
And instincts of the heart that teach the head?
What if the people have discerned at length
The dawn of the next nature, novel brain
Whose will they venture in the place of theirs,
Whose work, they trust, shall find them as novel ways
To untried heights which yet he only sees?
I felt it when you kissed me. See this Queen,
This people — in our phrase, this mass of men —
See how the mass lies passive to my hand
Now that my hand is plastic, with you by
To make the muscles iron! Oh, an end
Shall crown this issue as this crowns the first!
My will be on this people! then, the strain,
The grappling of the potter with his clay,
The long uncertain struggle, — the success
And consummation of the spirit-work,
Some vase shaped to the curl of the god's lip,
While rounded fair for human sense to see
The Graces in a dance men recognize
With turbulent applause and laughs of heart!
So triumph ever shall renew itself;
Ever shall end in efforts higher yet,
Ever begin . . .
    Con.   I ever helping?
    Nor.   Thus!
            [*As he embraces her, the* QUEEN *enters.*
Con. Hist, madam! So have I performed my part.
You see your gratitude's true decency,
Norbert? A little slow in seeing it!
Begin, to end the sooner! What's a kiss?

Nor. Constance?
Con.   Why, must I teach it you again?
You want a witness to your dulness, sir?
What was I saying these ten minutes long?
Then I repeat — when some young handsome man
Like you has acted out a part like yours,
Is pleased to fall in love with one beyond,
So very far beyond him, as he says —
So hopelessly in love that but to speak
Would prove him mad, — he thinks judiciously,
And makes some insignificant good soul,
Like me, his friend, adviser, confidant,
And very stalking-horse to cover him
In following after what he dares not face —
When his end's gained — (sir, do you understand?)
When she, he dares not face, has loved him first,
— May I not say so, madam? — tops his hope,
And overpasses so his wildest dream,
With glad consent of all, and most of her
The confidant who brought the same about —
Why, in the moment when such joy explodes,
I do hold that the merest gentleman
Will not start rudely from the stalking-horse,
Dismiss it with a " There, enough of you! "
Forget it, show his back unmannerly;
But like a liberal heart will rather turn
And say, " A tingling time of hope was ours;
Betwixt the fears and falterings, we two lived
A chanceful time in waiting for the prize:
The confidant, the Constance, served not ill.
And though I shall forget her in due time,
Her use being answered now, as reason bids,
Nay as herself bids from her heart of hearts, —
Still, she has rights, the first thanks go to her,
The first good praise goes to the prosperous tool,
And the first — which is the last — rewarding kiss."
    Nor. Constance, it is a dream — ah, see, you smile!
    Con. So, now his part being properly performed,
Madam, I turn to you and finish mine
As duly; I do justice in my turn.
Yes, madam, he has loved you — long and well;
He could not hope to tell you so — 't was I
Who served to prove your soul accessible,
I led his thoughts on, drew them to their place
When they had wandered else into despair,
And kept love constant toward its natural aim.

Enough, my part is played; you stoop half-way
And meet us royally and spare our fears:
'T is like yourself. He thanks you, so do I.
Take him — with my full heart! my work is praised
By what comes of it. Be you happy, both!
Yourself — the only one on earth who can —
Do all for him, much more than a mere heart
Which though warm is not useful in its warmth
As the silk vesture of a queen! fold that
Around him gently, tenderly. For him —
For him, — he knows his own part!
  Nor.   Have you done?
I take the jest at last. Should I speak now?
Was yours the wager, Constance, foolish child,
Or did you but accept it? Well — at least
You lose by it.
  Con.   Nay, madam, 't is your turn!
Restrain him still from speech a little more,
And make him happier as more confident!
Pity him, madam, he is timid yet!
Mark, Norbert! Do not shrink now! Here I yield
My whole right in you to the Queen, observe!
With her go put in practice the great schemes
You teem with, follow the career else closed —
Be all you cannot be except by her!
Behold her! — Madam, say for pity's sake
Anything — frankly say you love him! Else
He'll not believe it: there's more earnest in
His fear than you conceive: I know the man!
  Nor. I know the woman somewhat, and confess
I thought she had jested better: she begins
To overcharge her part. I gravely wait
Your pleasure, madam: where is my reward?
  Queen. Norbert, this wild girl (whom I recognize
Scarce more than you do, in her fancy-fit,
Eccentric speech and variable mirth,
Not very wise perhaps and somewhat bold,
Yet suitable, the whole night's work being strange)
— May still be right: I may do well to speak
And make authentic what appears a dream
To even myself. For, what she says is true:
Yes, Norbert — what you spoke just now of love,
Devotion, stirred no novel sense in me,
But justified a warmth felt long before.
Yes, from the first — I loved you, I shall say:
Strange! but I do grow stronger, now 't is said.

IN A BALCONY

Your courage helps mine: you did well to speak
To-night, the night that crowns your twelvemonths' toil:
But still I had not waited to discern
Your heart so long, believe me! From the first
The source of so much zeal was almost plain,
In absence even of your own words just now
Which hazarded the truth. 'T is very strange,
But takes a happy ending — in your love
Which mine meets: be it so! as you chose me,
So I choose you.
    Nor.   And worthily you choose.
I will not be unworthy your esteem,
No, madam. I do love you; I will meet
Your nature, now I know it. This was well.
I see, — you dare and you are justified :
But none had ventured such experiment,
Less versed than you in nobleness of heart,
Less confident of finding such in me.
I joy that thus you test me ere you grant
The dearest richest beauteousest and best
Of women to my arms: 't is like yourself.
So — back again into my part's set words —
Devotion to the uttermost is yours,
But no, you cannot, madam, even you,
Create in me the love our Constance does.
Or — something truer to the tragic phrase —
Not yon magnolia-bell superb with scent
Invites a certain insect — that 's myself —
But the small eye-flower nearer to the ground.
I take this lady.
    Con.   Stay — not hers, the trap —
Stay, Norbert — that mistake were worst of all!
He is too cunning, madam! It was I,
I, Norbert, who . . .
    Nor.   You, was it, Constance? Then,
But for the grace of this divinest hour
Which gives me you, I might not pardon here!
I am the Queen's; she only knows my brain :
She may experiment upon my heart
And I instruct her too by the result.
But you, Sweet, you who know me, who so long
Have told my heartbeats over, held my life
In those white hands of yours, — it is not well!
    Con. Tush! I have said it, did I not say it all?
The life, for her — the heartbeats, for her sake!
    Nor. Enough! my cheek grows red, I think. Your test

There's not the meanest woman in the world,
Not she I least could love in all the world,
Whom, did she love me, had love proved itself,
I dare insult as you insult me now.
Constance, I could say, if it must be said,
"Take back the soul you offer, I keep mine!"
But — "Take the soul still quivering on your hand,
The soul so offered, which I cannot use,
And, please you, give it to some playful friend,
For — what's the trifle he requites me with?"
I, tempt a woman, to amuse a man,
That two may mock her heart if it succumb?
No: fearing God and standing 'neath his heaven,
I would not dare insult a woman so,
Were she the meanest woman in the world,
And he, I cared to please, ten emperors!
  Con. Norbert!
  Nor.   I love once as I live but once.
What case is this to think or talk about?
I love you. Would it mend the case at all
If such a step as this killed love in me?
Your part were done: account to God for it!
But mine — could murdered love get up again,
And kneel to whom you please to designate,
And make you mirth? It is too horrible.
You did not know this, Constance? now you know
That body and soul have each one life, but one:
And here's my love, here, living, at your feet.
  Con. See the Queen! Norbert — this one more last word —
If thus you have taken jest for earnest — thus
Loved me in earnest . . .
  Nor.   Ah, no jest holds here!
Where is the laughter in which jests break up,
And what this horror that grows palpable?
Madam — why grasp you thus the balcony?
Have I done ill? Have I not spoken truth?
How could I other? Was it not your test,
To try me, what my love for Constance meant?
Madam, your royal soul itself approves,
The first, that I should choose thus! so one takes
A beggar, — asks him, what would buy his child?
And then approves the expected laugh of scorn
Returned as something noble from the rags.
Speak, Constance, I'm the beggar! Ha, what's this?
You two glare each at each like panthers now.
Constance, the world fades; only you stand there!

You did not, in to-night's wild whirl of things,
Sell me — your soul of souls, for any price?
No — no — 't is easy to believe in you !
Was it your love's mad trial to o'ertop
Mine by this vain self-sacrifice ? well, still —
Though I might curse, I love you. I am love
And cannot change : love's self is at your feet !
                                              [*The* QUEEN *goes out.*
  Con. Feel my heart; let it die against your own !
  Nor. Against my own. Explain not; let this be !
This is life's height.
  Con.   Yours, yours, yours !
  Nor.   You and I —
Why care by what meanders we are here
I' the centre of the labyrinth ? Men have died
Trying to find this place, which we have found.
  Con. Found, found !
  Nor.   Sweet, never fear what she can do !
We are past harm now.
  Con.   On the breast of God.
I thought of men — as if you were a man.
Tempting him with a crown !
  Nor.   This must end here :
It is too perfect.
  Con.   There 's the music stopped.
What measured heavy tread ? It is one blaze
About me and within me.
  Nor.   Oh, some death
Will run its sudden finger round this spark
And sever us from the rest !
  Con.   And so do well.
Now the doors open.
  Nor.   'T is the guard comes.
  Con.   Kiss !

DRAMATIS PERSONÆ

1864.

JAMES LEE'S WIFE.

I.

JAMES LEE'S WIFE SPEAKS AT THE WINDOW.

I.

Ah, Love, but a day
  And the world has changed!
The sun's away,
  And the bird estranged;
The wind has dropped,
  And the sky's deranged:
Summer has stopped.

II.

Look in my eyes!
  Wilt thou change too?
Should I fear surprise?
  Shall I find aught new
In the old and dear,
  In the good and true,
With the changing year?

III.

Thou art a man,
  But I am thy love.
For the lake, its swan;
  For the dell, its dove;
And for thee — (oh, haste!)
  Me, to bend above,
Me, to hold embraced.

II.

BY THE FIRESIDE.

I.

Is all our fire of shipwreck wood,
    Oak and pine?
Oh, for the ills half-understood,
    The dim dead woe
    Long ago
Befallen this bitter coast of France!
Well, poor sailors took their chance;
    I take mine.

II.

A ruddy shaft our fire must shoot
    O'er the sea:
Do sailors eye the casement — mute
    Drenched and stark,
    From their bark —
And envy, gnash their teeth for hate
O' the warm safe house and happy freight
    — Thee and me?

III.

God help you, sailors, at your need!
    Spare the curse!
For some ships, safe in port indeed,
    Rot and rust,
    Run to dust,
All through worms i' the wood, which crept,
Gnawed our hearts out while we slept:
    That is worse.

IV.

Who lived here before us two?
    Old-world pairs.
Did a woman ever — would I knew! —
    Watch the man
    With whom began
Love's voyage full-sail, — (now, gnash your teeth!)
When planks start, open hell beneath
    Unawares?

III.

IN THE DOORWAY.

I.

THE swallow has set her six young on the rail,
    And looks sea-ward:
The water's in stripes like a snake, olive-pale
    To the leeward, —
On the weather-side, black, spotted white with the wind.
"Good fortune departs, and disaster's behind," —
Hark, the wind with its wants and its infinite wail!

II.

Our fig-tree, that leaned for the saltness, has furled
    Her five fingers,
Each leaf like a hand opened wide to the world
    Where there lingers
No glint of the gold, Summer sent for her sake:
How the vines writhe in rows, each impaled on its stake!
My heart shrivels up and my spirit shrinks curled.

III.

Yet here are we two; we have love, house enough,
    With the field there,
This house of four rooms, that field red and rough,
    Though it yield there,
For the rabbit that robs, scarce a blade or a bent;
If a magpie alight now, it seems an event;
And they both will be gone at November's rebuff.

IV.

But why must cold spread? but wherefore bring change
    To the spirit,
God meant should mate his with an infinite range,
    And inherit
His power to put life in the darkness and cold?
Oh, live and love worthily, bear and be bold!
Whom Summer made friends of, let Winter estrange!

IV.

ALONG THE BEACH.

I.

I WILL be quiet and talk with you,
 And reason why you are wrong.
You wanted my love — is that much true?
And so I did love, so I do:
 What has come of it all along?

II.

I took you — how could I otherwise?
 For a world to me, and more;
For all, love greatens and glorifies
Till God's aglow, to the loving eyes,
 In what was mere earth before.

III.

Yes, earth — yes, mere ignoble earth!
 Now do I mis-state, mistake?
Do I wrong your weakness and call it worth?
Expect all harvest, dread no dearth,
 Seal my sense up for your sake?

IV.

Oh, Love, Love, no, Love! not so, indeed!
 You were just weak earth, I knew:
With much in you waste, with many a weed,
And plenty of passions run to seed,
 But a little good grain too.

V.

And such as you were, I took you for mine:
 Did not you find me yours,
To watch the olive and wait the vine,
And wonder when rivers of oil and wine
 Would flow, as the Book assures?

VI.

Well, and if none of these good things came.
 What did the failure prove?
The man was my whole world, all the same.

VII.

Yet this turns now to a fault — there! there!
    That I do love, watch too long,
And wait too well, and weary and wear;
And 't is all an old story, and my despair
    Fit subject for some new song:

VIII.

" How the light, light love, he has wings to fly
    At suspicion of a bond:
My wisdom has bidden your pleasure good-bye,
Which will turn up next in a laughing eye,
    And why should you look beyond?"

V.

ON THE CLIFF.

I.

I LEANED on the turf,
I looked at a rock
Left dry by the surf;
For the turf, to call it grass were to mock:
Dead to the roots, so deep was done
The work of the summer sun.

II.

And the rock lay flat
As an anvil's face:
No iron like that!
Baked dry; of a weed, of a shell, no trace:
Sunshine outside, but ice at the core,
Death's altar by the lone shore.

III.

On the turf, sprang gay
With his films of blue,
No cricket, I 'll say,
But a warhorse, barded and chanfroned too,
The gift of a quixote-mage to his knight,
Real fairy, with wings all right.

IV.

On the rock, they scorch
Like a drop of fire
From a brandished torch,
Fall two red fans of a butterfly :
No turf, no rock: in their ugly stead,
See, wonderful blue and red !

V.

Is it not so
With the minds of men ?
The level and low,
The burnt and bare, in themselves ; but then
With such a blue and red grace, not theirs, —
Love settling unawares !

VI.

READING A BOOK, UNDER THE CLIFF.

I.

"Still ailing, Wind ? Wilt be appeased or no ?
   Which needs the other's office, thou or I ?
Dost want to be disburdened of a woe,
   And can, in truth, my voice untie
Its links, and let it go ?

II.

"Art thou a dumb, wronged thing that would be righted,
   Entrusting thus thy cause to me ? Forbear !
No tongue can mend such pleadings; faith, requited
   With falsehood, — love, at last aware
Of scorn, — hopes, early blighted, —

III.

"We have them ; but I know not any tone
   So fit as thine to falter forth a sorrow:
Dost think men would go mad without a moan,
   If they knew any way to borrow
A pathos like thy own ?

IV.

"Which sigh wouldst mock, of all the sighs? The one
  So long escaping from lips starved and blue,
That lasts while on her pallet-bed the nun
  Stretches her length; her foot comes through
The straw she shivers on;

V.

"You had not thought she was so tall: and spent,
  Her shrunk lids open, her lean fingers shut
Close, close, their sharp and livid nails indent
  The clammy palm; then all is mute:
That way, the spirit went.

VI.

"Or wouldst thou rather that I understand
  Thy will to help me? — like the dog I found
Once, pacing sad this solitary strand,
  Who would not take my food, poor hound,
But whined and licked my hand."

VII.

All this, and more, comes from some young man's pride
  Of power to see, — in failure and mistake,
Relinquishment, disgrace, on every side, —
  Merely examples for his sake,
Helps to his path untried:

VIII.

Instances he must — simply recognize?
  Oh, more than so! — must, with a learner's zeal,
Make doubly prominent, twice emphasize,
  By added touches that reveal
The god in babe's disguise.

IX.

Oh, he knows what defeat means, and the rest!
  Himself the undefeated that shall be:
Failure, disgrace, he flings them you to test, —
  His triumph, in eternity
Too plainly manifest!

X.

Whence, judge if he learn forthwith what the wind
    Means in its moaning — by the happy prompt
Instinctive way of youth, I mean ; for kind
    Calm years, exacting their accompt
Of pain, mature the mind :

XI.

And some midsummer morning, at the lull
    Just about daybreak, as he looks across
A sparkling foreign country, wonderful
    To the sea's edge for gloom and gloss,
Next minute must annul, —

XII.

Then, when the wind begins among the vines,
    So low, so low, what shall it say but this?
"Here is the change beginning, here the lines
    Circumscribe beauty, set to bliss
The limit time assigns."

XIII.

Nothing can be as it has been before ;
    Better, so call it, only not the same.
To draw one beauty into our hearts' core,
    And keep it changeless ! such our claim ;
So answered, — Nevermore !

XIV.

Simple ? Why this is the old woe o' the world ;
    Tune, to whose rise and fall we live and die.
Rise with it, then ! Rejoice that man is hurled
    From change to change unceasingly,
His soul's wings never furled !

XV.

That 's a new question ; still replies the fact,
    Nothing endures : the wind moans, saying so ;
We moan in acquiescence : there 's life's pact.
    Perhaps probation — do *I* know?
God does : endure his act !

XVI.

Only, for man, how bitter not to grave
    On his soul's hands' palms one fair good wise thing

Just as he grasped it! For himself, death's wave;
　While time first washes — ah, the sting! —
O'er all he 'd sink to save.

VII.

AMONG THE ROCKS.

I.

OH, good gigantic smile o' the brown old earth,
　This autumn morning! How he sets his bones
To bask i' the sun, and thrusts out knees and feet
For the ripple to run over in its mirth;
　Listening the while, where on the heap of stones
The white breast of the sea-lark twitters sweet.

II.

That is the doctrine, simple, ancient, true;
　Such is life's trial, as old earth smiles and knows.
If you loved only what were worth your love,
Love were clear gain, and wholly well for you:
　Make the low nature better by your throes!
Give earth yourself, go up for gain above!

VIII.

BESIDE THE DRAWING-BOARD.

I.

"As like as a Hand to another Hand!"
　Whoever said that foolish thing,
Could not have studied to understand
　The counsels of God in fashioning,
Out of the infinite love of his heart,
This Hand, whose beauty I praise, apart
From the world of wonder left to praise,
If I tried to learn the other ways
Of love in its skill, or love in its power.
　"As like as a Hand to another Hand:"
　Who said that, never took his stand,
Found and followed, like me, an hour,
The beauty in this, — how free, how fine

To fear, almost, — of the limit-line !
As I looked at this, and learned and drew,
 Drew and learned, and looked again,
While fast the happy minutes flew,
 Its beauty mounted into my brain,
And a fancy seized me ; I was fain
To efface my work, begin anew,
Kiss what before I only drew ;
Ay, laying the red chalk 'twixt my lips,
 With soul to help if the mere lips failed,
I kissed all right where the drawing ailed,
Kissed fast the grace that somehow slips
Still from one's soulless finger-tips.

II.

'T is a clay cast, the perfect thing,
 From Hand live once, dead long ago :
Princess-like it wears the ring
 To fancy's eye, by which we know
That here at length a master found
 His match, a proud lone soul its mate,
As soaring genius sank to ground,
 And pencil could not emulate
The beauty in this, — how free, how fine
To fear almost ! — of the limit-line.
Long ago the god, like me
The worm, learned, each in our degree :
Looked and loved, learned and drew,
 Drew and learned and loved again,
While fast the happy minutes flew,
 Till beauty mounted into his brain
And on the finger which outvied
 His art he placed the ring that 's there,
Still by fancy's eye descried,
 In token of a marriage rare :
For him on earth, his art's despair,
For him in heaven, his soul's fit bride.

III.

Little girl with the poor coarse hand
 I turned from to a cold clay cast —
I have my lesson, understand
 The worth of flesh and blood at last !
Nothing but beauty in a Hand ?
 Because he could not change the hue,
 Mend the lines and make them true

To this which met his soul's demand, —
   Would Da Vinci turn from you?
I hear him laugh my woes to scorn —
" The fool forsooth is all forlorn
Because the beauty, she thinks best,
Lived long ago or was never born, —
Because no beauty bears the test
In this rough peasant Hand! Confessed
' Art is null and study void!'
So sayest thou? So said not I,
Who threw the faulty pencil by,
And years instead of hours employed,
Learning the veritable use
Of flesh and bone and nerve beneath
Lines and hue of the outer sheath,
If haply I might reproduce
One motive of the powers profuse,
Flesh and bone and nerve that make
The poorest coarsest human hand
An object worthy to be scanned
A whole life long for their sole sake.
Shall earth and the cramped moment-space
Yield the heavenly crowning grace?
Now the parts and then the whole!
Who art thou, with stinted soul
And stunted body, thus to cry,
'I love, — shall that be life's strait dole?
I must live beloved or die!'
This peasant hand that spins the wool
And bakes the bread, why lives it on,
Poor and coarse with beauty gone, —
What use survives the beauty?" Fool!

Go, little girl with the poor coarse hand!
I have my lesson, shall understand.

IX.

ON DECK.

I.

THERE is nothing to remember in me,
   Nothing I ever said with a grace,
Nothing I did that you care to see,

Nothing I was that deserves a place
In your mind, now I leave you, set you free.

II.

Conceded! In turn, concede to me,
Such things have been as a mutual flame.
Your soul's locked fast; but, love for a key,
You might let it loose, till I grew the same
In your eyes, as in mine you stand : strange plea!

III.

For then, then, what would it matter to me
That I was the harsh, ill-favored one?
We both should be like as pea and pea;
It was ever so since the world begun :
So, let me proceed with my reverie.

IV.

How strange it were if you had all me,
As I have all you in my heart and brain,
You, whose least word brought gloom or glee,
Who never lifted the hand in vain —
Will hold mine yet, from over the sea!

V.

Strange, if a face, when you thought of me,
Rose like your own face present now,
With eyes as clear in their due degree,
Much such a mouth, and as bright a brow,
Till you saw yourself, while you cried " 'T is She!"

VI.

Well, you may, you must, set down to me
Love that was life, life that was love;
A tenure of breath at your lips' decree,
A passion to stand as your thoughts approve,
A rapture to fall where your foot might be.

VII.

But did one touch of such love for me
Come in a word or a look of yours,
Whose words and looks will, circling, flee
Round me and round while life endures, —
Could I fancy " As I feel, thus feels He ; "

VIII.

Why, fade you might to a thing like me,
 And your hair grow these coarse hanks of hair,
Your skin, this bark of a gnarled tree, —
 You might turn myself! — should I know or care,
When I should be dead of joy, James Lee?

GOLD HAIR.

A STORY OF PORNIC.

I.

OH, the beautiful girl, too white,
 Who lived at Pornic, down by the sea,
Just where the sea and the Loire unite!
 And a boasted name in Brittany
She bore, which I will not write.

II.

Too white, for the flower of life is red;
 Her flesh was the soft seraphic screen
Of a soul that is meant (her parents said)
 To just see earth, and hardly be seen,
And blossom in heaven instead.

III.

Yet earth saw one thing, one how fair!
 One grace that grew to its full on earth:
Smiles might be sparse on her cheek so spare,
 And her waist want half a girdle's girth,
But she had her great gold hair.

IV.

Hair, such a wonder of flix and floss,
 Freshness and fragrance — floods of it, too!
Gold, did I say? Nay, gold's mere dross:
 Here, Life smiled, "Think what I meant to do!"
And Love sighed, "Fancy my loss!"

V.

So, when she died, it was scarce more strange
 Than that, when delicate evening dies,

And you follow its spent sun's pallid range,
  There 's a shoot of color startles the skies
With sudden, violent change, —

VI.

That, while the breath was nearly to seek,
  As they put the little cross to her lips,
She changed; a spot came out on her cheek,
  A spark from her eye in mid-eclipse,
And she broke forth, "I must speak!"

VII.

"Not my hair!" made the girl her moan —
  "All the rest is gone or to go;
But the last, last grace, my all, my own,
  Let it stay in the grave, that the ghosts may know!
Leave my poor gold hair alone!"

VIII.

The passion thus vented, dead lay she;
  Her parents sobbed their worst on that;
All friends joined in, nor observed degree:
  For indeed the hair was to wonder at,
As it spread — not flowing free,

IX.

But curled around her brow, like a crown,
  And coiled beside her cheeks, like a cap,
And calmed about her neck — ay, down
  To her breast, pressed flat, without a gap
I' the gold, it reached her gown.

X.

All kissed that face, like a silver wedge
  'Mid the yellow wealth, nor disturbed its hair:
E'en the priest allowed death's privilege,
  As he planted the crucifix with care
On her breast, 'twixt edge and edge.

XI.

And thus was she buried, inviolate
  Of body and soul, in the very space
By the altar; keeping saintly state
  In Pornic church, for her pride of race,
Pure life and piteous fate.

XII.

And in after-time would your fresh tear fall,
  Though your mouth might twitch with a dubious smile,
As they told you of gold, both robe and pall,
  How she prayed them leave it alone awhile,
So it never was touched at all.

XIII.

Years flew; this legend grew at last
  The life of the lady; all she had done,
All been, in the memories fading fast
  Of lover and friend, was summed in one
Sentence survivors passed:

XIV.

To wit, she was meant for heaven, not earth;
  Had turned an angel before the time:
Yet, since she was mortal, in such dearth
  Of frailty, all you could count a crime
Was — she knew her gold hair's worth.

XV.

At little pleasant Pornic church,
  It chanced, the pavement wanted repair,
Was taken to pieces: left in the lurch,
  A certain sacred space lay bare,
And the boys began research.

XVI.

'T was the space where our sires would lay a saint,
  A benefactor, — a bishop, suppose,
A baron with armor-adornments quaint,
  Dame with chased ring and jewelled rose,
Things sanctity saves from taint;

XVII.

So we come to find them in after-days
  When the corpse is presumed to have done with gauds
Of use to the living, in many ways:
  For the boys get pelf, and the town applauds,
And the church deserves the praise.

XVIII.

They grubbed with a will: and at length — *O cor
    Humanum, pectora cœca,* and the rest ! —
They found — no gaud they were prying for,
    No ring, no rose, but — who would have guessed ? —
A double Louis-d'or !

XIX.

Here was a case for the priest: he heard,
    Marked, inwardly digested, laid
Finger on nose, smiled, " There 's a bird
    Chirps in my ear : " then, " Bring a spade,
Dig deeper ! " — he gave the word.

XX.

And lo, when they came to the coffin-lid,
    Or rotten planks which composed it once,
Why, there lay the girl's skull wedged amid
    A mint of money, it served for the nonce
To hold in its hair-heaps hid !

XXI.

Hid there ? Why ? Could the girl be wont
    (She the stainless soul) to treasure up
Money, earth's trash and heaven's affront ?
    Had a spider found out the communion-cup,
Was a toad in the christening-font ?

XXII.

Truth is truth : too true it was.
    Gold ! She hoarded and hugged it first,
Longed for it, leaned o'er it, loved it — alas —
    Till the humor grew to a head and burst,
And she cried, at the final pass, —

XXIII.

" Talk not of God, my heart is stone !
    Nor lover nor friend — be gold for both !
Gold I lack ; and, my all, my own,
    It shall hide in my hair. I scarce die loth
If they let my hair alone ! "

XXIV.

Louis-d'or, some six times five,
    And duly double, every piece.

Now, do you see? With the priest to shrive,
  With parents preventing her soul's release
By kisses that kept alive, —

XXV.

With heaven's gold gates about to ope,
  With friends' praise, gold-like, lingering still,
An instinct had bidden the girl's hand grope
  For gold, the true sort — " Gold in heaven, if you will ;
But I keep earth's too, I hope."

XXVI.

Enough ! The priest took the grave's grim yield :
  The parents, they eyed that price of sin
As if *thirty pieces* lay revealed
  On the place *to bury strangers in*,
The hideous Potter's Field.

XXVII.

But the priest bethought him : " ' Milk that 's spilt '
  — You know the adage ! Watch and pray !
Saints tumble to earth with so slight a tilt !
  It would build a new altar ; that, we may ! "
And the altar therewith was built.

XXVIII.

Why I deliver this horrible verse ?
  As the text of a sermon, which now I preach :
Evil or good may be better or worse
  In the human heart, but the mixture of each
Is a marvel and a curse.

XXIX.

The candid incline to surmise of late
  That the Christian faith proves false, I find ;
For our Essays-and-Reviews' debate
  Begins to tell on the public mind,
And Colenso's words have weight :

XXX.

I still, to suppose it true, for my part,
  See reasons and reasons ; this, to begin :
'T is the faith that launched point-blank her dart
  At the head of a lie — taught Original Sin,
The Corruption of Man's Heart.

THE WORST OF IT.

I.

Would it were I had been false, not you!
I that am nothing, not you that are all:
I, never the worse for a touch or two
  On my speckled hide; not you, the pride
Of the day, my swan, that a first fleck's fall
  On her wonder of white must unswan, undo!

II.

I had dipped in life's struggle and, out again,
  Bore specks of it here, there, easy to see,
When I found my swan and the cure was plain;
  The dull turned bright as I caught your white
On my bosom: you saved me — saved in vain
  If you ruined yourself, and all through me!

III.

Yes, all through the speckled beast that I am,
  Who taught you to stoop; you gave me yourself,
And bound your soul by the vows that damn:
  Since on better thought you break, as you ought,
Vows — words, no angel set down, some elf
  Mistook, — for an oath, an epigram!

IV.

Yes, might I judge you, here were my heart,
  And a hundred its like, to treat as you pleased!
I choose to be yours, for my proper part,
  Yours, leave or take, or mar me or make;
If I acquiesce, why should you be teased
  With the conscience-prick and the memory-smart?

V.

But what will God say? Oh, my sweet,
  Think, and be sorry you did this thing!
Though earth were unworthy to feel your feet,
  There's a heaven above may deserve your love:
Should you forfeit heaven for a snapt gold ring
  And a promise broke, were it just or meet?

VI.

And I to have tempted you! I, who tried
  Your soul, no doubt, till it sank! Unwise,

I loved, and was lowly, loved and aspired,
  Loved, grieving or glad, till I made you mad,
And you meant to have hated and despised —
  Whereas, you deceived me nor inquired!

VII.

She, ruined? How? No heaven for her?
  Crowns to give, and none for the brow
That looked like marble and smelt like myrrh?
  Shall the robe be worn, and the palm-branch borne,
And she go graceless, she graced now
  Beyond all saints, as themselves aver?

VIII.

Hardly! That must be understood!
  The earth is your place of penance, then;
And what will it prove? I desire your good,
  But, plot as I may, I can find no way
How a blow should fall, such as falls on men,
  Nor prove too much for your womanhood.

IX.

It will come, I suspect, at the end of life,
  When you walk alone, and review the past;
And I, who so long shall have done with strife,
  And journeyed my stage and earned my wage
And retired as was right, — I am called at last
  When the devil stabs you, to lend the knife.

X.

He stabs for the minute of trivial wrong,
  Nor the other hours are able to save,
The happy, that lasted my whole life long:
  For a promise broke, not for first words spoke,
The true, the only, that turn my grave
  To a blaze of joy and a crash of song.

XI.

Witness beforehand! Off I trip
  On a safe path gay through the flowers you flung:
My very name made great by your lip,
  And my heart aglow with the good I know
Of a perfect year when we both were young,
  And I tasted the angels' fellowship.

XII.

And witness, moreover . . . Ah, but wait!
I spy the loop whence an arrow shoots!
It may be for yourself, when you meditate,
  That you grieve — for slain ruth, murdered truth:
"Though falsehood escape in the end, what boots?
  How truth would have triumphed!" — you sigh too late.

XIII.

Ay, who would have triumphed like you, I say!
  Well, it is lost now; well, you must bear,
Abide and grow fit for a better day:
  You should hardly grudge, could I be your judge!
But hush! For you, can be no despair:
  There's amends: 't is a secret: hope and pray!

XIV.

For I was true at least — oh, true enough!
  And, Dear, truth is not as good as it seems!
Commend me to conscience! Idle stuff!
  Much help is in mine, as I mope and pine,
And skulk through day, and scowl in my dreams
  At my swan's obtaining the crow's rebuff.

XV.

Men tell me of truth now — "False!" I cry:
  Of beauty — "A mask, friend! Look beneath!"
We take our own method, the devil and I,
  With pleasant and fair and wise and rare:
And the best we wish to what lives, is — death;
  Which even in wishing, perhaps we lie!

XVI.

Far better commit a fault and have done —
  As you, Dear! — forever; and choose the pure,
And look where the healing waters run,
  And strive and strain to be good again,
And a place in the other world ensure,
  All glass and gold, with God for its sun.

XVII.

Misery! What shall I say or do?
  I cannot advise, or, at least, persuade:
Most like, you are glad you deceived me — rue
  No whit of the wrong: you endured too long,

Have done no evil and want no aid,
  Will live the old life out and chance the new.

XVIII.

And your sentence is written all the same,
  And I can do nothing, — pray, perhaps:
But somehow the world pursues its game, —
  If I pray, if I curse, — for better or worse:
And my faith is torn to a thousand scraps,
  And my heart feels ice while my words breathe flame.

XIX.

Dear, I look from my hiding-place.
  Are you still so fair? Have you still the eyes?
Be happy! Add but the other grace,
  Be good! Why want what the angels vaunt?
I knew you once: but in Paradise,
  If we meet, I will pass nor turn my face.

DÎS ALITER VISUM;

OR,

LE BYRON DE NOS JOURS.

I.

Stop, let me have the truth of that!
  Is that all true? I say, the day
Ten years ago when both of us
  Met on a morning, friends — as thus
We meet this evening, friends or what? —

II.

Did you — because I took your arm
  And sillily smiled, "A mass of brass
That sea looks, blazing underneath!"
  While up the cliff-road edged with heath,
We took the turns nor came to harm —

III.

Did you consider, "Now makes twice
  That I have seen her, walked and talked
With this poor pretty thoughtful thing,
  Whose worth I weigh: she tries to sing;
Draws, hopes in time the eye grows nice;

IV.

"Reads verse and thinks she understands;
  Loves all, at any rate, that's great,
Good, beautiful; but much as we
  Down at the bath-house love the sea,
Who breathe its salt and bruise its sands:

V.

"While . . . do but follow the fishing-gull
  That flaps and floats from wave to cave!
There's the sea-lover, fair my friend!
  What then? Be patient, mark and mend!
Had you the making of your skull?"

VI.

And did you, when we faced the church
  With spire and sad slate roof, aloof
From human fellowship so far,
  Where a few graveyard crosses are,
And garlands for the swallows' perch, —

VII.

Did you determine, as we stepped
  O'er the lone stone fence, "Let me get
Her for myself, and what's the earth
  With all its art, verse, music, worth —
Compared with love, found, gained, and kept?

VIII.

"Schumann's our music-maker now;
  Has his march-movement youth and mouth?
Ingres's the modern man that paints;
  Which will lean on me, of his saints?
Heine for songs; for kisses, how?"

IX.

And did you, when we entered, reached
  The votive frigate, soft aloft
Riding on air this hundred years,
  Safe-smiling at old hopes and fears, —
Did you draw profit while she preached?

X.

Resolving, "Fools we wise men grow!
  Yes, I could easily blurt out curt

Some question that might find reply
　　As prompt in her stopped lips, dropped eye,
And rush of red to cheek and brow:

XI.

"Thus were a match made, sure and fast,
　　'Mid the blue weed-flowers round the mound
Where, issuing, we shall stand and stay
　　For one more look at baths and bay,
Sands, sea-gulls, and the old church last —

XII.

" A match 'twixt me, bent, wigged and lamed,
　　Famous, however, for verse and worse,
Sure of the Fortieth spare Arm-chair
　　When gout and glory seat me there,
So, one whose love-freaks pass unblamed, —

XIII.

" And this young beauty, round and sound
　　As a mountain-apple, youth and truth
With loves and doves, at all events
　　With money in the Three per Cents;
Whose choice of me would seem profound: —

XIV.

"She might take me as I take her.
　　Perfect the hour would pass, alas!
Climb high, love high, what matter?　Still,
　　Feet, feelings, must descend the hill:
An hour's perfection can't recur.

XV.

" Then follows Paris and full time
　　For both to reason: 'Thus with us!'
She 'll sigh, 'Thus girls give body and soul
　　At first word, think they gain the goal,
When 't is the starting-place they climb!

XVI.

" ' My friend makes verse and gets renown;
　　Have they all fifty years, his peers?
He knows the world, firm, quiet and gay;
　　Boys will become as much one day:
They 're fools; he cheats, with beard less brown.

XVII.

"'For boys say, *Love me or I die!*
   He did not say, *The truth is, youth
I want, who am old and know too much ;
   I'd catch youth : lend me sight and touch!
Drop heart's blood where life's wheels grate dry!*'

XVIII.

"While I should make rejoinder " — (then
   It was, no doubt, you ceased that least
Light pressure of my arm in yours) —
   "' I can conceive of cheaper cures
For a yawning-fit o'er books and men.

XIX.

"'What? All I am, was, and might be,
   All, books taught, art brought, life's whole strife,
Painful results since precious, just
   Were fitly exchanged, in wise disgust,
For two cheeks freshened by youth and sea?

XX.

"'All for a nosegay! — what came first ;
   With fields on flower, untried each side ;
I rally, need my books and men,
   And find a nosegay :' drop it, then,
No match yet made for best or worst!'"

XXI.

That ended me. You judged the porch
   We left by, Norman ; took our look
At sea and sky ; wondered so few
   Find out the place for air and view ;
Remarked the sun began to scorch ;

XXII.

Descended, soon regained the baths,
   And then, good-bye! Years ten since then :
Ten years! We meet : you tell me, now,
   By a window-seat for that cliff-brow,
On carpet-stripes for those sand-paths.

XXIII.

Now I may speak : you fool, for all
   Your lore! Who made things plain in vain?

DÍS ALITER VISUM

What was the sea for? What, the gray
  Sad church, that solitary day,
Crosses and graves and swallows' call?

XXIV.

Was there nought better than to enjoy?
  No feat which, done, would make time break,
And let us pent-up creatures through
  Into eternity, our due?
No forcing earth teach heaven's employ?

XXV.

No wise beginning, here and now,
  What cannot grow complete (earth's feat)
And heaven must finish, there and then?
  No tasting earth's true food for men,
Its sweet in sad, its sad in sweet?

XXVI.

No grasping at love, gaining a share
  O' the sole spark from God's life at strife
With death, so, sure of range above
  The limits here? For us and love,
Failure; but, when God fails, despair.

XXVII.

This you call wisdom? Thus you add
  Good unto good again, in vain?
You loved, with body worn and weak;
  I loved, with faculties to seek:
Were both loves worthless since ill-clad?

XXVIII.

Let the mere star-fish in his vault
  Crawl in a wash of weed, indeed,
Rose-jacynth to the finger-tips:
  He, whole in body and soul, outstrips
Man, found with either in default.

XXIX.

But what's whole, can increase no more,
  Is dwarfed and dies, since here's its sphere.
The devil laughed at you in his sleeve!
  You knew not? That I well believe;
Or you had saved two souls: nay, four.

XXX.

For Stephanie sprained last night her wrist,
  Ankle or something. " Pooh," cry you ?
At any rate she danced, all say,
  Vilely ; her vogue has had its day.
Here comes my husband from his whist.

TOO LATE.

I.

HERE was I with my arm and heart
  And brain, all yours for a word, a want
Put into a look — just a look, your part, —
  While mine, to repay it . . . vainest vaunt,
Were the woman, that's dead, alive to hear,
  Had her lover, that's lost, love's proof to show!
But I cannot show it ; you cannot speak
  From the churchyard neither, miles removed,
Though I feel by a pulse within my cheek,
  Which stabs and stops, that the woman I loved
Needs help in her grave and finds none near,
  Wants warmth from the heart which sends it — so!

II.

Did I speak once angrily, all the drear days
  You lived, you woman I loved so well,
Who married the other ? Blame or praise,
  Where was the use then ? Time would tell,
And the end declare what man for you,
  What woman for me, was the choice of God.
But, Edith dead ! no doubting more !
  I used to sit and look at my life
As it rippled and ran till, right before,
  A great stone stopped it : oh, the strife
Of waves at the stone some devil threw
  In my life's midcurrent, thwarting God !

III.

But either I thought, " They may churn and chide
  Awhile, my waves which came for their joy
And found this horrible stone full-tide :
  Yet I see just a thread escape, deploy
Through the evening-country, silent and safe,

And it suffers no more till it finds the sea."
Or else I would think, " Perhaps some night
    When new things happen, a meteor-ball
May slip through the sky in a line of light,
    And earth breathe hard, and landmarks fall,
And my waves no longer champ nor chafe,
    Since a stone will have rolled from its place : let be ! "

IV.

But, dead ! All's done with : wait who may,
    Watch and wear and wonder who will.
Oh, my whole life that ends to-day !
    Oh, my soul's sentence, sounding still,
" The woman is dead, that was none of his ;
    And the man, that was none of hers, may go ! "
There's only the past left : worry that !
    Wreak, like a bull, on the empty coat,
Rage, its late wearer is laughing at !
    Tear the collar to rags, having missed his throat ;
Strike stupidly on — " This, this and this,
    Where I would that a bosom received the blow ! "

V.

I ought to have done more : once my speech,
    And once your answer, and there, the end,
And Edith was henceforth out of reach !
    Why, men do more to deserve a friend,
Be rid of a foe, get rich, grow wise,
    Nor, folding their arms, stare fate in the face.
Why, better even have burst like a thief
    And borne you away to a rock for us two,
In a moment's horror, bright, bloody and brief,
    Then changed to myself again — " I slew
Myself in that moment ; a ruffian lies
    Somewhere : your slave, see, born in his place ! "

VI.

What did the other do ? You be judge !
    Look at us, Edith ! Here are we both !
Give him his six whole years : I grudge
    None of the life with you, nay, loathe
Myself that I grudged his start in advance
    Of me who could overtake and pass.
But, as if he loved you ! No, not he,
    Nor any one else in the world, 't is plain :
Who ever heard that another, free

As I, young, prosperous, sound and sane,
Poured life out, proffered it — " Half a glance
Of those eyes of yours and I drop the glass ! "

VII.

Handsome, were you ? 'T is more than they held,
More than they said ; I was 'ware and watched :
I was the scapegrace, this rat belled
The cat, this fool got his whiskers scratched :
The others ? No head that was turned, no heart
Broken, my lady, assure yourself !
Each soon made his mind up ; so and so
Married a dancer, such and such
Stole his friend's wife, stagnated slow,
Or maundered, unable to do as much,
And muttered of peace where he had no part :
While, hid in the closet, laid on the shelf, —

VIII.

On the whole, you were let alone, I think !
So, you looked to the other, who acquiesced ;
My rival, the proud man, — prize your pink
Of poets ! A poet he was ! I've guessed :
He rhymed you his rubbish nobody read,
Loved you and doved you — did not I laugh !
There was a prize ! But we both were tried.
Oh, heart of mine, marked broad with her mark,
Tekel, found wanting, set aside,
Scorned ! See, I bleed these tears in the dark
Till comfort come and the last be bled :
He ? He is tagging your epitaph.

IX.

If it would only come over again !
— Time to be patient with me, and probe
This heart till you punctured the proper vein,
Just to learn what blood is : twitch the robe
From that blank lay-figure your fancy draped,
Prick the leathern heart till the — verses spirt !
And late it was easy ; late, you walked
Where a friend might meet you ; Edith's name
Arose to one's lip if one laughed or talked ;
If I heard good news, you heard the same ;
When I woke, I knew that your breath escaped ;
I could bide my time, keep alive, alert.

X.

And alive I shall keep and long, you will see!
I knew a man, was kicked like a dog
From gutter to cesspool; what cared he
  So long as he picked from the filth his prog?
He saw youth, beauty and genius die,
  And jollily lived to his hundredth year.
But I will live otherwise: none of such life!
  At once I begin as I mean to end.
Go on with the world, get gold in its strife,
  Give your spouse the slip and betray your friend!
There are two who decline, a woman and I,
  And enjoy our death in the darkness here.

XI.

I liked that way you had with your curls
  Wound to a ball in a net behind:
Your cheek was chaste as a Quaker-girl's,
  And your mouth — there was never, to my mind,
Such a funny mouth, for it would not shut;
  And the dented chin too — what a chin!
There were certain ways when you spoke, some words
  That you know you never could pronounce:
You were thin, however; like a bird's
  Your hand seemed — some would say, the pounce
Of a scaly-footed hawk — all but!
  The world was right when it called you thin.

XII.

But I turn my back on the world: I take
  Your hand, and kneel, and lay to my lips.
Bid me live, Edith! Let me slake
  Thirst at your presence! Fear no slips:
'T is your slave shall pay, while his soul endures,
  Full due, love's whole debt, *summum jus*.
My queen shall have high observance, planned
  Courtship made perfect, no least line
Crossed without warrant. There you stand,
  Warm too, and white too: would this wine
Had washed all over that body of yours,
  Ere I drank it, and you down with it, thus!

ABT VOGLER.

(AFTER HE HAS BEEN EXTEMPORIZING UPON THE MUSICAL
INSTRUMENT OF HIS INVENTION.)

I.

WOULD that the structure brave, the manifold music I build,
  Bidding my organ obey, calling its keys to their work,
Claiming each slave of the sound, at a touch, as when Solomon willed
Armies of angels that soar, legions of demons that lurk,
Man, brute, reptile, fly,—alien of end and of aim,
  Adverse, each from the other heaven-high, hell-deep removed,—
Should rush into sight at once as he named the ineffable Name,
  And pile him a palace straight, to pleasure the princess he loved!

II.

Would it might tarry like his, the beautiful building of mine,
  This which my keys in a crowd pressed and importuned to raise!
Ah, one and all, how they helped, would dispart now and now combine,
  Zealous to hasten the work, heighten their master his praise!
And one would bury his brow with a blind plunge down to hell,
  Burrow awhile and build, broad on the roots of things,
Then up again swim into sight, having based me my palace well,
  Founded it, fearless of flame, flat on the nether springs.

III.

And another would mount and march, like the excellent minion he was,
  Ay, another and yet another, one crowd but with many a crest,
Raising my rampired walls of gold as transparent as glass,
  Eager to do and die, yield each his place to the rest:
For higher still and higher (as a runner tips with fire,
  When a great illumination surprises a festal night—
Outlining round and round Rome's dome from space to spire)
  Up, the pinnacled glory reached, and the pride of my soul was in sight.

IV.

In sight? Not half! for it seemed, it was certain, to match
    man's birth,
Nature in turn conceived, obeying an impulse as I;
And the emulous heaven yearned down, made effort to reach
    the earth,
  As the earth had done her best, in my passion, to scale the
    sky:
Novel splendors burst forth, grew familiar and dwelt with mine,
  Not a point nor peak but found and fixed its wandering star;
Meteor-moons, balls of blaze: and they did not pale nor pine,
  For earth had attained to heaven, there was no more near
    nor far.

V.

Nay more; for there wanted not who walked in the glare and
    glow,
  Presences plain in the place; or, fresh from the Protoplast,
Furnished for ages to come, when a kindlier wind should blow,
  Lured now to begin and live, in a house to their liking at
    last;
Or else the wonderful Dead who have passed through the body
    and gone,
  But were back once more to breathe in an old world worth
    their new:
What never had been, was now; what was, as it shall be anon;
  And what is, — shall I say, matched both? for I was made
    perfect too.

VI.

All through my keys that gave their sounds to a wish of my
    soul,
  All through my soul that praised as its wish flowed visibly
    forth,
All through music and me! For think, had I painted the
    whole,
  Why, there it had stood, to see, nor the process so wonder-
    worth:
Had I written the same, made verse — still, effect proceeds from
    cause,
  Ye know why the forms are fair, ye hear how the tale is told;
It is all triumphant art, but art in obedience to laws,
  Painter and poet are proud in the artist-list enrolled:—

VII.

But here is the finger of God, a flash of the will that can,
    Existent behind all laws, that made them and, lo, they are!
And I know not if, save in this, such gift be allowed to man,
    That out of three sounds he frame, not a fourth sound, but a star.
Consider it well: each tone of our scale in itself is nought;
    It is everywhere in the world — loud, soft, and all is said:
Give it to me to use! I mix it with two in my thought:
    And, there! Ye have heard and seen: consider and bow the head!

VIII.

Well, it is gone at last, the palace of music I reared;
    Gone! and the good tears start, the praises that come too slow;
For one is assured at first, one scarce can say that he feared,
    That he even gave it a thought, the gone thing was to go.
Never to be again! But many more of the kind
    As good, nay, better perchance: is this your comfort to me?
To me, who must be saved because I cling with my mind
    To the same, same self, same love, same God: ay, what was, shall be.

IX.

Therefore to whom turn I but to Thee, the ineffable Name?
    Builder and maker, Thou, of houses not made with hands!
What, have fear of change from Thee who art ever the same?
    Doubt that Thy power can fill the heart that Thy power expands?
There shall never be one lost good! What was, shall live as before;
    The evil is null, is nought, is silence implying sound;
What was good, shall be good, with, for evil, so much good more;
    On the earth the broken arcs; in the heaven, a perfect round.

X.

All we have willed or hoped or dreamed of good, shall exist;
    Not its semblance, but itself; no beauty, nor good, nor power
Whose voice has gone forth, but each survives for the melodist
    When eternity affirms the conception of an hour.
The high that proved too high, the heroic for earth too hard,
    The passion that left the ground to lose itself in the sky,
Are music sent up to God by the lover and the bard;
    Enough that he heard it once: we shall hear it by-and-by.

XI.

And what is our failure here but a triumph's evidence
  For the fulness of the days? Have we withered or agonized?
Why else was the pause prolonged but that singing might issue
      thence?
  Why rushed the discords in, but that harmony should be
      prized?
Sorrow is hard to bear, and doubt is slow to clear,
  Each sufferer says his say, his scheme of the weal and woe:
But God has a few of us whom he whispers in the ear;
  The rest may reason and welcome: 't is we musicians know.

XII.

Well, it is earth with me; silence resumes her reign:
  I will be patient and proud, and soberly acquiesce.
Give me the keys. I feel for the common chord again,
  Sliding by semitones, till I sink to the minor, — yes,
And I blunt it into a ninth, and I stand on alien ground,
  Surveying awhile the heights I rolled from into the deep;
Which, hark, I have dared and done, for my resting-place is
      found,
  The C Major of this life: so, now I will try to sleep.

RABBI BEN EZRA.

I.

GROW old along with me!
The best is yet to be,
The last of life, for which the first was made:
Our times are in His hand
Who saith, "A whole I planned,
Youth shows but half; trust God: see all, nor be afraid!"

II.

Not that, amassing flowers,
Youth sighed, "Which rose make ours,
Which lily leave and then as best recall?"
Not that, admiring stars,
It yearned, "Nor Jove, nor Mars;
Mine be some figured flame which blends, transcends them all!"

III.

Not for such hopes and fears
Annulling youth's brief years,

Do I remonstrate: folly wide the mark!
Rather I prize the doubt
Low kinds exist without,
Finished and finite clods, untroubled by a spark.

IV.

Poor vaunt of life indeed,
Were man but formed to feed
On joy, to solely seek and find and feast;
Such feasting ended, then
As sure an end to men;
Irks care the crop full bird? Frets doubt the maw-crammed beast?

V.

Rejoice we are allied
To That which doth provide
And not partake, effect and not receive!
A spark disturbs our clod;
Nearer we hold of God
Who gives, than of His tribes that take, I must believe.

VI.

Then, welcome each rebuff
That turns earth's smoothness rough,
Each sting that bids nor sit nor stand but go!
Be our joys three-parts pain!
Strive, and hold cheap the strain;
Learn, nor account the pang; dare, never grudge the throe!

VII.

For thence, — a paradox
Which comforts while it mocks, —
Shall life succeed in that it seems to fail:
What I aspired to be,
And was not, comforts me:
A brute I might have been, but would not sink i' the scale.

VIII.

What is he but a brute
Whose flesh has soul to suit,
Whose spirit works lest arms and legs want play?
To man, propose this test —
Thy body at its best,
How far can that project thy soul on its lone way?

IX.

Yet gifts should prove their use:
I own the Past profuse
Of power each side, perfection every turn:
Eyes, ears took in their dole,
Brain treasured up the whole;
Should not the heart beat once "How good to live and learn"?

X.

Not once beat " Praise be Thine!
I see the whole design,
I, who saw power, see now Love perfect too:
Perfect I call Thy plan:
Thanks that I was a man!
Maker, remake, complete, — I trust what Thou shalt do!"

XI.

For pleasant is this flesh;
Our soul, in its rose-mesh
Pulled ever to the earth, still yearns for rest:
Would we some prize might hold
To match those manifold
Possessions of the brute, — gain most, as we did best!

XII.

Let us not always say,
"Spite of this flesh to-day
I strove, made head, gained ground upon the whole!"
As the bird wings and sings,
Let us cry, " All good things
Are ours, nor soul helps flesh more, now, than flesh helps soul!"

XIII.

Therefore I summon age
To grant youth's heritage,
Life's struggle having so far reached its term:
Thence shall I pass, approved
A man, for aye removed
From the developed brute; a God though in the germ.

XIV.

And I shall thereupon
Take rest, ere I be gone
Once more on my adventure brave and new:
Fearless and unperplexed,

When I wage battle next,
What weapons to select, what armor to indue.

XV.

Youth ended, I shall try
My gain or loss thereby;
Leave the fire-ashes, what survives is gold:
And I shall weigh the same,
Give life its praise or blame:
Young, all lay in dispute; I shall know, being old.

XVI.

For note, when evening shuts,
A certain moment cuts
The deed off, calls the glory from the gray:
A whisper from the west
Shoots — "Add this to the rest,
Take it and try its worth: here dies another day."

XVII.

So, still within this life,
Though lifted o'er its strife,
Let me discern, compare, pronounce at last,
"This rage was right i' the main,
That acquiescence vain:
The Future I may face now I have proved the Past."

XVIII.

For more is not reserved
To man, with soul just nerved
To act to-morrow what he learns to-day:
Here, work enough to watch
The Master work, and catch
Hints of the proper craft, tricks of the tool's true play.

XIX.

As it was better, youth
Should strive, through acts uncouth,
Toward making, than repose on aught found made:
So, better, age, exempt
From strife, should know, than tempt
Further. Thou waitedst age: wait death nor be afraid!

XX.

Enough now, if the Right
And Good and Infinite

Be named here, as thou callest thy hand thine own,
With knowledge absolute,
Subject to no dispute
From fools that crowded youth, nor let thee feel alone.

XXI.

Be there, for once and all,
Severed great minds from small,
Announced to each his station in the Past!
Was I, the world arraigned,
Were they, my soul disdained,
Right? Let age speak the truth and give us peace at last!

XXII.

Now, who shall arbitrate?
Ten men love what I hate,
Shun what I follow, slight what I receive;
Ten, who in ears and eyes
Match me: we all surmise,
They this thing, and I that: whom shall my soul believe?

XXIII.

Not on the vulgar mass
Called "work," must sentence pass,
Things done, that took the eye and had the price;
O'er which, from level stand,
The low world laid its hand,
Found straightway to its mind, could value in a trice:

XXIV.

But all, the world's coarse thumb
And finger failed to plumb,
So passed in making up the main account;
All instincts immature,
All purposes unsure,
That weighed not as his work, yet swelled the man's amount:

XXV.

Thoughts hardly to be packed
Into a narrow act,
Fancies that broke through language and escaped;
All I could never be,
All, men ignored in me,
This, I was worth to God, whose wheel the pitcher shaped.

XXVI.

Ay, note that Potter's wheel,
That metaphor! and feel
Why time spins fast, why passive lies our clay, —
Thou, to whom fools propound,
When the wine makes its round,
" Since life fleets, all is change ; the Past gone, seize to-day ! "

XXVII.

Fool! All that is, at all,
Lasts ever, past recall;
Earth changes, but thy soul and God stand sure :
What entered into thee,
That was, is, and shall be :
Time's wheel runs back or stops : Potter and clay endure.

XXVIII.

He fixed thee 'mid this dance
Of plastic circumstance,
This Present, thou, forsooth, wouldst fain arrest :
Machinery just meant
To give thy soul its bent,
Try thee and turn thee forth, sufficiently impressed.

XXIX.

What though the earlier grooves,
Which ran the laughing loves
Around thy base, no longer pause and press ?
What though, about thy rim,
Scull-things in order grim
Grow out, in graver mood, obey the sterner stress ?

XXX.

Look not thou down but up!
To uses of a cup,
The festal board, lamp's flash and trumpet's peal,
The new wine's foaming flow,
The Master's lips aglow!
Thou, heaven's consummate cup, what needst thou with earth's
    wheel?

XXXI.

But I need, now as then,
Thee, God, who mouldest men ;
And since, not even while the whirl was worst,

Did I — to the wheel of life
With shapes and colors rife,
Bound dizzily — mistake my end, to slake Thy thirst:

XXXII.

So, take and use Thy work:
Amend what flaws may lurk,
What strain o' the stuff, what warpings past the aim!
My times be in Thy hand!
Perfect the cup as planned!
Let age approve of youth, and death complete the same!

A DEATH IN THE DESERT.

[SUPPOSED of Pamphylax the Antiochene:
It is a parchment, of my rolls the fifth,
Hath three skins glued together, is all Greek,
And goeth from *Epsilon* down to *Mu*:
Lies second in the surnamed Chosen Chest,
Stained and conserved with juice of terebinth,
Covered with cloth of hair, and lettered *Xi*,
From Xanthus, my wife's uncle, now at peace:
Mu and *Epsilon* stand for my own name.
I may not write it, but I make a cross
To show I wait His coming, with the rest,
And leave off here: beginneth Pamphylax.]

I said, "If one should wet his lips with wine,
And slip the broadest plantain-leaf we find,
Or else the lappet of a linen robe,
Into the water-vessel, lay it right,
And cool his forehead just above the eyes,
The while a brother, kneeling either side,
Should chafe each hand and try to make it warm, —
He is not so far gone but he might speak."

This did not happen in the outer cave,
Nor in the secret chamber of the rock,
Where, sixty days since the decree was out,
We had him, bedded on a camel-skin,
And waited for his dying all the while;
But in the midmost grotto: since noon's light
Reached there a little, and we would not lose
The last of what might happen on his face.

I at the head, and Xanthus at the feet,
With Valens and the Boy, had lifted him,
And brought him from the chamber in the depths,
And laid him in the light where we might see:
For certain smiles began about his mouth,
And his lids moved, presageful of the end.

Beyond, and halfway up the mouth o' the cave,
The Bactrian convert, having his desire,
Kept watch, and made pretence to graze a goat
That gave us milk, on rags of various herb,
Plantain and quitch, the rocks' shade keeps alive:
So that if any thief or soldier passed,
(Because the persecution was aware,)
Yielding the goat up promptly with his life,
Such man might pass on, joyful at a prize,
Nor care to pry into the cool o' the cave.
Outside was all noon and the burning blue.

"Here is wine," answered Xanthus, — dropped a drop;
I stooped and placed the lap of cloth aright,
Then chafed his right hand, and the Boy his left:
But Valens had bethought him, and produced
And broke a ball of nard, and made perfume.
Only, he did — not so much wake, as — turn
And smile a little, as a sleeper does
If any dear one call him, touch his face —
And smiles and loves, but will not be disturbed.

Then Xanthus said a prayer, but still he slept:
It is the Xanthus that escaped to Rome,
Was burned, and could not write the chronicle.

Then the Boy sprang up from his knees, and ran,
Stung by the splendor of a sudden thought,
And fetched the seventh plate of graven lead
Out of the secret chamber, found a place,
Pressing with finger on the deeper dints,
And spoke, as 't were his mouth proclaiming first,
"I am the Resurrection and the Life."

Whereat he opened his eyes wide at once,
And sat up of himself, and looked at us;
And thenceforth nobody pronounced a word:
Only, outside, the Bactrian cried his cry
Like the lone desert-bird that wears the ruff,
As signal we were safe, from time to time.

First he said, " If a friend declared to me,
This my son Valens, this my other son,
Were James and Peter, — nay, declared as well
This lad was very John, — I could believe !
— Could, for a moment, doubtlessly believe :
So is myself withdrawn into my depths,
The soul retreated from the perished brain
Whence it was wont to feel and use the world
Through these dull members, done with long ago.
Yet I myself remain ; I feel myself :
And there is nothing lost. Let be, awhile ! "

[This is the doctrine he was wont to teach,
How divers persons witness in each man,
Three souls which make up one soul : first, to wit,
A soul of each and all the bodily parts,
Seated therein, which works, and is what Does,
And has the use of earth, and ends the man
Downward : but, tending upward for advice,
Grows into, and again is grown into
By the next soul, which, seated in the brain,
Useth the first with its collected use,
And feeleth, thinketh, willeth, — is what Knows :
Which, duly tending upward in its turn,
Grows into, and again is grown into
By the last soul, that uses both the first,
Subsisting whether they assist or no,
And, constituting man's self, is what Is —
And leans upon the former, makes it play,
As that played off the first : and, tending up,
Holds, is upheld by, God, and ends the man
Upward in that dread point of intercourse,
Nor needs a place, for it returns to Him.
What Does, what Knows, what Is ; three souls, one man.
I give the glossa of Theotypas.]

And then, " A stick, once fire from end to end ;
Now, ashes save the tip that holds a spark !
Yet, blow the spark, it runs back, spreads itself
A little where the fire was : thus I urge
The soul that served me, till it task once more
What ashes of my brain have kept their shape,
And these make effort on the last o' the flesh,
Trying to taste again the truth of things — "
(He smiled) — " their very superficial truth ;
As that ye are my sons, that it is long

Since James and Peter had release by death,
And I am only he, your brother John,
Who saw and heard, and could remember all.
Remember all! It is not much to say.
What if the truth broke on me from above
As once and ofttimes? Such might hap again:
Doubtlessly He might stand in presence here,
With head wool-white, eyes flame, and feet like brass,
The sword and the seven stars, as I have seen —
I who now shudder only and surmise
'How did your brother bear that sight and live?'

"If I live yet, it is for good, more love
Through me to men: be nought but ashes here
That keep awhile my semblance, who was John, —
Still, when they scatter, there is left on earth
No one alive who knew (consider this!)
— Saw with his eyes and handled with his hands
That which was from the first, the Word of Life.
How will it be when none more saith 'I saw'?

"Such ever was love's way: to rise, it stoops.
Since I, whom Christ's mouth taught, was bidden teach,
I went, for many years, about the world,
Saying 'It was so; so I heard and saw,'
Speaking as the case asked: and men believ·
Afterward came the message to myself
In Patmos isle; I was not bidden teach,
But simply listen, take a book and write,
Nor set down other than the given word,
With nothing left to my arbitrament
To choose or change: I wrote, and men believed.
Then, for my time grew brief, no message more,
No call to write again, I found a way,
And, reasoning from my knowledge, merely taught
Men should, for love's sake, in love's strength, believe;
Or I would pen a letter to a friend
And urge the same as friend, nor less nor more:
Friends said I reasoned rightly, and believed.
But at the last, why, I seemed left alive
Like a sea-jelly weak on Patmos strand,
To tell dry sea-beach gazers how I fared
When there was mid-sea, and the mighty things;
Left to repeat, 'I saw, I heard, I knew,'
And go all over the old ground again,
With Antichrist already in the world,

And many Antichrists, who answered prompt,
' Am I not Jasper as thyself art John?
Nay, young, whereas through age thou mayest forget:
Wherefore, explain, or how shall we believe?'
I never thought to call down fire on such,
Or, as in wonderful and early days,
Pick up the scorpion, tread the serpent dumb;
But patient stated much of the Lord's life
Forgotten or misdelivered, and let it work:
Since much that at the first, in deed and word,
Lay simply and sufficiently exposed,
Had grown (or else my soul was grown to match,
Fed through such years, familiar with such light,
Guarded and guided still to see and speak)
Of new significance and fresh result;
What first were guessed as points, I now knew stars,
And named them in the Gospel I have writ.
For men said, ' It is getting long ago:
Where is the promise of His coming?'— asked
These young ones in their strength, as loth to wait,
Of me who, when their sires were born, was old.
I, for I loved them, answered, joyfully,
Since I was there, and helpful in my age;
And, in the main, I think such men believed.
Finally, thus endeavoring, I fell sick,
Ye brought me here, and I supposed the end,
And went to sleep with one thought that, at least,
Though the whole earth should lie in wickedness,
We had the truth, might leave the rest to God.
Yet now I wake in such decrepitude
As I had slidden down and fallen afar,
Past even the presence of my former self,
Grasping the while for stay at facts which snap,
Till I am found away from my own world,
Feeling for foothold through a blank profound,
Along with unborn people in strange lands,
Who say — I hear said or conceive they say —
' Was John at all, and did he say he saw?
Assure us, ere we ask what he might see!'

" And how shall I assure them? Can they share
—They, who have flesh, a veil of youth and strength
About each spirit, that needs must bide its time,
Living and learning still as years assist
Which wear the thickness thin, and let man see —
With me who hardly am withheld at all,

But shudderingly, scarce a shred between,
Lie bare to the universal prick of light?
Is it for nothing we grow old and weak,
We whom God loves? When pain ends, gain ends too.
To me, that story — ay, that Life and Death
Of which I wrote ' it was ' — to me, it is ;
— Is, here and now : I apprehend nought else.
Is not God now i' the world His power first made?
Is not His love at issue still with sin,
Visibly when a wrong is done on earth ?
Love, wrong, and pain, what see I else around ?
Yea, and the Resurrection and Uprise
To the right hand of the throne — what is it beside,
When such truth, breaking bounds, o'erfloods my soul,
And, as I saw the sin and death, even so
See I the need yet transiency of both,
The good and glory consummated thence ?
I saw the power ; I see the Love, once weak,
Resume the Power : and in this word ' I see,'
Lo, there is recognized the Spirit of both
That moving o'er the spirit of man, unblinds
His eye and bids him look. These are, I see ;
But ye, the children, His beloved ones too,
Ye need, — as I should use an optic glass
I wondered at erewhile, somewhere i' the world,
It had been given a crafty smith to make ;
A tube, he turned on objects brought too close,
Lying confusedly insubordinate
For the unassisted eye to master once :
Look through his tube, at distance now they lay,
Become succinct, distinct, so small, so clear !
Just thus, ye needs must apprehend what truth
I see, reduced to plain historic fact,
Diminished into clearness, proved a point
And far away : ye would withdraw your sense
From out eternity, strain it upon time,
Then stand before that fact, that Life and Death,
Stay there at gaze, till it dispart, dispread,
As though a star should open out, all sides,
Grow the world on you, as it is my world.

" For life, with all it yields of joy and woe,
 And hope and fear, — believe the aged friend, —
Is just our chance o' the prize of learning love,
How love might be, hath been indeed, and is ;
And that we hold thenceforth to the uttermost

Such prize despite the envy of the world,
And, having gained truth, keep truth : that is all.
But see the double way wherein we are led,
How the soul learns diversely from the flesh!
With flesh, that hath so little time to stay,
And yields mere basement for the soul's emprise,
Expect prompt teaching. Helpful was the light,
And warmth was cherishing and food was choice
To every man's flesh, thousand years ago,
As now to yours and mine; the body sprang
At once to the height, and stayed : but the soul, — no!
Since sages who, this noontide, meditate
In Rome or Athens, may descry some point
Of the eternal power, hid yestereve;
And, as thereby the power's whole mass extends,
So much extends the æther floating o'er
The love that tops the might, the Christ in God.
Then, as new lessons shall be learned in these
Till earth's work stop and useless time run out,
So duly, daily, needs provision be
For keeping the soul's prowess possible,
Building new barriers as the old decay,
Saving us from evasion of life's proof,
Putting the question ever, ' Does God love,
And will ye hold that truth against the world?'
Ye know there needs no second proof with good
Gained for our flesh from any earthly source :
We might go freezing, ages, — give us fire,
Thereafter we judge fire at its full worth,
And guard it safe through every chance, ye know!
That fable of Prometheus and his theft,
How mortals gained Jove's fiery flower, grows old
(I have been used to hear the pagans own)
And out of mind; but fire, howe'er its birth,
Here is it, precious to the sophist now
Who laughs the myth of Æschylus to scorn,
As precious to those satyrs of his play,
Who touched it in gay wonder at the thing.
While were it so with the soul, — this gift of truth
Once grasped, were this our soul's gain safe, and sure
To prosper as the body's gain is wont, —
Why, man's probation would conclude, his earth
Crumble; for he both reasons and decides,
Weighs first, then chooses : will he give up fire
For gold or purple once he knows its worth?
Could he give Christ up were His worth as plain?

Therefore, I say, to test man, the proofs shift,
Nor may he grasp that fact like other fact,
And straightway in his life acknowledge it,
As, say, the indubitable bliss of fire.
Sigh ye, ' It had been easier once than now ? '
To give you answer I am left alive ;
Look at me who was present from the first !
Ye know what things I saw ; then came a test,
My first, befitting me who so had seen :
' Forsake the Christ thou sawest transfigured, Him
Who trod the sea and brought the dead to life ?
What should wring this from thee ! ' — ye laugh and ask.
What wrung it ?   Even a torchlight and a noise,
The sudden Roman faces, violent hands,
And fear of what the Jews might do !   Just that,
And it is written, ' I forsook and fled : '
There was my trial, and it ended thus.
Ay, but my soul had gained its truth, could grow :
Another year or two, — what little child,
What tender woman that had seen no least
Of all my sights, but barely heard them told,
Who did not clasp the cross with a light laugh,
Or wrap the burning robe round, thanking God ?
Well, was truth safe forever, then ?   Not so.
Already had begun the silent work
Whereby truth, deadened of its absolute blaze,
Might need love's eye to pierce the o'erstretched doubt.
Teachers were busy, whispering ' All is true
As the aged ones report ; but youth can reach
Where age gropes dimly, weak with stir and strain,
And the full doctrine slumbers till to-day.'
Thus, what the Roman's lowered spear was found,
A bar to me who touched and handled truth,
Now proved the glozing of some new shrewd tongue,
This Ebion, this Cerinthus or their mates,
Till imminent was the outcry ' Save our Christ ! '
Whereon I stated much of the Lord's life
Forgotten or misdelivered, and let it work.
Such work done, as it will be, what comes next ?
What do I hear say, or conceive men say,
' Was John at all, and did he say he saw ?
Assure us, ere we ask what he might see ! '

" Is this indeed a burden for late days,
   And may I help to bear it with you all,
   Using my weakness which becomes your strength ?

For if a babe were born inside this grot,
Grew to a boy here, heard us praise the sun,
Yet had but yon sole glimmer in light's place, —
One loving him and wishful he should learn,
Would much rejoice himself was blinded first
Month by month here, so made to understand
How eyes, born darkling, apprehend amiss :
I think I could explain to such a child
There was more glow outside than gleams he caught,
Ay, nor need urge 'I saw it, so believe !'
It is a heavy burden you shall bear
In latter days, new lands, or old grown strange,
Left without me, which must be very soon.
What is the doubt, my brothers ?   Quick with it !
I see you stand conversing, each new face,
Either in fields, of yellow summer eves,
On islets yet unnamed amid the sea;
Or pace for shelter 'neath a portico
Out of the crowd in some enormous town
Where now the larks sing in a solitude ;
Or muse upon blank heaps of stone and sand
Idly conjectured to be Ephesus :
And no one asks his fellow any more
'Where is the promise of His coming?' but
'Was He revealed in any of His lives,
   As Power, as Love, as Influencing Soul?'

"Quick, for time presses, tell the whole mind out,
   And let us ask and answer and be saved !
My book speaks on, because it cannot pass ;
One listens quietly, nor scoffs but pleads,
'Here is a tale of things done ages since;
What truth was ever told the second day ?
Wonders, that would prove doctrine, go for nought.
Remains the doctrine, love; well, we must love,
And what we love most, power and love in one,
Let us acknowledge on the record here,
Accepting these in Christ: must Christ then be ?
Has He been ?   Did not we ourselves make Him ?
Our mind receives but what it holds, no more.
First of the love, then ; we acknowledge Christ —
A proof we comprehend His love, a proof
We had such love already in ourselves,
Knew first what else we should not recognize.
'T is mere projection from man's inmost mind,
And, what he loves, thus falls reflected back,

Becomes accounted somewhat out of him ;
He throws it up in air, it drops down earth's,
With shape, name, story added, man's old way.
How prove you Christ came otherwise at least?
Next try the power: He made and rules the world:
Certes there is a world once made, now ruled,
Unless things have been ever as we see.
Our sires declared a charioteer's yoked steeds
Brought the sun up the east and down the west,
Which only of itself now rises, sets,
As if a hand impelled it and a will, —
Thus they long thought, they who had will and hands:
But the new question's whisper is distinct,
Wherefore must all force needs be like ourselves?
We have the hands, the will; what made and drives
The sun is force, is law, is named, not known,
While will and love we do know; marks of these,
Eye-witnesses attest, so books declare —
As that, to punish or reward our race,
The sun at undue times arose or set
Or else stood still: what do not men affirm?
But earth requires as urgently reward
Or punishment to-day as years ago,
And none expects the sun will interpose:
Therefore it was mere passion and mistake,
Or erring zeal for right, which changed the truth.
Go back, far, farther, to the birth of things;
Ever the will, the intelligence, the love,
Man's! — which he gives, supposing he but finds,
As late he gave head, body, hands and feet,
To help these in what forms he called his gods.
First, Jove's brow, Juno's eyes were swept away,
But Jove's wrath, Juno's pride continued long;
As last, will, power, and love discarded these,
So law in turn discards power, love, and will.
What proveth God is otherwise at least?
All else, projection from the mind of man!'

" Nay, do not give me wine, for I am strong,
But place my gospel where I put my hands.

" I say that man was made to grow, not stop;
That help, he needed once, and needs no more,
Having grown but an inch by, is withdrawn:
For he hath new needs, and new helps to these.
This imports solely, man should mount on each

A DEATH IN THE DESERT

New height in view; the help whereby he mounts,
The ladder-rung his foot has left, may fall,
Since all things suffer change save God the Truth.
Man apprehends Him newly at each stage
Whereat earth's ladder drops, its service done;
And nothing shall prove twice what once was proved.
You stick a garden-plot with ordered twigs
To show inside lie germs of herbs unborn,
And check the careless step would spoil their birth;
But when herbs wave, the guardian twigs may go,
Since should ye doubt of virtues, question kinds,
It is no longer for old twigs ye look,
Which proved once underneath lay store of seed,
But to the herb's self, by what light ye boast,
For what fruit's signs are. This book's fruit is plain,
Nor miracles need prove it any more.
Doth the fruit show? Then miracles bade 'ware
At first of root and stem, saved both till now
From trampling ox, rough boar and wanton goat.
What? Was man made a wheelwork to wind up,
And be discharged, and straight wound up anew?
No! — grown, his growth lasts; taught, he ne'er forgets:
May learn a thousand things, not twice the same.

"This might be pagan teaching: now hear mine.

"I say, that as the babe, you feed awhile,
Becomes a boy and fit to feed himself,
So, minds at first must be spoon-fed with truth:
When they can eat, babe's nurture is withdrawn.
I fed the babe whether it would or no:
I bid the boy or feed himself or starve.
I cried once, 'That ye may believe in Christ,
Behold this blind man shall receive his sight!'
I cry now, 'Urgest thou, *for I am shrewd
And smile at stories how John's word could cure —
Repeat that miracle and take my faith?*'
I say, that miracle was duly wrought
When, save for it, no faith was possible.
Whether a change were wrought i' the shows o' the world,
Whether the change came from our minds which see
Of shows o' the world so much as and no more
Than God wills for His purpose, — (what do I
See now, suppose you, there where you see rock
Round us?) — I know not; such was the effect,
So faith grew, making void more miracles

Because too much : they would compel, not help.
I say, the acknowledgment of God in Christ
Accepted by thy reason, solves for thee
All questions in the earth and out of it,
And has so far advanced thee to be wise.
Wouldst thou unprove this to re-prove the proved ?
In life's mere minute, with power to use that proof,
Leave knowledge and revert to how it sprung?
Thou hast it ; use it and forthwith, or die !

" For I say, this is death and the sole death,
When a man's loss comes to him from his gain,
Darkness from light, from knowledge ignorance,
And lack of love from love made manifest ;
A lamp's death when, replete with oil, it chokes ;
A stomach's when, surcharged with food, it starves.
With ignorance was surety of a cure.
When man, appalled at nature, questioned first,
' What if there lurk a might behind this might ? '
He needed satisfaction God could give,
And did give, as ye have the written word :
But when he finds might still redouble might,
Yet asks, ' Since all is might, what use of will ? '
— Will, the one source of might, — he being man
With a man's will and a man's might, to teach
In little how the two combine in large, —
That man has turned round on himself and stands,
Which in the course of nature is, to die.

" And when man questioned, ' What if there be love
Behind the will and might, as real as they ? ' —
He needed satisfaction God could give,
And did give, as ye have the written word :
But when, beholding that love everywhere,
He reasons, ' Since such love is everywhere,
And since ourselves can love and would be loved,
We ourselves make the love, and Christ was not,' —
How shall ye help this man who knows himself,
That he must love and would be loved again,
Yet, owning his own love that proveth Christ,
Rejecteth Christ through very need of Him ?
The lamp o'erswims with oil, the stomach flags
Loaded with nurture, and that man's soul dies.

" If he rejoin, ' But this was all the while
A trick ; the fault was, first of all, in thee,

Thy story of the places, names and dates,
Where, when and how the ultimate truth had rise,
— Thy prior truth, at last discovered none,
Whence now the second suffers detriment.
What good of giving knowledge if, because
O' the manner of the gift, its profit fail?
And why refuse what modicum of help
Had stopped the after-doubt, impossible
I' the face of truth — truth absolute, uniform?
Why must I hit of this and miss of that,
Distinguish just as I be weak or strong,
And not ask of thee and have answer prompt,
Was this once, was it not once? — then and now
And evermore, plain truth from man to man.
Is John's procedure just the heathen bard's?
Put question of his famous play again
How for the ephemerals' sake, Jove's fire was filched,
And carried in a cane and brought to earth:
The fact is in the fable, cry the wise,
Mortals obtained the boon, so much is fact,
Though fire be spirit and produced on earth.
As with the Titan's, so now with thy tale:
Why breed in us perplexity, mistake,
Nor tell the whole truth in the proper words?'

"I answer, Have ye yet to argue out
The very primal thesis, plainest law,
— Man is not God but hath God's end to serve,
A master to obey, a course to take,
Somewhat to cast off, somewhat to become?
Grant this, then man must pass from old to new,
From vain to real, from mistake to fact,
From what once seemed good, to what now proves best.
How could man have progression otherwise?
Before the point was mooted 'What is God?'
No savage man inquired 'What am myself?'
Much less replied, 'First, last, and best of things.'
Man takes that title now if he believes
Might can exist with neither will nor love,
In God's case — what he names now Nature's Law —
While in himself he recognizes love
No less than might and will: and rightly takes.
Since if man prove the sole existent thing
Where these combine, whatever their degree,
However weak the might or will or love,
So they be found there, put in evidence, —

He is as surely higher in the scale
Than any might with neither love nor will,
As life, apparent in the poorest midge,
(When the faint dust-speck flits, ye guess its wing,)
Is marvellous beyond dead Atlas' self —
Given to the nobler midge for resting-place!
Thus, man proves best and highest — God, in fine,
And thus the victory leads but to defeat,
The gain to loss, best rise to the worst fall,
His life becomes impossible, which is death.

" But if, appealing thence, he cower, avouch
He is mere man, and in humility
Neither may know God nor mistake himself;
I point to the immediate consequence
And say, by such confession straight he falls
Into man's place, a thing nor God nor beast,
Made to know that he can know and not more:
Lower than God who knows all and can all,
Higher than beasts which know and can so far
As each beast's limit, perfect to an end,
Nor conscious that they know, nor craving more;
While man knows partly but conceives beside,
Creeps ever on from fancies to the fact,
And in this striving, this converting air
Into a solid he may grasp and use,
Finds progress, man's distinctive mark alone,
Not God's, and not the beasts': God is, they are,
Man partly is and wholly hopes to be.
Such progress could no more attend his soul
Were all it struggles after found at first
And guesses changed to knowledge absolute,
Than motion wait his body, were all else
Than it the solid earth on every side,
Where now through space he moves from rest to rest.
Man, therefore, thus conditioned, must expect
He could not, what he knows now, know at first;
What he considers that he knows to-day,
Come but to-morrow, he will find misknown;
Getting increase of knowledge, since he learns
Because he lives, which is to be a man,
Set to instruct himself by his past self:
First, like the brute, obliged by facts to learn,
Next, as man may, obliged by his own mind,
Bent, habit, nature, knowledge turned to law.
God's gift was that man should conceive of truth

And yearn to gain it, catching at mistake,
As midway help till he reach fact indeed.
The statuary ere he mould a shape
Boasts a like gift, the shape's idea, and next
The aspiration to produce the same;
So, taking clay, he calls his shape thereout,
Cries ever ' Now I have the thing I see : '
Yet all the while goes changing what was wrought,
From falsehood like the truth, to truth itself.
How were it had he cried, ' I see no face,
No breast, no feet i' the ineffectual clay ' ?
Rather commend him that he clapped his hands,
And laughed ' It is my shape and lives again ! '
Enjoyed the falsehood, touched it on to truth,
Until yourselves applaud the flesh indeed
In what is still flesh-imitating clay.
Right in you, right in him, such way be man's!
God only makes the live shape at a jet.
Will ye renounce this pact of creatureship?
The pattern on the Mount subsists no more,
Seemed awhile, then returned to nothingness;
But copies, Moses strove to make thereby,
Serve still and are replaced as time requires :
By these, make newest vessels, reach the type!
If ye demur, this judgment on your head,
Never to reach the ultimate, angels' law,
Indulging every instinct of the soul
There where law, life, joy, impulse are one thing!

"Such is the burden of the latest time.
I have survived to hear it with my ears,
Answer it with my lips : does this suffice?
For if there be a further woe than such,
Wherein my brothers struggling need a hand,
So long as any pulse is left in mine,
May I be absent even longer yet,
Plucking the blind ones back from the abyss,
Though I should tarry a new hundred years ! "

But he was dead : 'twas about noon, the day
Somewhat declining : we five buried him
That eve, and then, dividing, went five ways,
And I, disguised, returned to Ephesus.

By this, the cave's mouth must be filled with sand.
Valens is lost, I know not of his trace;

The Bactrian was but a wild childish man,
And could not write nor speak, but only loved:
So, lest the memory of this go quite,
Seeing that I to-morrow fight the beasts,
I tell the same to Phœbas, whom believe!
For many look again to find that face,
Beloved John's to whom I ministered,
Somewhere in life about the world; they err:
Either mistaking what was darkly spoke
At ending of his book, as he relates,
Or misconceiving somewhat of this speech
Scattered from mouth to mouth, as I suppose.
Believe ye will not see him any more
About the world with his divine regard!
For all was as I say, and now the man
Lies as he lay once, breast to breast with God.

[Cerinthus read and mused; one added this:

"If Christ, as thou affirmest, be of men
Mere man, the first and best but nothing more, —
Account Him, for reward of what He was,
Now and forever, wretchedest of all.
For see; Himself conceived of life as love,
Conceived of love as what must enter in,
Fill up, make one with His each soul He loved:
Thus much for man's joy, all men's joy for Him.
Well, He is gone, thou sayest, to fit reward.
But by this time are many souls set free,
And very many still retained alive:
Nay, should His coming be delayed awhile,
Say, ten years longer (twelve years, some compute),
See if, for every finger of thy hands,
There be not found, that day the world shall end,
Hundreds of souls, each holding by Christ's word
That He will grow incorporate with all,
With me as Pamphylax, with him as John,
Groom for each bride! Can a mere man do this?
Yet Christ saith, this He lived and died to do.
Call Christ, then, the illimitable God,
Or lost!"

But 't was Cerinthus that is lost.]

CALIBAN UPON SETEBOS;

OR,

NATURAL THEOLOGY IN THE ISLAND.

"Thou thoughtest that I was altogether such an one as thyself."

['WILL sprawl, now that the heat of day is best,
Flat on his belly in the pit's much mire,
With elbows wide, fists clenched to prop his chin.
And, while he kicks both feet in the cool slush,
And feels about his spine small eft-things course,
Run in and out each arm, and make him laugh:
And while above his head a pompion-plant,
Coating the cave-top as a brow its eye,
Creeps down to touch and tickle hair and beard,
And now a flower drops with a bee inside,
And now a fruit to snap at, catch and crunch, —
He looks out o'er yon sea which sunbeams cross
And recross till they weave a spider-web,
(Meshes of fire, some great fish breaks at times,)
And talks to his own self, howe'er he please,
Touching that other, whom his dam called God.
Because to talk about Him, vexes — ha,
Could He but know! and time to vex is now,
When talk is safer than in winter-time.
Moreover Prosper and Miranda sleep
In confidence he drudges at their task,
And it is good to cheat the pair, and gibe,
Letting the rank tongue blossom into speech.]

Setebos, Setebos, and Setebos!
'Thinketh, He dwelleth i' the cold o' the moon.

'Thinketh He made it, with the sun to match,
But not the stars; the stars came otherwise;
Only made clouds, winds, meteors, such as that:
Also this isle, what lives and grows thereon,
And snaky sea which rounds and ends the same.

'Thinketh, it came of being ill at ease:
He hated that He cannot change His cold,
Nor cure its ache. 'Hath spied an icy fish
That longed to 'scape the rock-stream where she lived,
And thaw herself within the lukewarm brine
O' the lazy sea her stream thrusts far amid,

A crystal spike 'twixt two warm walls of wave;
Only, she ever sickened, found repulse
At the other kind of water, not her life,
(Green-dense and dim-delicious, bred o' the sun,)
Flounced back from bliss she was not born to breathe,
And in her old bounds buried her despair,
Hating and loving warmth alike: so He.

'Thinketh, He made thereat the sun, this isle,
Trees and the fowls here, beast and creeping thing.
You otter, sleek-wet, black, lithe as a leech;
Yon auk, one fire-eye in a ball of foam,
That floats and feeds; a certain badger brown
He hath watched hunt with that slant white-wedge eye
By moonlight; and the pie with the long tongue
That pricks deep into oakwarts for a worm,
And says a plain word when she finds her prize,
But will not eat the ants; the ants themselves
That build a wall of seeds and settled stalks
About their hole — He made all these and more,
Made all we see, and us, in spite: how else?
He could not, Himself, make a second self
To be His mate; as well have made Himself:
He would not make what He mislikes or slights,
An eyesore to Him, or not worth His pains:
But did, in envy, listlessness or sport,
Make what Himself would fain, in a manner, be —
Weaker in most points, stronger in a few,
Worthy, and yet mere playthings all the while,
Things He admires and mocks too, — that is it.
Because, so brave, so better though they be,
It nothing skills if He begin to plague.
Look now, I melt a gourd-fruit into mash,
Add honeycomb and pods, I have perceived,
Which bite like finches when they bill and kiss, —
Then, when froth rises bladdery, drink up all,
Quick, quick, till maggots scamper through my brain;
Last, throw me on my back i' the seeded thyme,
And wanton, wishing I were born a bird.
Put case, unable to be what I wish,
I yet could make a live bird out of clay:
Would not I take clay, pinch my Caliban
Able to fly? — for, there, see, he hath wings,
And great comb like the hoopoe's to admire,
And there, a sting to do his foes offence,
There, and I will that he begin to live,

Fly to yon rock-top, nip me off the horns
Of grigs high up that make the merry din,
Saucy through their veined wings, and mind me not.
In which feat, if his leg snapped, brittle clay,
And he lay stupid-like, — why, I should laugh;
And if he, spying me, should fall to weep,
Beseech me to be good, repair his wrong,
Bid his poor leg smart less or grow again, —
Well, as the chance were, this might take or else
Not take my fancy: I might hear his cry,
And give the manikin three sound legs for one,
Or pluck the other off, leave him like an egg,
And lessoned he was mine and merely clay.
Were this no pleasure, lying in the thyme,
Drinking the mash, with brain become alive,
Making and marring clay at will? So He.

'Thinketh, such shows nor right nor wrong in Him,
Nor kind, nor cruel: He is strong and Lord.
'Am strong myself compared to yonder crabs
That march now from the mountain to the sea;
'Let twenty pass, and stone the twenty-first,
Loving not, hating not, just choosing so.
'Say, the first straggler that boasts purple spots
Shall join the file, one pincer twisted off;
'Say, this bruised fellow shall receive a worm,
And two worms he whose nippers end in red;
As it likes me each time, I do: so He.

Well then, 'supposeth He is good i' the main,
Placable if His mind and ways were guessed,
But rougher than His handiwork, be sure!
Oh, He hath made things worthier than Himself,
And envieth that, so helped, such things do more
Than He who made them! What consoles but this?
That they, unless through Him, do nought at all,
And must submit: what other use in things?
'Hath cut a pipe of pithless elder-joint
That, blown through, gives exact the scream o' the jay
When from her wing you twitch the feathers blue:
Sound this, and little birds that hate the jay
Flock within stone's throw, glad their foe is hurt:
Put case such pipe could prattle and boast forsooth,
" I catch the birds, I am the crafty thing,
 I make the cry my maker cannot make
 With his great round mouth; he must blow through mine!"
Would not I smash it with my foot? So He.

But wherefore rough, why cold and ill at ease ?
Aha, that is a question ! Ask, for that,
What knows,— the something over Setebos
That made Him, or He, may be, found and fought,
Worsted, drove off and did to nothing, perchance.
There may be something quiet o'er His head,
Out of His reach, that feels nor joy nor grief,
Since both derive from weakness in some way.
I joy because the quails come ; would not joy
Could I bring quails here when I have a mind :
This Quiet, all it hath a mind to, doth.
'Esteemeth stars the outposts of its couch,
But never spends much thought nor care that way.
It may look up, work up,— the worse for those
It works on ! 'Careth but for Setebos
The many-handed as a cuttle-fish,
Who, making Himself feared through what He does,
Looks up, first, and perceives he cannot soar
To what is quiet and hath happy life ;
Next looks down here, and out of very spite
Makes this a bauble-world to ape yon real,
These good things to match those as hips do grapes.
'T is solace making baubles, ay, and sport.
Himself peeped late, eyed Prosper at his books
Careless and lofty, lord now of the isle :
Vexed, 'stitched a book of broad leaves, arrow-shaped,
Wrote thereon, he knows what, prodigious words ;
Has peeled a wand and called it by a name ;
Weareth at whiles for an enchanter's robe
The eyed skin of a supple ocelot ;
And hath an ounce sleeker than youngling mole,
A four-legged serpent he makes cower and couch,
Now snarl, now hold its breath and mind his eye,
And saith she is Miranda and my wife :
'Keeps for his Ariel a tall pouch-bill crane
He bids go wade for fish and straight disgorge ;
Also a sea-beast, lumpish, which he snared,
Blinded the eyes of, and brought somewhat tame,
And split its toe-webs, and now pens the drudge
In a hole o' the rock and calls him Caliban ;
A bitter heart that bides its time and bites.
'Plays thus at being Prosper in a way,
Taketh his mirth with make-believes : so He.

His dam held that the Quiet made all things
Which Setebos vexed only : 'holds not so.

Who made them weak, meant weakness He might vex.
Had He meant other, while His hand was in,
Why not make horny eyes no thorn could prick,
Or plate my scalp with bone against the snow,
Or overscale my flesh 'neath joint and joint,
Like an orc's armor? Ay, — so spoil His sport!
He is the One now: only He doth all.

'Saith, He may like, perchance, what profits Him.
Ay, himself loves what does him good; but why?
'Gets good no otherwise. This blinded beast
Loves whoso places flesh-meat on his nose,
But, had he eyes, would want no help, but hate
Or love, just as it liked him: He hath eyes.
Also it pleaseth Setebos to work,
Use all His hands, and exercise much craft,
By no means for the love of what is worked.
'Tasteth, himself, no finer good i' the world
When all goes right, in this safe summer-time,
And he wants little, hungers, aches not much,
Than trying what to do with wit and strength.
'Falls to make something: 'piled yon pile of turfs,
And squared and stuck there squares of soft white chalk,
And, with a fish-tooth, scratched a moon on each,
And set up endwise certain spikes of tree,
And crowned the whole with a sloth's skull a-top,
Found dead i' the woods, too hard for one to kill.
No use at all i' the work, for work's sole sake;
'Shall some day knock it down again: so He.

'Saith He is terrible: watch His feats in proof!
One hurricane will spoil six good months' hope.
He hath a spite against me, that I know,
Just as He favors Prosper, who knows why?
So it is, all the same, as well I find.
'Wove wattles half the winter, fenced them firm
With stone and stake to stop she-tortoises
Crawling to lay their eggs here: well, one wave,
Feeling the foot of Him upon its neck,
Gaped as a snake does, lolled out its large tongue,
And licked the whole labor flat: so much for spite.

'Saw a ball flame down late (yonder it lies)
Where, half an hour before, I slept i' the shade:
Often they scatter sparkles: there is force!
'Dug up a newt He may have envied once

And turned to stone, shut up inside a stone.
Please Him and hinder this? — What Prosper does?
Aha, if He would tell me how! Not He!
There is the sport: discover how or die!
All need not die, for of the things o' the isle
Some flee afar, some dive, some run up trees;
Those at His mercy, — why, they please Him most
When . . . when . . . well, never try the same way twice
Repeat what act has pleased, He may grow wroth.
You must not know His ways, and play Him off,
Sure of the issue. 'Doth the like himself:
'Spareth a squirrel that it nothing fears
But steals the nut from underneath my thumb,
And when I threat, bites stoutly in defence:
'Spareth an urchin that contrariwise,
Curls up into a ball, pretending death
For fright at my approach: the two ways please.
But what would move my choler more than this,
That either creature counted on its life
To-morrow and next day and all days to come,
Saying, forsooth, in the inmost of its heart,
" Because he did so yesterday with me,
And otherwise with such another brute,
So must he do henceforth and always." — Ay?
Would teach the reasoning couple what " must " means!
'Doth as he likes, or wherefore Lord? So He.

'Conceiveth all things will continue thus,
And we shall have to live in fear of Him
So long as He lives, keeps His strength: no change,
If He have done His best, make no new world
To please Him more, so leave off watching this, —
If He surprise not even the Quiet's self
Some strange day, — or, suppose, grow into it
As grubs grow butterflies: else, here are we,
And there is He, and nowhere help at all.

'Believeth with the life, the pain shall stop.
His dam held different, that after death
He both plagued enemies and feasted friends:
Idly! He doth His worst in this our life,
Giving just respite lest we die through pain,
Saving last pain for worst, — with which, an end.
Meanwhile, the best way to escape His ire
Is, not to seem too happy. 'Sees, himself,
Yonder two flies, with purple films and pink,

Bask on the pompion-bell above: kills both.
'Sees two black painful beetles roll their ball
On head and tail as if to save their lives :
Moves them the stick away they strive to clear.

Even so, 'would have Him misconceive, suppose
This Caliban strives hard and ails no less,
And always, above all else, envies Him ;
Wherefore he mainly dances on dark nights,
Moans in the sun, gets under holes to laugh,
And never speaks his mind save housed as now :
Outside, 'groans, curses. If He caught me here,
O'erheard this speech, and asked " What chucklest at ? "
'Would, to appease Him, cut a finger off,
Or of my three kid yearlings burn the best,
Or let the toothsome apples rot on tree,
Or push my tame beast for the orc to taste :
While myself lit a fire, and made a song
And sung it, " *What I hate, be consecrate
To celebrate Thee and Thy state, no mate
For Thee ; what see for envy in poor me ?* "
Hoping the while, since evils sometimes mend,
Warts rub away and sores are cured with slime,
That some strange day, will either the Quiet catch
And conquer Setebos, or likelier He
Decrepit may doze, doze, as good as die.

[What, what? A curtain o'er the world at once !
Crickets stop hissing ; not a bird — or, yes,
There scuds His raven that has told Him all !
It was fool's play, this prattling ! Ha ! The wind
Shoulders the pillared dust, death's house o' the move,
And fast invading fires begin ! White blaze —
A tree's head snaps — and there, there, there, there, there,
His thunder follows ! Fool to gibe at Him !
Lo ! 'Lieth flat and loveth Setebos !
'Maketh his teeth meet through his upper lip,
Will let those quails fly, will not eat this month
One little mess of whelks, so he may 'scape !]

CONFESSIONS.

I.

What is he buzzing in my ears?
  "Now that I come to die,
Do I view the world as a vale of tears?"
  Ah, reverend sir, not I!

II.

What I viewed there once, what I view again
  Where the physic bottles stand
On the table's edge, — is a suburb lane,
  With a wall to my bedside hand.

III.

That lane sloped, much as the bottles do,
  From a house you could descry
O'er the garden-wall: is the curtain blue
  Or green to a healthy eye?

IV.

To mine, it serves for the old June weather
  Blue above lane and wall;
And that farthest bottle labelled "Ether"
  Is the house o'ertopping all.

V.

At a terrace, somewhere near the stopper,
  There watched for me, one June,
A girl: I know, sir, it's improper,
  My poor mind's out of tune.

VI.

Only, there was a way . . . you crept
  Close by the side, to dodge
Eyes in the house, two eyes except:
  They styled their house "The Lodge."

VII.

What right had a lounger up their lane?
  But, by creeping very close,
With the good wall's help, — their eyes might strain
  And stretch themselves to Oes,

VIII.

Yet never catch her and me together,
   As she left the attic, there,
By the rim of the bottle labelled " Ether,"
   And stole from stair to stair,

IX.

And stood by the rose-wreathed gate. Alas,
   We loved, sir — used to meet:
How sad and bad and mad it was —
   But then, how it was sweet!

MAY AND DEATH.

I.

I WISH that when you died last May,
   Charles, there had died along with you
Three parts of spring's delightful things;
   Ay, and, for me, the fourth part too.

II.

A foolish thought, and worse, perhaps!
   There must be many a pair of friends
Who, arm in arm, deserve the warm
   Moon-births and the long evening-ends.

III.

So, for their sake, be May still May!
   Let their new time, as mine of old,
Do all it did for me: I bid
   Sweet sights and sounds throng manifold.

IV.

Only, one little sight, one plant,
   Woods have in May, that starts up green
Save a sole streak which, so to speak,
   Is spring's blood, spilt its leaves between, —

V.

That, they might spare; a certain wood
   Might miss the plant; their loss were small:
But I, — whene'er the leaf grows there,
   Its drop comes from my heart, that's all.

DEAF AND DUMB.

A GROUP BY WOOLNER.

ONLY the prism's obstruction shows aright
   The secret of a sunbeam, breaks its light
Into the jewelled bow from blankest white;
   So may a glory from defect arise:
Only by Deafness may the vexed Love wreak
   Its insuppressive sense on brow and cheek,
Only by Dumbness adequately speak
   As favored mouth could never, through the eyes.

PROSPICE.

FEAR death? — to feel the fog in my throat,
   The mist in my face,
When the snows begin, and the blasts denote
   I am nearing the place,
The power of the night, the press of the storm,
   The post of the foe;
Where he stands, the Arch Fear in a visible form,
   Yet the strong man must go:
For the journey is done and the summit attained,
   And the barriers fall,
Though a battle's to fight ere the guerdon be gained,
   The reward of it all.
I was ever a fighter, so — one fight more,
   The best and the last!
I would hate that death bandaged my eyes, and forbore,
   And bade me creep past.
No! let me taste the whole of it, fare like my peers
   The heroes of old,
Bear the brunt, in a minute pay glad life's arrears
   Of pain, darkness and cold.
For sudden the worst turns the best to the brave,
   The black minute's at end,
And the elements' rage, the fiend-voices that rave,
   Shall dwindle, shall blend,
Shall change, shall become first a peace out of pain,
   Then a light, then thy breast,
O thou soul of my soul! I shall clasp thee again,
   And with God be the rest!

EURYDICE TO ORPHEUS.

A PICTURE BY LEIGHTON.

But give them me, the mouth, the eyes, the brow!
Let them once more absorb me! One look now
Will lap me round forever, not to pass
Out of its light, though darkness lie beyond:
Hold me but safe again within the bond
Of one immortal look! All woe that was,
Forgotten, and all terror that may be,
Defied, — no past is mine, no future: look at me!

YOUTH AND ART.

I.

It once might have been, once only:
  We lodged in a street together,
You, a sparrow on the housetop lonely,
  I, a lone she-bird of his feather.

II.

Your trade was with sticks and clay,
  You thumbed, thrust, patted and polished,
Then laughed "They will see some day
  Smith made, and Gibson demolished."

III.

My business was song, song, song;
  I chirped, cheeped, trilled and twittered,
"Kate Brown's on the boards ere long,
  And Grisi's existence embittered!"

IV.

I earned no more by a warble
  Than you by a sketch in plaster;
You wanted a piece of marble,
  I needed a music-master.

V.

We studied hard in our styles,
  Chipped each at a crust like Hindoos,
For air, looked out on the tiles,
  For fun, watched each other's windows

VI.

You lounged, like a boy of the South,
    Cap and blouse — nay, a bit of beard too;
Or you got it, rubbing your mouth
    With fingers the clay adhered to.

VII.

And I — soon managed to find
    Weak points in the flower-fence facing,
Was forced to put up a blind
    And be safe in my corset-lacing.

VIII.

No harm! It was not my fault
    If you never turned your eye's tail up
As I shook upon E *in alt.*,
    Or ran the chromatic scale up:

IX.

For spring bade the sparrows pair,
    And the boys and girls gave guesses,
And stalls in our street looked rare
    With bulrush and watercresses.

X.

Why did not you pinch a flower
    In a pellet of clay and fling it?
Why did not I put a power
    Of thanks in a look, or sing it?

XI.

I did look, sharp as a lynx,
    (And yet the memory rankles,)
When models arrived, some minx
    Tripped up-stairs, she and her ankles.

XII.

But I think I gave you as good!
    "That foreign fellow, — who can know
How she pays, in a playful mood,
    For his tuning her that piano?"

XIII.

Could you say so, and never say,
    "Suppose we join hands and fortunes,

    And I fetch her from over the way,
      Her, piano, and long tunes and short tunes "?

XIV.

No, no: you would not be rash,
  Nor I rasher and something over:
You 've to settle yet Gibson's hash,
  And Grisi yet lives in clover.

XV.

But you meet the Prince at the Board,
  I 'm queen myself at *bals-paré*,
I 've married a rich old lord,
  And you 're dubbed knight and an R. A.

XVI.

Each life unfulfilled, you see;
  It hangs still, patchy and scrappy:
We have not sighed deep, laughed free,
  Starved, feasted, despaired, — been happy.

XVII.

And nobody calls you a dunce,
  And people suppose me clever:
This could but have happened once,
  And we missed it, lost it forever.

A FACE.

IF one could have that little head of hers
Painted upon a background of pale gold,
Such as the Tuscan's early art prefers!
No shade encroaching on the matchless mould
Of those two lips, which should be opening soft
In the pure profile; not as when she laughs,
For that spoils all: but rather as if aloft
Yon hyacinth, she loves so, leaned its staff's
Burden of honey-colored buds to kiss
And capture 'twixt the lips apart for this.
Then her lithe neck, three fingers might surround,
How it should waver on the pale gold ground
Up to the fruit-shaped, perfect chin it lifts!
I know, Correggio loves to mass, in rifts
Of heaven, his angel faces, orb on orb

Breaking its outline, burning shades absorb:
But these are only massed there, I should think,
Waiting to see some wonder momently
Grow out, stand full, fade slow against the sky
(That's the pale ground you'd see this sweet face by),
All heaven, meanwhile, condensed into one eye
Which fears to lose the wonder, should it wink.

A LIKENESS.

SOME people hang portraits up
In a room where they dine or sup:
And the wife clinks tea-things under,
And her cousin, he stirs his cup,
Asks, "Who was the lady, I wonder?"
"'T is a daub John bought at a sale,"
Quoth the wife, — looks black as thunder.
"What a shade beneath her nose!
Snuff-taking, I suppose," —
Adds the cousin, while John's corns ail.

Or else, there's no wife in the case,
But the portrait's queen of the place,
Alone 'mid the other spoils
Of youth, — masks, gloves and foils,
And pipe-sticks, rose, cherry-tree, jasmine,
And the long whip, the tandem-lasher,
And the cast from a fist ("not, alas! mine,
But my master's, the Tipton Slasher"),
And the cards where pistol-balls mark ace,
And a satin shoe used for cigar-case,
And the chamois-horns ("shot in the Chablais"),
And prints — Rarey drumming on Cruiser,
And Sayers, our champion, the bruiser,
And the little edition of Rabelais:
Where a friend, with both hands in his pockets,
May saunter up close to examine it,
And remark a good deal of Jane Lamb in it,
"But the eyes are half out of their sockets;
That hair's not so bad, where the gloss is,
But they've made the girl's nose a proboscis:
Jane Lamb, that we danced with at Vichy!
What, is not she Jane? Then, who is she?"

A LIKENESS

All that I own is a print,
An etching, a mezzotint;
'T is a study, a fancy, a fiction,
Yet a fact (take my conviction)
Because it has more than a hint
Of a certain face, I never
Saw elsewhere touch or trace of
In women I've seen the face of:
Just an etching, and, so far, clever.

I keep my prints, an imbroglio,
Fifty in one portfolio.
When somebody tries my claret,
We turn round chairs to the fire,
Chirp over days in a garret,
Chuckle o'er increase of salary,
Taste the good fruits of our leisure,
Talk about pencil and lyre,
And the National Portrait Gallery:
Then I exhibit my treasure.
After we've turned over twenty,
And the debt of wonder my crony owes
Is paid to my Marc Antonios,
He stops me — "*Festina lentè!*
What's that sweet thing there, the etching?"
How my waistcoat-strings want stretching,
How my cheeks grow red as tomatos,
How my heart leaps! But hearts, after leaps, ache.

"By the by, you must take, for a keepsake,
That other, you praised, of Volpato's."
The fool! would he try a flight further and say —
He never saw, never before to-day,
What was able to take his breath away,
A face to lose youth for, to occupy age
With the dream of, meet death with, — why, I'll not engage
But that, half in a rapture and half in a rage,
I should toss him the thing's self — "'T is only a duplicate,
A thing of no value! Take it, I supplicate!"

MR. SLUDGE, "THE MEDIUM."

Now, don't, sir! Don't expose me! Just this once!
This was the first and only time, I'll swear, —
Look at me, — see, I kneel, — the only time,
I swear, I ever cheated, — yes, by the soul
Of Her who hears — (your sainted mother, sir!)
All, except this last accident, was truth —
This little kind of slip! — and even this,
It was your own wine, sir, the good champagne,
(I took it for Catawba, you're so kind,)
Which put the folly in my head!

                         " Get up ? "
You still inflict on me that terrible face?
You show no mercy? — Not for Her dear sake,
The sainted spirit's, whose soft breath even now
Blows on my cheek — (don't you feel something, sir?)
You'll tell?

                Go tell, then! Who the devil cares
What such a rowdy chooses to . . .
                               Aie — aie — aie!
Please, sir! your thumbs are through my windpipe, sir!
Ch—ch!

            Well, sir, I hope you've done it now!
Oh Lord! I little thought, sir, yesterday,
When your departed mother spoke those words
Of peace through me, and moved you, sir, so much,
You gave me — (very kind it was of you)
These shirt-studs — (better take them back again,
Please, sir) — yes, little did I think so soon
A trifle of trick, all through a glass too much
Of his own champagne, would change my best of friends
Into an angry gentleman!

                    Though, 't was wrong.
I don't contest the point; your anger's just:
Whatever put such folly in my head,
I know 't was wicked of me. There's a thick
Dusk undeveloped spirit (I've observed)
Owes me a grudge — a negro's, I should say,
Or else an Irish emigrant's; yourself
Explained the case so well last Sunday, sir,

When we had summoned Franklin to clear up
A point about those shares i' the telegraph:
Ay, and he swore . . . or might it be Tom Paine? . .
Thumping the table close by where I crouched,
He'd do me soon a mischief: that's come true!
Why, now your face clears! I was sure it would!
Then, this one time . . . don't take your hand away,
Through yours I surely kiss your mother's hand . . .
You'll promise to forgive me? — or, at least,
Tell nobody of this? Consider, sir!
What harm can mercy do? Would but the shade
Of the venerable dead-one just vouchsafe
A rap or tip! What bit of paper's here?
Suppose we take a pencil, let her write,
Make the least sign, she urges on her child
Forgiveness? There now! Eh? Oh! 'T was your foot,
And not a natural creak, sir?

      Answer, then!
Once, twice, thrice . . . see, I'm waiting to say "thrice
All to no use? No sort of hope for me?
It's all to post to Greeley's newspaper?

What? If I told you all about the tricks?
Upon my soul! — the whole truth, and nought else,
And how there's been some falsehood — for your part,
Will you engage to pay my passage out,
And hold your tongue until I'm safe on board?
England's the place, not Boston — no offence!
I see what makes you hesitate: don't fear!
I mean to change my trade and cheat no more,
Yes, this time really it's upon my soul!
Be my salvation! — under Heaven, of course.
I'll tell some queer things. Sixty Vs must do.
A trifle, though, to start with! We'll refer
The question to this table?

      How you're changed!
Then split the difference; thirty more, we'll say.
Ay, but you leave my presents! Else I'll swear
'T was all through those: you wanted yours again,
So, picked a quarrel with me, to get them back!
Tread on a worm, it turns, sir! If I turn,
Your fault! 'T is you'll have forced me! Who's obliged
To give up life yet try no self-defence?
At all events, I'll run the risk. Eh?

Done!
May I sit, sir? This dear old table, now!
Please, sir, a parting eggnog and cigar!
I've been so happy with you! Nice stuffed chairs,
And sympathetic sideboards; what an end
To all the instructive evenings! (It's alight.)
Well, nothing lasts, as Bacon came and said.
Here goes, — but keep your temper, or I'll scream!

Fol-lol-the-rido-liddle-iddle-ol!
You see, sir, it's your own fault more than mine;
It's all your fault, you curious gentlefolk!
You're prigs, — excuse me, — like to look so spry,
So clever, while you cling by half a claw
To the perch whereon you puff yourselves at roost,
Such piece of self-conceit as serves for perch
Because you chose it, so it must be safe.
Oh, otherwise you're sharp enough! You spy
Who slips, who slides, who holds by help of wing,
Wanting real foothold, — who can't keep upright
On the other perch, your neighbor chose, not you:
There's no outwitting you respecting him!
For instance, men love money — that, you know —
And what men do to gain it: well, suppose
A poor lad, say a help's son in your house,
Listening at keyholes, hears the company
Talk grand of dollars, V-notes, and so forth,
How hard they are to get, how good to hold,
How much they buy, — if, suddenly, in pops he —
"*I* 've got a V-note!" — what do you say to him?
What's your first word which follows your last kick?
"Where did you steal it, rascal?" That's because
He finds you, fain would fool you, off your perch,
Not on the special piece of nonsense, sir,
Elected your parade-ground: let him try
Lies to the end of the list, — "He picked it up,
His cousin died and left it him by will,
The President flung it to him, riding by,
An actress trucked it for a curl of his hair,
He dreamed of luck and found his shoe enriched,
He dug up clay, and out of clay made gold" —
How would you treat such possibilities?
Would not you, prompt, investigate the case
With cowhide? "Lies, lies, lies," you'd shout: and why?
Which of the stories might not prove mere truth?
This last, perhaps, that clay was turned to coin!

Let's see, now, give him me to speak for him!
How many of your rare philosophers,
In plaguy books I've had to dip into,
Believed gold could be made thus, saw it made,
And made it? Oh, with such philosophers
You're on your best behavior! While the lad —
With him, in a trice, you settle likelihoods,
Nor doubt a moment how he got his prize:
In his case, you hear, judge and execute,
All in a breath: so would most men of sense.

But let the same lad hear you talk as grand
At the same keyhole, you and company,
Of signs and wonders, the invisible world;
How wisdom scouts our vulgar unbelief
More than our vulgarest credulity;
How good men have desired to see a ghost,
What Johnson used to say, what Wesley did,
Mother Goose thought, and fiddle-diddle-dee: —
If he break in with, "Sir, *I* saw a ghost!"
Ah, the ways change! He finds you perched and prim;
It's a conceit of yours that ghosts may be:
There's no talk now of cowhide. "Tell it out!
Don't fear us! Take your time and recollect!
Sit down first: try a glass of wine, my boy!
And, David, (is not that your Christian name?)
Of all things, should this happen twice — it may —
Be sure, while fresh in mind, you let us know!"
Does the boy blunder, blurt out this, blab that,
Break down in the other, as beginners will?
All's candor, all's considerateness — "No haste!
Pause and collect yourself! We understand!
That's the bad memory, or the natural shock,
Or the unexplained *phenomena!*"

                                  Egad,
The boy takes heart of grace; finds, never fear,
The readiest way to ope your own heart wide,
Show — what I call your peacock-perch, pet post
To strut, and spread the tail, and squawk upon!
'Just as you thought, much as you might expect!
There be more things in heaven and earth, Horatio," . . .
And so on. Shall not David take the hint,
Grow bolder, stroke you down at quickened rate?
If he ruffle a feather, it's, "Gently, patiently!
Manifestations are so weak at first!

Doubting, moreover, kills them, cuts all short,
Cures with a vengeance!"

       There, sir, that's your style
You and your boy — such pains bestowed on him,
Or any headpiece of the average worth,
To teach, say, Greek, would perfect him apace,
Make him a Person (" Porson ? " thank you, sir !)
Much more, proficient in the art of lies.
You never leave the lesson ! Fire alight,
Catch you permitting it to die ! You 've friends ;
There 's no withholding knowledge, — least from those
Apt to look elsewhere for their souls' supply :
Why should not you parade your lawful prize ?
Who finds a picture, digs a medal up,
Hits on a first edition, — he henceforth
Gives it his name, grows notable : how much more,
Who ferrets out a " medium " ? " David 's yours,
You highly-favored man ? Then, pity souls
Less privileged ! Allow us share your luck ! "
So, David holds the circle, rules the roast,
Narrates the vision, peeps in the glass ball,
Sets-to the spirit-writing, hears the raps,
As the case may be.

       Now mark ! To be precise —
Though I say, " lies " all these, at this first stage,
'T is just for science' sake : I call such grubs
By the name of what they 'll turn to, dragon-flies.
Strictly, it 's what good people style untruth ;
But yet, so far, not quite the full-grown thing :
It 's fancying, fable-making, nonsense-work —
What never meant to be so very bad —
The knack of story-telling, brightening up
Each dull old bit of fact that drops its shine.
One does see somewhat when one shuts one's eyes,
If only spots and streaks ; tables do tip
In the oddest way of themselves : and pens, good Lord,
Who knows if you drive them or they drive you ?
'T is but a foot in the water and out again ;
Not that duck-under which decides your dive.
Note this, for it 's important : listen why.

I 'll prove, you push on David till he dives
And ends the shivering. Here 's your circle, now :
Two-thirds of them, with heads like you their host,

Turn up their eyes, and cry, as you expect,
" Lord, who 'd have thought it ! " But there 's always one
Looks wise, compassionately smiles, submits,
" Of your veracity no kind of doubt,
But — do you feel so certain of that boy's ?
Really, I wonder ! I confess myself
More chary of my faith ! " That 's galling, sir !
What, he the investigator, he the sage,
When all 's done ? Then, you just have shut your eyes,
Opened your mouth, and gulped down David whole,
You ! Terrible were such catastrophe !
So, evidence is redoubled, doubled again,
And doubled besides ; once more, " He heard, we heard,
You and they heard, your mother and your wife,
Your children and the stranger in your gates :
Did they or did they not ? " So much for him,
The black sheep, guest without the wedding-garb,
The doubting Thomas ! Now 's your turn to crow :
" He 's kind to think you such a fool : Sludge cheats ?
Leave you alone to take precautions ! "

            Straight
The rest join chorus. Thomas stands abashed,
Sips silent some such beverage as this,
Considers if it be harder, shutting eyes
And gulping David in good fellowship,
Than going elsewhere, getting, in exchange,
With no eggnog to lubricate the food,
Some just as tough a morsel. Over the way,
Holds Captain Sparks his court : is it better there ?
Have not you hunting-stories, scalping-scenes,
And Mexican War exploits to swallow plump
If you 'd be free o' the stove-side, rocking-chair,
And trio of affable daughters ?

           Doubt succumbs !
Victory ! All your circle 's yours again !
Out of the clubbing of submissive wits,
David's performance rounds, each chink gets patched,
Every protrusion of a point 's filed fine,
All 's fit to set a-rolling round the world,
And then return to David finally,
Lies seven feet thick about his first half-inch.
Here 's a choice birth o' the supernatural,
Poor David 's pledged to ! You 've employed no tool
That laws exclaim at, save the devil's own,

Yet screwed him into henceforth gulling you
To the top o' your bent, — all out of one half-lie!

You hold, if there 's one half or a hundredth part
Of a lie, that 's his fault, — his be the penalty!
I dare say! You 'd prove firmer in his place?
You 'd find the courage, — that first flurry over,
That mild bit of romancing-work at end, —
To interpose with "It gets serious, this;
Must stop here. Sir, I saw no ghost at all.
Inform your friends I made . . . well, fools of them,
And found you ready made. I 've lived in clover
These three weeks: take it out in kicks of me!"
I doubt it. Ask your conscience! Let me know,
Twelve months hence, with how few embellishments
You 've told almighty Boston of this passage
Of arms between us, your first taste o' the foil
From Sludge who could not fence, sir! Sludge, your boy!
I lied, sir, — there! I got up from my gorge
On offal in the gutter, and preferred
Your canvas-backs: I took their carver's size,
Measured his modicum of intelligence,
Tickled him on the cockles of his heart
With a raven feather, and next week found myself
Sweet and clean, dining daintily, dizened smart,
Set on a stool buttressed by ladies' knees,
Every soft smiler calling me her pet,
Encouraging my story to uncoil
And creep out from its hole, inch after inch,
"How last night, I no sooner snug in bed,
Tucked up, just as they left me, — than came raps!
While a light whisked" . . . "Shaped somewhat like a star?"
"Well, like some sort of stars, ma'am." — "So we thought!
And any voice? Not yet? Try hard, next time,
If you can't hear a voice; we think you may:
At least, the Pennsylvanian 'mediums' did."
Oh, next time comes the voice! "Just as we hoped!"
Are not the hopers proud now, pleased, profuse
O' the natural acknowledgment?

         Of course!
So, off we push, illy-oh-yo, trim the boat,
On we sweep with a cataract ahead,
We 're midway to the Horse-shoe: stop, who can.
The dance of bubbles gay about our prow!
Experiences become worth waiting for,

Spirits now speak up, tell their inmost mind,
And compliment the "medium" properly,
Concern themselves about his Sunday coat,
See rings on his hand with pleasure. Ask yourself
How you'd receive a course of treats like these!
Why, take the quietest hack and stall him up,
Cram him with corn a month, then out with him
Among his mates on a bright April morn,
With the turf to tread; see if you find or no
A caper in him, if he bucks or bolts!
Much more a youth whose fancies sprout as rank
As toadstool-clump from melon-bed. 'T is soon,
"Sirrah, you spirit, come, go, fetch and carry,
Read, write, rap, rub-a-dub, and hang yourself!"
I'm spared all further trouble; all's arranged;
Your circle does my business; I may rave
Like an epileptic dervish in the books,
Foam, fling myself flat, rend my clothes to shreds;
No matter: lovers, friends and countrymen
Will lay down spiritual laws, read wrong things right
By the rule o' reverse. If Francis Verulam
Styles himself Bacon, spells the name beside
With a y and a k, says he drew breath in York,
Gave up the ghost in Wales when Cromwell reigned,
(As, sir, we somewhat fear he was apt to say,
Before I found the useful book that knows) —
Why, what harm's done? The circle smiles apace,
"It was not Bacon, after all, you see!
We understand; the trick's but natural:
Such spirits' individuality
Is hard to put in evidence: they incline
To gibe and jeer, these undeveloped sorts.
You see, their world's much like a jail broke loose,
While this of ours remains shut, bolted, barred,
With a single window to it. Sludge, our friend,
Serves as this window, whether thin or thick,
Or stained or stainless; he's the medium-pane
Through which, to see us and be seen, they peep:
They crowd each other, hustle for a chance,
Tread on their neighbor's kibes, play tricks enough!
Does Bacon, tired of waiting, swerve aside?
Up in his place jumps Barnum — 'I'm your man,
I'll answer you for Bacon!' Try once more!"

Or else it's — "What's a 'medium'? He's a means,
Good, bad, indifferent, still the only means

Spirits can speak by; he may misconceive,
Stutter and stammer, — he 's their Sludge and drudge,
Take him or leave him; they must hold their peace,
Or else, put up with having knowledge strained
To half-expression through his ignorance.
Suppose, the spirit Beethoven wants to shed
New music he 's brimful of; why, he turns
The handle of this organ, grinds with Sludge,
And what he poured in at the mouth o' the mill
As a Thirty-third Sonata, (fancy now!)
Comes from the hopper as bran-new Sludge, nought else,
The Shakers' Hymn in G, with a natural F,
Or the 'Stars and Stripes' set to consecutive fourths."

Sir, where 's the scrape you did not help me through,
You that are wise? And for the fools, the folk
Who came to see, — the guests, (observe that word!)
Pray do you find guests criticise your wine,
Your furniture, your grammar, or your nose?
Then, why your "medium"? What 's the difference?
Prove your madeira red-ink and gamboge, —
Your Sludge, a cheat — then, somebody 's a goose
For vaunting both as genuine. "Guests!" Don't fear!
They 'll make a wry face, nor too much of that,
And leave you in your glory.

      "No, sometimes
They doubt and say as much!" Ay, doubt they do!
And what 's the consequence? "Of course they doubt" —
(You triumph) — "that explains the hitch at once!
Doubt posed our 'medium,' puddled his pure mind;
He gave them back their rubbish: pitch chaff in,
Could flour come out o' the honest mill?" So, prompt
Applaud the faithful: cases flock in point,
"How, when a mocker willed a 'medium' once
Should name a spirit James whose name was George,
'James,' cried the 'medium,' — 't was the test of truth!"
In short, a hit proves much, a miss proves more.
Does this convince? The better: does it fail?
Time for the double-shotted broadside, then —
The grand means, last resource. Look black and big!
"You style us idiots, therefore — why stop short?
Accomplices in rascality: this we hear
In our own house, from our invited guest
Found brave enough to outrage a poor boy
Exposed by our good faith! Have you been heard?

Now, then, hear us; one man's not quite worth twelve.
You see a cheat? Here's some twelve see an ass:
Excuse me if I calculate: good day!"
Out slinks the sceptic, all the laughs explode,
Sludge waves his hat in triumph!

                            Or — he don't.
There's something in real truth (explain who can!)
One casts a wistful eye at, like the horse
Who mopes beneath stuffed hay-racks and won't munch
Because he spies a corn-bag: hang that truth,
It spoils all dainties proffered in its place!
I've felt at times when, cockered, cosseted
And coddled by the aforesaid company,
Bidden enjoy their bullying, — never fear,
But o'er their shoulders spit at the flying man, —
I've felt a child; only, a fractious child
That, dandled soft by nurse, aunt, grandmother,
Who keep him from the kennel, sun and wind,
Good fun and wholesome mud, — enjoined be sweet,
And comely and superior, — eyes askance
The ragged sons o' the gutter at their game,
Fain would be down with them i' the thick o' the filth,
Making dirt-pies, laughing free, speaking plain,
And calling granny the gray old cat she is.
I've felt a spite, I say, at you, at them,
Huggings and humbug — gnashed my teeth to mark
A decent dog pass! It's too bad, I say,
Ruining a soul so!

                    But what's "so," what's fixed,
Where may one stop? Nowhere! The cheating's nursed
Out of the lying, softly and surely spun
To just your length, sir! I'd stop soon enough:
But you're for progress. "All old, nothing new?
Only the usual talking through the mouth,
Or writing by the hand? I own, I thought
This would develop, grow demonstrable,
Make doubt absurd, give figures we might see,
Flowers we might touch. There's no one doubts you, Sludge!
You dream the dreams, you see the spiritual sights,
The speeches come in your head, beyond dispute.
Still, for the sceptics' sake, to stop all mouths,
We want some outward manifestation! — well,
The Pennsylvanians gained such; why not Sludge?
He may improve with time!"

                    Ay, that he may!
He sees his lot: there's no avoiding fate.
'T is a trifle at first. "Eh, David? Did you hear?
You jogged the table, your foot caused the squeak,
This time you 're . . . joking, are you not, my boy?"
"N-n-no!"— and I 'm done for, bought and sold henceforth
The old good easy jog-trot way, the . . . eh?
The . . . not so very false, as falsehood goes,
The spinning out and drawing fine, you know, —
Really mere novel-writing of a sort,
Acting, or improvising, make-believe,
Surely not downright cheatery, — anyhow,
'T is done with and my lot cast; Cheat's my name:
The fatal dash of brandy in your tea
Has settled what you 'll have the souchong's smack:
The caddy gives way to the dram-bottle.

Then, it's so cruel easy! Oh, those tricks
That can't be tricks, those feats by sleight of hand,
Clearly no common conjuror's!— no, indeed!
A conjuror? Choose me any craft i' the world
A man puts hand to; and with six months' pains,
I 'll play you twenty tricks miraculous
To people untaught the trade: have you seen glass blown,
Pipes pierced? Why, just this biscuit that I chip,
Did you ever watch a baker toss one flat
To the oven? Try and do it! Take my word,
Practise but half as much, while limbs are lithe,
To turn, shove, tilt a table, crack your joints,
Manage your feet, dispose your hands aright,
Work wires that twitch the curtains, play the glove
At end o' your slipper, — then put out the lights
And . . . there, there, all you want you 'll get, I hope!
I found it slip, easy as an old shoe.

Now, lights on table again! I 've done my part,
You take my place while I give thanks and rest.
"Well, Judge Humgruffin, what's your verdict, sir?
You, hardest head in the United States, —
Did you detect a cheat here? Wait! Let's see!
Just an experiment first, for candor's sake!
I 'll try and cheat you, Judge! The table tilts:
Is it I that move it? Write! I 'll press your hand:
Cry when I push, or guide your pencil, Judge!"
Sludge still triumphant! "That a rap, indeed?
That, the real writing? Very like a whale!
Then, if, sir, you — a most distinguished man,

And, were the Judge not here, I'd say, . . . no matter!
Well, sir, if you fail, you can't take us in, —
There's little fear that Sludge will!"

         Won't he, ma'am?
But what if our distinguished host, like Sludge,
Bade God bear witness that he played no trick,
While you believed that what produced the raps
Was just a certain child who died, you know,
And whose last breath you thought your lips had felt?
Eh? That's a capital point, ma'am: Sludge begins
At your entreaty with your dearest dead,
The little voice set lisping once again,
The tiny hand made feel for yours once more,
The poor lost image brought back, plain as dreams,
Which image, if a word had chanced recall,
The customary cloud would cross your eyes,
Your heart return the old tick, pay its pang!
A right mood for investigation, this!
One's at one's ease with Saul and Jonathan,
Pompey and Cæsar: but one's own lost child . . .
I wonder, when you heard the first clod drop
From the spadeful at the grave-side, felt you free
To investigate who twitched your funeral scarf
Or brushed your flounces? Then, it came of course,
You should be stunned and stupid; then (how else?)
Your breath stopped with your blood, your brain struck work.
But now, such causes fail of such effects,
All's changed, — the little voice begins afresh,
Yet you, calm, consequent, can test and try
And touch the truth. " Tests? Did n't the creature tell
Its nurse's name, and say it lived six years,
And rode a rocking-horse? Enough of tests!
Sludge never could learn that!"

        He could not, eh?
You compliment him. "Could not?" Speak for yourself!
I'd like to know the man I ever saw
Once, — never mind where, how, why, when, — once saw,
Of whom I do not keep some matter in mind
He'd swear I "could not" know, sagacious soul!
What? Do you live in this world's blow of blacks,
Palaver, gossipry, a single hour
Nor find one smut has settled on your nose,
Of a smut's worth, no more, no less? — one fact
Out of the drift of facts, whereby you learn

What someone was, somewhere, somewhen, somewhy?
You don't tell folk — " See what has stuck to me!
Judge Humgruffin, our most distinguished man,
Your uncle was a tailor, and your wife
Thought to have married Miggs, missed him, hit you!" —
Do you, sir, though you see him twice a-week?
" No," you reply, " what use retailing it?
Why should I?" But, you see, one day you *should*,
Because one day there's much use, — when this fact
Brings you the Judge upon both gouty knees
Before the supernatural; proves that Sludge
Knows, as you say, a thing he " could not " know:
Will not Sludge thenceforth keep an outstretched face,
The way the wind drives?

     " Could not!" Look you now,
I'll tell you a story! There's a whiskered chap,
A foreigner, that teaches music here
And gets his bread, — knowing no better way:
He says, the fellow who informed of him
And made him fly his country and fall West,
Was a hunchback cobbler, sat, stitched soles and sang,
In some outlandish place, the city Rome,
In a cellar by their Broadway, all day long;
Never asked questions, stopped to listen or look,
Nor lifted nose from lapstone; let the world
Roll round his three-legged stool, and news run in
The ears he hardly seemed to keep pricked up.
Well, that man went on Sundays, touched his pay,
And took his praise from government, you see;
For something like two dollars every week,
He'd engage tell you some one little thing
Of some one man, which led to many more,
(Because one truth leads right to the world's end,)
And make you that man's master — when he dined
And on what dish, where walked to keep his health
And to what street. His trade was, throwing thus
His sense out, like an ant-eater's long tongue,
Soft, innocent, warm, moist, impassible,
And when 't was crusted o'er with creatures — slick,
Their juice enriched his palate. " Could not Sludge!"

I'll go yet a step further, and maintain,
Once the imposture plunged its proper depth
I' the rotten of your natures, all of you, —
(If one's not mad nor drunk, and hardly then)

It 's impossible to cheat — that 's, be found out!
Go tell your brotherhood this first slip of mine,
All to-day's tale, how you detected Sludge,
Behaved unpleasantly, till he was fain confess,
And so has come to grief! You 'll find, I think,
Why Sludge still snaps his fingers in your face.
There now, you 've told them! What 's their prompt reply?
" Sir, did that youth confess he had cheated me,
I 'd disbelieve him. He may cheat at times ;
That 's in the 'medium'-nature, thus they 're made,
Vain and vindictive, cowards, prone to scratch.
And so all cats are ; still, a cat 's the beast
You coax the strange electric sparks from out,
By rubbing back its fur ; not so a dog,
Nor lion, nor lamb : 't is the cat's nature, sir !
Why not the dog's? Ask God, who made them beasts!
D' ye think the sound, the nicely-balanced man
(Like me," — aside) — " like you yourself," — (aloud)
" — He 's stuff to make a 'medium'? Bless your soul,
'T is these hysteric, hybrid half-and-halfs,
Equivocal, worthless vermin yield the fire!
We take such as we find them, 'ware their tricks,
Wanting their service. Sir, Sludge took in you —
How, I can't say, not being there to watch :
He was tried, was tempted by your easiness, —
He did not take in me!"

     Thank you for Sludge!
I 'm to be grateful to such patrons, eh,
When what you hear 's my best word ? 'T is a challenge,
" Snap at all strangers, half-tamed prairie-dog,
So you cower duly at your keeper's beck!
Cat, show what claws were made for, muffling them
Only to me! Cheat others if you can,
Me, if you dare!" And, my wise sir, I dared—
Did cheat you first, made you cheat others next,
And had the help o' your vaunted manliness
To bully the incredulous. You used me?
Have not I used you, taken full revenge,
Persuaded folk they knew not their own name,
And straight they 'd own the error! Who was the fool
When, to an awe-struck wide-eyed open-mouthed
Circle of sages, Sludge would introduce
Milton composing baby-rhymes, and Locke
Reasoning in gibberish, Homer writing Greek
In noughts and crosses, Asaph setting psalms

To crotchet and quaver? I 've made a spirit squeak
In sham voice for a minute, then outbroke
Bold in my own, defying the imbeciles —
Have copied some ghost's pothooks, half a page,
Then ended with my own scrawl undisguised.
"All right! The ghost was merely using Sludge,
Suiting itself from his imperfect stock!"
Don't talk of gratitude to me! For what?
For being treated as a showman's ape,
Encouraged to be wicked and make sport,
Fret or sulk, grin or whimper, any mood
So long as the ape be in it and no man —
Because a nut pays every mood alike.
Curse your superior, superintending sort,
Who, since you hate smoke, send up boys that climb
To cure your chimney, bid a "medium" lie
To sweep you truth down! Curse your women too,
Your insolent wives and daughters, that fire up
Or faint away if a male hand squeeze theirs,
Yet, to encourage Sludge, may play with Sludge
As only a "medium," only the kind of thing
They must humor, fondle . . . oh, to misconceive
Were too preposterous! But I 've paid them out!
They 've had their wish — called for the naked truth,
And in she tripped, sat down and bade them stare:
They had to blush a little and forgive!
"The fact is, children talk so; in next world
All our conventions are reversed, — perhaps
Made light of: something like old prints, my dear!
The Judge has one, he brought from Italy,
A metropolis in the background, — o'er a bridge,
A team of trotting roadsters, — cheerful groups
Of wayside travellers, peasants at their work,
And, full in front, quite unconcerned, why not?
Three nymphs conversing with a cavalier,
And never a rag among them: 'fine,' folk cry —
And heavenly manners seem not much unlike!
Let Sludge go on; we 'll fancy it 's in print!"
If such as came for wool, sir, went home shorn,
Where is the wrong I did them? 'T was their choice;
They tried the adventure, ran the risk, tossed up
And lost, as some one 's sure to do in games;
They fancied I was made to lose, — smoked glass
Useful to spy the sun through, spare their eyes:
And had I proved a red-hot iron plate
They thought to pierce, and, for their pains, grew blind,

Whose were the fault but theirs? While, as things go,
Their loss amounts to gain, the more 's the shame!
They 've had their peep into the spirit-world,
And all this world may know it! They 've fed fat
Their self-conceit which else had starved : what chance
Save this, of cackling o'er a golden egg
And compassing distinction from the flock,
Friends of a feather? Well, they paid for it,
And not prodigiously ; the price o' the play,
Not counting certain pleasant interludes,
Was scarce a vulgar play's worth. When you buy
The actor's talent, do you dare propose
For his soul beside? Whereas, my soul you buy!
Sludge acts Macbeth, obliged to be Macbeth,
Or you 'll not hear his first word! Just go through
That slight formality, swear himself 's the Thane,
And thenceforth he may strut and fret his hour,
Spout, spawl, or spin his target, no one cares!
Why had n't I leave to play tricks, Sludge as Sludge?
Enough of it all! I 've wiped out scores with you —
Vented your fustian, let myself be streaked
Like tom-fool with your ochre and carmine,
Worn patchwork your respectable fingers sewed
To metamorphose somebody, — yes, I 've earned
My wages, swallowed down my bread of shame,
And shake the crumbs off — where but in your face?

As for religion — why, I served it, sir!
I 'll stick to that! With my *phenomena*
I laid the atheist sprawling on his back,
Propped up Saint Paul, or, at least, Swedenborg!
In fact, it 's just the proper way to balk
These troublesome fellows — liars, one and all,
Are not these sceptics? Well, to baffle them,
No use in being squeamish : lie yourself!
Erect your buttress just as wide o' the line,
Your side, as they build up the wall on theirs ;
Where both meet, midway in a point, is truth,
High overhead : so, take your room, pile bricks,
Lie! Oh, there 's titillation in all shame!
What snow may lose in white, snow gains in rose!
Miss Stokes turns — Rahab, — nor a bad exchange!
Glory be on her, for the good she wrought,
Breeding belief anew 'neath ribs of death,
Browbeating now the unabashed before,
Ridding us of their whole life's gathered straws

By a live coal from the altar! Why, of old,
Great men spent years and years in writing books
To prove we 've souls, and hardly proved it then:
Miss Stokes with her live coal, for you and me!
Surely, to this good issue, all was fair—
Not only fondling Sludge, but, even suppose
He let escape some spice of knavery,— well,
In wisely being blind to it! Don't you praise
Nelson for setting spy-glass to blind eye
And saying . . . what was it— that he could not see
The signal he was bothered with? Ay, indeed!

I 'll go beyond: there 's a real love of a lie,
Liars find ready-made for lies they make,
As hand for glove, or tongue for sugar-plum.
At best, 't is never pure and full belief;
Those furthest in the quagmire,— don't suppose
They strayed there with no warning, got no chance
Of a filth-speck in their face, which they clenched teeth,
Bent brow against! Be sure they had their doubts,
And fears, and fairest challenges to try
The floor o' the seeming solid sand! But no!
Their faith was pledged, acquaintance too apprised,
All but the last step ventured, kerchiefs waved,
And Sludge called "pet:" 't was easier marching on
To the promised land; join those who, Thursday next,
Meant to meet Shakespeare; better follow Sludge —
Prudent, oh sure!— on the alert, how else?
But making for the mid-bog, all the same!
To hear your outcries, one would think I caught
Miss Stokes by the scruff o' the neck, and pitched her flat,
Foolish-face-foremost! Hear these simpletons,
That 's all I beg, before my work 's begun,
Before I 've touched them with my finger-tip!
Thus they await me (do but listen, now!
It 's reasoning, this is,— I can't imitate
The baby voice, though),— "In so many tales
Must be some truth, truth though a pin-point big,
Yet, some: a single man 's deceived, perhaps —
Hardly, a thousand: to suppose one cheat
Can gull all these, were more miraculous far
Than aught we should confess a miracle," —
And so on. Then the Judge sums up — (it 's rare)
Bids you respect the authorities that leap
To the judgment-seat at once,— why don't you note
The limpid nature, the unblemished life,

The spotless honor, indisputable sense
Of the first upstart with his story? What —
Outrage a boy on whom you ne'er till now
Set eyes, because he finds raps trouble him?

Fools, these are: ay, and how of their opposites
Who never did, at bottom of their hearts,
Believe for a moment? — Men emasculate,
Blank of belief, who played, as eunuchs use,
With superstition safely, — cold of blood,
Who saw what made for them i' the mystery,
Took their occasion, and supported Sludge
— As proselytes? No, thank you, far too shrewd!
— But promisers of fair play, encouragers
O' the claimant; who in candor needs must hoist
Sludge up on Mars' Hill, get speech out of Sludge
To carry off, criticise, and cant about!
Did n't Athens treat Saint Paul so? — at any rate,
It's "a new thing," philosophy fumbles at.
Then there's the other picker-out of pearl
From dungheaps, — ay, your literary man,
Who draws on his kid gloves to deal with Sludge
Daintily and discreetly, — shakes a dust
O' the doctrine, flavors thence, he well knows how,
The narrative or the novel, — half-believes,
All for the book's sake, and the public's stare,
And the cash that's God's sole solid in this world!
Look at him! Try to be too bold, too gross
For the master! Not you! He's the man for muck;
Shovel it forth, full-splash, he'll smooth your brown
Into artistic richness, never fear!
Find him the crude stuff; when you recognize
Your lie again, you'll doff your hat to it,
Dressed out for company! "For company,"
I say, since there's the relish of success:
Let all pay due respect, call the lie truth,
Save the soft silent smirking gentleman
Who ushered in the stranger: you must sigh
"How melancholy, he, the only one,
Fails to perceive the bearing of the truth
Himself gave birth to!" — There's the triumph's smack!
That man would choose to see the whole world roll
I' the slime o' the slough, so he might touch the tip
Of his brush with what I call the best of browns —
Tint ghost-tales, spirit-stories, past the power
Of the outworn umber and bistre!

                                    Yet I think
There 's a more hateful form of foolery —
The social sage's, Solomon of saloons
And philosophic diner-out, the fribble
Who wants a doctrine for a chopping-block
To try the edge of his faculty upon,
Prove how much common sense he 'll hack and hew
I' the critical minute 'twixt the soup and fish!
These were my patrons: these, and the like of them
Who, rising in my soul now, sicken it, —
These I have injured! Gratitude to these?
The gratitude, forsooth, of a prostitute
To the greenhorn and the bully — friends of hers,
From the wag that wants the queer jokes for his club,
To the snuffbox-decorator, honest man,
Who just was at his wits' end where to find
So genial a Pasiphae! All and each
Pay, compliment, protect from the police:
And how she hates them for their pains, like me!
So much for my remorse at thanklessness
Toward a deserving public!

                                    But, for God?
Ay, that 's a question! Well, sir, since you press —
(How you do tease the whole thing out of me!
I don't mean you, you know, when I say "them:"
Hate you, indeed! But that Miss Stokes, that Judge!
Enough, enough — with sugar: thank you, sir!)
Now for it, then! Will you believe me, though?
You 've heard what I confess; I don't unsay
A single word: I cheated when I could,
Rapped with my toe-joints, set sham hands at work,
Wrote down names weak in sympathetic ink,
Rubbed odic lights with ends of phosphor-match,
And all the rest; believe that: believe this,
By the same token, though it seem to set
The crooked straight again, unsay the said,
Stick up what I 've knocked down; I can't help that
It 's truth! I somehow vomit truth to-day.
This trade of mine — I don't know, can't be sure
But there was something in it, tricks and all!
Really, I want to light up my own mind.
They were tricks, — true, but what I mean to add
Is also true. First, — don't it strike you, sir?
Go back to the beginning, — the first fact
We 're taught is, there 's a world beside this world,
With spirits, not mankind, for tenantry;

That much within that world once sojourned here,
That all upon this world will visit there,
And therefore that we, bodily here below,
Must have exactly such an interest
In learning what may be the ways o' the world
Above us, as the disembodied folk
Have (by all analogic likelihood)
In watching how things go in the old home
With us, their sons, successors, and what not.
Oh, yes, with added powers probably,
Fit for the novel state, — old loves grown pure,
Old interests understood aright, — they watch!
Eyes to see, ears to hear, and hands to help,
Proportionate to advancement: they're ahead,
That's all — do what we do, but noblier done —
Use plate, whereas we eat our meals off delf,
(To use a figure.)

Concede that, and I ask
Next what may be the mode of intercourse
Between us men here, and those once-men there?
First comes the Bible's speech; then, history
With the supernatural element, — you know —
All that we sucked in with our mothers' milk,
Grew up with, got inside of us at last,
Till it's found bone of bone and flesh of flesh.
See now, we start with the miraculous,
And know it used to be, at all events:
What's the first step we take, and can't but take,
In arguing from the known to the obscure?
Why this: "What was before, may be to-day.
Since Samuel's ghost appeared to Saul, — of course
My brother's spirit may appear to me."
Go tell your teacher that! What's his reply?
What brings a shade of doubt for the first time
O'er his brow late so luminous with faith?
"Such things have been," says he, "and there's no doubt
Such things may be: but I advise mistrust
Of eyes, ears, stomach, and, more than all, your brain,
Unless it be of your great-grandmother,
Whenever they propose a ghost to you!"
The end is, there's a composition struck;
'T is settled, we've some way of intercourse
Just as in Saul's time; only, different:
How, when and where, precisely, — find it out!
I want to know, then, what's so natural

As that a person born into this world
And seized on by such teaching, should begin
With firm expectancy and a frank look-out
For his own allotment, his especial share
I' the secret, — his particular ghost, in fine?
I mean, a person born to look that way,
Since natures differ: take the painter-sort,
One man lives fifty years in ignorance
Whether grass be green or red, — "No kind of eye
For color," say you; while another picks
And puts away even pebbles, when a child,
Because of bluish spots and pinky veins —
"Give him forthwith a paint-box!" Just the same
Was I born . . . "medium," you won't let me say, —
Well, seer of the supernatural
Everywhen, everyhow, and everywhere, —
Will that do?

      I and all such boys of course
Started with the same stock of Bible-truth;
Only, — what in the rest you style their sense,
Instinct, blind reasoning but imperative,
This, betimes, taught them the old world had one law
And ours another: "New world, new laws," cried they:
"None but old laws, seen everywhere at work,"
Cried I, and by their help explained my life
The Jews' way, still a working way to me.
Ghosts made the noises, fairies waved the lights,
Or Santaclaus slid down on New Year's Eve
And stuffed with cakes the stocking at my bed,
Changed the worn shoes, rubbed clean the fingered slate
O' the sum that came to grief the day before.

This could not last long: soon enough I found
Who had worked wonders thus, and to what end:
But did I find all easy, like my mates?
Henceforth no supernatural any more?
Not a whit: what projects the billiard-balls?
"A cue," you answer. "Yes, a cue," said I;
"But what hand, off the cushion, moved the cue?
What unseen agency, outside the world,
Prompted its puppets to do this and that,
Put cakes and shoes and slates into their mind,
These mothers and aunts, nay even schoolmasters?"
Thus high I sprang, and there have settled since.
Just so I reason, in sober earnest still,

About the greater godsends, what you call
The serious gains and losses of my life.
What do I know or care about your world
Which either is or seems to be? This snap
O' my fingers, sir! My care is for myself;
Myself am whole and sole reality
Inside a raree-show and a market-mob
Gathered about it: that's the use of things.
'T is easy saying they serve vast purposes,
Advantage their grand selves: be it true or false,
Each thing may have two uses. What's a star?
A world, or a world's sun: does n't it serve
As taper also, timepiece, weather-glass,
And almanac? Are stars not set for signs
When we should shear our sheep, sow corn, prune trees?
The Bible says so.

     Well, I add one use
To all the acknowledged uses, and declare
If I spy Charles's Wain at twelve to-night,
It warns me, "Go, nor lose another day,
And have your hair cut, Sludge!" You laugh: and why?
Were such a sign too hard for God to give?
No: but Sludge seems too little for such grace:
Thank you, sir! So you think, so does not Sludge!
When you and good men gape at Providence,
Go into history and bid us mark
Not merely powder-plots prevented, crowns
Kept on kings' heads by miracle enough,
But private mercies — oh, you 've told me, sir,
Of such interpositions! How yourself
Once, missing on a memorable day
Your handkerchief — just setting out, you know, —
You must return to fetch it, lost the train,
And saved your precious self from what befell
The thirty-three whom Providence forgot.
You tell, and ask me what I think of this?
Well, sir, I think then, since you needs must know,
What matter had you and Boston city to boot
Sailed skyward, like burnt onion-peelings? Much
To you, no doubt: for me — undoubtedly
The cutting of my hair concerns me more,
Because, however sad the truth may seem,
Sludge is of all-importance to himself.
You set apart that day in every year
For special thanksgiving, were a heathen else:

Well, I who cannot boast the like escape,
Suppose I said, " I don't thank Providence
For my part, owing it no gratitude " ?
" Nay, but you owe as much," — you 'd tutor me,
" You, every man alive, for blessings gained
In every hour o' the day, could you but know!
I saw my crowning mercy: all have such,
Could they but see!" Well, sir, why don't they see?
" Because they won't look, — or, perhaps, they can't."
Then, sir, suppose I can, and will, and do
Look, microscopically as is right,
Into each hour with its infinitude
Of influences at work to profit Sludge?
For that 's the case: I 've sharpened up my sight
To spy a providence in the fire's going out,
The kettle's boiling, the dime's sticking fast
Despite the hole i' the pocket. Call such facts
Fancies, too petty a work for Providence,
And those same thanks which you exact from me
Prove too prodigious payment: thanks for what,
If nothing guards and guides us little men?
No, no, sir! You must put away your pride,
Resolve to let Sludge into partnership!
I live by signs and omens: looked at the roof
Where the pigeons settle — " If the further bird,
The white, takes wing first, I 'll confess when thrashed;
Not, if the blue does," — so I said to myself
Last week, lest you should take me by surprise:
Off flapped the white, — and I 'm confessing, sir!
Perhaps 't is Providence's whim and way
With only me, i' the world: how can you tell?
"Because unlikely!" Was it likelier, now,
That this our one out of all worlds beside,
The what-d'you-call-'em millions, should be just
Precisely chosen to make Adam for,
And the rest o' the tale? Yet the tale 's true, you know:
Such undeserving clod was graced so once;
Why not graced likewise undeserving Sludge?
Are we merit-mongers, flaunt we filthy rags?
All you can bring against my privilege
Is, that another way was taken with you, —
Which I don't question. It 's pure grace, my luck:
I 'm broken to the way of nods and winks,
And need no formal summoning. You 've a help;
Holloa his name or whistle, clap your hands,
Stamp with your foot or pull the bell: all 's one,

He understands you want him, here he comes.
Just so, I come at the knocking: you, sir, wait
The tongue o' the bell, nor stir before you catch
Reason's clear tingle, nature's clapper brisk,
Or that traditional peal was wont to cheer
Your mother's face turned heavenward: short of these
There 's no authentic intimation, eh?
Well, when you hear, you 'll answer them, start up
And stride into the presence, top of toe,
And there find Sludge beforehand, Sludge that sprang
At noise o' the knuckle on the partition-wall!
I think myself the more religious man.
Religion 's all or nothing; it 's no mere smile
O' contentment, sigh of aspiration, sir —
No quality o' the finelier-tempered clay
Like its whiteness or its lightness; rather, stuff
O' the very stuff, life of life, and self of self.
I tell you, men won't notice; when they do,
They 'll understand. I notice nothing else:
I 'm eyes, ears, mouth of me, one gaze and gape,
Nothing eludes me, everything 's a hint,
Handle and help. It 's all absurd, and yet
There 's something in it all, I know: how much?
No answer! What does that prove? Man 's still man,
Still meant for a poor blundering piece of work
When all 's done; but, if somewhat 's done, like this,
Or not done, is the case the same? Suppose
I blunder in my guess at the true sense
O' the knuckle-summons, nine times out of ten, —
What if the tenth guess happen to be right?
If the tenth shovel-load of powdered quartz
Yield me the nugget? I gather, crush, sift all,
Pass o'er the failure, pounce on the success.
To give you a notion, now — (let who wins, laugh!)
When first I see a man, what do I first?
Why, count the letters which make up his name,
And as their number chances, even or odd,
Arrive at my conclusion, trim my course:
Hiram H. Horsefall is your honored name,
And have n't I found a patron, sir, in you?
"Shall I cheat this stranger?" I take apple-pips,
Stick one in either *canthus* of my eye,
And if the left drops first — (your left, sir, stuck)
I 'm warned, I let the trick alone this time.
You, sir, who smile, superior to such trash,
You judge of character by other rules:

Don't your rules sometimes fail you ? Pray, what rule
Have you judged Sludge by hitherto ?

                                      Oh, be sure,
You, everybody blunders, just as I,
In simpler things than these by far! For see:
I knew two farmers, — one, a wiseacre
Who studied seasons, rummaged almanacs,
Quoted the dew-point, registered the frost,
And then declared, for outcome of his pains,
Next summer must be dampish: 't was a drought.
His neighbor prophesied such drought would fall,
Saved hay and corn, made cent. per cent. thereby,
And proved a sage indeed: how came his lore ?
Because one brindled heifer, late in March,
Stiffened her tail of evenings, and somehow
He got into his head that drought was meant!
I don't expect all men can do as much:
Such kissing goes by favor. You must take
A certain turn of mind for this, — a twist
I' the flesh, as well. Be lazily alive,
Open-mouthed, like my friend the ant-eater,
Letting all nature's loosely-guarded motes
Settle and, slick, be swallowed! Think yourself
The one i' the world, the one for whom the world
Was made, expect it tickling at your mouth!
Then will the swarm of busy buzzing flies,
Clouds of coincidence, break egg-shell, thrive,
Breed, multiply, and bring you food enough.

I can't pretend to mind your smiling, sir!
Oh, what you mean is this! Such intimate way,
Close converse, frank exchange of offices,
Strict sympathy of the immeasurably great
With the infinitely small, betokened here
By a course of signs and omens, raps and sparks, —
How does it suit the dread traditional text
O' the " Great and Terrible Name "? Shall the Heaven
    of Heavens
Stoop to such child's play ?

                             Please, sir, go with me
A moment, and I 'll try to answer you.
The " *Magnum et terribile* " (is that right ?)
Well, folk began with this in the early day ;
And all the acts they recognized in proof

Were thunders, lightnings, earthquakes, whirlwinds, dealt
Indisputably on men whose death they caused.
There, and there only, folk saw Providence
At work, — and seeing it, 't was right enough
All heads should tremble, hands wring hands amain,
And knees knock hard together at the breath
O' the Name's first letter; why, the Jews, I 'm told,
Won't write it down, no, to this very hour,
Nor speak aloud : you know best if 't be so.
Each ague-fit of fear at end, they crept
(Because somehow people once born must live)
Out of the sound, sight, swing and sway o' the Name,
Into a corner, the dark rest of the world,
And safe space where as yet no fear had reached ;
'T was there they looked about them, breathed again,
And felt indeed at home, as we might say.
The current o' common things, the daily life,
This had their due contempt ; no Name pursued
Man from the mountain-top where fires abide,
To his particular mouse-hole at its foot
Where he ate, drank, digested, lived in short :
Such was man's vulgar business, far too small
To be worth thunder : " small," folk kept on, " small,"
With much complacency in those great days!
A mote of sand, you know, a blade of grass —
What was so despicable as mere grass,
Except perhaps the life o' the worm or fly
Which fed there? These were "small" and men were
    great.
Well, sir, the old way 's altered somewhat since,
And the world wears another aspect now :
Somebody turns our spyglass round, or else
Puts a new lens in it : grass, worm, fly grow big :
We find great things are made of little things,
And little things go lessening till at last
Comes God behind them. Talk of mountains now ?
We talk of mould that heaps the mountain, mites
That throng the mould, and God that makes the mites.
The Name comes close behind a stomach-cyst,
The simplest of creations, just a sac
That 's mouth, heart, legs and belly at once, yet lives
And feels, and could do neither, we conclude,
If simplified still further one degree :
The small becomes the dreadful and immense !
Lightning, forsooth? No word more upon that!
A tin-foil bottle, a strip of greasy silk,

With a bit of wire and knob of brass, and there's
Your dollar's-worth of lightning! But the cyst—
The life of the least of the little things?

          No, no!
Preachers and teachers try another tack,
Come near the truth this time: they put aside
Thunder and lightning. "That's mistake," they cry;
" Thunderbolts fall for neither fright nor sport,
But do appreciable good, like tides,
Changes o' the wind, and other natural facts—
'Good' meaning good to man, his body or soul.
Mediate, immediate, all things minister
To man,—that's settled: be our future text
'We are His children!'" So, they now harangue
About the intention, the contrivance, all
That keeps up an incessant play of love,—
See the Bridgewater book.

         Amen to it!
Well, sir, I put this question: I'm a child?
I lose no time, but take you at your word:
How shall I act a child's part properly?
Your sainted mother, sir,—used you to live
With such a thought as this a-worrying you?
" She has it in her power to throttle me,
Or stab or poison: she may turn me out,
Or lock me in,—nor stop at this to-day,
But cut me off to-morrow from the estate
I look for "—(long may you enjoy it, sir!)
" In brief, she may unchild the child I am."
You never had such crotchets? Nor have I!
Who, frank confessing childship from the first,
Cannot both fear and take my ease at once,
So, don't fear,—know what might be, well enough,
But know too, child-like, that it will not be,
At least in my case, mine, the son and heir
O' the kingdom, as yourself proclaim my style.
But do you fancy I stop short at this?
Wonder if suit and service, son and heir
Needs must expect, I dare pretend to find?
If, looking for signs proper to such an one,
I straight perceive them irresistible?
Concede that homage is a son's plain right,
And, never mind the nods and raps and winks,
'T is the pure obvious supernatural

Steps forward, does its duty: why, of course!
I have presentiments; my dreams come true:
I fancy a friend stands whistling all in white
Blithe as a boblink, and he's dead I learn.
I take dislike to a dog my favorite long,
And sell him; he goes mad next week and snaps.
I guess that stranger will turn up to-day
I have not seen these three years; there's his knock.
I wager "sixty peaches on that tree!" —
That I pick up a dollar in my walk,
That your wife's brother's cousin's name was George —
And win on all points. Oh, you wince at this?
You'd fain distinguish between gift and gift,
Washington's oracle and Sludge's itch
O' the elbow when at whist he ought to trump?
With Sludge it's too absurd? *Fine, draw the line
Somewhere, but, sir, your somewhere is not mine!*

Bless us, I'm turning poet! It's time to end.
How you have drawn me out, sir! All I ask
Is — am I heir or not heir? If I'm he,
Then, sir, remember, that same personage
(To judge by what we read i' the newspaper)
Requires, beside one nobleman in gold
To carry up and down his coronet,
Another servant, probably a duke,
To hold eggnog in readiness: why want
Attendance, sir, when helps in his father's house
Abound, I'd like to know?

      Enough of talk!
My fault is that I tell too plain a truth.
Why, which of those who say they disbelieve,
Your clever people, but has dreamed his dream,
Caught his coincidence, stumbled on his fact
He can't explain, (he'll tell you smilingly,)
Which he's too much of a philosopher
To count as supernatural, indeed,
So calls a puzzle and problem, proud of it:
Bidding you still be on your guard, you know,
Because one fact don't make a system stand,
Nor prove this an occasional escape
Of spirit beneath the matter: that's the way!
Just so wild Indians picked up, piece by piece,
The fact in California, the fine gold
That underlay the gravel — hoarded these,

But never made a system stand, nor dug!
So wise men hold out in each hollowed palm
A handful of experience, sparkling fact
They can't explain; and since their rest of life
Is all explainable, what proof in this?
Whereas I take the fact, the grain of gold,
And fling away the dirty rest of life,
And add this grain to the grain each fool has found
O' the million other such philosophers, —
Till I see gold, all gold and only gold,
Truth questionless though unexplainable,
And the miraculous proved the commonplace!
The other fools believed in mud, no doubt —
Failed to know gold they saw: was that so strange?
Are all men born to play Bach's fiddle-fugues,
"Time" with the foil in carte, jump their own height,
Cut the mutton with the broadsword, skate a five,
Make the red hazard with the cue, clip nails
While swimming, in five minutes row a mile,
Pull themselves three feet up with the left arm,
Do sums of fifty figures in their head,
And so on, by the scores of instances?
The Sludge with luck, who sees the spiritual facts,
His fellows strive and fail to see, may rank
With these, and share the advantage.

Ay, but share
The drawback! Think it over by yourself;
I have not heart, sir, and the fire's gone gray.
Defect somewhere compensates for success,
Every one knows that. Oh, we're equals, sir!
The big-legged fellow has a little arm
And a less brain, though big legs win the race:
Do you suppose I 'scape the common lot?
Say, I was born with flesh so sensitive,
Soul so alert, that, practice helping both,
I guess what's going on outside the veil,
Just as a prisoned crane feels pairing-time
In the islands where his kind are, so must fall
To capering by himself some shiny night,
As if your back-yard were a plot of spice —
Thus am I 'ware o' the spirit-world: while you,
Blind as a beetle that way, — for amends,
Why, you can double fist and floor me, sir!
Ride that hot hardmouthed horrid horse of yours,
Laugh while it lightens, play with the great dog,

Speak your mind though it vex some friend to hear,
Never brag, never bluster, never blush, —
In short, you've pluck, when I'm a coward — there!
I know it, I can't help it, — folly or no,
I'm paralyzed, my hand's no more a hand,
Nor my head, a head, in danger: you can smile
And change the pipe in your cheek. Your gift's not mine.
Would you swap for mine? No! but you'd add my gift
To yours: I dare say! I too sigh at times,
Wish I were stouter, could tell truth nor flinch,
Kept cool when threatened, did not mind so much
Being dressed gayly, making strangers stare,
Eating nice things; when I'd amuse myself,
I shut my eyes and fancy in my brain,
I'm — now the President, now Jenny Lind,
Now Emerson, now the Benicia Boy —
With all the civilized world a-wondering
And worshipping. I know it's folly and worse;
I feel such tricks sap, honeycomb the soul,
But I can't cure myself, — despond, despair,
And then, hey, presto, there's a turn o' the wheel,
Under comes uppermost, fate makes full amends;
Sludge knows and sees and hears a hundred things
You all are blind to, — I've my taste of truth,
Likewise my touch of falsehood, — vice no doubt,
But you've your vices also: I'm content.

What, sir? You won't shake hands? "Because I cheat!"
"You've found me out in cheating!" That's enough
To make an apostle swear! Why, when I cheat,
*Mean to cheat, do cheat, and am caught in the act,
Are you, or rather, am I sure o' the fact?*
(There's verse again, but I'm inspired somehow.)
Well then I'm not sure! I may be, perhaps,
Free as a babe from cheating: how it began,
My gift, — no matter; what 't is got to be
In the end now, that's the question; answer that!
Had I seen, perhaps, what hand was holding mine,
Leading me whither, I had died of fright:
So, I was made believe I led myself.
If I should lay a six-inch plank from roof
To roof, you would not cross the street, one step,
Even at your mother's summons: but, being shrewd,
If I paste paper on each side the plank
And swear 't is solid pavement, why, you'll cross
Humming a tune the while, in ignorance

Beacon Street stretches a hundred feet below:
I walked thus, took the paper-cheat for stone.
Some impulse made me set a thing o' the move
Which, started once, ran really by itself;
Beer flows thus, suck the siphon; toss the kite,
It takes the wind and floats of its own force.
Don't let truth's lump rot stagnant for the lack
Of a timely helpful lie to leaven it!
Put a chalk-egg beneath the clucking hen,
She 'll lay a real one, laudably deceived,
Daily for weeks to come. I 've told my lie,
And seen truth follow, marvels none of mine;
All was not cheating, sir, I 'm positive!
I don't know if I move your hand sometimes
When the spontaneous writing spreads so far,
If my knee lifts the table all that height,
Why the inkstand don't fall off the desk a-tilt,
Why the accordion plays a prettier waltz
Than I can pick out on the pianoforte,
Why I speak so much more than I intend,
Describe so many things I never saw.
I tell you, sir, in one sense, I believe
Nothing at all, — that everybody can,
Will, and does cheat: but in another sense
I 'm ready to believe my very self —
That every cheat 's inspired, and every lie
Quick with a germ of truth.

       You ask perhaps
Why I should condescend to trick at all
If I know a way without it? This is why!
There 's a strange secret sweet self-sacrifice
In any desecration of one's soul
To a worthy end, — is n't it Herodotus
(I wish I could read Latin!) who describes
The single gift o' the land's virginity,
Demanded in those old Egyptian rites,
(I 've but a hazy notion — help me, sir!)
For one purpose in the world, one day in a life,
One hour in a day — thereafter, purity,
And a veil thrown o'er the past forevermore!
Well now, they understood a many things
Down by Nile city, or wherever it was!
I 've always vowed, after the minute's lie,
And the end's gain, — truth should be mine henceforth.
This goes to the root o' the matter, sir, — this plain

Plump fact: accept it and unlock with it
The wards of many a puzzle!

                        Or, finally,
Why should I set so fine a gloss on things?
What need I care? I cheat in self-defence,
And there's my answer to a world of cheats!
Cheat? To be sure, sir! What's the world worth else?
Who takes it as he finds, and thanks his stars?
Don't it want trimming, turning, furbishing up
And polishing over? Your so-styled great men,
Do they accept one truth as truth is found,
Or try their skill at tinkering? What's your world?
Here are you born, who are, I'll say at once,
Of the luckiest kind, whether in head and heart,
Body and soul, or all that helps them both.
Well, now, look back: what faculty of yours
Came to its full, had ample justice done
By growing when rain fell, biding its time,
Solidifying growth when earth was dead,
Spiring up, broadening wide, in seasons due?
Never! You shot up and frost nipped you off,
Settled to sleep when sunshine bade you sprout;
One faculty thwarted its fellow: at the end,
All you boast is, "I had proved a topping tree
In other climes,"—yet this was the right clime
Had you foreknown the seasons. Young, you've force
Wasted like well-streams: old,—oh, then indeed,
Behold a labyrinth of hydraulic pipes
Through which you'd play off wondrous waterwork;
Only, no water's left to feed their play.
Young,—you've a hope, an aim, a love; it's tossed
And crossed and lost: you struggle on, some spark
Shut in your heart against the puffs around,
Through cold and pain; these in due time subside,
Now then for age's triumph, the hoarded light
You mean to loose on the altered face of things,—
Up with it on the tripod! It's extinct.
Spend your life's remnant asking, which was best,
Light smothered up that never peeped forth once,
Or the cold cresset with full leave to shine?
Well, accept this too,—seek the fruit of it
Not in enjoyment, proved a dream on earth,
But knowledge, useful for a second chance,
Another life,—you've lost this world—you've gained
Its knowledge for the next.—What knowledge, sir,

Except that you know nothing? Nay, you doubt
Whether 't were better have made you man or brute,
If aught be true, if good and evil clash.
No foul, no fair, no inside, no outside,
There 's your world!

      Give it me! I slap it brisk
With harlequin's pasteboard sceptre: what 's it now?
Changed like a rock-flat, rough with rusty weed,
At first wash-over o' the returning wave!
All the dry dead impracticable stuff
Starts into life and light again; this world
Pervaded by the influx from the next.
I cheat, and what 's the happy consequence?
You find full justice straightway dealt you out,
Each want supplied, each ignorance set at ease,
Each folly fooled. No life-long labor now
As the price of worse than nothing! No mere film
Holding you chained in iron, as it seems,
Against the outstretch of your very arms
And legs i' the sunshine moralists forbid!
What would you have? Just speak and, there, you see!
You 're supplemented, made a whole at last,
Bacon advises, Shakespeare writes you songs,
And Mary Queen of Scots embraces you.
Thus it goes on, not quite like life perhaps,
But so near, that the very difference piques,
Shows that e'en better than this best will be —
This passing entertainment in a hut
Whose bare walls take your taste since, one stage more,
And you arrive at the palace: all half real,
And you, to suit it, less than real beside,
In a dream, lethargic kind of death in life,
That helps the interchange of natures, flesh
Transfused by souls, and such souls! Oh, 't is choice!
And if at whiles the bubble, blown too thin,
Seem nigh on bursting, — if you nearly see
The real world through the false, — what *do* you see?
Is the old so ruined? You find you 're in a flock
O' the youthful, earnest, passionate — genius, beauty,
Rank and wealth also, if you care for these·
And all depose their natural rights, hail you
(That 's me, sir) as their mate and yoke-fellow.
Participate in Sludgehood — nay, grow mine,
I veritably possess them — banish doubt,
And reticence and modesty alike!

Why, here's the Golden Age, old Paradise
Or new Utopia! Here's true life indeed,
And the world well won now, mine for the first time!

And all this might be, may be, and with good help
Of a little lying shall be: so, Sludge lies!
Why, he's at worst your poet who sings how Greeks
That never were, in Troy which never was,
Did this or the other impossible great thing!
He's Lowell — it's a world (you smile applause)
Of his own invention — wondrous Longfellow,
Surprising Hawthorne! Sludge does more than they,
And acts the books they write: the more his praise!

But why do I mount to poets? Take plain prose —
Dealers in common sense, set these at work,
What can they do without their helpful lies?
Each states the law and fact and face o' the thing
Just as he'd have them, finds what he thinks fit,
Is blind to what missuits him, just records
What makes his case out, quite ignores the rest.
It's a History of the World, the Lizard Age,
The Early Indians, the Old Country War,
Jerome Napoleon, whatsoever you please,
All as the author wants it. Such a scribe
You pay and praise for putting life in stones,
Fire into fog, making the past your world.
There's plenty of "How did you contrive to grasp
The thread which led you through this labyrinth?
How build such solid fabric out of air?
How on so slight foundation found this tale,
Biography, narrative?" or, in other words,
"How many lies did it require to make
The portly truth you here present us with?"
"Oh," quoth the penman, purring at your praise,
"'T is fancy all; no particle of fact:
I was poor and threadbare when I wrote that book
'Bliss in the Golden City.' I, at Thebes?
We writers paint out of our heads, you see!"
"— Ah, the more wonderful the gift in you,
The more creativeness and godlike craft!"
But I, do I present you with my piece,
It's "What, Sludge? When my sainted mother spoke
The verses Lady Jane Grey last composed
About the rosy bower in the seventh heaven
Where she and Queen Elizabeth keep house, —

You made the raps? 'T was your invention that?
Cur, slave, and devil!" — eight fingers and two thumbs
Stuck in my throat!

     Well, if the marks seem gone,
'T is because stiffish cocktail, taken in time,
Is better for a bruise than arnica.
There, sir! I bear no malice: 't is n't in me.
I know I acted wrongly: still, I 've tried
What I could say in my excuse, — to show
The devil 's not all devil . . . I don't pretend
He 's angel, much less such a gentleman
As you, sir! And I 've lost you, lost myself,
Lost all-l-l-l- . . .

     No — are you in earnest, sir?
Oh, yours, sir, is an angel's part! I know
What prejudice prompts, and what 's the common course
Men take to soothe their ruffled self-conceit:
Only you rise superior to it all!
No, sir, it don't hurt much; it 's speaking long
That makes me choke a little: the marks will go!
What? Twenty V-notes more, and outfit too,
And not a word to Greeley? One — one kiss
O' the haud that saves me! You 'll not let me speak,
I well know, and I 've lost the right, too true!
But I must say, sir, if She hears (she does)
Your sainted . . . Well, sir, — be it so! That 's, I think,
My bedroom candle. Good-night! Bl-l-less you, sir!

R-r-r, you brute-beast and blackguard! Cowardly scamp!
I only wish I dared burn down the house
And spoil your sniggering! Oh, what, you 're the man?
You 're satisfied at last? You 've found out Sludge?
We 'll see that presently: my turn, sir, next!
I too can tell my story: brute, — do you hear? —
You throttled your sainted mother, that old hag,
In just such a fit of passion: no, it was . . .
To get this house of hers, and many a note
Like these . . . I 'll pocket them, however . . . five,
Ten, fifteen . . . ay, you gave her throat the twist,
Or else you poisoned her! Confound the cuss!
Where was my head? I ought to have prophesied
He 'll die in a year and join her: that 's the way.

I don't know where my head is : what had I done?
How did it all go? I said he poisoned her,
And hoped he 'd have grace given him to repent,
Whereon he picked this quarrel, bullied me
And called me cheat : I thrashed him, — who could help?
He howled for mercy, prayed me on his knees
To cut and run and save him from disgrace :
I do so, and once off, he slanders me.
An end of him! Begin elsewhere anew!
Boston 's a hole, the herring-pond is wide,
V-notes are something, liberty still more.
Beside, is he the only fool in the world?

APPARENT FAILURE.

"We shall soon lose a celebrated building."
Paris Newspaper.

I.

No, for I 'll save it! Seven years since,
   I passed through Paris, stopped a day
To see the baptism of your Prince;
   Saw, made my bow, and went my way:
Walking the heat and headache off,
   I took the Seine-side, you surmise,
Thought of the Congress, Gortschakoff,
   Cavour's appeal and Buol's replies,
So sauntered till — what met my eyes?

II.

Only the Doric little Morgue!
   The dead-house where you show your drowned:
Petrarch's Vaucluse makes proud the Sorgue,
   Your Morgue has made the Seine renowned.
One pays one's debt in such a case;
   I plucked up heart and entered, — stalked,
Keeping a tolerable face
   Compared with some whose cheeks were chalked:
Let them! No Briton 's to be balked!

III.

First came the silent gazers; next,
   A screen of glass, we 're thankful for;
Last, the sight's self, the sermon's text,

The three men who did most abhor
Their life in Paris yesterday,
  So killed themselves : and now, enthroned
Each on his copper couch, they lay
  Fronting me, waiting to be owned.
I thought, and think, their sin 's atoned.

IV.

Poor men, God made, and all for that!
  The reverence struck me ; o'er each head
Religiously was hung its hat,
  Each coat dripped by the owner's bed,
Sacred from touch : each had his berth,
  His bounds, his proper place of rest,
Who last night tenanted on earth
  Some arch, where twelve such slept abreast, —
Unless the plain asphalte seemed best.

V.

How did it happen, my poor boy?
  You wanted to be Buonaparte
And have the Tuileries for toy,
  And could not, so it broke your heart?
You, old one by his side, I judge,
  Were, red as blood, a socialist,
A leveller! Does the Empire grudge
  You 've gained what no Republic missed?
Be quiet, and unclench your fist!

VI.

And this — why, he was red in vain,
  Or black, — poor fellow that is blue!
What fancy was it, turned your brain?
  Oh, women were the prize for you!
Money gets women, cards and dice
  Get money, and ill-luck gets just
The copper couch and one clear nice
  Cool squirt of water o'er your bust,
The right thing to extinguish lust!

VII.

It 's wiser being good than bad ;
  It 's safer being meek than fierce :
It 's fitter being sane than mad.
  My own hope is, a sun will pierce

The thickest cloud earth ever stretched;
That, after Last, returns the First,
Though a wide compass round be fetched;
That what began best, can't end worst,
Nor what God blessed once, prove accurst.

EPILOGUE.

FIRST SPEAKER, as *David*.

I.

ON the first of the Feast of Feasts,
   The Dedication Day,
When the Levites joined the Priests
   At the Altar in robed array,
Gave signal to sound and say, —

II.

When the thousands, rear and van,
   Swarming with one accord,
Became as a single man
   (Look, gesture, thought and word)
In praising and thanking the Lord, —

III.

When the singers lift up their voice,
   And the trumpets made endeavor,
Sounding, " In God rejoice ! "
   Saying, " In Him rejoice
Whose mercy endureth forever ! " —

IV.

Then the Temple filled with a cloud,
   Even the House of the Lord;
Porch bent and pillar bowed :
   For the presence of the Lord,
   In the glory of His cloud,
     Had filled the House of the Lord.

SECOND SPEAKER, as *Renan*.

Gone now ! All gone across the dark so far,
   Sharpening fast, shuddering ever, shutting still,

 Dwindling into the distance, dies that star
  Which came, stood, opened once! We gazed our fill
 With upturned faces on as real a Face
  That, stooping from grave music and mild fire,
 Took in our homage, made a visible place
  Through many a depth of glory, gyre on gyre,
 For the dim human tribute. Was this true?
  Could man indeed avail, mere praise of his,
 To help by rapture God's own rapture too,
  Thrill with a heart's red tinge that pure pale bliss?
 Why did it end? Who failed to beat the breast,
  And shriek, and throw the arms protesting wide,
 When a first shadow showed the star addressed
  Itself to motion, and on either side
 The rims contracted as the rays retired;
  The music, like a fountain's sickening pulse,
 Subsided on itself; awhile transpired
  Some vestige of a Face no pangs convulse,
 No prayers retard; then even this was gone,
  Lost in the night at last. We, lone and left
 Silent through centuries, ever and anon
  Venture to probe again the vault bereft
 Of all now save the lesser lights, a mist
  Of multitudinous points, yet suns, men say —
 And this leaps ruby, this lurks amethyst,
  But where may hide what came and loved our clay?
 How shall the sage detect in yon expanse
  The star which chose to stoop and stay for us?
 Unroll the records! Hailed ye such advance
  Indeed, and did your hope evanish thus?
 Watchers of twilight, is the worst averred?
  We shall not look up, know ourselves are seen,
 Speak, and be sure that we again are heard,
  Acting or suffering, have the disk's serene
 Reflect our life, absorb an earthly flame,
  Nor doubt that, were mankind inert and numb,
 Its core had never crimsoned all the same,
  Nor, missing ours, its music fallen dumb?
 Oh, dread succession to a dizzy post,
  Sad sway of sceptre whose mere touch appalls,
 Ghastly dethronement, cursed by those the most
  On whose repugnant brow the crown next falls!

EPILOGUE

THIRD SPEAKER.

I.

Witless alike of will and way divine,
How heaven's high with earth's low should intertwine!
Friends, I have seen through your eyes: now use mine!

II.

Take the least man of all mankind, as I ;
Look at his head and heart, find how and why
He differs from his fellows utterly:

III.

Then, like me, watch when nature by degrees
Grows alive round him, as in Arctic seas
(They said of old) the instinctive water flees

IV.

Toward some elected point of central rock,
As though, for its sake only, roamed the flock
Of waves about the waste : awhile they mock

V.

With radiance caught for the occasion, — hues
Of blackest hell now, now such reds and blues
As only heaven could fitly interfuse, —

VI.

The mimic monarch of the whirlpool, king
O' the current for a minute : then they wring
Up by the roots and oversweep the thing,

VII.

And hasten off, to play again elsewhere
The same part, choose another peak as bare,
They find and flatter, feast and finish there.

VIII.

When you see what I tell you, — nature dance
About each man of us, retire, advance,
As though the pageant's end were to enhance

IX.

His worth, and — once the life, his product, gained —
Roll away elsewhere, keep the strife sustained,
And show thus real, a thing the North but feigned —

X.

When you acknowledge that one world could do
All the diverse work, old yet ever new,
Divide us, each from other, me from you, —

XI.

Why, where's the need of Temple, when the walls
O' the world are that? What use of swells and falls
From Levites' choir, Priests' cries, and trumpet-calls?

XII.

That one Face, far from vanish, rather grows,
Or decomposes but to recompose,
Become my universe that feels and knows!

BALAUSTION'S ADVENTURE

INCLUDING

A TRANSCRIPT FROM EURIPIDES

Our Euripides, the Human,
With his droppings of warm tears,
And his touches of things common
Till they rose to touch the spheres.

TO THE COUNTESS COWPER.

If I mention the simple truth, that this poem absolutely owes its existence to you, — who not only suggested, but imposed on me as a task, what has proved the most delightful of May-month amusements, — I shall seem honest, indeed, but hardly prudent; for, how good and beautiful ought such a poem to be!

Euripides might fear little; but I, also, have an interest in the performance; and what wonder if I beg you to suffer that it make, in another and far easier sense, its nearest possible approach to those Greek qualities of goodness and beauty, by laying itself gratefully at your feet?

LONDON, July 23, 1871.   R. B.

ABOUT that strangest, saddest, sweetest song
I, when a girl, heard in Kameiros once,
And, after, saved my life by? Oh, so glad
To tell you the adventure!
                        Petalé,
Phullis, Charopé, Chrusion! You must know,
This "after" fell in that unhappy time
When poor reluctant Nikias, pushed by fate,
Went falteringly against Syracuse;
And there shamed Athens, lost her ships and men,
And gained a grave, or death without a grave.
I was at Rhodes — the isle, not Rhodes the town,
Mine was Kameiros — when the news arrived:
Our people rose in tumult, cried, "No more

Duty to Athens, let us join the League
And side with Sparta, share the spoil, — at worst,
Abjure a headship that will ruin Greece!"
And so, they sent to Knidos for a fleet
To come and help revolters. Ere help came, —
Girl as I was, and never out of Rhodes
The whole of my first fourteen years of life,
But nourished with Ilissian mother's-milk, —
I passionately cried to who would hear
And those who loved me at Kameiros — "No!
Never throw Athens off for Sparta's sake —
Never disloyal to the life and light
Of the whole world worth calling world at all!
Rather go die at Athens, lie outstretched
For feet to trample on, before the gate
Of Diomedes or the Hippadai,
Before the temples and among the tombs,
Than tolerate the grim felicity
Of harsh Lakonia! Ours the fasts and feasts,
Choës and Chutroi; ours the sacred grove,
Agora, Dikasteria, Poikilé,
Pnux, Keramikos; Salamis in sight,
Psuttalia, Marathon itself, not far!
Ours the great Dionusiac theatre,
And tragic triad of immortal fames,
Aischulos, Sophokles, Euripides!
To Athens, all of us that have a soul,
Follow me!" And I wrought so with my prayer,
That certain of my kinsfolk crossed the strait
And found a ship at Kaunos; well-disposed
Because the Captain — where did he draw breath
First but within Psuttalia? Thither fled
A few like-minded as ourselves. We turned
The glad prow westward, soon were out at sea,
Pushing, brave ship with the vermilion cheek,
Proud for our heart's true harbor. But a wind
Lay ambushed by Point Malea of bad fame,
And leapt out, bent us from our course. Next day
Broke stormless, so broke next blue day and next.
"But whither bound in this white waste?" we plagued
The pilot's old experience: "Cos or Crete?"
Because he promised us the land ahead.
While we strained eyes to share in what he saw,
The Captain's shout startled us; round we rushed:
What hung behind us but a pirate-ship
Panting for the good prize! "Row! harder row!

Row for dear life!" the Captain cried: "'t is Crete,
Friendly Crete looming large there! Beat this craft
That's but a keles, one-benched pirate-bark,
Lokrian, or that bad breed off Thessaly!
Only, so cruel are such water-thieves,
No man of you, no woman, child, or slave,
But falls their prey, once let them board our boat!"
So, furiously our oarsmen rowed and rowed;
And when the oars flagged somewhat, dash and dip,
As we approached the coast and safety, so
That we could hear behind us plain the threats
And curses of the pirate panting up
In one more throe and passion of pursuit, —
Seeing our oars flag in the rise and fall,
I sprang upon the altar by the mast
And sang aloft — some genius prompting me —
That song of ours which saved at Salamis:
"O sons of Greeks, go, set your country free,
Free your wives, free your children, free the fanes
O' the Gods, your fathers founded, — sepulchres
They sleep in! Or save all, or all be lost!"
Then, in a frenzy, so the noble oars
Churned the black water white, that well away
We drew, soon saw land rise, saw hills grow up,
Saw spread itself a sea-wide town with towers,
Not fifty stadia distant; and, betwixt
A large bay and a small, the islet-bar,
Even Ortugia's self — oh, luckless we!
For here was Sicily and Syracuse:
We ran upon the lion from the wolf.
Ere we drew breath, took counsel, out there came
A galley, hailed us. "Who asks entry here
In war-time? Are you Sparta's friend or foe?"
"Kaunians," — our Captain judged his best reply,
"The mainland-seaport that belongs to Rhodes;
Rhodes that casts in her lot now with the League,
Forsaking Athens, — you have heard belike!"
"Ay, but we heard all Athens in one ode
Just now! we heard her in that Aischulos!
You bring a boatful of Athenians here,
Kaunians although you be: and prudence bids,
For Kaunos' sake, why, carry them unhurt
To Kaunos, if you will: for Athens' sake,
Back must you, though ten pirates blocked the bay!
We want no colony from Athens here,
With memories of Salamis, forsooth,

To spirit up our captives, that pale crowd
I' the quarry, whom the daily pint of corn
Keeps in good order and submissiveness."
Then the gray Captain prayed them by the Gods,
And by their own knees, and their fathers' beards,
They should not wickedly thrust suppliants back,
But save the innocent on traffic bound —
Or, maybe, some Athenian family
Perishing of desire to die at home, —
From that vile foe still lying on its oars,
Waiting the issue in the distance. Vain!
Words to the wind! And we were just about
To turn and face the foe, as some tired bird
Barbarians pelt at, drive with shouts away
From shelter in what rocks, however rude,
She makes for, to escape the kindled eye,
Split beak, crook'd claw o' the creature, cormorant
Or ossifrage, that, hardly baffled, hangs
Afloat i' the foam, to take her if she turn.
So were we at destruction's very edge,
When those o' the galley, as they had discussed
A point, a question raised by somebody,
A matter mooted in a moment, — "Wait!"
Cried they (and wait we did, you may be sure).
" That song was veritable Aischulos,
Familiar to the mouth of man and boy,
Old glory: how about Euripides?
The newer and not yet so famous bard,
He that was born upon the battle-day
While that song and the salpinx sounded him
Into the world, first sound, at Salamis —
Might you know any of his verses too?"

Now, some one of the Gods inspired this speech:
Since ourselves knew what happened but last year —
How, when Gulippos gained his victory
Over poor Nikias, poor Demosthenes,
And Syracuse condemned the conquered force
To dig and starve i' the quarry, branded them —
Freeborn Athenians, brute-like in the front
With horse-head brands, — ah, "Region of the Steed"!
Of all these men immersed in misery,
It was found none had been advantaged so
By aught in the past life he used to prize
And pride himself concerning, — no rich man
By riches, no wise man by wisdom, no

Wiser man still (as who loved more the Muse)
By storing, at brain's edge and tip of tongue,
Old glory, great plays that had long ago
Made themselves wings to fly about the world, —
Not one such man was helped so at his need
As certain few that (wisest they of all)
Had, at first summons, oped heart, flung door wide
At the new knocking of Euripides,
Nor drawn the bolt with who cried "Decadence!
And, after Sophokles, be nature dumb!"
Such, — and I see in it God Bacchos' boon
To souls that recognized his latest child,
He who himself, born latest of the Gods,
Was stoutly held impostor by mankind, —
Such were in safety: any who could speak
A chorus to the end, or prologize,
Roll out a rhesis, wield some golden length
Stiffened by wisdom out into a line,
Or thrust and parry in bright monostich,
Teaching Euripides to Syracuse —
Any such happy man had prompt reward:
If he lay bleeding on the battlefield
They stanched his wounds and gave him drink and food;
If he were slave i' the house, for reverence
They rose up, bowed to who proved master now,
And bade him go free, thank Euripides!
Ay, and such did so: many such, he said,
Returning home to Athens, sought him out,
The old bard in the solitary house,
And thanked him ere they went to sacrifice.
I say, we knew that story of last year!

Therefore, at mention of Euripides,
The Captain crowed out, "Euoi, praise the God!
Oöp, boys, bring our owl-shield to the fore!
Out with our Sacred Anchor! Here she stands,
Balaustion! Strangers, greet the lyric girl!
Euripides? Babai! what a word there 'scaped
Your teeth's enclosure, quoth my grandsire's song!
Why, fast as snow in Thrace, the voyage through,
Has she been falling thick in flakes of him!
Frequent as figs at Kaunos, Kaunians said.
Balaustion, stand forth and confirm my speech!
Now it was some whole passion of a play;
Now, peradventure, but a honey-drop
That slipt its comb i' the chorus. If there rose

A star, before I could determine steer
Southward or northward — if a cloud surprised
Heaven, ere I fairly hollaed ' Furl the sail ! ' —
She had at finger's end both cloud and star ;
Some thought that perched there, tame and tunable,
Fitted with wings ; and still, as off it flew,
' So sang Euripides,' she said, ' so sang
The meteoric poet of air and sea,
Planets and the pale populace of heaven,
The mind of man, and all that 's made to soar ! '
And so, although she has some other name,
We only call her Wild-pomegranate-flower,
Balaustion ; since, where'er the red bloom burns
I' the dull dark verdure of the bounteous tree,
Dethroning, in the Rosy Isle, the rose,
You shall find food, drink, odor, all at once ;
Cool leaves to bind about an aching brow,
And, never much away, the nightingale.
Sing them a strophe, with the turn-again,
Down to the verse that ends all, proverb-like,
And save us, thou Balaustion, bless the name ! "

But I cried, " Brother Greek ! better than so, —
Save us, and I have courage to recite
The main of a whole play from first to last ;
That strangest, saddest, sweetest song of his,
ALKESTIS ; which was taught, long years ago,
At Athens, in Glaukinos' archonship,
But only this year reached our Isle o' the Rose.
I saw it at Kameiros ; played the same,
They say, as for the right Lenean feast
In Athens ; and beside the perfect piece —
Its beauty and the way it makes you weep, —
There is much honor done your own loved God
Herakles, whom you house i' the city here
Nobly, the Temple wide Greece talks about !
I come a suppliant to your Herakles !
Take me and put me on his temple-steps,
To tell you his achievement as I may,
And, that told, he shall bid you set us free ! "

Then, because Greeks are Greeks, and hearts are hearts,
And poetry is power, — they all outbroke
In a great joyous laughter with much love :
" Thank Herakles for the good holiday !
Make for the harbor ! Row, and let voice ring,

' In we row, bringing more Euripides ! ' "
All the crowd, as they lined the harbor now,
" More of Euripides ! " — took up the cry.
We landed; the whole city, soon astir,
Came rushing out of gates in common joy
To the suburb temple; there they stationed me
O' the topmost step : and plain I told the play,
Just as I saw it; what the actors said,
And what I saw, or thought I saw the while,
At our Kameiros theatre, clean-scooped
Out of a hillside, with the sky above
And sea before our seats in marble row :
Told it, and, two days more, repeated it,
Until they sent us on our way again
With good words and great wishes.
        Oh, for me —
A wealthy Syracusan brought a whole
Talent and bade me take it for myself :
I left it on the tripod in the fane,
— For had not Herakles a second time
Wrestled with Death and saved devoted ones ? —
Thank-offering to the hero. And a band
Of captives, whom their lords grew kinder to
Because they called the poet countryman,
Sent me a crown of wild-pomegranate-flower :
So, I shall live and die Balaustion now.
But one — one man — one youth, — three days, each day,
(If, ere I lifted up my voice to speak,
I gave a downward glance by accident,)
Was found at foot o' the temple. When we sailed,
There, in the ship too, was he found as well,
Having a hunger to see Athens too.
We reached Peiraieus; when I landed — lo,
He was beside me. Anthesterion-month
Is just commencing : when its moon rounds full,
We are to marry. O Euripides !

I saw the master : when we found ourselves
(Because the young man needs must follow me)
Firm on Peiraieus, I demanded first
Whither to go and find him. Would you think ?
The story how he saved us made some smile :
They wondered strangers were exorbitant
In estimation of Euripides.
He was not Aischulos nor Sophokles :
— " Then, of our younger bards who boast the bay,
Had I sought Agathon, or Iophon,

Or, what now had it been Kephisophon?
A man that never kept good company,
The most unsociable of poet-kind,
All beard that was not freckle in his face!"

I soon was at the tragic house, and saw
The master, held the sacred hand of him
And laid it to my lips. Men love him not:
How should they? Nor do they much love his friend
Sokrates: but those two have fellowship:
Sokrates often comes to hear him read,
And never misses if he teach a piece.
Both, being old, will soon have company,
Sit with their peers above the talk. Meantime,
He lives as should a statue in its niche;
Cold walls enclose him, mostly darkness there,
Alone, unless some foreigner uncouth
Breaks in, sits, stares an hour, and so departs,
Brain-stuffed with something to sustain his life,
Dry to the marrow 'mid much merchandise.
How should such know and love the man?
            Why, mark!
Even when I told the play and got the praise,
There spoke up a brisk little somebody,
Critic and whippersnapper, in a rage
To set things right: "The girl departs from truth!
Pretends she saw what was not to be seen,
Making the mask of the actor move, forsooth!
'Then a fear flitted o'er the wife's white face,' —
'Then frowned the father,' — 'then the husband shook,' —
'Then from the festal forehead slipt each spray,
And the heroic mouth's gay grace was gone;' —
As she had seen each naked fleshly face,
And not the merely-painted mask it wore!"
Well, is the explanation difficult?
What's poetry except a power that makes?
And, speaking to one sense, inspires the rest,
Pressing them all into its service; so
That who sees painting, seems to hear as well
The speech that's proper for the painted mouth;
And who hears music, feels his solitude
Peopled at once — for how count heartbeats plain
Unless a company, with hearts which beat,
Come close to the musician, seen or no?
And who receives true verse at eye or ear,
Takes in (with verse) time, place, and person too,

So, links each sense on to its sister-sense,
Grace-like: and what if but one sense of three
Front you at once? The sidelong pair conceive
Through faintest touch of finest finger-tips, —
Hear, see and feel, in faith's simplicity,
Alike, what one was sole recipient of:
Who hears the poem, therefore, sees the play.

Enough and too much! Hear the play itself!
Under the grape-vines, by the streamlet-side,
Close to Baccheion; till the cool increase,
And other stars steal on the evening-star,
And so, we homeward flock i' the dusk, we five!
You will expect, no one of all the words
O' the play but is grown part now of my soul,
Since the adventure. 'T is the poet speaks:
But if I, too, should try and speak at times,
Leading your love to where my love, perchance,
Climbed earlier, found a nest before you knew —
Why, bear with the poor climber, for love's sake!
Look at Baccheion's beauty opposite,
The temple with the pillars at the porch!
See you not something beside masonry?
What if my words wind in and out the stone
As yonder ivy, the God's parasite?
Though they leap all the way the pillar leads,
Festoon about the marble, foot to frieze,
And serpentiningly enrich the roof,
Toy with some few bees and a bird or two, —
What then? The column holds the cornice up!

There slept a silent palace in the sun,
With plains adjacent and Thessalian peace —
Pherai, where King Admetos ruled the land.

Out from the portico there gleamed a God,
Apollon: for the bow was in his hand,
The quiver at his shoulder, all his shape
One dreadful beauty. And he hailed the house,
As if he knew it well and loved it much:
"O Admeteian domes, where I endured,
Even the God I am, to drudge awhile,
Do righteous penance for a reckless deed,
Accepting the slaves' table thankfully!"

Then told how Zeus had been the cause of all,
Raising the wrath in him which took revenge
And slew those forgers of the thunderbolt
Wherewith Zeus blazed the life from out the breast
Of Phoibos' son Asklepios (I surmise,
Because he brought the dead to life again),
And so, for punishment, must needs go slave,
God as he was, with a mere mortal lord :
— Told how he came to King Admetos' land,
And played the ministrant, was herdsman there,
Warding all harm away from him and his
Till now ; "For, holy as I am," said he,
"The lord I chanced upon was holy too :
Whence I deceived the Moirai, drew from death
My master, this same son of Pheres, — ay,
The Goddesses conceded him escape
From Hades, when the fated day should fall,
Could he exchange lives, find some friendly one
Ready, for his sake, to content the grave.
But trying all in turn, the friendly list,
Why, he found no one, none who loved so much,
Nor father, nor the aged mother's self
That bore him, no, not any save his wife,
Willing to die instead of him and watch
Never a sunrise nor a sunset more :
And she is even now within the house,
Upborne by pitying hands, the feeble frame
Gasping its last of life out ; since to-day
Destiny is accomplished, and she dies,
And I, lest here pollution light on me,
Leave, as ye witness, all my wonted joy
In this dear dwelling. Ay, — for here comes Death
Close on us of a sudden ! who, pale priest
Of the mute people, means to bear his prey
To the house of Hades. The symmetric step !
How he treads true to time and place and thing,
Dogging day, hour and minute, for death's-due !"

And we observed another Deity,
Half in, half out the portal, — watch and ward, —
Eying his fellow : formidably fixed,
Yet faltering too at who affronted him,
As somehow disadvantaged, should they strive.
Like some dread heapy blackness, ruffled wing,
Convulsed and cowering head that is all eye,
Which proves a ruined eagle who, too blind
Swooping in quest o' the quarry, fawn or kid,

Descried deep down the chasm 'twixt rock and rock,
Has wedged and mortised, into either wall
O' the mountain, the pent earthquake of his power;
So lies, half hurtless yet still terrible,
Just when — who stalks up, who stands front to front,
But the great lion-guarder of the gorge,
Lord of the ground, a stationed glory there!
Yet he too pauses ere he try the worst
O' the frightful unfamiliar nature, new
To the chasm, indeed, but elsewhere known enough,
Among the shadows and the silences
Above i' the sky: so, each antagonist
Silently faced his fellow and forbore.
Till Death shrilled, hard and quick, in spite and fear:

"Ha, ha, and what mayst thou do at the domes,
Why hauntest here, thou Phoibos? Here again
At the old injustice, limiting our rights,
Balking of honor due us Gods o' the grave?
Was 't not enough for thee to have delayed
Death from Admetos, — with thy crafty art
Cheating the very Fates, — but thou must arm
The bow-hand and take station, press 'twixt me
And Pelias' daughter, who then saved her spouse, —
Did just that, now thou comest to undo, —
Taking his place to die, Alkestis here?"
But the God sighed, "Have courage! All my arms,
This time, are simple justice and fair words."

Then each plied each with rapid interchange:

"What need of bow, were justice arms enough?"

"Ever it is my wont to bear the bow."

"Ay, and with bow, not justice, help this house!"

"I help it, since a friend's woe weighs me too."

"And now, — wilt force from me this second corpse?"

"By force I took no corpse at first from thee."

"How then is he above ground, not beneath?"

"He gave his wife instead of him, thy prey."

"And prey, this time at least, I bear below!"

"Go take her! — for I doubt persuading thee . . ."

"To kill the doomed one? What my function else?"

"No! Rather, to dispatch the true mature."

"Truly I take thy meaning, see thy drift!"

"Is there a way then she may reach old age?"

"No way! I glad me in my honors too!"

"But, young or old, thou tak'st one life, no more!"

"Younger they die, greater my praise redounds!"

"If she die old, — the sumptuous funeral!"

"Thou layest down a law the rich would like."

"How so? Did wit lurk there and 'scape thy sense?"

"Who could buy substitutes would die old men."

"It seems thou wilt not grant me, then, this grace?"

"This grace I will not grant: thou know'st my ways."

"Ways harsh to men, hateful to Gods, at least!"

"All things thou canst not have: my rights for me!"

 And then Apollon prophesied, — I think,
More to himself than to impatient Death,
Who did not hear or would not heed the while, —
For he went on to say, " Yet even so,
Cruel above the measure, thou shalt clutch
No life here! Such a man do I perceive
Advancing to the house of Pheres now,
Sent by Eurustheus to bring out of Thrace,
The winter world, a chariot with its steeds!
He indeed, when Admetos proves the host,
And he the guest, at the house here, — he it is
Shall bring to bear such force, and from thy hands

Rescue this woman! Grace no whit to me
Will that prove, since thou dost thy deed the same,
And earnest too my hate, and all for nought!"

But how should Death or stay or understand?
Doubtless, he only felt the hour was come,
And the sword free; for he but flung some taunt—
"Having talked much, thou wilt not gain the more!
This woman, then, descends to Hades' hall
Now that I rush on her, begin the rites
O' the sword; for sacred, to us Gods below,
That head whose hair this sword shall sanctify!"

And, in the fire-flash of the appalling sword,
The uprush and the outburst, the onslaught
Of Death's portentous passage through the door,
Apollon stood a pitying moment-space:
I caught one last gold gaze upon the night
Nearing the world now: and the God was gone,
And mortals left to deal with misery,
As in came stealing slow, now this, now that
Old sojourner throughout the country-side,
Servants grown friends to those unhappy here:
And, cloudlike in their increase, all these griefs
Broke and began the over-brimming wail,
Out of a common impulse, word by word.

"What now may mean the silence at the door?
Why is Admetos' mansion stricken dumb?
Not one friend near, to say if we should mourn
Our mistress dead, or if Alkestis lives
And sees the light still, Pelias' child — to me,
To all, conspicuously the best of wives
That ever was toward husband in this world!
Hears anyone or wail beneath the roof,
Or hands that strike each other, or the groan
Announcing all is done and nought to dread?
Still not a servant stationed at the gates!
O Paian, that thou would'st dispart the wave
O' the woe, be present! Yet, had woe o'erwhelmed
The housemates, they were hardly silent thus:
It cannot be, the dead is forth and gone.
Whence comes thy gleam of hope? I dare not hope:
What is the circumstance that heartens thee?
How could Admetos have dismissed a wife
So worthy, unescorted to the grave?

Before the gates I see no hallowed vase
Of fountain-water, such as suits death's door;
Nor any clipt locks strew the vestibule,
Though surely these drop when we grieve the dead,
Nor hand sounds smitten against youthful hand,
The women's way. And yet — the appointed time —
How speak the word ? — this day is even the day
Ordained her for departing from its light.
O touch calamitous to heart and soul !
Needs must one, when the good are tortured so,
Sorrow, — one reckoned faithful from the first."

Then their souls rose together, and one sigh
Went up in cadence from the common mouth :
How " Vainly — anywhither in the world
Directing or land-labor or sea-search —
To Lukia or the sand-waste, Ammon's seat —
Might you set free their hapless lady's soul
From the abrupt Fate's footstep instant now.
Not a sheep-sacrificer at the hearths
Of Gods had they to go to : one there was
Who, if his eyes saw light still, — Phoibos' son, —
Had wrought so, she might leave the shadowy place
And Hades' portal ; for he propped up Death's
Subdued ones, till the Zeus-flung thunder-flame
Struck him ; and now what hope of life were hailed
With open arms ? For, all the king could do
Is done already, — not one God whereof
The altar fails to reek with sacrifice :
And for assuagement of these evils — nought ! "

But here they broke off, for a matron moved
Forth from the house : and, as her tears flowed fast,
They gathered round. "What fortune shall we hear?
For mourning thus, if aught affect thy lord,
We pardon thee : but lives the lady yet
Or has she perished ? — that we fain would know ! "

"Call her dead, call her living, each style serves,"
The matron said : " though grave-ward bowed, she breathed:
Nor knew her husband what the misery meant
Before he felt it : hope of life was none :
The appointed day pressed hard ; the funeral pomp
He had prepared too."
     When the friends broke out,
" Let her in dying know herself at least

Sole wife, of all the wives 'neath the sun wide,
For glory and for goodness!" — "Ah, how else
Than best? who controverts the claim?" quoth she:
" What kind of creature should the woman prove
That has surpassed Alkestis? — surelier shown
Preference for her husband to herself
Than by determining to die for him?
But so much all our city knows indeed:
Hear what she did indoors and wonder then!
For, when she felt the crowning day was come,
She washed with river-waters her white skin,
And, taking from the cedar closets forth
Vesture and ornament, bedecked herself
Nobly, and stood before the hearth, and prayed:
'Mistress, because I now depart the world,
Falling before thee the last time, I ask —
Be mother to my orphans! wed the one
To a kind wife, and make the other's mate
Some princely person: nor, as I who bore
My children perish, suffer that they too
Die all untimely, but live, happy pair,
Their full glad life out in the fatherland!'
And every altar through Admetos' house
She visited and crowned and prayed before,
Stripping the myrtle-foliage from the boughs,
Without a tear, without a groan, — no change
At all to that skin's nature, fair to see,
Caused by the imminent evil. But this done, —
Reaching her chamber, falling on her bed,
There, truly, burst she into tears and spoke:
'O bride-bed, where I loosened from my life
Virginity for that same husband's sake
Because of whom I die now — fare thee well!
Since nowise do I hate thee: me alone
Hast thou destroyed; for, shrinking to betray
Thee and my spouse, I die: but thee, O bed,
Some other woman shall possess as wife —
Truer, no! but of better fortune, say!'
— So falls on, kisses it till all the couch
Is moistened with the eyes' sad overflow.
But when of many tears she had her fill,
She flings from off the couch, goes headlong forth,
Yet — forth the chamber — still keeps turning back
And casts her on the couch again once more.
Her children, clinging to their mother's robe,
Wept meanwhile: but she took them in her arms,

And, as a dying woman might, embraced
Now one and now the other: 'neath the roof,
All of the household servants wept as well,
Moved to compassion for their mistress; she
Extended her right hand to all and each,
And there was no one of such low degree
She spoke not to nor had an answer from.
Such are the evils in Admetos' house.
Dying, — why, he had died; but, living, gains
Such grief as this he never will forget!"
And when they questioned of Admetos, "Well —
Holding his dear wife in his hands, he weeps;
Entreats her not to give him up, and seeks
The impossible, in fine: for there she wastes
And withers by disease, abandoned now,
A mere dead weight upon her husband's arm.
Yet, none the less, although she breathe so faint,
Her will is to behold the beams o' the sun:
Since never more again, but this last once,
Shall she see sun, its circlet or its ray.
But I will go, announce your presence, — friends
Indeed; since 't is not all so love their lords
As seek them in misfortune, kind the same:
But you are the old friends I recognize."

And at the word she turned again to go:
The while they waited, taking up the plaint
To Zeus again: "What passage from this strait?
What loosing of the heavy fortune fast
About the palace? Will such help appear,
Or must we clip the locks and cast around
Each form already the black peplos' fold?
Clearly the black robe, clearly! All the same,
Pray to the Gods! — like Gods' no power so great!
O thou king Paian, find some way to save!
Reveal it, yea, reveal it! Since of old
Thou found'st a cure, why, now again become
Releaser from the bonds of Death, we beg,
And give the sanguinary Hades pause!"
So the song dwindled into a mere moan,
How dear the wife, and what her husband's woe;
When suddenly —

"Behold, behold!" breaks forth:
"Here is she coming from the house indeed!
Her husband comes, too! Cry aloud, lament,
Pheraian land, this best of women, bound —

So is she withered by disease away —
For realms below and their infernal king!
Never will we affirm there 's more of joy
Than grief in marriage ; making estimate
Both from old sorrows anciently observed,
And this misfortune of the king we see —
Admetos who, of bravest spouse bereaved,
Will live life's remnant out, no life at all! "

So wailed they, while a sad procession wound
Slow from the innermost o' the palace, stopped
At the extreme verge of the platform-front :
There opened, and disclosed Alkestis' self,
The consecrated lady, borne to look
Her last — and let the living look their last —
She at the sun, we at Alkestis.
                                    We!
For would you note a memorable thing?
We grew to see in that severe regard, —
Hear in that hard dry pressure to the point,
Word slow pursuing word in monotone, —
What Death meant when he called her consecrate
Henceforth to Hades. I believe, the sword —
Its office was to cut the soul at once
From life, — from something in this world which hides
Truth, and hides falsehood, and so lets us live
Somehow. Suppose a rider furls a cloak
About a horse's head ; unfrightened, so,
Between the menace of a flame, between
Solicitation of the pasturage,
Untempted equally, he goes his gait
To journey's end : then pluck the pharos off!
Show what delusions steadied him i' the straight
O' the path, made grass seem fire and fire seem grass,
All through a little bandage o'er the eyes!
As certainly with eyes unbandaged now
Alkestis looked upon the action here,
Self-immolation for Admetos' sake ;
Saw, with a new sense, all her death would do,
And which of her survivors had the right,
And which the less right, to survive thereby.
For, you shall note, she uttered no one word
Of love more to her husband, though he wept
Plenteously, waxed importunate in prayer —
Folly's old fashion when its seed bears fruit.
I think she judged that she had bought the ware

O' the seller at its value, — nor praised him
Nor blamed herself, but, with indifferent eye,
Saw him purse money up, prepare to leave
The buyer with a solitary bale —
True purple — but in place of all that coin,
Had made a hundred others happy too,
If so willed fate or fortune! What remained
To give away, should rather go to these
Than one with coin to clink and contemplate.
Admetos had his share and might depart,
The rest was for her children and herself.
(Charopé makes a face: but wait awhile!)
She saw things plain as Gods do: by one stroke
O' the sword that rends the life-long veil away.
(Also Euripides saw plain enough:
But you and I, Charopé! — you and I
Will trust his sight until our own grow clear.)

" Sun, and thou light of day, and heavenly dance
O' the fleet cloud-figure!" (so her passion paused,
While the awe-stricken husband made his moan,
Muttered now this now that ineptitude:
" Sun that sees thee and me, a suffering pair,
Who did the Gods no wrong whence thou should'st die!")
Then, as if caught up, carried in their course,
Fleeting and free as cloud and sunbeam are,
She missed no happiness that lay beneath:
" O thou wide earth, from these my palace roofs,
To distant nuptial chambers once my own
In that Iolkos of my ancestry!" —
There the flight failed her. " Raise thee, wretched one!
Give us not up! Pray pity from the Gods!" .

Vainly Admetos: for " I see it — see
The two-oared boat! The ferryer of the dead,
Charon, hand hard upon the boatman's-pole,
Calls me — even now calls — ' Why delayest thou?
Quick! Thou obstructest all made ready here
For prompt departure: quick, then!'"
       " Woe is me!
A bitter voyage this to undergo,
Even i' the telling! Adverse Powers above,
How do ye plague us!"
       Then a shiver ran:
" He has me — seest not? — hales me, — who is it? —
To the hall o' the Dead — ah, who but Hades' self,

He, with the wings there, glares at me, one gaze
All that blue brilliance, under the eyebrow!
What wilt thou do? Unhand me! Such a way
I have to traverse, all unhappy one!"

" Way — piteous to thy friends, but, most of all,
Me and thy children: ours assuredly
A common partnership in grief like this!"

Whereat they closed about her; but "Let be!
Leave, let me lie now! Strength forsakes my feet.
Hades is here, and shadowy on my eyes
Comes the night creeping. Children — children, now
Indeed, a mother is no more for you!
Farewell, O children, long enjoy the light!"

" Ah me, the melancholy word I hear,
Oppressive beyond every kind of death!
No, by the Deities, take heart nor dare
To give me up — no, by our children too
Made orphans of! But rise, be resolute,
Since, thou departed, I no more remain!
For in thee are we bound up, to exist
Or cease to be — so we adore thy love!"

— Which brought out truth to judgment. At this word
And protestation, all the truth in her
Claimed to assert itself: she waved away
The blue-eyed black-wing'd phantom, held in check
The advancing pageantry of Hades there,
And, with no change in her own countenance,
She fixed her eyes on the protesting man,
And let her lips unlock their sentence, — so!
" Admetos, — how things go with me thou seest, —
I wish to tell thee, ere I die, what things
I will should follow. I — to honor thee,
Secure for thee, by my own soul's exchange,
Continued looking on the daylight here —
Die for thee — yet, if so I pleased, might live,
Nay, wed what man of Thessaly I would,
And dwell i' the dome with pomp and queenliness.
I would not, — would not live bereft of thee,
With children orphaned, neither shrank at all,
Though having gifts of youth wherein I joyed.
Yet, who begot thee and who gave thee birth,
Both of these gave thee up; no less, a term
Of life was reached when death became them well,

Ay, well — to save their child and glorious die:
Since thou wast all they had, nor hope remained
Of having other children in thy place.
So, I and thou had lived out our full time,
Nor thou, left lonely of thy wife, wouldst groan
With children reared in orphanage: but thus
Some God disposed things, willed they so should be.
Be they so! Now do thou remember this,
Do me in turn a favor — favor, since
Certainly I shall never claim my due,
For nothing is more precious than a life:
But a fit favor, as thyself wilt say,
Loving our children here no less than I,
If head and heart be sound in thee at least.
Uphold them, make them masters of my house,
Nor wed and give a step-dame to the pair,
Who, being a worse wife than I, through spite
Will raise her hand against both thine and mine.
Never do this at least, I pray to thee!
For hostile the new-comer, the step-dame,
To the old brood — a very viper she
For gentleness! Here stand they, boy and girl;
The boy has got a father, a defence
Tower-like, he speaks to and has answer from:
But thou, my girl, how will thy virginhood
Conclude itself in marriage fittingly?
Upon what sort of sire-found yoke-fellow
Art thou to chance? with all to apprehend —
Lest, casting on thee some unkind report,
She blast thy nuptials in the bloom of youth.
For neither shall thy mother watch thee wed,
Nor hearten thee in childbirth, standing by
Just when a mother's presence helps the most!
No, for I have to die: and this my ill
Comes to me, nor to-morrow, no, nor yet
The third day of the month, but now, even now,
I shall be reckoned among those no more.
Farewell, be happy! And to thee, indeed,
Husband, the boast remains permissible
Thou hadst a wife was worthy! and to you,
Children; as good a mother gave you birth."

"Have courage!" interposed the friends. "For him
I have no scruple to declare — all this
Will he perform, except he fail of sense."

"All this shall be — shall be!" Admetos sobbed:
"Fear not! And, since I had thee living, dead
Alone wilt thou be called my wife: no fear
That some Thessalian ever styles herself
Bride, hails this man for husband in thy place!
No woman, be she of such lofty line
Or such surpassing beauty otherwise!
Enough of children: gain from these I have,
Such only may the Gods grant! since in thee
Absolute is our loss, where all was gain.
And I shall bear for thee no year-long grief,
But grief that lasts while my own days last, love!
Love! For my hate is she who bore me, now:
And him I hate, my father: loving-ones
Truly, in word not deed! But thou didst pay
All dearest to thee down, and buy my life,
Saving me so! Is there not cause enough
That I who part with such companionship
In thee, should make my moan? I moan, and more!
For I will end the feastings — social flow
O' the wine friends flock for, garlands and the Muse
That graced my dwelling. Never now for me
To touch the lyre, to lift my soul in song
At summons of the Lydian flute; since thou
From out my life hast emptied all the joy!
And this thy body, in thy likeness wrought
By some wise hand of the artificers,
Shall lie disposed within my marriage-bed:
This I will fall on, this enfold about,
Call by thy name, — my dear wife in my arms
Even though I have not, I shall seem to have —
A cold delight, indeed, but all the same
So should I lighten of its weight my soul!
And, wandering my way in dreams perchance,
Thyself wilt bless me: for, come when they will,
Even by night our loves are sweet to see.
But were the tongue and tune of Orpheus mine,
So that to Koré crying, or her lord,
In hymns, from Hades I might rescue thee —
Down would I go, and neither Plouton's dog
Nor Charon, he whose oar sends souls across,
Should stay me till again I made thee stand
Living, within the light! But, failing this,
There, where thou art, await me when I die,
Make ready our abode, my housemate still!
For in the selfsame cedar, me with thee

Will I provide that these our friends shall place,
My side lay close by thy side! Never, corpse
Although I be, would I division bear
From thee, my faithful one of all the world!"

So he stood sobbing: nowise insincere,
But somehow child-like, like his children, like
Childishness the world over. What was new
In this announcement that his wife must die?
What particle of pain beyond the pact
He made, with eyes wide open, long ago —
Made and was, if not glad, content to make?
Now that the sorrow, he had called for, came,
He sorrowed to the height: none heard him say,
However, what would seem so pertinent,
"To keep this pact, I find surpass my power:
Rescind it, Moirai! Give me back her life,
And take the life I kept by base exchange!
Or, failing that, here stands your laughing-stock
Fooled by you, worthy just the fate o' the fool
Who makes a pother to escape the best
And gain the worst you wiser Powers allot!"
No, not one word of this: nor did his wife
Despite the sobbing, and the silence soon
To follow, judge so much was in his thought —
Fancy that, should the Moirai acquiesce,
He would relinquish life nor let her die.
The man was like some merchant who, in storm,
Throws the freight over to redeem the ship:
No question, saving both were better still.
As it was, — why, he sorrowed, which sufficed.
So, all she seemed to notice in his speech
Was what concerned her children. Children, too,
Bear the grief and accept the sacrifice.
Rightly rules nature: does the blossomed bough
O' the grape-vine, or the dry grape's self, bleed wine?

So, bending to her children all her love,
She fastened on their father's only word
To purpose now, and followed it with this:
"O children, now yourselves have heard these things —
Your father saying he will never wed
Another woman to be over you,
Nor yet dishonor me!"
      "And now at least
I say it, and I will accomplish too!"

"Then, for such promise of accomplishment,
Take from my hand these children!"

"Thus I take —
Dear gift from the dear hand!"

"Do thou become
Mother, now, to these children in my place!"

"Great the necessity I should be so,
At least, to these bereaved of thee!"

"Child — child!
Just when I needed most to live, below
Am I departing from you both!"

"Ah me!
And what shall I do, then, left lonely thus?"

"Time will appease thee: who is dead is nought."

"Take me with thee — take, by the Gods below!"

"We are sufficient, we who die for thee."

"Oh, Powers, ye widow me of what a wife!"

"And truly the dimmed eye draws earthward now!"

"Wife, if thou leav'st me, I am lost indeed!"

"She once was — now is nothing, thou mayst say."

"Raise thy face, nor forsake thy children thus!"

"Ah, willingly indeed I leave them not!
But — fare ye well, my children!"

"Look on them —
Look!"
"I am nothingness."

"What dost thou? Leav'st . . ."
"Farewell!"
And in the breath she passed away.
"Undone — me miserable!" moaned the king,

While friends released the long-suspended sigh.
"Gone is she: no wife for Admetos more!"

Such was the signal: how the woe broke forth,
Why tell? — or how the children's tears ran fast
Bidding their father note the eyelids' stare,
Hands' droop, each dreadful circumstance of death.

"Ay, she hears not, she sees not: I and you,
'T is plain, are stricken hard and have to bear!"
Was all Admetos answered; for, I judge,
He only now began to taste the truth:
The thing done lay revealed, which undone thing,
Rehearsed for fact by fancy, at the best,
Never can equal. He had used himself
This long while (as he muttered presently)
To practise with the terms, the blow involved
By the bargain, sharp to bear, but bearable
Because of plain advantage at the end.
Now that, in fact not fancy, the blow fell —
Needs must he busy him with the surprise.
"Alkestis — not to see her nor be seen,
Hear nor be heard of by her, any more
To-day, to-morrow, to the end of time —
Did I mean this should buy my life?" thought he.

So, friends came round him, took him by the hand,
Bade him remember our mortality,
Its due, its doom: how neither was he first,
Nor would be last, to thus deplore the loved.

"I understand," slow the words came at last.
"Nor of a sudden did the evil here
Fly on me: I have known it long ago,
Ay, and essayed myself in misery;
Nothing is new. You have to stay, you friends,
Because the next need is to carry forth
The corpse here: you must stay and do your part,
Chant proper pæan to the God below;
Drink-sacrifice he likes not. I decree
That all Thessalians over whom I rule
Hold grief in common with me; let them shear
Their locks, and be the peplos black they show!
And you who to the chariot yoke your steeds,
Or manage steeds one-frontleted, — I charge,
Clip from each neck with steel the mane away!

And through my city, nor of flute nor lyre
Be there a sound till twelve full moons succeed.
For I shall never bury any corpse
Dearer than this to me, nor better friend:
One worthy of all honor from me, since
Me she has died for, she and she alone."

With that, he sought the inmost of the house,
He and his dead, to get grave's garniture,
While the friends sang the pæan that should peal.
" Daughter of Pelias, with farewell from me,
I' the house of Hades have thy unsunned home!
Let Hades know, the dark-haired deity, —
And he who sits to row and steer alike,
Old corpse-conductor, let him know he bears
Over the Acherontian lake, this time,
I' the two-oared boat, the best — oh, best by far
Of womankind! For thee, Alkestis Queen!
Many a time those haunters of the Muse
Shall sing thee to the seven-stringed mountain-shell,
And glorify in hymns that need no harp,
At Sparta when the cycle comes about,
And that Karneian month wherein the moon
Rises and never sets the whole night through:
So too at splendid and magnificent
Athenai. Such the spread of thy renown,
And such the lay that, dying, thou hast left
Singer and sayer. O that I availed
Of my own might to send thee once again
From Hades' hall, Kokutos' stream, by help
O' the oar that dips the river, back to day!"

So, the song sank to prattle in her praise:
" Light, from above thee, lady, fall the earth,
Thou only one of womankind to die,
Wife for her husband! If Admetos take
Anything to him like a second spouse —
Hate from his offspring and from us shall be
His portion, let the king assure himself!
No mind his mother had to hide in earth
Her body for her son's sake, nor his sire
Had heart to save whom he begot, — not they,
The white-haired wretches! only thou it was,
I' the bloom of youth, didst save him and so die!
Might it be mine to chance on such a mate
And partner! For there 's penury in life

Of such allowance: were she mine at least,
So wonderful a wife, assuredly
She would companion me throughout my days
And never once bring sorrow!"
                              A great voice —
"My hosts here!"
                    Oh, the thrill that ran through us!
Never was aught so good and opportune
As that great interrupting voice! For see!
Here maundered this dispirited old age
Before the palace; whence a something crept
Which told us well enough without a word
What was a-doing inside, — every touch
O' the garland on those temples, tenderest
Disposure of each arm along its side,
Came putting out what warmth i' the world was left.
Then, as it happens at a sacrifice
When, drop by drop, some lustral bath is brimmed:
Into the thin and clear and cold, at once
They slaughter a whole wine-skin; Bacchos' blood
Sets the white water all aflame: even so,
Sudden into the midst of sorrow, leapt
Along with the gay cheer of that great voice,
Hope, joy, salvation: Herakles was here!
Himself, o' the threshold, sent his voice on first
To herald all that human and divine
I' the weary happy face of him, — half God,
Half man, which made the god-part God the more.

"Hosts mine," he broke upon the sorrow with,
"Inhabitants of this Pheraian soil,
Chance I upon Admetos inside here?"

The irresistible sound wholesome heart
O' the hero, — more than all the mightiness
At labor in the limbs that, for man's sake,
Labored and meant to labor their life-long, —
This drove back, dried up sorrow at its source.
How could it brave the happy weary laugh
Of who had bantered sorrow "Sorrow here?
What have you done to keep your friend from harm?
Could no one give the life I see he keeps?
Or, say there's sorrow here past friendly help,
Why waste a word or let a tear escape
While other sorrows wait you in the world,
And want the life of you, though helpless here?"

Clearly there was no telling such an one
How, when their monarch tried who loved him more
Than he loved them, and found they loved, as he,
Each man, himself, and held, no otherwise,
That, of all evils in the world, the worst
Was — being forced to die, whate'er death gain:
How all this selfishness in him and them
Caused certain sorrow which they sang about, —
I think that Herakles, who held his life
Out on his hand, for any man to take —
I think his laugh had marred their threnody.

"He is in the house," they answered. After all,
They might have told the story, talked their best
About the inevitable sorrow here,
Nor changed nor checked the kindly nature, — no!
So long as men were merely weak, not bad,
He loved men: were they Gods he used to help?
"Yea, Pheres' son is in-doors, Herakles.
But say, what sends thee to Thessalian soil,
Brought by what business to this Pherai town?"

"A certain labor that I have to do
Eurustheus the Tirunthian," laughed the God.

"And whither wendest — on what wandering
Bound now?" (they had an instinct, guessed what meant
Wanderings, labors, in the God's light mouth.)

"After the Thrakian Diomedes' car
With the four horses."

      "Ah, but canst thou that?
Art inexperienced in thy host to be?"

"All-inexperienced: I have never gone
As yet to the land o' the Bistones."

       "Then, look
By no means to be master of the steeds
Without a battle!"
    "Battle there may be:
I must refuse no labor, all the same."

"Certainly, either having slain a foe
Wilt thou return to us, or, slain thyself,
Stay there!"

"And, even if the game be so,
The risk in it were not the first I run."

"But, say thou overpower the lord o' the place,
What more advantage dost expect thereby?"

"I shall drive off his horses to the king."

"No easy handling them to bit the jaw!"

"Easy enough; except, at least, they breathe
Fire from their nostrils!"
       "But they mince up men
With those quick jaws!"
        "You talk of provender
For mountain-beasts, and not mere horses' food!"

"Thou mayst behold their mangers caked with gore!"

"And of what sire does he who bred them boast
Himself the son?"
       "Of Ares, king o' the targe —
Thrakian, of gold throughout."
         Another laugh.
"Why, just the labor, just the lot for me
Dost thou describe in what I recognize!
Since hard and harder, high and higher yet,
Truly this lot of mine is like to go
If I must needs join battle with the brood
Of Ares: ay, I fought Lukaon first,
And again, Kuknos: now engage in strife
This third time, with such horses and such lord.
But there is nobody shall ever see
Alkmené's son shrink foemen's hand before!"

— "Or ever hear him say" (the Chorus thought)
"That death is terrible; and help us so
To chime in — 'terrible beyond a doubt,
And, if to thee, why, to ourselves much more:
Know what has happened, then, and sympathize'!"
Therefore they gladly stopped the dialogue,
Shifted the burthen to new shoulder straight,
As, "Look where comes the lord o' the land, himself,
Admetos, from the palace!" they outbroke
In some surprise, as well as much relief.
What had induced the king to waive his right

And luxury of woe in loneliness?

Out he came quietly; the hair was clipt,
And the garb sable; else no outward sign
Of sorrow as he came and faced his friend.
Was truth fast terrifying tears away?
"Hail, child of Zeus, and sprung from Perseus too!"
The salutation ran without a fault.

"And thou, Admetos, King of Thessaly!"

"Would, as thou wishest me, the grace might fall!
But my good-wisher, that thou art, I know."

"What's here? these shorn locks, this sad show of thee?"

"I must inter a certain corpse to-day."

"Now, from thy children God avert mischance!"

"They live, my children; all are in the house!"

"Thy father — if 't is he departs indeed,
His age was ripe at least."

"My father lives,
And she who bore me lives too, Herakles."

"It cannot be thy wife Alkestis gone?"

"Twofold the tale is, I can tell of her."

"Dead dost thou speak of her, or living yet?"

"She is — and is not: hence the pain to me!"

"I learn no whit the more, so dark thy speech!"

"Know'st thou not on what fate she needs must fall?"

"I know she is resigned to die for thee."

"How lives she still, then, if submitting so?"

"Eh, weep her not beforehand! wait till then!"

"Who is to die is dead; doing is done."

"To be and not to be are thought diverse."

"Thou judgest this — I, that way, Herakles!"

"Well, but declare what causes thy complaint!
Who is the man has died from out thy friends?"

"No man: I had a woman in my mind."

"Alien, or some one born akin to thee?"

"Alien: but still related to my house."

"How did it happen then that here-she died?"

"Her father dying left his orphan here."

"Alas, Admetos — would we found thee gay,
Not grieving!"

"What as if about to do
Subjoinest thou that comment?"

"I shall seek
Another hearth, proceed to other hosts."

"Never, O king, shall that be! No such ill
Betide me!"

"Nay, to mourners should there come
A guest, he proves importunate!"

"The dead —
Dead are they: but go thou within my house!"

"'T is base carousing beside friends who mourn."

"The guest-rooms, whither we shall lead thee, lie
Apart from ours."

"Nay, let me go my way!
Ten-thousandfold the favor I shall thank!"

"It may not be thou goest to the hearth
Of any man but me!" so made an end
Admetos, softly and decisively,
Of the altercation. Herakles forbore:
And the king bade a servant lead the way,
Open the guest-rooms ranged remote from view
O' the main hall, tell the functionaries, next,

They had to furnish forth a plenteous feast:
And then shut close the doors o' the hall, midway,
" Because it is not proper friends who feast
Should hear a groaning or be grieved," quoth he.

Whereat the hero, who was truth itself,
Let out the smile again, repressed awhile
Like fountain-brilliance one forbids to play.
He did too many grandnesses, to note
Much in the meaner things about his path:
And stepping there, with face towards the sun,
Stopped seldom to pluck weeds or ask their names.
Therefore he took Admetos at the word:
This trouble must not hinder any more
A true heart from good will and pleasant ways.
And so, the great arm, which had slain the snake,
Strained his friend's head a moment in embrace
On that broad breast beneath the lion's hide,
Till the king's cheek winced at the thick rough gold;
And then strode off, with who had care of him,
To the remote guest-chamber: glad to give
Poor flesh and blood their respite and relief
In the interval 'twixt fight and fight again —
All for the world's sake. Our eyes followed him,
Be sure, till those mid-doors shut us outside.
The king, too, watched great Herakles go off
All faith, love, and obedience to a friend.

And when they questioned him, the simple ones,
" What dost thou? Such calamity to face,
Lies full before thee — and thou art so bold
As play the host, Admetos? Hast thy wits?"
He replied calmly to each chiding tongue:
" But if from house and home I forced away
A coming guest, wouldst thou have praised me more?
No, truly! since calamity were mine,
Nowise diminished; while I showed myself
Unhappy and inhospitable too:
So adding to my ills this other ill,
That mine were styled a stranger-hating house.
Myself have ever found this man the best
Of entertainers when I went his way
To parched and thirsty Argos."
                              " If so be —
Why didst thou hide what destiny was here,
When one came that was kindly, as thou say'st?"

" He never would have willed to cross my door
Had he known aught of my calamities.
And probably to some of you I seem
Unwise enough in doing what I do;
Such will scarce praise me: but these halls of mine
Know not to drive off and dishonor guests."

And so, the duty done, he turned once more
To go and busy him about his dead.
As for the sympathizers left to muse,
There was a change, a new light thrown on things,
Contagion from the magnanimity
O' the man whose life lay on his hand so light,
As up he stepped, pursuing duty still
" Higher and harder," as he laughed and said.
Somehow they found no folly now in the act
They blamed erewhile: Admetos' private grief
Shrank to a somewhat pettier obstacle
I' the way o' the world: they saw good days had been,
And good days, peradventure, still might be,
Now that they overlooked the present cloud
Heavy upon the palace opposite.
And soon the thought took words and music thus: —

" Harbor of many a stranger, free to friend,
Ever and always, O thou house o' the man
We mourn for! Thee, Apollon's very self,
The lyric Puthian, deigned inhabit once,
Become a shepherd here in thy domains,
And pipe, adown the winding hillside paths,
Pastoral marriage-poems to thy flocks
At feed: while with them fed in fellowship,
Through joy i' the music, spot-skin lynxes; ay,
And lions too, the bloody company,
Came, leaving Othrus' dell; and round thy lyre,
Phoibos, there danced the speckle-coated fawn,
Pacing on lightsome fetlock past the pines
Tress-topped, the creature's natural boundary,
Into the open everywhere; such heart
Had she within her, beating joyous beats,
At the sweet reassurance of thy song!
Therefore the lot o' the master is, to live
In a home multitudinous with herds,
Along by the fair-flowing Boibian lake,
Limited, that ploughed land and pasture-plain,
Only where stand the sun's steeds, stabled west
I' the cloud, by that mid-air which makes the clime

Of those Molossoi: and he rules as well
O'er the Aigaian, up to Pelion's shore, —
Sea-stretch without a port! Such lord have we:
And here he opens house now, as of old,
Takes to the heart of it a guest again:
Though moist the eyelid of the master, still
Mourning his dear wife's body, dead but now!"

And they admired: nobility of soul
Was self-impelled to reverence, they saw:
The best men ever prove the wisest too:
Something instinctive guides them still aright.
And on each soul this boldness settled now,
That one who reverenced the Gods so much
Would prosper yet: (or — I could wish it ran —
Who venerates the Gods i' the main will still
Practise things honest though obscure to judge.)

They ended, for Admetos entered now;
Having disposed all duteously indoors,
He came into the outside world again,
Quiet as ever: but a quietude
Bent on pursuing its descent to truth,
As who must grope until he gain the ground
O' the dungeon doomed to be his dwelling now.
Already high o'er head was piled the dusk,
When something pushed to stay his downward step,
Pluck back despair just reaching its repose.
He would have bidden the kind presence there
Observe that, — since the corpse was coming out,
Cared for in all things that befit the case,
Carried aloft, in decency and state,
To the last burial-place and burning pile, —
'T were proper friends addressed, as custom prompts,
Alkestis bound on her last journeying.

"Ay, for we see thy father," they subjoined,
"Advancing as the aged foot best may;
His servants, too: each bringing in his hand
Adornments for thy wife, all pomp that's due
To the downward-dwelling people." And in truth,
By slow procession till they filled the stage,
Came Pheres, and his following, and their gifts.
You see, the worst of the interruption was,
It plucked back, with an over-hasty hand,
Admetos from descending to the truth,

(I told you) — put him on the brink again,
Full i' the noise and glare where late he stood:
With no fate fallen and irrevocable,
But all things subject still to chance and change:
And that chance — life, and that change — happiness.
And with the low strife came the little mind:
He was once more the man might gain so much,
Life too and wife too, would his friends but help!
All he felt now was that there faced him one
Supposed the likeliest, in emergency,
To help: and help, by mere self-sacrifice
So natural, it seemed as if the sire
Must needs lie open still to argument,
Withdraw the rash decision, not to die
But rather live, though death would save his son: —
Argument like the ignominious grasp
O' the drowner whom his fellow grasps as fierce,
Each marvelling that the other needs must hold
Head out of water, though friend choke thereby.

And first the father's salutation fell.
Burthened he came, in common with his child,
Who lost, none would gainsay, a good chaste spouse:
Yet such things must be borne, though hard to bear.
"So, take this tribute of adornment, deep
In the earth let it descend along with her!
Behooves we treat the body with respect
— Of one who died, at least, to save thy life,
Kept me from being childless, nor allowed
That I, bereft of thee, should peak and pine
In melancholy age! she, for the sex,
All of her sisters, put in evidence,
By daring such a feat, that female life
Might prove more excellent than men suppose.
O thou Alkestis!" out he burst in fine,
"Who, while thou savedst this my son, didst raise
Also myself from sinking, — hail to thee!
Well be it with thee even in the house
Of Hades! I maintain, if mortals must
Marry, this sort of marriage is the sole
Permitted those among them who are wise!"

So his oration ended. Like hates like:
Accordingly Admetos, — full i' the face
Of Pheres, his true father, outward shape
And inward fashion, body matching soul, —

Saw just himself when years should do their work
And reinforce the selfishness inside
Until it pushed the last disguise away:
As when the liquid metal cools i' the mould,
Stands forth a statue: bloodless, hard, cold bronze.
So, in old Pheres, young Admetos showed,
Pushed to completion: and a shudder ran,
And his repugnance soon had vent in speech:
Glad to escape outside, nor, pent within,
Find itself there fit food for exercise.

"Neither to this interment called by me
Comest thou, nor thy presence I account
Among the covetable proofs of love.
As for thy tribute of adornment, — no!
Ne'er shall she don it, ne'er in debt to thee
Be buried! What is thine, that keep thou still!
Then it behooved thee to commiserate
When I was perishing: but thou — who stood'st
Foot-free o' the snare, wast acquiescent then
That I, the young, should die, not thou, the old —
Wilt thou lament this corpse thyself hast slain?
Thou wast not, then, true father to this flesh;
Nor she, who makes profession of my birth
And styles herself my mother, neither she
Bore me: but, come of slave's blood, I was cast
Stealthily 'neath the bosom of thy wife!
Thou showedst, put to touch, the thing thou art,
Nor I esteem myself born child of thee!
Otherwise, thine is the preëminence
O'er all the world in cowardice of soul:
Who, being the old man thou art, arrived
Where life should end, didst neither will nor dare
Die for thy son, but left the task to her,
The alien woman, whom I well might think
Own, only mother both and father too!
And yet a fair strife had been thine to strive,
— Dying for thy own child; and brief for thee
In any case, the rest of time to live;
While I had lived, and she, our rest of time,
Nor I been left to groan in solitude.
Yet certainly all things which happy man
Ought to experience, thy experience grasped.
Thou wast a ruler through the bloom of youth,
And I was son to thee, recipient due
Of sceptre and demesne, — no need to fear
That dying thou shouldst leave an orphan house

For strangers to despoil. Nor yet wilt thou
Allege that as dishonoring, forsooth,
Thy length of days, I gave thee up to die, —
I, who have held thee in such reverence !
And in exchange for it, such gratitude
Thou, father, — thou award'st me, mother mine !
Go, lose no time, then, in begetting sons
Shall cherish thee in age, and, when thou diest,
Deck up and lay thee out as corpses claim !
For never I, at least, with this my hand
Will bury thee: it is myself am dead
So far as lies in thee. But if I light
Upon another savior, and still see
The sunbeam, — his, the child I call myself,
His, the old age that claims my cherishing.
How vainly do these aged pray for death,
Abuse the slow drag of senility !
But should death step up, nobody inclines
To die, nor age is now the weight it was ! "

You see what all this poor pretentious talk
Tried at, — how weakness strove to hide itself
In bluster against weakness, — the loud word
To hide the little whisper, not so low
Already in that heart beneath those lips !
Ha, could it be, who hated cowardice
Stood confessed craven, and who lauded so
Self-immolating love, himself had pushed
The loved one to the altar in his place?
Friends interposed, would fain stop further play
O' the sharp-edged tongue: they felt love's champion here
Had left an undefended point or two,
The antagonist might profit by ; bade "Pause !
Enough the present sorrow ! Nor, O son,
Whet thus against thyself thy father's soul ! "

Ay, but old Pheres was the stouter stuff !
Admetos, at the flintiest of the heart,
Had so much soft in him as held a fire :
The other was all iron, clashed from flint
Its fire, but shed no spark and showed no bruise.
Did Pheres crave instruction as to facts ?
He came, content, the ignoble word, for him,
Should lurk still in the blackness of each breast,
As sleeps the water-serpent half-surmised :
Not brought up to the surface at a bound,
By one touch of the idly-probing spear,

Reed-like against unconquerable scale.
He came pacific, rather, as strength should,
Bringing the decent praise, the due regret,
And each banality prescribed of old.
Did he commence " Why let her die for you ?"
And rouse the coiled and quiet ugliness
" What is so good to man as man's own life ? "
No : but the other did : and, for his pains,
Out, full in face of him, the venom leapt.

" And whom dost thou make bold, son — Ludian slave,
Or Phrugian whether, money made thy ware,
To drive at with revilings ? Know'st thou not
I, a Thessalian, from Thessalian sire
Spring and am born legitimately free ?
Too arrogant art thou ; and, youngster words
Casting against me, having had thy fling,
Thou goest not off as all were ended so !
I gave thee birth indeed and mastership
I' the mansion, brought thee up to boot : there ends
My owing, nor extends to die for thee !
Never did I receive it as a law
Hereditary, no, nor Greek at all,
That sires in place of sons were bound to die.
For, to thy sole and single self wast thou
Born, with whatever fortune, good or bad ;
Such things as bear bestowment, those thou hast ;
Already ruling widely, broad lands, too,
Doubt not but I shall leave thee in due time :
For why ? My father left me them before.
Well then, where wrong I thee ? — of what defraud ?
Neither do thou die for this man, myself,
Nor let him die for thee ! — is all I beg.
Thou joyest seeing daylight : dost suppose
Thy father joys not too ? Undoubtedly,
Long I account the time to pass below,
And brief my span of days ; yet sweet the same :
Is it otherwise to thee who, impudent,
Didst fight off this same death, and livest now
Through having sneaked past fate apportioned thee,
And slain thy wife so ? Cryest cowardice
On me, I wonder, thou — whom, poor poltroon,
A very woman worsted, daring death
Just for the sake of thee, her handsome spark ?
Shrewdly hast thou contrived how not to die
Forevermore now : 't is but still persuade

The wife, for the time being, to take thy place!
What, and thy friends who would not do the like,
These dost thou carp at, craven thus thyself?
Crouch and be silent, craven! Comprehend
That, if thou lovest so that life of thine,
Why, everybody loves his own life too:
So, good words, henceforth! If thou speak us ill,
Many and true an ill thing shalt thou hear!"

There you saw leap the hydra at full length!
Only, the old kept glorying the more,
The more the portent thus uncoiled itself,
Whereas the young man shuddered head to foot,
And shrank from kinship with the creature. Why
Such horror, unless what he hated most,
Vaunting itself outside, might fairly claim
Acquaintance with the counterpart at home?
I would the Chorus here had plucked up heart,
Spoken out boldly and explained the man,
If not to men, to Gods. That way, I think,
Sophokles would have led their dance and song.
Here, they said simply, "Too much evil spoke
On both sides!" As the young before, so now
They bade the old man leave abusing thus.

"Let him speak, — I have spoken!" said the youth:
And so died out the wrangle by degrees,
In wretched bickering. "If thou wince at fact,
Behoved thee not prove faulty to myself!"

"Had I died for thee I had faulted more!"

"All's one, then, for youth's bloom and age to die?"

"Our duty is to live one life, not two!"

"Go then, and outlive Zeus, for aught I care!"

"What, curse thy parents with no sort of cause?"

"Curse, truly! All thou lovest is long life!"

"And dost not thou, too, all for love of life,
Carry out now, in place of thine, this corpse?"

"Monument, rather, of thy cowardice,
Thou worst one!"

"Not for me she died, I hope!
That, thou wilt hardly say!"
"No; simply this:
Would, some day, thou mayst come to need myself!"

"Meanwhile, woo many wives — the more will die!"

"And so shame thee who never dared the like!"

"Dear is this light o' the sun-god — dear, I say!"

"Proper conclusion for a beast to draw!"

"One thing is certain: there's no laughing now,
As out thou bearest the poor dead old man!"

"Die when thou wilt, thou wilt die infamous!"

"And once dead, whether famed or infamous,
I shall not care!"
"Alas and yet again!
How full is age of impudency!"
"True!
Thou couldst not call thy young wife impudent:
She was found foolish merely."
"Get thee gone!
And let me bury this my dead!"
"I go.
Thou buriest her whom thou didst murder first;
Whereof there's some account to render yet
Those kinsfolk by the marriage-side! I think,
Brother Akastos may be classed with me,
Among the beasts, not men, if he omit
Avenging upon thee his sister's blood!"

"Go to perdition, with thy housemate too!
Grow old all childlessly, with child alive,
Just as ye merit! for to me, at least,
Beneath the same roof ne'er do ye return.
And did I need by heralds' help renounce
The ancestral hearth, I had renounced the same!
But we — since this woe, lying at our feet
I' the path, is to be borne — let us proceed
And lay the body on the pyre."
I think,
What, through this wretched wrangle, kept the man

From seeing clear — beside the cause I gave —
Was, that the woe, himself described as full
I' the path before him, there did really lie —
Not roll into the abyss of dead and gone.
How, with Alkestis present, calmly crowned,
Was she so irrecoverable yet —
The bird, escaped, that's just on bough above,
The flower, let flutter half-way down the brink?
Not so detached seemed lifelessness from life
But — one dear stretch beyond all straining yet —
And he might have her at his heart once more,
When, in the critical minute, up there comes
The father and the fact, to trifle time!
"To the pyre!" an instinct prompted: pallid face,
And passive arm and pointed foot, when these
No longer shall absorb the sight, O friends,
Admetos will begin to see indeed
Who the true foe was, where the blows should fall!

So, the old selfish Pheres went his way,
Case-hardened as he came; and left the youth,
(Only half selfish now, since sensitive)
To go on learning by a light the more,
As friends moved off, renewing dirge the while:

"Unhappy in thy daring! Noble dame,
Best of the good, farewell! With favoring face
May Hermes the infernal, Hades too,
Receive thee! And if there, — ay, there, — some touch
Of further dignity await the good,
Sharing with them, mayst thou sit throned by her
The Bride of Hades, in companionship!"

Wherewith, the sad procession wound away,
Made slowly for the suburb sepulchre.
And lo, — while still one's heart, in time and tune,
Paced after that symmetric step of Death
Mute-marching, to the mind's eye, at the head
O' the mourners — one hand pointing out their path
With the long pale terrific sword we saw,
The other leading, with grim tender grace,
Alkestis quieted and consecrate, —
Lo, life again knocked laughing at the door!
The world goes on, goes ever, in and through,
And out again o' the cloud. We faced about,
Fronted the palace where the mid-hall-gate

Opened — not half, nor half of half, perhaps —
Yet wide enough to let out light and life,
And warmth, and bounty, and hope, and joy, at once.
Festivity burst wide, fruit rare and ripe
Crushed in the mouth of Bacchos, pulpy-prime,
All juice and flavor, save one single seed
Duly ejected from the God's nice lip,
Which lay o' the red edge, blackly visible —
To wit, a certain ancient servitor :
On whom the festal jaws o' the palace shut,
So, there he stood, a much-bewildered man.
Stupid? Nay, but sagacious in a sort :
Learned, life-long, i' the first outside of things,
Though bat for blindness to what lies beneath
And needs a nail-scratch ere 't is laid you bare.
This functionary was the trusted one
We saw deputed by Admetos late
To lead in Herakles and help him, soul
And body, to such snatched repose, snapped-up
Sustainment, as might do away the dust
O' the last encounter, knit each nerve anew
For that next onset sure to come at cry
O' the creature next assailed, — nay, should it prove
Only the creature that came forward now
To play the critic upon Herakles!

"Many the guests " — so he soliloquized
In musings burdensome to breast before,
When it seemed not too prudent tongue should wag —
" Many, and from all quarters of this world,
The guests I now have known frequent our house,
For whom I spread the banquet ; but than this,
Never a worse one did I yet receive
At the hearth here! One who seeing, first of all,
The master's sorrow, entered gate the same,
And had the hardihood to house himself.
Did things stop there! But, modest by no means,
He took what entertainment lay to hand,
Knowing of our misfortune, — did we fail
In aught of the fit service, urged us serve
Just as a guest expects! And in his hands
Taking the ivied goblet, drinks and drinks
The unmixed product of black mother-earth,
Until the blaze o' the wine went round about
And warmed him : then he crowns with myrtle sprigs
His head, and howls discordance — twofold lay
Was thereupon for us to listen to —

This fellow singing, namely, nor restrained
A jot by sympathy with sorrows here —
While we o' the household mourned our mistress — mourned,
That is to say, in silence — never showed
The eyes, which we kept wetting, to the guest —
For there Admetos was imperative.
And so, here am I helping make at home
A guest, some fellow ripe for wickedness,
Robber or pirate, while she goes her way
Out of our house : and neither was it mine
To follow in procession, nor stretch forth
Hand, wave my lady dear a last farewell,
Lamenting who to me and all of us
Domestics was a mother : myriad harms
She used to ward away from every one,
And mollify her husband's ireful mood.
I ask then, do I justly hate or no
This guest, this interloper on our grief ? "

" Hate him and justly ! " Here's the proper judge
Of what is due to the house from Herakles !
This man of much experience saw the first
O' the feeble duckings-down at destiny,
When King Admetos went his rounds, poor soul,
A-begging somebody to be so brave
As die for one afraid to die himself —
" Thou, friend ? Thou, love ? Father or mother, then !
None of you ? What, Alkestis must Death catch ?
O best of wives, one woman in the world !
But nowise droop : our prayers may still assist :
Let us try sacrifice ; if those avail
Nothing and Gods avert their countenance,
Why, deep and durable our grief will be ! "
Whereat the house, this worthy at its head,
Re-echoed " deep and durable our grief ! "
This sage, who justly hated Herakles,
Did he suggest once " Rather I than she ! "
Admonish the Turannos — " Be a man !
Bear thine own burden, never think to thrust
Thy fate upon another and thy wife !
It were a dubious gain could death be doomed
That other, and no passionatest plea
Of thine, to die instead, have force with fate ;
Seeing thou lov'st Alkestis : what were life
Unlighted by the loved one ? But to live —
Not merely live unsolaced by some thought,

Some word so poor — yet solace all the same —
As 'Thou i' the sepulchre, Alkestis, say!
Would I, or would not I, to save thy life,
Die, and die on, and die forevermore?'
No! but to read red-written up and down
The world 'This is the sunshine, this the shade,
This is some pleasure of earth, sky or sea,
Due to that other, dead that thou mayst live!'
Such were a covetable gain to thee?
Go die, fool, and be happy while 't is time!"
One word of counsel in this kind, methinks,
Had fallen to better purpose than Ai, ai,
Pheu, pheu, e, papai, and a pother of praise
O' the best, best, best one! Nothing was to hate
In King Admetos, Pheres, and the rest
O' the household down to his heroic self!
This was the one thing hateful: Herakles
Had flung into the presence, frank and free,
Out from the labor into the repose,
Ere out again and over head and ears
I' the heart of labor, all for love of men:
Making the most o' the minute, that the soul
And body, strained to height a minute since,
Might lie relaxed in joy, this breathing-space,
For man's sake more than ever; till the bow,
Restrung o' the sudden, at first cry for help,
Should send some unimaginable shaft
True to the aim and shatteringly through
The plate-mail of a monster, save man so.
He slew the pest o' the marish yesterday:
To-morrow he would bit the flame-breathed stud
That fed on man's-flesh: and this day between —
Because he held it natural to die,
And fruitless to lament a thing past cure,
So, took his fill of food, wine, song and flowers,
Till the new labor claimed him soon enough, —
"Hate him and justly!"
                        True, Charopé mine!
The man surmised not Herakles lay hid
I' the guest; or, knowing it, was ignorant
That still his lady lived — for Herakles;
Or else judged lightness needs must indicate
This or the other caitiff quality:
And therefore — had been right if not so wrong!
For who expects the sort of him will scratch
A nail's depth, scrape the surface just to see
What peradventure underlies the same?

So, he stood petting up his puny hate,
Parent-wise, proud of the ill-favored babe.
Not long! A great hand, careful lest it crush,
Startled him on the shoulder: up he stared,
And over him, who stood but Herakles!
There smiled the mighty presence, all one smile
And no touch more of the world-weary God,
Through the brief respite. Just a garland's grace
About the brow, a song to satisfy
Head, heart and breast, and trumpet-lips at once,
A solemn draught of true religious wine,
And — how should I know? — half a mountain-goat
Torn up and swallowed down, — the feast was fierce
But brief: all cares and pains took wing and flew,
Leaving the hero ready to begin
And help mankind, whatever woe came next,
Even though what came next should be nought more
Than the mean querulous mouth o' the man, remarked
Pursing its grievance up till patience failed
And the sage needs must rush out, as we saw,
To sulk outside and pet his hate in peace.
By no means would the Helper have it so:
He who was just about to handle brutes
In Thrace, and bit the jaws which breathed the flame, —
Well, if a good laugh and a jovial word
Could bridle age which blew bad humors forth,
That were a kind of help, too!
                              "Thou, there!" hailed
This grand benevolence the ungracious one —
"Why look'st so solemn and so thought-absorbed?
To guests a servant should not sour-faced be,
But do the honors with a mind urbane.
While thou, contrariwise, beholding here
Arrive thy master's comrade, hast for him
A churlish visage, all one beetle-brow —
Having regard to grief that's out-of-door!
Come hither, and so get to grow more wise!
Things mortal — know'st the nature that they have?
No, I imagine! whence could knowledge spring?
Give ear to me, then! For all flesh to die,
Is Nature's due; nor is there any one
Of mortals with assurance he shall last
The coming morrow: for, what's born of chance
Invisibly proceeds the way it will,
Not to be learned, no fortune-teller's prize.
This, therefore, having heard and known through me,

Gladden thyself! Drink! Count the day-by-day
Existence thine, and all the other — chance!
Ay, and pay homage also to by far
The sweetest of divinities for man,
Kupris! Benignant Goddess will she prove!
But as for aught else, leave and let things be!
And trust my counsel, if I seem to speak
To purpose — as I do, apparently.
Wilt not thou, then, — discarding overmuch
Mournfulness, do away with this shut door,
Come drink along with me, be-garlanded
This fashion? Do so, and — I well know what —
From this stern mood, this shrunk-up state of mind,
The pit-pat fall o' the flagon-juice down throat,
Soon will dislodge thee from bad harborage!
Men being mortal should think mortal-like:
Since to your solemn, brow-contracting sort,
All of them, — so I lay down law at least, —
Life is not truly life but misery."

Whereto the man with softened surliness:
"We know as much: but deal with matters, now,
Hardly befitting mirth and revelry."

"No intimate, this woman that is dead:
Mourn not too much! For, those o' the house itself,
Thy masters live, remember!"

      "Live indeed?
Ah, thou know'st nought o' the woe within these walls!"

"I do — unless thy master spoke me false
Somehow!"
    "Ay, ay, too much he loves a guest,
Too much, that master mine!" so muttered he.

"Was it improper he should treat me well,
Because an alien corpse was in the way?"

"No alien, but most intimate indeed!"

"Can it be, some woe was, he told me not?"

"Farewell and go thy way! Thy cares for thee —
To us, our master's sorrow is a care."

"This word begins no tale of alien woe!"

"Had it been other woe than intimate,
I could have seen thee feast, nor felt amiss."

"What! have I suffered strangely from my host?"

"Thou cam'st not at a fit reception-time:
With sorrow here beforehand: and thou seest
Shorn hair, black robes."
                      "But who is it that's dead?
Some child gone? or the aged sire perhaps?"

"Admetos' wife, then! she has perished, guest!"

"How sayest? And did ye house me, all the same?"

"Ay: for he had thee in that reverence
He dared not turn thee from his door away!"

"O hapless, and bereft of what a mate!"

"All of us now are dead, not she alone!"

"But I divined it! seeing, as I did,
His eye that ran with tears, his close-clipt hair,
His countenance! Though he persuaded me,
Saying it was a stranger's funeral
He went with to the grave: against my wish,
He forced on me that I should enter doors,
Drink in the hall o' the hospitable man
Circumstanced so! And do I revel yet
With wreath on head? But — thou to hold thy peace,
Nor tell me what a woe oppressed my friend!
Where is he gone to bury her? Where am I
To go and find her?"
                     "By the road that leads
Straight to Larissa, thou wilt see the tomb,
Out of the suburb, a carved sepulchre."

So said he, and therewith dismissed himself
Inside to his lamenting: somewhat soothed,
However, that he had adroitly spoilt
The mirth of the great creature: oh, he marked
The movement of the mouth, how lip pressed lip,
And either eye forgot to shine, as, fast,
He plucked the chaplet from his forehead, dashed
The myrtle-sprays down, trod them underfoot!

And all the joy and wonder of the wine
Withered away, like fire from off a brand
The wind blows over — beacon though it be,
Whose merry ardor only meant to make
Somebody all the better for its blaze,
And save lost people in the dark: quenched now!

Not long quenched! As the flame, just hurried off
The brand's edge, suddenly renews its bite,
Tasting some richness caked i' the core o' the tree, —
Pine, with a blood that's oil, — and triumphs up
Pillar-wise to the sky and saves the world:
So, in a spasm and splendor of resolve,
All at once did the God surmount the man.

"O much-enduring heart and hand of mine!
Now show what sort of son she bore to Zeus,
That daughter of Elektruon, Tiruns' child,
Alkmené! for that son must needs save now
The just-dead lady: ay, establish here
I' the house again Alkestis, bring about
Comfort and succor to Admetos so!
I will go lie in wait for Death, black-stoled
King of the corpses! I shall find him, sure,
Drinking, beside the tomb, o' the sacrifice:
And if I lie in ambuscade, and leap
Out of my lair, and seize — encircle him
Till one hand join the other round about —
There lives not who shall pull him out from me,
Rib-mauled, before he let the woman go!
But even say I miss the booty, — say,
Death comes not to the boltered blood, — why then,
Down go I, to the unsunned dwelling-place
Of Koré and the king there, — make demand,
Confident I shall bring Alkestis back,
So as to put her in the hands of him
My host, that housed me, never drove me off:
Though stricken with sore sorrow, hid the stroke,
Being a noble heart and honoring me!
Who of Thessalians, more than this man, loves
The stranger? Who, that now inhabits Greece?
Wherefore he shall not say the man was vile
Whom he befriended, — native noble heart!"

So, one look upward, as if Zeus might laugh
Approval of his human progeny, —

One summons of the whole magnific frame,
Each sinew to its service, — up he caught,
And over shoulder cast, the lion-shag,
Let the club go, — for had he not those hands?
And so went striding off, on that straight way
Leads to Larissa and the suburb tomb.
Gladness be with thee, Helper of our world!
I think this is the authentic sign and seal
Of Godship, that it ever waxes glad,
And more glad, until gladness blossoms, bursts
Into a rage to suffer for mankind,
And recommence at sorrow: drops like seed
After the blossom, ultimate of all.
Say, does the seed scorn earth and seek the sun?
Surely it has no other end and aim
Than to drop, once more die into the ground,
Taste cold and darkness and oblivion there:
And thence rise, tree-like grow through pain to joy,
More joy and most joy, — do man good again.

So, to the struggle off strode Herakles.
When silence closed behind the lion-garb,
Back came our dull fact settling in its place,
Though heartiness and passion half-dispersed
The inevitable fate. And presently
In came the mourners from the funeral,
One after one, until we hoped the last
Would be Alkestis and so end our dream.
Could they have really left Alkestis lone
I' the wayside sepulchre! Home, all save she!
And when Admetos felt that it was so,
By the stand-still: when he lifted head and face
From the two hiding hands and peplos' fold,
And looked forth, knew the palace, knew the hills,
Knew the plains, knew the friendly frequence there,
And no Alkestis any more again,
Why, the whole woe billow-like broke on him.

"O hateful entry, hateful countenance
O' the widowed halls!"—he moaned. "What was to be?
Go there? Stay here? Speak, not speak? All was now
Mad and impossible alike; one way
And only one was sane and safe — to die:
Now he was made aware how dear is death,
How lovable the dead are, how the heart
Yearns in us to go hide where they repose,

When we find sunbeams do no good to see,
Nor earth rests rightly where our footsteps fall.
His wife had been to him the very pledge,
Sun should be sun, earth — earth; the pledge was robbed,
Pact broken, and the world was left no world."
He stared at the impossible, mad life :
Stood, while they urged "Advance — advance !   Go deep
Into the utter dark, thy palace-core!"
They tried what they called comfort, "touched the quick
Of the ulceration in his soul," he said,
With memories, — " once thy joy was thus and thus !"
True comfort were to let him fling himself
Into the hollow grave o' the tomb, and so
Let him lie dead along with all he loved.

One bade him note that his own family
Boasted a certain father whose sole son,
Worthy bewailment, died : and yet the sire
Bore stoutly up against the blow and lived;
For all that he was childless now, and prone
Already to gray hairs, far on in life.
Could such a good example miss effect ?
Why fix foot, stand so, staring at the house,
Why not go in, as that wise kinsman would?

" O that arrangement of the house I know!
How can I enter, how inhabit thee
Now that one cast of fortune changes all ?
Oh me, for much divides the then from now!
Then — with those pine-tree torches, Pelian pomp
And marriage-hymns, I entered, holding high
The hand of my dear wife; while many-voiced
The revelry that followed me and her
That 's dead now, — friends felicitating both,
As who were lofty-lineaged, each of us
Born of the best, two wedded and made one;
Now — wail is wedding-chant's antagonist,
And, for white peplos, stoles in sable state
Herald my way to the deserted couch !"

The one word more they ventured was, "This grief
Befell thee witless of what sorrow means,
Close after prosperous fortune : but, reflect!
Thou hast saved soul and body.   Dead, thy wife —
Living, the love she left.   What 's novel here ?
Many the man, from whom Death long ago
Loosed the life-partner !"

Then Admetos spoke:
Turned on the comfort, with no tears, this time.
He was beginning to be like his wife.
I told you of that pressure to the point,
Word slow pursuing word in monotone,
Alkestis spoke with; so Admetos, now,
Solemnly bore the burden of the truth.
And as the voice of him grew, gathered strength,
And groaned on, and persisted to the end,
We felt how deep had been descent in grief,
And with what change he came up now to light,
And left behind such littleness as tears.

" Friends, I account the fortune of my wife
Happier than mine, though it seem otherwise:
For, her indeed no grief will ever touch,
And she from many a labor pauses now,
Renowned one! Whereas I, who ought not live,
But do live, by evading destiny,
Sad life am I to lead, I learn at last!
For how shall I bear going in-doors here?
Accosting whom? By whom saluted back,
Shall I have joyous entry? Whither turn?
Inside, the solitude will drive me forth,
When I behold the empty bed — my wife's —
The seat she used to sit upon, the floor
Unsprinkled as when dwellers loved the cool,
The children that will clasp my knees about,
Cry for their mother back: these servants too
Moaning for what a guardian they have lost!
Inside my house such circumstance awaits.
Outside, — Thessalian people's marriage-feasts
And gatherings for talk will harass me,
With overflow of women everywhere;
It is impossible I look on them —
Familiars of my wife and just her age!
And then, whoever is a foe of mine,
And lights on me — why, this will be his word —
' See there! alive ignobly, there he skulks
That played the dastard when it came to die,
And, giving her he wedded, in exchange,
Kept himself out of Hades safe and sound,
The coward! Do you call that creature — man?
He hates his parents for declining death,
Just as if he himself would gladly die!'
This sort of reputation shall I have,

Beside the other ills enough in store.
Ill-famed, ill-faring, — what advantage, friends,
Do you perceive I gain by life for death?"
That was the truth. Vexed waters sank to smooth:
'T was only when the last of bubbles broke,
The latest circlet widened all away
And left a placid level, that up swam
To the surface the drowned truth, in dreadful change.
So, through the quiet and submission, — ay,
Spite of some strong words — (for you miss the tone)
The grief was getting to be infinite —
Grief, friends fell back before. Their office shrank
To that old solace of humanity —
" Being born mortal, bear grief! Why born else?"
And they could only meditate anew.

" They, too, upborne by airy help of song,
And haply science, which can find the stars,
Had searched the heights: had sounded depths as well
By catching much at books where logic lurked,
Yet nowhere found they aught could overcome
Necessity: not any medicine served,
Which Thrakian tablets treasure, Orphic voice
Wrote itself down upon: nor remedy
Which Phoibos gave to the Asklepiadai;
Cutting the roots of many a virtuous herb
To solace overburdened mortals. None!
Of this sole goddess, never may we go
To altar nor to image: sacrifice
She hears not. All to pray for is — 'Approach!
But, oh, no harder on me, awful one,
Than heretofore! Let life endure thee still!
For, whatsoe'er Zeus' nod decree, that same
In concert with thee hath accomplishment.
Iron, the very stuff o' the Chaluboi,
Thou, by sheer strength, dost conquer and subdue;
Nor, of that harsh abrupt resolve of thine,
Any relenting is there!'
                                    " O my king!
Thee also, in the shackles of those hands,
Not to be shunned, the Goddess grasped! Yet, bear!
Since never wilt thou lead from underground
The dead ones, wail thy worst! If mortals die, —
The very children of immortals, too,
Dropped 'mid our darkness, these decay as sure!
Dear indeed was she while among us: dear,

Now she is dead, must she forever be:
Thy portion was to clasp, within thy couch,
The noblest of all women as a wife.
Nor be the tomb of her supposed some heap
That hides mortality: but like the Gods
Honored, a veneration to a world
Of wanderers! Oft the wanderer, struck thereby,
Who else had sailed past in his merchant-ship,
Ay, he shall leave ship, land, long wind his way
Up to the mountain-summit, till there break
Speech forth, 'So, this was she, then, died of old
To save her husband! now, a deity
She bends above us. Hail, benignant one!
Give good!' Such voices so will supplicate.
But — can it be? Alkmené's offspring comes,
Admetos! — to thy house advances here!"

I doubt not, they supposed him decently
Dead somewhere in that winter world of Thrace —
Vanquished by one o' the Bistones, or else
Victim to some mad steed's voracity —
For did not friends prognosticate as much?
It were a new example to the point,
That "children of immortals, dropped by stealth
Into our darkness, die as sure as we!"
A case to quote and comfort people with:
But, as for lamentation, ai and pheu,
Right-minded subjects kept them for their lord.

Ay, he it was advancing! In he strode,
And took his stand before Admetos, — turned
Now by despair to such a quietude,
He neither raised his face nor spoke, this time,
The while his friend surveyed him steadily.
That friend looked rough with fighting: had he strained
Worst brute to breast was ever strangled yet?
Somehow, a victory — for there stood the strength,
Happy, as always; something grave, perhaps;
The great vein-cordage on the fret-worked front,
Black-swollen, beaded yet with battle-dew
The yellow hair o' the hero! — his big frame
A-quiver with each muscle sinking back
Into the sleepy smooth it leaped from late.
Under the great guard of one arm, there leant
A shrouded something, live and woman-like,
Propped by the heartbeats 'neath the lion-coat.
When he had finished his survey, it seemed,

The heavings of the heart began subside,
The helpful breath returned, and last the smile
Shone out, all Herakles was back again,
As the words followed the saluting hand.

" To friendly man, behooves we freely speak,
Admetos! — nor keep buried, deep in breast,
Blame we leave silent. I assuredly
Judged myself proper, if I should approach
By accident calamities of thine,
To be demonstrably thy friend : but thou
Told'st me not of the corpse then claiming care,
That was thy wife's, but didst install me guest
I' the house here, as though busied with a grief
Indeed, but then, mere grief beyond thy gate :
And so, I crowned my head, and to the Gods
Poured my libations in thy dwelling-place,
With such misfortune round me. And I blame —
Certainly blame thee, having suffered thus!
But still I would not pain thee, pained enough :
So let it pass! Wherefore I seek thee now,
Having turned back again though onward bound,
That I will tell thee. Take and keep for me
This woman, till I come thy way again,
Driving before me, having killed the king
O' the Bistones, that drove of Thrakian steeds :
In such case, give the woman back to me!
But should I fare, — as fare I fain would not,
Seeing I hope to prosper and return, —
Then, I bequeath her as thy household slave.
She came into my hands with good hard toil!
For, what find I, when started on my course,
But certain people, a whole country-side,
Holding a wrestling-bout? as good to me
As a new labor : whence I took, and here
Come keeping with me, this, the victor's prize.
For, such as conquered in the easy work,
Gained horses which they drove away : and such
As conquered in the harder, — those who boxed
And wrestled, — cattle ; and, to crown the prize,
A woman followed. Chancing as I did,
Base were it to forego this fame and gain!
Well, as I said, I trust her to thy care :
No woman I have kidnapped, understand!
But good hard toil has done it : here I come!
Some day, who knows? even thou wilt praise the feat! "

Admetos raised his face and eyed the pair :
Then, hollowly and with submission, spoke,
And spoke again, and spoke time after time,
When he perceived the silence of his friend
Would not be broken by consenting word.
As a tired slave goes adding stone to stone
Until he stop some current that molests,
So poor Admetos piled up argument
Vainly against the purpose all too plain
In that great brow acquainted with command.

" Nowise dishonoring, nor amid my foes
Ranking thee, did I hide my wife's ill fate ;
But it were grief superimposed on grief,
Shouldst thou have hastened to another home.
My own woe was enough for me to weep !
But, for this woman, — if it so may be, —
Bid some Thessalian, — I entreat thee, king ! —
Keep her, — who has not suffered like myself !
Many of the Pheraioi welcome thee.
Be no reminder to me of my ills !
I could not, if I saw her come to live,
Restrain the tear ! Inflict on me, diseased,
No new disease : woe bends me down enough !
Then, where could she be sheltered in my house,
Female and young too ? For that she is young,
The vesture and adornment prove. Reflect !
Should such an one inhabit the same roof
With men ? And how, mixed up, a girl, with youths,
Shall she keep pure, in that case ? No light task
To curb the May-day youngster, Herakles !
I only speak because of care for thee.
Or must I, in avoidance of such harm,
Make her to enter, lead her life within
The chamber of the dead one, all apart ?
How shall I introduce this other, couch
This where Alkestis lay ? A double blame
I apprehend : first, from the citizens —
Lest some tongue of them taunt that I betray
My benefactress, fall into the snare
Of a new fresh face : then, the dead one's self, —
Will she not blame me likewise ? Worthy, sure,
Of worship from me ! circumspect my ways,
And jealous of a fault, are bound to be.
But thou, — O woman, whosoe'er thou art, —
Know, thou hast all the form, art like as like

Alkestis, in the bodily shape! Ah me!
Take — by the Gods — this woman from my sight,
Lest thou undo me, the undone before!
Since I seem — seeing her — as if I saw
My own wife! And confusions cloud my heart,
And from my eyes the springs break forth! Ah me
Unhappy — how I taste for the first time
My misery in all its bitterness!"

Whereat the friends conferred: "The chance, in truth,
Was an untoward one — none said otherwise.
Still, what a God comes giving, good or bad,
That, one should take and bear with. Take her, then!"

Herakles, — not unfastening his hold
On that same misery, beyond mistake
Hoarse in the words, convulsive in the face, —
" I would that I had such a power," said he,
" As to lead up into the light again
Thy very wife, and grant thee such a grace!"

" Well do I know thou wouldst: but where the hope?
There is no bringing back the dead to light."

" Be not extravagant in grief, no less!
Bear it, by augury of better things!"

" 'T is easier to advise 'bear up,' than bear!"

" But how carve way i' the life that lies before,
If bent on groaning ever for the past?"

" I myself know that: but a certain love
Allures me to the choice I shall not change."

" Ay, but, still loving dead ones, still makes weep."

" And let it be so! She has ruined me,
And still more than I say: that answers all."

" Oh, thou hast lost a brave wife: who disputes?"

" So brave a one — that he whom thou behold'st
Will never more enjoy his life again!"

" Time will assuage! The evil yet is young!"

"Time, thou mayst say, will; if time mean — to die."

"A wife — the longing for new marriage-joys
  Will stop thy sorrow!"
                      "Hush, friend, — hold thy peace!
  What hast thou said! I could not credit ear!"

"How then? Thou wilt not marry, then, but keep
  A widowed couch?"
                      "There is not any one
  Of womankind shall couch with whom thou seest!"

"Dost think to profit thus in any way
  The dead one?"
                      "Her, wherever she abide,
  My duty is to honor."
                      "And I praise —
  Indeed I praise thee! Still, thou hast to pay
  The price of it, in being held a fool!"

"Fool call me — only one name call me not!
  Bridegroom!"
                      "No: it was praise, I portioned thee,
  Of being good true husband to thy wife!"

"When I betray her, though she is no more,
  May I die!"
                      And the thing he said was true:
  For out of Herakles a great glow broke.
  There stood a victor worthy of a prize:
  The violet-crown that withers on the brow
  Of the half-hearted claimant. Oh, he knew
  The signs of battle hard fought and well won,
  This queller of the monsters! — knew his friend
  Planted firm foot, now, on the loathly thing
  That was Admetos late! "would die," he knew,
  Ere let the reptile raise its crest again.
  If that was truth, why try the true friend more?

"Then, since thou canst be faithful to the death,
  Take, deep into thy house, my dame!" smiled he.

"Not so! — I pray, by thy Progenitor!"

"Thou wilt mistake in disobeying me!"

"Obeying thee, I have to break my heart!"

"Obey me! Who knows but the favor done
May fall into its place as duty too?"

So, he was humble, would decline no more
Bearing a burden: he just sighed, "Alas!
Would thou hadst never brought this prize from game!"

"Yet, when I conquered there, thou conqueredst!"

"All excellently urged! Yet — spite of all,
Bear with me! let the woman go away!"

"She shall go, if needs must: but ere she go,
See if there *is* need!"
"Need there is! At least,
Except I make thee angry with me, so!"

"But I persist, because I have my spice
Of intuition likewise: take the dame!"

"Be thou the victor, then! But certainly
Thou dost thy friend no pleasure in the act!"

"Oh, time will come when thou shalt praise me! Now —
Only obey!"
"Then, servants, since my house
Must needs receive this woman, take her there!"

"I shall not trust this woman to the care
Of servants."
"Why, conduct her in, thyself,
If that seem preferable!"
"I prefer,
With thy good leave, to place her in thy hands!"

"I would not touch her! Entry to the house —
That, I concede thee."
"To thy sole right hand
I mean to trust her!"
"King! Thou wrenchest this
Out of me by main force, if I submit!"

"Courage, friend! Come, stretch hand forth! Good! Now
touch
The stranger-woman!"

"There! A hand I stretch —
As though it meant to cut off Gorgon's head!"

" Hast hold of her?"
"Fast hold."
"Why, then, hold fast
And have her! and, one day, asseverate
Thou wilt, I think, thy friend, the son of Zeus,
He was the gentle guest to entertain!
Look at her! See if she, in any way,
Present thee with resemblance of thy wife!"

Ah, but the tears come, find the words at fault!
There is no telling how the hero twitched
The veil off: and there stood, with such fixed eyes
And such slow smile, Alkestis' silent self!
It was the crowning grace of that great heart,
To keep back joy: procrastinate the truth
Until the wife, who had made proof and found
The husband wanting, might essay once more,
Hear, see, and feel him renovated now —
Able to do, now, all herself had done,
Risen to the height of her: so, hand in hand,
The two might go together, live and die.

Beside, when he found speech, you guess the speech.
He could not think he saw his wife again:
It was some mocking God that used the bliss
To make him mad! Till Herakles must help:
Assure him that no spectre mocked at all;
He was embracing whom he buried once.
Still, — did he touch, might he address the true, —
True eye, true body of the true live wife?

And Herakles said, smiling, "All was truth.
Spectre? Admetos had not made his guest
One who played ghost-invoker, or such cheat!
Oh, he might speak and have response, in time!
All heart could wish was gained now — life for death:
Only, the rapture must not grow immense:
Take care, nor wake the envy of the Gods!"

"Oh thou, of greatest Zeus true son," — so spoke
Admetos when the closing word must come,
"Go ever in a glory of success,
And save, that sire, his offspring to the end!

For thou hast — only thou — raised me and mine
Up again to this light and life!" Then asked
Tremblingly, how was trod the perilous path
Out of the dark into the light and life:
How it had happened with Alkestis there.

And Herakles said little, but enough —
How he engaged in combat with that king
O' the dæmons: how the field of contest lay
By the tomb's self: how he sprang from ambuscade,
Captured Death, caught him in that pair of hands.

But all the time, Alkestis moved not once
Out of the set gaze and the silent smile;
And a cold fear ran through Admetos' frame:
"Why does she stand and front me, silent thus?"

Herakles solemnly replied, "Not yet
Is it allowable thou hear the things
She has to tell thee; let evanish quite
That consecration to the lower Gods,
And on our upper world the third day rise!
Lead her in, meanwhile; good and true thou art,
Good, true, remain thou! Practise piety
To stranger-guests the old way! So, farewell!
Since forth I fare, fulfil my urgent task
Set by the king, the son of Sthenelos."

Fain would Admetos keep that splendid smile
Ever to light him. "Stay with us, thou heart!
Remain our house-friend!"
                          "At some other day!
Now, of necessity, I haste!" smiled he.

"But mayst thou prosper, go forth on a foot
 Sure to return! Through all the tetrarchy,
 Command my subjects that they institute
 Thanksgiving-dances for the glad event,
 And bid each altar smoke with sacrifice!
 For we are minded to begin a fresh
 Existence, better than the life before;
 Seeing I own myself supremely blest."

Whereupon all the friendly moralists
 Drew this conclusion: chirped, each beard to each:
"Manifold are thy shapings, Providence!

Many a hopeless matter Gods arrange.
What we expected never came to pass:
What we did not expect Gods brought to bear;
So have things gone, this whole experience through!"

Ah, but if you had seen the play itself!
They say, my poet failed to get the prize:
Sophokles got the prize, — great name! They say,
Sophokles also means to make a piece,
Model a new Admetos, a new wife:
Success to him! One thing has many sides.
The great name! But no good supplants a good,
Nor beauty undoes beauty. Sophokles
Will carve and carry a fresh cup, brimful
Of beauty and good, firm to the altar-foot,
And glorify the Dionusiac shrine:
Not clash against this crater in the place
Where the God put it when his mouth had drained,
To the last dregs, libation life-blood-like,
And praised Euripides forevermore —
The Human with his droppings of warm tears.

Still, since one thing may have so many sides,
I think I see how, — far from Sophokles, —
You, I, or any one might mould a new
Admetos, new Alkestis. Ah, that brave
Bounty of poets, the one royal race
That ever was, or will be, in this world!
They give no gift that bounds itself and ends
I' the giving and the taking: theirs so breeds
I' the heart and soul o' the taker, so transmutes
The man who only was a man before,
That he grows godlike in his turn, can give —
He also: share the poets' privilege,
Bring forth new good, new beauty, from the old.
As though the cup that gave the wine, gave, too,
The God's prolific giver of the grape,
That vine, was wont to find out, fawn around
His footstep, springing still to bless the dearth,
At bidding of a Mainad. So with me:
For I have drunk this poem, quenched my thirst,
Satisfied heart and soul — yet more remains!
Could we too make a poem? Try at least,
Inside the head, what shape the rose-mists take!

When God Apollon took, for punishment,
A mortal form and sold himself a slave
To King Admetos till a term should end, —
Not only did he make, in servitude,
Such music, while he fed the flocks and herds,
As saved the pasturage from wrong or fright,
Curing rough creatures of ungentleness :
Much more did that melodious wisdom work
Within the heart o' the master : there, ran wild
Many a lust and greed that grow to strength
By preying on the native pity and care,
Would else, all undisturbed, possess the land.

And these, the God so tamed, with golden tongue,
That, in the plenitude of youth and power,
Admetos vowed himself to rule thenceforth
In Pherai solely for his people's sake,
Subduing to such end each lust and greed
That dominates the natural charity.

And so the struggle ended.   Right ruled might :
And soft yet brave, and good yet wise, the man
Stood up to be a monarch ; having learned
The worth of life, life's worth would he bestow
On all whose lot was cast, to live or die,
As he determined for the multitude.
So stands a statue : pedestalled sublime,
Only that it may wave the thunder off,
And ward, from winds that vex, a world below.

And then, — as if a whisper found its way
E'en to the sense o' the marble, — " Vain thy vow !
The royalty of its resolve, that head
Shall hide within the dust ere day be done :
That arm, its outstretch of beneficence,
Shall have a speedy ending on the earth :
Lie patient, prone, while light some cricket leaps
And takes possession of the masterpiece,
To sit, sing louder as more near the sun.
For why ?   A flaw was in the pedestal ;
Who knows ?   A worm's work !   Sapped, the certain fate
O' the statue is to fall, and thine to die ! "

Whereat the monarch, calm, addressed himself
To die, but bitterly the soul outbroke —
" O prodigality of life, blind waste

I' the world, of power profuse without the will
To make life do its work, deserve its day!
My ancestors pursued their pleasure, poured
The blood o' the people out in idle war,
Or took occasion of some weary peace
To bid men dig down deep or build up high,
Spend bone and marrow that the king might feast
Intrenched and buttressed from the vulgar gaze.
Yet they all lived, nay, lingered to old age:
As though Zeus loved that they should laugh to scorn
The vanity of seeking other ends
In rule, than just the ruler's pastime. They
Lived; I must die."
      And, as some long last moan
Of a minor suddenly is propped beneath
By note which, new-struck, turns the wail, that was,
Into a wonder and a triumph, so
Began Alkestis: "Nay, thou art to live!
The glory that, in the disguise of flesh,
Was helpful to our house,—he prophesied
The coming fate: whereon, I pleaded sore
That he,—I guessed a God, who to his couch
Amid the clouds must go and come again,
While we were darkling,—since he loved us both,
He should permit thee, at whatever price,
To live and carry out to heart's content
Soul's purpose, turn each thought to very deed,
Nor let Zeus lose the monarch meant in thee.

" To which Apollon, with a sunset smile,
Sadly—'And so should mortals arbitrate!
It were unseemly if they aped us Gods,
And, mindful of our chain of consequence,
Lost care of the immediate earthly link:
Forewent the comfort of life's little hour,
In prospect of some cold abysmal blank
Alien eternity,—unlike the time
They know, and understand to practise with,—
No,—our eternity—no heart's blood, bright
And warm outpoured in its behoof, would tinge
Never so palely, warm a whit the more:
Whereas retained and treasured—left to beat
Joyously on, a life's length, in the breast
O' the loved and loving—it would throb itself
Through, and suffuse the earthly tenement,
Transform it, even as your mansion here

Is love-transformed into a temple-home
Where I, a God, forget the Olumpian glow,
I' the feel of human richness like the rose:
Your hopes and fears, so blind and yet so sweet
With death about them. Therefore, well in thee
To look, not on eternity, but time:
To apprehend that, should Admetos die,
All, we Gods purposed in him, dies as sure:
That, life's link snapping, all our chain is lost.
And yet a mortal glance might pierce, methinks,
Deeper into the seeming dark of things,
And learn, no fruit, man's life can bear, will fade:
Learn, if Admetos die now, so much more
Will pity for the frailness found in flesh,
Will terror at the earthly chance and change
Frustrating wisest scheme of noblest soul,
Will these go wake the seeds of good asleep
Throughout the world: as oft a rough wind sheds
The unripe promise of some field-flower, — true!
But loosens too the level, and lets breathe
A thousand captives for the year to come.
Nevertheless, obtain thy prayer, stay fate!
Admetos lives — if thou wilt die for him!'

"So was the pact concluded that I die,
And thou live on, live for thyself, for me,
For all the world. Embrace and bid me hail,
Husband, because I have the victory —
Am, heart, soul, head to foot, one happiness!"

Whereto Admetos, in a passionate cry:
"Never, by that true word Apollon spoke!
All the unwise wish is unwished, O wife!
Let purposes of Zeus fulfil themselves,
If not through me, then through some other man!
Still, in myself he had a purpose too,
Inalienably mine, to end with me:
This purpose — that, throughout my earthly life,
Mine should be mingled and made up with thine, —
And we two prove one force and play one part
And do one thing. Since death divides the pair,
'T is well that I depart and thou remain
Who wast to me as spirit is to flesh:
Let the flesh perish, be perceived no more,
So thou, the spirit that informed the flesh,
Bend yet awhile, a very flame above

The rift I drop into the darkness by, —
And bid remember, flesh and spirit once
Worked in the world, one body, for man's sake.
Never be that abominable show
Of passive death without a quickening life —
Admetos only, no Alkestis now!"

Then she: "O thou Admetos, must the pile
Of truth on truth, which needs but one truth more
To tower up in completeness, trophy-like,
Emprise of man, and triumph of the world,
Must it go ever to the ground again
Because of some faint heart or faltering hand,
Which we, that breathless world about the base,
Trusted should carry safe to altitude,
Superimpose o' the summit, our supreme
Achievement, our victorious coping-stone?
Shall thine, Beloved, prove the hand and heart
That fail again, flinch backward at the truth
Would cap and crown the structure this last time, —
Precipitate our monumental hope
And strew the earth ignobly yet once more?
See how, truth piled on truth, the structure wants,
Waits just the crowning truth I claim of thee!
Wouldst thou, for any joy to be enjoyed,
For any sorrow that thou mightst escape,
Unwill thy will to reign a righteous king?
Nowise! And were there two lots, death and life, —
Life, wherein good resolve should go to air,
Death, whereby finest fancy grew plain fact
I' the reign of thy survivor, — life or death?
Certainly death, thou choosest. Here stand I
The wedded, the beloved one: hadst thou loved
Her who less worthily could estimate
Both life and death than thou? Not so should say
Admetos, whom Apollon made come court
Alkestis in a car, submissive brutes
Of blood were yoked to, symbolizing soul
Must dominate unruly sense in man.
Then, shall Admetos and Alkestis see
Good alike, and alike choose, each for each,
Good, — and yet, each for other, at the last,
Choose evil? What? thou soundest in my soul
To depths below the deepest, reachest good
In evil, that makes evil good again,
And so allottest to me that I live

And not die — letting die, not thee alone,
But all true life that lived in both of us?
Look at me once ere thou decree the lot!"

Therewith her whole soul entered into his,
He looked the look back, and Alkestis died.

And even while it lay, i' the look of him,
Dead, the dimmed body, bright Alkestis' soul
Had penetrated through the populace
Of ghosts, was got to Koré, — throned and crowned
The pensive queen o' the twilight, where she dwells
Forever in a muse, but half away
From flowery earth she lost and hankers for, —
And there demanded to become a ghost
Before the time.
     Whereat the softened eyes
Of the lost maidenhood that lingered still
Straying among the flowers in Sicily,
Sudden was startled back to Hades' throne
By that demand: broke through humanity
Into the orbed omniscience of a God,
Searched at a glance Alkestis to the soul,
And said — while a long slow sigh lost itself
I' the hard and hollow passage of a laugh:

"Hence, thou deceiver! This is not to die,
If, by the very death which mocks me now,
The life, that's left behind and past my power,
Is formidably doubled. Say, there fight
Two athletes, side by side, each athlete armed
With only half the weapons, and no more,
Adequate to a contest with their foe:
If one of these should fling helm, sword and shield
To fellow — shieldless, swordless, helmless late —
And so leap naked o'er the barrier, leave
A combatant equipped from head to heel,
Yet cry to the other side, 'Receive a friend
Who fights no longer!' 'Back, friend, to the fray!'
Would be the prompt rebuff; I echo it.
Two souls in one were formidable odds:
Admetos must not be himself and thou!"

And so, before the embrace relaxed a whit,
The lost eyes opened, still beneath the look;

And lo, Alkestis was alive again,
And of Admetos' rapture who shall speak?

So, the two lived together long and well.
But never could I learn, by word of scribe
Or voice of poet, rumor wafts our way,
That — of the scheme of rule in righteousness,
The bringing back again the Golden Age,
Which, rather than renounce, our pair would die —
That ever one faint particle came true,
With both alive to bring it to effect:
Such is the envy Gods still bear mankind!

So might our version of the story prove,
And no Euripidean pathos plague
Too much my critic-friend of Syracuse.

"Besides your poem failed to get the prize:
(That is, the first prize: second prize is none.)
Sophokles got it!" Honor the great name!
All cannot love two great names; yet some do:
I know the poetess who graved in gold,
Among her glories that shall never fade,
This style and title for Euripides,
The Human with his droppings of warm tears.

I know, too, a great Kaunian painter, strong
As Herakles, though rosy with a robe
Of grace that softens down the sinewy strength:
And he has made a picture of it all.
There lies Alkestis dead, beneath the sun,
She longed to look her last upon, beside
The sea, which somehow tempts the life in us
To come trip over its white waste of waves,
And try escape from earth, and fleet as free.
Behind the body, I suppose there bends
Old Pheres in his hoary impotence;
And women-wailers, in a corner crouch
— Four, beautiful as you four — yes, indeed! —
Close, each to other, agonizing all,
As fastened, in fear's rhythmic sympathy,
To two contending opposite. There strains
The might o' the hero 'gainst his more than match,
— Death, dreadful not in thew and bone, but like
The envenomed substance that exudes some dew
Whereby the merely honest flesh and blood

Will fester up and run to ruin straight,
Ere they can close with, clasp and overcome
The poisonous impalpability
That simulates a form beneath the flow
Of those gray garments; I pronounce that piece
Worthy to set up in our Poikilé!

And all came, — glory of the golden verse,
And passion of the picture, and that fine
Frank outgush of the human gratitude
Which saved our ship and me, in Syracuse, —
Ay, and the tear or two which slipt perhaps
Away from you, friends, while I told my tale,
— It all came of this play that gained no prize!
Why crown whom Zeus has crowned in soul before?

PRINCE HOHENSTIEL-SCHWANGAU

SAVIOR OF SOCIETY

[1871]

*Ὕδραν φονεύσας, μυρίων τ' ἄλλων πόνων
διῆλθον ἀγέλας . . .
τὸ λοίσθιον δὲ τόνδ' ἔτλην τάλας πόνον,
. . . δῶμα θριγκῶσαι κακοῖς.*

I slew the Hydra, and from labor pass'd
To labor — tribes of labors! Till, at last,
Attempting one more labor, in a trice,
Alack, with ills I *crowned the edifice.*

YOU have seen better days, dear? So have I —
And worse too, for they brought no such bud-mouth
As yours to lisp " You wish you knew me ! " Well,
Wise men, 't is said, have sometimes wished the same,
And wished and had their trouble for their pains.
Suppose my Œdipus should lurk at last
Under a pork-pie hat and crinoline,
And, latish, pounce on Sphinx in Leicester Square?
Or likelier, what if Sphinx in wise old age,
Grown sick of snapping foolish people's heads,
And jealous for her riddle's proper rede, —
Jealous that the good trick which served the turn
Have justice rendered it, nor class one day
With friend Home's stilts and tongs and medium-ware, —
What if the once redoubted Sphinx, I say,
(Because night draws on, and the sands increase,
And desert-whispers grow a prophecy,)
Tell all to Corinth of her own accord,
Bright Corinth, not dull Thebes, for Laïs' sake,
Who finds me hardly gray, and likes my nose,
And thinks a man of sixty at the prime?
Good! It shall be! Revealment of myself!

But listen, for we must co-operate ;
I don't drink tea : permit me the cigar !

First, how to make the matter plain, of course —
What was the law by which I lived. Let's see:
Ay, we must take one instant of my life
Spent sitting by your side in this neat room :
Watch well the way I use it, and don't laugh !
Here's paper on the table, pen and ink :
Give me the soiled bit — not the pretty rose !
See ! having sat an hour, I'm rested now,
Therefore want work : and spy no better work
For eye and hand and mind that guides them both,
During this instant, than to draw my pen
From blot One — thus — up, up to blot Two — thus —
Which I at last reach, thus, and here's my line
Five inches long and tolerably straight :
Better to draw than leave undrawn, I think,
Fitter to do than let alone, I hold,
Though better, fitter, by but one degree.
Therefore it was that, rather than sit still
Simply, my right-hand drew it while my left
Pulled smooth and pinched the moustache to a point.

Now I permit your plump lips to unpurse :
" So far, one possibly may understand
Without recourse to witchcraft ! " True, my dear.
Thus folks begin with Euclid, — finish, how ?
Trying to square the circle ! — at any rate,
Solving abstruser problems than this first,
" How find the nearest way 'twixt point and point."
Deal but with moral mathematics so —
Master one merest moment's work of mine,
Even this practising with pen and ink, —
Demonstrate why I rather plied the quill
Than left the space a blank, — you gain a fact,
And God knows what a fact's worth ! So proceed
By inference from just this moral fact
— I don't say, to that plaguy quadrature,
" What the whole man meant, whom you wish you knew,"
But, what meant certain things he did of old,
Which puzzled Europe, — why, you'll find them plain,
This way, not otherwise : I guarantee,
Understand one, you comprehend the rest.
Rays from all round converge to any point :
Study the point then ere you track the rays'

The size o' the circle's nothing; subdivide
Earth, and earth's smallest grain of mustard-seed,
You count as many parts, small matching large,
If you can use the mind's eye: otherwise,
Material optics, being gross at best,
Prefer the large and leave our mind the small —
And pray how many folk have minds can see?
Certainly you — and somebody in Thrace
Whose name escapes me at the moment. You —
Lend me your mind then! Analyze with me
This instance of the line 'twixt blot and blot
I rather chose to draw than leave a blank,
Things else being equal. You are taught thereby
That 't is my nature, when I am at ease,
Rather than idle out my life too long,
To want to do a thing — to put a thought,
Whether a great thought or a little one,
Into an act, as nearly as may be.
Make what is absolutely new — I can't,
Mar what is made already well enough —
I won't: but turn to best account the thing
That's half-made — that I can. Two blots, you saw
I knew how to extend into a line
Symmetric on the sheet they blurred before —
Such little act sufficed, this time, such thought.

Now, we 'll extend rays, widen out the verge,
Describe a larger circle; leave this first
Clod of an instance we began with, rise
To the complete world many clods effect.
Only continue patient while I throw,
Delver-like, spadeful after spadeful up,
Just as truths come, the subsoil of me, mould
Whence spring my moods: your object, — just to find,
Alike from handlift and from barrow-load,
What salts and silts may constitute the earth —
If it be proper stuff to blow man glass,
Or bake him pottery, bear him oaks or wheat —
What's born of me, in brief; which found, all's known.
If it were genius did the digging-job,
Logic would speedily sift its product smooth
And leave the crude truths bare for poetry;
But I'm no poet, and am stiff i' the back.
What one spread fails to bring, another may.
In goes the shovel and out comes scoop — as here!

I live to please myself. I recognize
Power passing mine, immeasurable, God —
Above me, whom He made, as heaven beyond
Earth — to use figures which assist our sense.
I know that He is there as I am here,
By the same proof, which seems no proof at all,
It so exceeds familiar forms of proof.
Why "there," not "here"? Because, when I say "there"
I treat the feeling with distincter shape
That space exists between us: I, — not He, —
Live, think, do human work here — no machine,
His will moves, but a being by myself,
His, and not He who made me for a work,
Watches my working, judges its effect,
But does not interpose. He did so once,
And probably will again some time — not now,
Life being the minute of mankind, not God's,
In a certain sense, like time before and time
After man's earthly life, so far as man
Needs apprehend the matter. Am I clear?
Suppose I bid a courier take to-night —
(. . . Once for all, let me talk as if I smoked
Yet in the Residenz, a personage:
I must still represent the thing I was,
Galvanically make dead muscle play,
Or how shall I illustrate muscle's use?)
I could then, last July, bid courier take
Message for me, post-haste, a thousand miles.
I bid him, since I have the right to bid,
And, my part done so far, his part begins;
He starts with due equipment, will and power,
Means he may use, misuse, not use at all,
At his discretion, at his peril too.
I leave him to himself: but, journey done,
I count the minutes, call for the result
In quickness and the courier quality,
Weigh its worth, and then punish or reward
According to proved service; not before.
Meantime, he sleeps through noontide, rides till dawn,
Sticks to the straight road, tries the crooked path,
Measures and manages resource, trusts, doubts
Advisers by the wayside, does his best
At his discretion, lags or launches forth,
(He knows and I know) at his peril too.
You see? Exactly thus men stand to God:
I with my courier, God with me. Just so

I have His bidding to perform; but mind
And body, all of me, though made and meant
For that sole service, must consult, concert
With my own self and nobody beside,
How to effect the same: God helps not else.
'T is I who, with my stock of craft and strength,
Choose the directer cut across the hedge,
Or keep the foot-track that respects a crop.
Lie down and rest, rise up and run, — live spare,
Feed free, — all that's my business: but, arrive,
Deliver message, bring the answer back,
And make my bow, I must: then God will speak,
Praise me or haply blame as service proves.
To other men, to each and every one,
Another law! what likelier? God, perchance,
Grants each new man, by some as new a mode,
Intercommunication with Himself,
Wreaking on finiteness infinitude;
By such a series of effects, gives each
Last His own imprint: old yet ever new
The process: 't is the way of Deity.
How it succeeds, He knows: I only know
That varied modes of creatureship abound,
Implying just as varied intercourse
For each with the creator of them all.
Each has his own mind and no other's mode.
What mode may yours be? I shall sympathize!
No doubt, you, good young lady that you are,
Despite a natural naughtiness or two,
Turn eyes up like a Pradier Magdalen
And see an outspread providential hand
Above the owl's-wing aigrette — guard and guide —
Visibly o'er your path, about your bed,
Through all your practisings with London-town.
It points, you go; it stays fixed, and you stop;
You quicken its procedure by a word
Spoken, a thought in silence, prayer and praise.
Well, I believe that such a hand may stoop,
And such appeals to it may stave off harm,
Pacify the grim guardian of this Square,
And stand you in good stead on quarter-day:
Quite possible in your case; not in mine.
" Ah, but I choose to make the difference,
Find the emancipation?" No, I hope!
If I deceive myself, take noon for night,
Please to become determinedly blind

To the true ordinance of human life,
Through mere presumption — that is my affair,
And truly a grave one; but as grave I think
Your affair, yours, the specially observed, —
Each favored person that perceives his path
Pointed him, inch by inch, and looks above
For guidance, through the mazes of this world,
In what we call its meanest life-career
— Not how to manage Europe properly,
But how keep open shop, and yet pay rent,
Rear household, and make both ends meet, the same.
I say, such man is no less tasked than I
To duly take the path appointed him
By whatsoever sign he recognize.
Our insincerity on both our heads!
No matter what the object of a life,
Small work or large, — the making thrive a shop,
Or seeing that an empire take no harm, —
There are known fruits to judge obedience by.
You 've read a ton's weight, now, of newspaper —
Lives of me, gabble about the kind of prince —
You know my work i' the rough; I ask you, then,
Do I appear subordinated less
To hand-impulsion, one prime push for all,
Than little lives of men, the multitude
That cried out, every quarter of an hour,
For fresh instructions, did or did not work,
And praised in the odd minutes?

       Eh, my dear?
Such is the reason why I acquiesced
In doing what seemed best for me to do,
So as to please myself on the great scale,
Having regard to immortality
No less than life — did that which head and heart
Prescribed my hand, in measure with its means
Of doing — used my special stock of power —
Not from the aforesaid head and heart alone,
But every sort of helpful circumstance,
Some problematic and some nondescript:
All regulated by the single care
I' the last resort — that I made thoroughly serve
The when and how, toiled where was need, reposed
As resolutely at the proper point,
Braved sorrow, courted joy, to just one end:
Namely, that just the creature I was bound

To be, I should become, nor thwart at all
God's purpose in creation. I conceive
No other duty possible to man, —
Highest mind, lowest mind, — no other law
By which to judge life failure or success:
What folk call being saved or cast away.

Such was my rule of life; I worked my best,
Subject to ultimate judgment, God's not man's.
Well then, this settled, — take your tea, I beg,
And meditate the fact, 'twixt sip and sip, —
This settled — why I pleased myself, you saw,
By turning blot and blot into a line,
O' the little scale, — we'll try now (as your tongue
Tries the concluding sugar-drop) what's meant
To please me most o' the great scale. Why, just now,
With nothing else to do within my reach,
Did I prefer making two blots one line
To making yet another separate
Third blot, and leaving those I found unlinked?
It meant, I like to use the thing I find,
Rather than strive at unfound novelty:
I make the best of the old, nor try for new.
Such will to act, such choice of action's way,
Constitute — when at work on the great scale,
Driven to their farthest natural consequence
By all the help from all the means — my own
Particular faculty of serving God,
Instinct for putting power to exercise
Upon some wish and want o' the time, I prove
Possible to mankind as best I may.
This constitutes my mission, — grant the phrase, —
Namely, to rule men — men within my reach,
To order, influence and dispose them so
As render solid and stabilify
Mankind in particles, the light and loose,
For their good and my pleasure in the act.
Such good accomplished proves twice good to me —
Good for its own sake, as the just and right,
And, in the effecting also, good again
To me its agent, tasked as suits my taste.

Is this much easy to be understood
At first glance? Now begin the steady gaze!

My rank — (if I must tell you simple truth —
Telling were else not worth the whiff o' the weed

I lose for the tale's sake) — dear, my rank i' the world
Is hard to know and name precisely : err
I may, but scarcely over-estimate
My style and title. Do I class with men
Most useful to their fellows ? Possibly, —
Therefore, in some sort, best; but, greatest mind
And rarest nature ? Evidently no.
A conservator, call me, if you please,
Not a creator nor destroyer : one
Who keeps the world safe. I profess to trace
The broken circle of society,
Dim actual order, I can redescribe
Not only where some segment silver-true
Stays clear, but where the breaks of black commence
Baffling you all who want the eye to probe —
As I make out yon problematic thin
White paring of your thumb-nail outside there,
Above the plaster-monarch on his steed —
See an inch, name an ell, and prophesy
O' the rest that ought to follow, the round moon
Now hiding in the night of things : that round,
I labor to demonstrate moon enough
For the month's purpose, — that society,
Render efficient for the age's need :
Preserving you in either case the old,
Nor aiming at a new and greater thing,
A sun for moon, a future to be made
By first abolishing the present law :
No such proud task for me by any means !
History shows you men whose master-touch
Not so much modifies as makes anew :
Minds that transmute nor need restore at all.
A breath of God made manifest in flesh
Subjects the world to change, from time to time,
Alters the whole conditions of our race
Abruptly, not by unperceived degrees
Nor play of elements already there,
But quite new leaven, leavening the lump,
And liker, so, the natural process. See !
Where winter reigned for ages — by a turn
I' the time, some star-change, (ask geologists,)
The ice-tracts split, clash, splinter and disperse,
And there's an end of immobility,
Silence, and all that tinted pageant, base
To pinnacle, one flush from fairy-land
Dead-asleep and deserted somewhere, — see ! —

As a fresh sun, wave, spring and joy outburst.
Or else the earth it is, time starts from trance,
Her mountains tremble into fire, her plains
Heave blinded by confusion : what result ?
New teeming growth, surprises of strange life
Impossible before, a world broke up
And re-made, order gained by law destroyed.
Not otherwise, in our society
Follow like portents, all as absolute
Regenerations : they have birth at rare
Uncertain unexpected intervals
O' the world, by ministry impossible
Before and after fulness of the days :
Some dervish desert-spectre, swordsman, saint,
Lawgiver, lyrist, — oh, we know the names !
Quite other these than I. Our time requires
No such strange potentate, — who else would dawn, —
No fresh force till the old have spent itself.
Such seems the natural economy.
To shoot a beam into the dark, assists :
To make that beam do fuller service, spread
And utilize such bounty to the height,
That assists also, — and that work is mine.
I recognize, contemplate, and approve
The general compact of society,
Not simply as I see effected good,
But good i' the germ, each chance that's possible
I' the plan traced so far : all results, in short,
For better or worse of the operation due
To those exceptional natures, unlike mine,
Who, helping, thwarting, conscious, unaware,
Did somehow manage to so far describe
This diagram left ready to my hand,
Waiting my turn of trial. I see success,
See failure, see what makes or mars throughout.
How shall I else but help complete this plan
Of which I know the purpose and approve,
By letting stay therein what seems to stand,
And adding good thereto of easier reach
To-day than yesterday ?

      So much, no more !
Whereon, " No more than that ? " — inquire aggrieved
Half of my critics : "nothing new at all ?
The old plan saved, instead of a sponged slate
And fresh-drawn figure ? " — while, " So much as that ? "

Object their fellows of the other faith:
"Leave uneffaced the crazy labyrinth
Of alteration and amendment, lines
Which every dabster felt in duty bound
To signalize his power of pen and ink
By adding to a plan once plain enough?
Why keep each fool's bequeathment, scratch and blur
Which overscrawl and underscore the piece —
Nay, strengthen them by touches of your own?"

Well, that's my mission, so I serve the world,
Figure as man o' the moment, — in default
Of somebody inspired to strike such change
Into society — from round to square,
The ellipsis to the rhomboid, how you please,
As suits the size and shape o' the world he finds.
But this I can, — and nobody my peer, —
Do the best with the least change possible:
Carry the incompleteness on, a stage,
Make what was crooked straight, and roughness smooth,
And weakness strong: wherein if I succeed,
It will not prove the worst achievement, sure,
In the eyes at least of one man, one I look
Nowise to catch in critic company:
To wit, the man inspired, the genius' self
Destined to come and change things thoroughly.
He, at least, finds his business simplified,
Distinguishes the done from undone, reads
Plainly what meant and did not mean this time
We live in, and I work on, and transmit
To such successor: he will operate
On good hard substance, not mere shade and shine.
Let all my critics, born to idleness
And impotency, get their good, and have
Their hooting at the giver: I am deaf —
Who find great good in this society,
Great gain, the purchase of great labor. Touch
The work I may and must, but — reverent
In every fall o' the finger-tip, no doubt.
Perhaps I find all good there's warrant for
I' the world as yet: nay, to the end of time, —
Since evil never means part company
With mankind, only shift side and change shape.
I find advance i' the main, and notably
The Present an improvement on the Past,
And promise for the Future — which shall prove

Only the Present with its rough made smooth,
Its indistinctness emphasized; I hope
No better, nothing newer for mankind,
But something equably smoothed everywhere,
Good, reconciled with hardly-quite-as-good,
Instead of good and bad each jostling each.
"And that's all?" Ay, and quite enough for me!
We have toiled so long to gain what gain I find
I' the Present,—let us keep it! We shall toil
So long before we gain—if gain God grant—
A Future with one touch of difference
I' the heart of things, and not their outside face,—
Let us not risk the whiff of my cigar
For Fourier, Comte, and all that ends in smoke!

This I see clearest probably of men
With power to act and influence, now alive:
Juster than they to the true state of things;
In consequence, more tolerant that, side
By side, shall co-exist and thrive alike
In the age, the various sorts of happiness
Moral, mark! — not material — moods o' the mind
Suited to man and man his opposite:
Say, minor modes of movement — hence to there,
Or thence to here, or simply round about —
So long as each toe spares its neighbor's kibe,
Nor spoils the major march and main advance.
The love of peace, care for the family,
Contentment with what's bad but might be worse —
Good movements these! and good, too, discontent,
So long as that spurs good, which might be best,
Into becoming better, anyhow:
Good — pride of country, putting hearth and home
I' the background, out of undue prominence:
Good — yearning after change, strife, victory,
And triumph. Each shall have its orbit marked,
But no more, — none impede the other's path
In this wide world, — though each and all alike,
Save for me, fain would spread itself through space
And leave its fellow not an inch of way.
I rule and regulate the course, excite,
Restrain: because the whole machine should march
Impelled by those diversely-moving parts,
Each blind to aught beside its little bent.
Out of the turnings round and round inside,
Comes that straightforward world-advance, I want,

And none of them supposes God wants too
And gets through just their hindrance and my help.
I think that to have held the balance straight
For twenty years, say, weighing claim and claim
And giving each its due, no less no more,
This was good service to humanity,
Right usage of my power in head and heart,
And reasonable piety beside.
Keep those three points in mind while judging me!
You stand, perhaps, for some one man, not men, —
Represent this or the other interest,
Nor mind the general welfare, — so, impugn
My practice and dispute my value: why?
You man of faith, I did not tread the world
Into a paste, and thereof make a smooth
Uniform mound whereon to plant your flag,
The lily-white, above the blood and brains!
Nor yet did I, you man of faithlessness,
So roll things to the level which you love,
That you could stand at ease there and survey
The universal Nothing undisgraced
By pert obtrusion of some old church-spire
I' the distance! Neither friend would I content,
Nor, as the world were simply meant for him,
Thrust out his fellow and mend God's mistake.
Why, you two fools, — my dear friends all the same, —
Is it some change o' the world and nothing else
Contents you? Should whatever was, not be?
How thanklessly you view things! There's the root
Of the evil, source of the entire mistake:
You see no worth i' the world, nature and life,
Unless we change what is to what may be,
Which means, — may be, i' the brain of one of you!
"Reject what is?" — all capabilities —
Nay, you may style them chances if you choose —
All chances, then, of happiness that lie
Open to anybody that is born,
Tumbles into this life and out again, —
All that may happen, good and evil too,
I' the space between, to each adventurer
Upon this 'sixty, Anno Domini:
A life to live — and such a life! a world
To learn, one's lifetime in, — and such a world!
How did the foolish ever pass for wise
By calling life a burden, man a fly
Or worm or what's most insignificant?

"O littleness of man!" deplores the bard;
And then, for fear the Powers should punish him,
"O grandeur of the visible universe
Our human littleness contrasts withal!
O sun, O moon, ye mountains and thou sea,
Thou emblem of immensity, thou this,
That and the other,—what impertinence
In man to eat and drink and walk about
And have his little notions of his own,
The while some wave sheds foam upon the shore!"
First of all, 't is a lie some three-times thick:
The bard,—this sort of speech being poetry,—
The bard puts mankind well outside himself
And then begins instructing them: "This way
I and my friend the sea conceive of you!
What would you give to think such thoughts as ours
Of you and the sea together?" Down they go
On the humbled knees of them: at once they draw
Distinction, recognize no mate of theirs
In one, despite his mock humility,
So plain a match for what he plays with. Next,
The turn of the great ocean-playfellow,
When the bard, leaving Bond Street very far
From ear-shot, cares not to ventriloquize,
But tells the sea its home-truths: "You, my match?
You, all this terror and immensity
And what not? Shall I tell you what you are?
Just fit to hitch into a stanza, so
Wake up and set in motion who's asleep
O' the other side of you in England, else
Unaware, as folk pace their Bond Street now,
Somebody here despises them so much!
Between us,—they are the ultimate! to them
And their perception go these lordly thoughts:
Since what were ocean—mane and tail, to boot—
Mused I not here, how make thoughts thinkable?
Start forth my stanza and astound the world!
Back, billows, to your insignificance!
Deep, you are done with!"

       Learn, my gifted friend,
There are two things i' the world, still wiser folk
Accept—intelligence and sympathy.
You pant about unutterable power
I' the ocean, all you feel but cannot speak?
Why, that's the plainest speech about it all.

You did not feel what was not to be felt.
Well, then, all else but what man feels is nought —
The wash o' the liquor that o'erbrims the cup
Called man, and runs to waste adown his side,
Perhaps to feed a cataract, — who cares?
I'll tell you: all the more I know mankind,
The more I thank God, like my grandmother,
For making me a little lower than
The angels, honor-clothed and glory-crowned:
This is the honor, — that no thing I know,
Feel or conceive, but I can make my own
Somehow, by use of hand or head or heart:
This is the glory, — that in all conceived,
Or felt or known, I recognize a mind
Not mine but like mine, — for the double joy, —
Making all things for me and me for Him.
There's folly for you at this time of day!
So think it! and enjoy your ignorance
Of what — no matter for the worthy's name —
Wisdom set working in a noble heart,
When he, who was earth's best geometer
Up to that time of day, consigned his life
With its results into one matchless book,
The triumph of the human mind so far,
All in geometry man yet could do:
And then wrote on the dedication-page
In place of name the universe applauds,
"But, God, what a geometer art Thou!"
I suppose Heaven is, through Eternity,
The equalizing, ever and anon,
In momentary rapture, great with small,
Omniscience with intelligency, God
With man, — the thunder-glow from pole to pole
Abolishing, a blissful moment-space,
Great cloud alike and small cloud, in one fire —
As sure to ebb as sure again to flow
When the new receptivity deserves
The new completion. There's the Heaven for me.
And I say, therefore, to live out one's life
I' the world here, with the chance, — whether by pain
Or pleasure be the process, long or short
The time, august or mean the circumstance
To human eye, — of learning how set foot
Decidedly on some one path to Heaven,
Touch segment in the circle whence all lines
Lead to the centre equally, red lines

Or black lines, so they but produce themselves —
This, I do say, — and here my sermon ends, —
This makes it worth our while to tenderly
Handle a state of things which mend we might,
Mar we may, but which meanwhile helps so far.
Therefore my end is — save society!

" And that's all?" twangs the never-failing taunt
O' the foe — " No novelty, creativeness,
Mark of the master that renews the age?"
"Nay, all that?" rather will demur my judge
I look to hear some day, nor friend nor foe —
" Did you attain, then, to perceive that God
Knew what He undertook when He made things?"
Ay: that my task was to co-operate
Rather than play the rival, chop and change
The order whence comes all the good we know,
With this, — good's last expression to our sense, —
That there's a further good conceivable
Beyond the utmost earth can realize:
And, therefore, that to change the agency,
The evil whereby good is brought about —
Try to make good do good as evil does —
Were just as if a chemist, wanting white,
And knowing black ingredients bred the dye,
Insisted these too should be white forsooth!
Correct the evil, mitigate your best,
Blend mild with harsh, and soften black to gray
If gray may follow with no detriment
To the eventual perfect purity!
But as for hazarding the main result
By hoping to anticipate one half
In the intermediate process, — no, my friends!
This bad world, I experience and approve;
Your good world, — with no pity, courage, hope,
Fear, sorrow, joy, — devotedness, in short,
Which I account the ultimate of man,
Of which there's not one day nor hour but brings,
In flower or fruit, some sample of success,
Out of this same society I save —
None of it for me! That I might have none,
I rapped your tampering knuckles twenty years.
Such was the task imposed me, such my end.

Now for the means thereto. Ah, confidence —
Keep we together or part company?

This is the critical minute! " Such my end ? "
Certainly ; how could it be otherwise ?
Can there be question which was the right task —
To save or to destroy society ?
Why, even prove that, by some miracle,
Destruction were the proper work to choose,
And that a torch best remedies what 's wrong
I' the temple, whence the long procession wound
Of powers and beauties, earth's achievements all,
The human strength that strove and overthrew, —
The human love that, weak itself, crowned strength, —
The instinct crying, " God is whence I came ! " —
The reason laying down the law, " And such
His will i' the world must be ! " — the leap and shout
Of genius, " For I hold His very thoughts,
The meaning of the mind of Him ! " — nay, more
The ingenuities, each active force
That turning in a circle on itself
Looks neither up nor down but keeps the spot,
Mere creature-like and, for religion, works,
Works only and works ever, makes and shapes
And changes, still wrings more of good from less,
Still stamps some bad out, where was worst before,
So leaves the handiwork, the act and deed,
Were it but house and land and wealth, to show
Here was a creature perfect in the kind —
Whether as bee, beaver, or behemoth,
What 's the importance ? he has done his work
For work's sake, worked well, earned a creature's praise ; —
I say, concede that same fane, whence deploys
Age after age, all this humanity,
Diverse but ever dear, out of the dark
Behind the altar into the broad day
By the portal — enter, and, concede there mocks
Each lover of free motion and much space
A perplexed length of apse and aisle and nave, —
Pillared roof and carved screen, and what care I ? —
Which irk the movement and impede the march, —
Nay, possibly, bring flat upon his nose
At some odd breakneck angle, by some freak
Of old-world artistry, that personage
Who, could he but have kept his skirts from grief
And catching at the hooks and crooks about,
Had stepped out on the daylight of our time
Plainly the man of the age, — still, still, I bar
Excessive conflagration in the case.

"Shake the flame freely!" shout the multitude:
The architect approves I stuck my torch
Inside a good stout lantern, hung its light
Above the hooks and crooks, and ended so.
To save society was well: the means
Whereby to save it, — there begins the doubt
Permitted you, imperative on me;
Were mine the best means? Did I work aright
With powers appointed me? — since powers denied
Concern me nothing.
     Well, my work reviewed
Fairly, leaves more hope than discouragement.
First, there's the deed done: what I found, I leave, —
What tottered, I kept stable: if it stand
One month, without sustainment, still thank me
The twenty years' sustainer! Now, observe,
Sustaining is no brilliant self-display
Like knocking down or even setting up:
Much bustle these necessitate; and still
To vulgar eye, the mightier of the myth
Is Hercules, who substitutes his own
For Atlas' shoulder and supports the globe
A whole day, — not the passive and obscure
Atlas who bore, ere Hercules was born,
And is to go on bearing that same load
When Hercules turns ash on Œta's top.
'T is the transition-stage, the tug and strain,
That strike men: standing still is stupid-like.
My pressure was too constant on the whole
For any part's eruption into space
'Mid sparkles, crackling, and much praise of me.
I saw that, in the ordinary life,
Many of the little make a mass of men
Important beyond greatness here and there;
As certainly as, in life exceptional,
When old things terminate and new commence,
A solitary great man's worth the world.
God takes the business into His own hands
At such time: who creates the novel flower
Contrives to guard and give it breathing-room:
I merely tend the cornfield, care for crop,
And weed no acre thin to let emerge
What prodigy may stifle there perchance,
— No, though my eye have noted where he lurks.
Oh those mute myriads that spoke loud to me —

The eyes that craved to see the light, the mouths
That sought the daily bread and nothing more,
The hands that supplicated exercise,
Men that had wives, and women that had babes,
And all these making suit to only live!
Was I to turn aside from husbandry,
Leave hope of harvest for the corn, my care,
To play at horticulture, rear some rose
Or poppy into perfect leaf and bloom
When, 'mid the furrows, up was pleased to sprout
Some man, cause, system, special interest
I ought to study, stop the world meanwhile?
"But I am Liberty, Philanthropy,
Enlightenment, or Patriotism, the power
Whereby you are to stand or fall!" cries each:
"Mine and mine only be the flag you flaunt!"
And, when I venture to object, "Meantime,
What of yon myriads with no flag at all —
My crop which, who flaunts flag must tread across?"
"Now, this it is to have a puny mind!"
Admire my mental prodigies: "down — down —
Ever at home o' the level and the low,
There bides he brooding! Could he look above,
With less of the owl and more of the eagle eye,
He'd see there's no way helps the little cause
Like the attainment of the great. Dare first
The chief emprise; dispel yon cloud between
The sun and us; nor fear that, though our heads
Find earlier warmth and comfort from his ray,
What lies about our feet, the multitude,
Will fail of benefaction presently.
Come now, let each of us awhile cry truce
To special interests, make common cause
Against the adversary — or perchance
Mere dullard to his own plain interest!
Which of us will you choose? — since needs must be
Some one o' the warring causes you incline
To hold, i' the main, has right and should prevail:
Why not adopt and give it prevalence?
Choose strict Faith or lax Incredulity, —
King, Caste, and Cultus — or the Rights of Man,
Sovereignty of each Proudhon o'er himself,
And all that follows in just consequence!
Go free the stranger from a foreign yoke;
Or stay, concentrate energy at home;
Succeed! — when he deserves, the stranger will.

Comply with the Great Nation's impulse, print
By force of arms, — since reason pleads in vain,
And, 'mid the sweet compulsion, pity weeps, —
Hohenstiel-Schwangau on the universe!
Snub the Great Nation, cure the impulsive itch
With smartest fillip on a restless nose
Was ever launched by thumb and finger! Bid
Hohenstiel-Schwangau first repeal the tax
On pig-tails and pomatum, and then mind
Abstruser matters for next century!
Is your choice made? Why then, act up to choice!
Leave the illogical touch now here now there
I' the way of work, the tantalizing help
First to this, then the other opposite:
The blowing hot and cold, sham policy,
Sure ague of the mind and nothing more,
Disease of the perception or the will,
That fain would hide in a fine name! Your choice,
Speak it out and condemn yourself thereby!"

Well, Leicester Square is not the Residenz:
Instead of shrugging shoulder, turning friend
The deaf ear, with a wink to the police —
I'll answer — by a question, wisdom's mode.
How many years, o' the average, do men
Live in this world? Some score, say computists.
Quintuple me that term and give mankind
The likely hundred, and with all my heart
I'll take your task upon me, work your way,
Concentrate energy on some one cause:
Since, counseller, I also have my cause,
My flag, my faith in its effect, my hope
In its eventual triumph for the good
O' the world. And once upon a time, when I
Was like all you, mere voice and nothing more,
Myself took wings, soared sunward, and thence sang,
"Look where I live i' the loft, come up to me,
Groundlings, nor grovel longer! gain this height,
And prove you breathe here better than below!
Why, what emancipation far and wide
Will follow in a trice! They too can soar,
Each tenant of the earth's circumference
Claiming to elevate humanity,
They also must attain such altitude,
Live in the luminous circle that surrounds
The planet, not the leaden orb itself

Press out, each point, from surface to yon verge
Which one has gained and guaranteed your realm!"
Ay, still my fragments wander, music-fraught,
Sighs of the soul, mine once, mine now, and mine
Forever! Crumbled arch, crushed aqueduct,
Alive with tremors in the shaggy growth
Of wild-wood, crevice-sown, that triumphs there
Imparting exultation to the hills!
Sweep of the swathe when only the winds walk
And waft my words above the grassy sea
Under the blinding blue that basks o'er Rome, —
Hear ye not still — " Be Italy again " ?
And ye, what strikes the panic to your heart ?
Decrepit council-chambers, — where some lamp
Drives the unbroken black three paces off
From where the graybeards huddle in debate,
Dim cowls and capes, and midmost glimmers one
Like tarnished gold, and what they say is doubt,
And what they think is fear, and what suspends
The breath in them is not the plaster-patch
Time disengages from the painted wall
Where Rafael moulderingly bids adieu,
Nor tick of the insect turning tapestry
Which a queen's finger traced of old, to dust ;
But some word, resonant, redoubtable,
Of who once felt upon his head a hand
Whereof the head now apprehends his foot.
" Light in Rome, Law in Rome, and Liberty
O' the soul in Rome — the free Church, the free State!
Stamp out the nature that 's best typified
By its embodiment in Peter's Dome,
The scorpion-body with the greedy pair
Of outstretched nippers, either colonnade
Agape for the advance of heads and hearts!"
There 's one cause for you! one and only one,
For I am vocal through the universe,
I' the workshop, manufactory, exchange
And market-place, sea-port and custom-house
O' the frontier : listen if the echoes die —
" Unfettered commerce! Power to speak and hear,
And print and read! The universal vote!
Its rights for labor!" This, with much beside,
I spoke when I was voice and nothing more,
But altogether such an one as you
My censors. " Voice, and nothing more, indeed!"
Re-echoes round me : " that 's the censure, there 's

Involved the ruin of you soon or late!
Voice, — when its promise beat the empty air:
And nothing more, — when solid earth 's your stage,
And we desiderate performance, deed
For word, the realizing all you dreamed
In the old days: now, for deed, we find at door
O' the council-chamber posted, mute as mouse,
Hohenstiel-Schwangau, sentry and safeguard
O' the graybeards all a-chuckle, cowl to cape,
Who challenge Judas, — that 's endearment's style, —
To stop their mouths or let escape grimace,
While they keep cursing Italy and him.
The power to speak, hear, print and read is ours?
Ay, we learn where and how, when clapped inside
A convict-transport bound for cool Cayenne!
The universal vote we have: its urn,
We also have where votes drop, fingered-o'er
By the universal Prefect. Say, Trade 's free
And Toil turned master out o' the slave it was:
What then? These feed man's stomach, but his soul
Craves finer fare, nor lives by bread alone,
As somebody says somewhere. Hence you stand
Proved and recorded either false or weak,
Faulty in promise or performance: which?"
Neither, I hope. Once pedestalled on earth,
To act not speak, I found earth was not air.
I saw that multitude of mine, and not
The nakedness and nullity of air
Fit only for a voice to float in free.
Such eyes I saw that craved the light alone,
Such mouths that wanted bread and nothing else,
Such hands that supplicated handiwork,
Men with the wives, and women with the babes,
Yet all these pleading just to live, not die!
Did I believe one whit less in belief,
Take truth for falsehood, wish the voice revoked
That told the truth to heaven for earth to hear?
No, this should be, and shall; but when and how?
At what expense to these who average
Your twenty years of life, my computists?
"Not bread alone," but bread before all else
For these: the bodily want serve first, said I;
If earth-space and the lifetime help not here,
Where is the good of body having been?
But, helping body, if we somewhat balk
The soul of finer fare, such food 's to find

Elsewhere and afterward — all indicates,
Even this selfsame fact that soul can starve
Yet body still exist its twenty years :
While, stint the body, there's an end at once
O' the revel in the fancy that Rome's free,
And superstition's fettered, and one prints
Whate'er one pleases, and who pleases reads
The same, and speaks out and is spoken to,
And divers hundred thousand fools may vote
A vote untampered with by one wise man,
And so elect Barabbas deputy
In lieu of his concurrent. I who trace
The purpose written on the face of things,
For my behoof and guidance — (whoso needs
No such sustainment, sees beneath my signs,
Proves, what I take for writing, penmanship,
Scribble and flourish with no sense for me
O' the sort I solemnly go spelling out, —
Let him! there's certain work of mine to show
Alongside his work : which gives warranty
Of shrewder vision in the workman — judge!)
I who trace Providence without a break
I' the plan of things, drop plumb on this plain print
Of an intention with a view to good,
That man is made in sympathy with man
At outset of existence, so to speak ;
But in dissociation, more and more,
Man from his fellow, as their lives advance
In culture ; still humanity, that's born
A mass, keeps flying off, fining away
Ever into a multitude of points,
And ends in isolation, each from each :
Peerless above i' the sky, the pinnacle, —
Absolute contact, fusion, all below
At the base of being. How comes this about?
This stamp of God characterizing man
And nothing else but man in the universe —
That, while he feels with man (to use man's speech)
I' the little things of life, its fleshly wants
Of food and rest and health and happiness,
Its simplest spirit-motions, loves and hates,
Hopes, fears, soul-cravings on the ignoblest scale,
O' the fellow-creature, — owns the bond at base, —
He tends to freedom and divergency
In the upward progress, plays the pinnacle
When life's at greatest (grant again the phrase!

Because there's neither great nor small in life).
" Consult thou for thy kind that have the eyes
To see, the mouths to eat, the hands to work,
Men with the wives, and women with the babes!"
Prompts Nature. " Care thou for thyself alone
I' the conduct of the mind God made thee with!
Think, as if man had never thought before!
Act, as if all creation hung attent
On the acting of such faculty as thine,
To take prime pattern from thy masterpiece!"
Nature prompts also: neither law obeyed
To the uttermost by any heart and soul
We know or have in record: both of them
Acknowledged blindly by whatever man
We ever knew or heard of in this world.
" Will you have why and wherefore, and the fact
Made plain as pikestaff?" modern Science asks.
" That mass man sprung from was a jelly-lump
Once on a time; he kept an after-course
Through fish and insect, reptile, bird and beast,
Till he attained to be an ape at last
Or last but one. And if this doctrine shock
In aught the natural pride" . . . Friend, banish fear,
The natural humility replies.
Do you suppose, even I, poor potentate,
Hohenstiel-Schwangau, who once ruled the roast, —
I was born able at all points to ply
My tools? or did I have to learn my trade,
Practise as exile ere perform as prince?
The world knows something of my ups and downs:
But grant me time, give me the management
And manufacture of a model me,
Me fifty-fold, a prince without a flaw, —
Why, there's no social grade, the sordidest,
My embryo potentate should blink and 'scape.
King, all the better he was cobbler once,
He should know, sitting on the throne, how tastes
Life to who sweeps the doorway. But life's hard,
Occasion rare; you cut probation short,
And, being half-instructed, on the stage
You shuffle through your part as best you can,
And bless your stars, as I do. God takes time.
I like the thought He should have lodged me once
I' the hole, the cave, the hut, the tenement,
The mansion and the palace; made me learn
The feel o' the first, before I found myself

Loftier i' the last, not more emancipate ;
From first to last of lodging, I was I,
And not at all the place that harbored me.
Do I refuse to follow farther yet
I' the backwardness, repine if tree and flower,
Mountain or streamlet were my dwelling-place
Before I gained enlargement, grew mollusk ?
As well account that way for many a thrill
Of kinship, I confess to, with the powers
Called Nature : animate, inanimate,
In parts or in the whole, there 's something there
Man-like that somehow meets the man in me.
My pulse goes altogether with the heart
O' the Persian, that old Xerxes, when he stayed
His march to conquest of the world, a day
I' the desert, for the sake of one superb
Plane-tree which queened it there in solitude :
Giving her neck its necklace, and each arm
Its armlet, suiting soft waist, snowy side,
With cincture and apparel. Yes, I lodged
In those successive tenements ; perchance
Taste yet the straitness of them while I stretch
Limb and enjoy new liberty the more.
And some abodes are lost or ruinous ;
Some, patched-up and pieced-out, and so transformed
They still accommodate the traveller
His day of lifetime. Oh you count the links,
Descry no bar of the unbroken man ?
Yes, — and who welds a lump of ore, suppose
He likes to make a chain and not a bar,
And reach by link on link, link small, link large,
Out to the due length — why, there 's forethought still
Outside o' the series, forging at one end,
While at the other there 's — no matter what
The kind of critical intelligence
Believing that last link had last but one
For parent, and no link was, first of all,
Fitted to anvil, hammered into shape.
Else, I accept the doctrine, and deduce
This duty, that I recognize mankind,
In all its height and depth and length and breadth.
Mankind i' the main have little wants, not large :
I, being of will and power to help, i' the main,
Mankind, must help the least wants first. My friend,
That is, my foe, without such power and will,
May plausibly concentrate all he wields,

And do his best at helping some large want,
Exceptionally noble cause, that's seen
Subordinate enough from where I stand.
As he helps, I helped once, when like himself,
Unable to help better, work more wide;
And so would work with heart and hand to-day,
Did only computists confess a fault,
And multiply the single score by five,
Five only, give man's life its hundred years.
Change life, in me shall follow change to match!
Time were then, to work here, there, everywhere,
By turns and try experiment at ease!
Full time to mend as well as mar: why wait
The slow and sober uprise all around
O' the building? Let us run up, right to roof,
Some sudden marvel, piece of perfectness,
And testify what we intend the whole!
Is the world losing patience? "Wait!" say we:
"There's time: no generation needs to die
Unsolaced; you've a century in store!"
But, no: I sadly let the voices wing
Their way i' the upper vacancy, nor test
Truth on this solid as I promised once.
Well, and what is there to be sad about?
The world's the world, life's life, and nothing else.
'T is part of life, a property to prize,
That those o' the higher sort engaged i' the world,
Should fancy they can change its ill to good,
Wrong to right, ugliness to beauty: find
Enough success in fancy turning fact,
To keep the sanguine kind in countenance
And justify the hope that busies them:
Failure enough, — to who can follow change
Beyond their vision, see new good prove ill
I' the consequence, see blacks and whites of life
Shift square indeed, but leave the checkered face
Unchanged i' the main, — failure enough for such,
To bid ambition keep the whole from change,
As their best service. I hope nought beside.
No, my brave thinkers, whom I recognize,
Gladly, myself the first, as, in a sense,
All that our world's worth, flower and fruit of man!
Such minds myself award supremacy
Over the common insignificance,
When only Mind's in question, — Body bows
To quite another government, you know.

Be Kant crowned king o' the castle in the air!
Hans Slouch — his own, and children's mouths to feed
I' the hovel on the ground — wants meat, nor chews
"The Critique of Pure Reason" in exchange.
But, now, — suppose I could allow your claims
And quite change life to please you, — would it please?
Would life comport with change and still be life?
Ask, now, a doctor for a remedy:
There's his prescription. Bid him point you out
Which of the five or six ingredients saves
The sick man. "Such the efficacity?
Then why not dare and do things in one dose
Simple and pure, all virtue, no alloy
Of the idle drop and powder?" What's his word?
The efficacity, neat, were neutralized:
It wants dispersing and retarding, — nay,
Is put upon its mettle, plays its part
Precisely through such hindrance everywhere,
Finds some mysterious give and take i' the case,
Some gain by opposition, he foregoes
Should he unfetter the medicament.
So with this thought of yours that fain would work
Free in the world: it wants just what it finds —
The ignorance, stupidity, the hate,
Envy and malice and uncharitableness
That bar your passage, break the flow of you
Down from those happy heights where many a cloud
Combined to give you birth and bid you be
The royalest of rivers: on you glide
Silverly till you reach the summit-edge,
Then over, on to all that ignorance,
Stupidity, hate, envy, bluffs and blocks,
Posted to fret you into foam and noise.
What of it? Up you mount in minute mist,
And bridge the chasm that crushed your quietude,
A spirit-rainbow, earthborn jewelry
Outsparkling the insipid firmament
Blue above Terni and its orange-trees.
Do not mistake me! You, too, have your rights!
Hans must not burn Kant's house above his head
Because he cannot understand Kant's book:
And still less must Hans' pastor burn Kant's self
Because Kant understands some books too well.
But, justice seen to on this little point,
Answer me, is it manly, is it sage
To stop and struggle with arrangements here

It took so many lives, so much of toil,
To tinker up into efficiency?
Can't you contrive to operate at once, —
Since time is short and art is long, — to show
Your quality i' the world, whate'er you boast,
Without this fractious call on folks to crush
The world together just to set you free,
Admire the capers you will cut perchance,
Nor mind the mischief to your neighbors?

"Age!
Age and experience bring discouragement,"
You taunt me: I maintain the opposite.
Am I discouraged who — perceiving health,
Strength, beauty, as they tempt the eye of soul,
Are uncombinable with flesh and blood —
Resolve to let my body live its best,
And leave my soul what better yet may be
Or not be, in this life or afterward?
— In either fortune, wiser than who waits
Till magic art procure a miracle.
In virtue of my very confidence
Mankind ought to outgrow its babyhood;
I prescribe rocking, deprecate rough hands,
While thus the cradle holds it past mistake.
Indeed, my task's the harder — equable
Sustainment everywhere, all strain, no push —
Whereby friends credit me with indolence,
Apathy, hesitation. "Stand stock-still
If able to move briskly? 'All a-strain' —
So must we compliment your passiveness?
Sound asleep, rather!"

Just the judgment passed
Upon a statue, luckless like myself,
I saw at Rome once! 'T was some artist's whim
To cover all the accessories close
I' the group, and leave you only Laocoön
With neither sons nor serpents to denote
The purpose of his gesture. Then a crowd
Was called to try the question, criticise
Wherefore such energy of legs and arms,
Nay, eyeballs, starting from the socket. One —
I give him leave to write my history —
Only one said, "I think the gesture strives
Against some obstacle we cannot see."

All the rest made their minds up. "'T is a yawn
Of sheer fatigue subsiding to repose :
The statue 's ' Somnolency ' clear enough ! "

There, my arch stranger-friend, my audience both
And arbitress, you have one half your wish,
At least : you know the thing I tried to do !
All, so far, to my praise and glory — all
Told as befits the self-apologist, —
Who ever promises a candid sweep
And clearance of those errors miscalled crimes
None knows more, none laments so much as he,
And ever rises from confession, proved
A god whose fault was — trying to be man.
Just so, fair judge, — if I read smile aright —
I condescend to figure in your eyes
As biggest heart and best of Europe's friends,
And hence my failure. God will estimate
Success one day ; and, in the mean time — you !

I daresay there 's some fancy of the sort
Frolicking round this final puff I send
To die up yonder in the ceiling-rose, —
Some consolation-stakes, we losers win !
A plague of the return to " I — I — I
Did this, meant that, hoped, feared the other thing ! "
Autobiography, adieu ! The rest
Shall make amends, be pure blame, history
And falsehood : not the ineffective truth,
But Thiers-and-Victor-Hugo exercise.
Hear what I never was, but might have been
I' the better world where goes tobacco-smoke !
Here lie the dozen volumes of my life :
(Did I say " lie " ? the pregnant word will serve.)
Cut on to the concluding chapter, though !
Because the little hours begin to strike.
Hurry Thiers-Hugo to the labor's end !

Something like this the unwritten chapter reads.

Exemplify the situation thus !
Hohenstiel-Schwangau, being, no dispute,
Absolute mistress, chose the Assembly, first,
To serve her : chose this man, its President
Afterward, to serve also, — specially
To see that folk did service one and all.

And now the proper term of years was out,
When the Head-servant must vacate his place ;
And nothing lay so patent to the world
As that his fellow-servants one and all
Were — mildly to make mention — knaves or fools,
Each of them with his promise flourished full
I' the face of you by word and impudence,
Or filtered slyly out by nod and wink
And nudge upon your sympathetic rib —
That not one minute more did knave or fool
Mean to keep faith and serve as he had sworn
Hohenstiel-Schwangau, once her Head away.
Why should such swear except to get the chance,
When time should ripen and confusion bloom,
Of putting Hohenstielers-Schwangauese
To the true use of human property —
Restoring souls and bodies, this to Pope,
And that to King, that other to his planned
Perfection of a Share-and-share-alike,
That other still, to Empire absolute
In shape of the Head-servant's very self
Transformed to Master whole and sole? each scheme
Discussible, concede one circumstance —
That each scheme's parent were, beside himself,
Hohenstiel-Schwangau, not her serving-man
Sworn to do service in the way she chose
Rather than his way : way superlative,
Only, — by some infatuation, — his
And his and his and everyone's but hers
Who stuck to just the Assembly and the Head.
I make no doubt the Head, too, had his dream
Of doing sudden duty swift and sure
On all that heap of untrustworthiness —
Catching each vaunter of the villany
He meant to perpetrate when time was ripe,
Once the Head-servant fairly out of doors, —
And, caging here a knave and there a fool,
Cry, " Mistress of your servants, these and me,
Hohenstiel-Schwangau ! I, their trusty Head,
Pounce on a pretty scheme concocting here
That's stopped, extinguished by my vigilance.
Your property is safe again : but mark !
Safe in these hands, not yours, who lavish trust
Too lightly. Leave my hands their charge awhile !
I know your business better than yourself:
Let me alone about it ! Some fine day,

Once we are rid of the embarrassment,
You shall look up and see your longings crowned!"
Such fancy might have tempted him be false,
But this man chose truth and was wiser so.
He recognized that for great minds i' the world
There is no trial like the appropriate one
Of leaving little minds their liberty
Of littleness to blunder on through life,
Now aiming at right ends by foolish means,
Now, at absurd achievement through the aid
Of good and wise endeavor — to acquiesce
In folly's life-long privilege, though with power
To do the little minds the good they need,
Despite themselves, by just abolishing
Their right to play the part and fill the place
I' the scheme of things He schemed who made alike
Great minds and little minds, saw use for each.
Could the orb sweep those puny particles
It just half-lights at distance, hardly leads
I' the leash — sweep out each speck of them from space
They anticise in with their days and nights
And whirlings round and dancings off, forsooth,
And all that fruitless individual life
One cannot lend a beam to but they spoil —
Sweep them into itself and so, one star,
Preponderate henceforth i' the heritage
Of heaven! No! in less senatorial phrase,
The man endured to help, not save outright
The multitude by substituting him
For them, his knowledge, will and way, for God's:
Nor change the world, such as it is, and was
And will be, for some other, suiting all
Except the purpose of the maker. No!
He saw that weakness, wickedness will be,
And therefore should be : that the perfect man,
As we account perfection — at most pure
O' the special gold, whate'er the form it take,
Head-work or heart-work, fined and thrice-refined
I' the crucible of life, whereto the powers
Of the refiner, one and all, are flung
To feed the flame, he saw that e'en the block,
Such perfect man holds out triumphant, breaks
Into some poisonous ore, gold's opposite,
At the very purest, so compensating
Man's Adversary — what if we believe?
For earlier stern exclusion of his stuff.

See the sage, with the hunger for the truth,
And see his system that's all true, except
The one weak place that's stanchioned by a lie!
The moralist, who walks with head erect
I' the crystal clarity of air so long,
Until a stumble, and the man's one mire!
Philanthropy undoes the social knot
With axe-edge, makes love room 'twixt head and trunk:
Religion — but, enough, the thing's too clear!
Well, if these sparks break out i' the greenest tree,
Our topmost of performance, yours and mine,
What will be done i' the dry ineptitude
Of ordinary mankind, bark and bole,
All seems ashamed of but their mother-earth?
Therefore throughout Head's term of servitude
He did the appointed service, and forbore
Extraneous action that were duty else,
Done by some other servant, idle now
Or mischievous: no matter, each his own —
Own task, and, in the end, own praise or blame!
He suffered them strut, prate, and brag their best,
Squabble at odds on every point save one,
And there shake hands, — agree to trifle time,
Obstruct advance with, each, his cricket-cry,
"Wait till the Head be off the shoulders here!
Then comes my King, my Pope, my Autocrat,
My Socialist Republic to her own —
To-wit, that property of only me,
Hohenstiel-Schwangau who conceits herself
Free, forsooth, and expects I keep her so!"
— Nay, suffered when, perceiving with dismay
Head's silence paid no tribute to their noise,
They turned on him. "Dumb menace in that mouth,
Malice in that unstridulosity!
He cannot but intend some stroke of state
Shall signalize his passage into peace
Out of the creaking, — hinder transference
O' the Hohenstielers-Schwangauese to king,
Pope, autocrat, or socialist republic! That's
Exact the cause his lips unlocked would cry!
Therefore be stirring: brave, beard, bully him!
Dock, by the million, of its friendly joints,
The electoral body short at once! who did,
May do again, and undo us beside;
Wrest from his hands the sword for self-defence,
The right to parry any thrust in play

We peradventure please to meditate! "
And so forth ; creak, creak, creak : and ne'er a line
His locked mouth oped the wider, till at last
O' the long degraded and insulting day,
Sudden the clock told it was judgment-time.
Then he addressed himself to speak indeed
To the fools, not knaves : they saw him walk straight down
Each step of the eminence, as he first engaged,
And stand at last o' the level, — all he swore.
" People, and not the people's varletry,
This is the task you set myself and these !
Thus I performed my part of it, and thus
They thwarted me throughout, here, here, and here :
Study each instance ! yours the loss, not mine.
What they intend now is demonstrable
As plainly : here 's such man, and here 's such mode
Of making you some other than the thing
You, wisely or unwisely, choose to be,
And only set him up to keep you so.
Do you approve this ? Yours the loss, not mine.
Do you condemn it ? There 's a remedy.
Take me — who know your mind, and mean your good,
With clearer brain and stouter arm than they,
Or you, or haply anybody else —
And make me master for the moment ! Choose
What time, what power you trust me with : I too
Will choose as frankly ere I trust myself
With time and power : they must be adequate
To the end and aim, since mine the loss, with yours,
If means be wanting ; once their worth approved,
Grant them, and I shall forthwith operate —
Ponder it well ! — to the extremest stretch
O' the power you trust me : if with unsuccess,
God wills it, and there 's nobody to blame."

Whereon the people answered with a shout,
" The trusty one ! no tricksters any more ! "
How could they other ? He was in his place.

What followed ? Just what he foresaw, what proved
The soundness of both judgments, — his, o' the knaves
And fools, each trickster with his dupe, — and theirs,
The people's, in what head and arm could help.
There was uprising, masks dropped, flags unfurled,
Weapons outflourished in the wind, my faith !
Heavily did he let his fist fall plumb

On each perturber of the public peace,
No matter whose the wagging head it broke —
From bald-pate craft and greed and impudence
Of night-hawk at first chance to prowl and prey
For glory and a little gain beside,
Passing for eagle in the dusk of the age, —
To florid head-top, foamy patriotism
And tribunitial daring, breast laid bare
Through confidence in rectitude, with hand
On private pistol in the pocket: these
And all the dupes of these, who lent themselves
As dust and feather do, to help offence
O' the wind that whirls them at you, then subsides
In safety somewhere, leaving filth afloat,
Annoyance you may brush from eyes and beard, —
These he stopped: bade the wind's spite howl or whine
Its worst outside the building, wind conceives
Meant to be pulled together and become
Its natural playground so. What foolishness
Of dust or feather proved importunate
And fell 'twixt thumb and finger, found them gripe
To detriment of bulk and buoyancy.
Then followed silence and submission. Next,
The inevitable comment came on work
And work's cost: he was censured as profuse
Of human life and liberty: too swift
And thorough his procedure, who had lagged
At the outset, lost the opportunity
Through timid scruples as to right and wrong.
"There's no such certain mark of a small mind"
(So did Sagacity explain the fault)
"As when it needs must square away and sink
To its own small dimensions, private scale
Of right and wrong, — humanity i' the large,
The right and wrong of the universe, forsooth!
This man addressed himself to guard and guide
Hohenstiel-Schwangau. When the case demands
He frustrate villany in the egg, unhatched,
With easy stamp and minimum of pang
E'en to the punished reptile, 'There's my oath
Restrains my foot,' objects our guide and guard,
'I must leave guardianship and guidance now:
Rather than stretch one handbreadth of the law,
I am bound to see it break from end to end.
First show me death i' the body politic:
Then prescribe pill and potion, what may please

Hohenstiel-Schwangau ! all is for her sake :
'T was she ordained my service should be so.
What if the event demonstrate her unwise,
If she unwill the thing she willed before ?
I hold to the letter and obey the bond
And leave her to perdition loyally.'
Whence followed thrice the expenditure we blame
Of human life and liberty : for want
O' the by-blow, came deliberate butcher's-work ! "
" Elsewhere go carry your complaint ! " bade he.
" Least, largest, there 's one law for all the minds,
Here or above : be true at any price !
'T is just o' the great scale, that such happy stroke
Of falsehood would be found a failure.   Truth
Still stands unshaken at her base by me,
Reigns paramount i' the world, for the large good
O' the long late generations, — I and you
Forgotten like this buried foolishness !
Not so the good I rooted in its grave."

This is why he refused to break his oath,
Rather appealed to the people, gained the power
To act as he thought best, then used it, once
For all, no matter what the consequence
To knaves and fools.   As thus began his sway,
So, through its twenty years, one rule of right
Sufficed him : govern for the many first,
The poor mean multitude, all mouths and eyes :
Bid the few, better favored in the brain,
Be patient, nor presume on privilege,
Help him or else be quiet, — never crave
That he help them, — increase, forsooth, the gulf
Yawning so terribly 'twixt mind and mind
I' the world here, which his purpose was to block
At bottom, were it by an inch, and bridge,
If by a filament, no more, at top.
Equalize things a little !   And the way
He took to work that purpose out, was plain
Enough to intellect and honesty
And — superstition, style it if you please,
So long as you allow there was no lack
O' the quality imperative in man —
Reverence.   You see deeper ? thus saw he,
And by the light he saw, must walk : how else
Was he to do his part ? a man's, with might
And main, and not a faintest touch of fear,

Sure he was in the hand of God who comes
Before and after, with a work to do
Which no man helps nor hinders. Thus the man, —
So timid when the business was to touch
The uncertain order of humanity,
Imperil, for a problematic cure
Of grievance on the surface, any good
I' the deep of things, dim yet discernible, —
This same man, so irresolute before,
Show him a true excrescence to cut sheer,
A devil's graft on God's foundation-stock,
Then — no complaint of indecision more!
He wrenched out the whole canker, root and branch,
Deaf to who cried that earth would tumble in
At its four corners if he touched a twig.
Witness that lie of lies, arch-infamy,
When the Republic, with her life involved
In just this law — " Each people rules itself
Its own way, not as any stranger please " —
Turned, and for first proof she was living, bade
Hohenstiel-Schwangau fasten on the throat
Of the first neighbor that claimed benefit
O' the law herself established : " Hohenstiel
For Hohenstielers! Rome, by parity
Of reasoning, for Romans? That's a jest
Wants proper treatment, — lancet-puncture suits
The proud flesh: Rome ape Hohenstiel forsooth! "
And so the siege and slaughter and success
Whereof we nothing doubt that Hohenstiel
Will have to pay the price, in God's good time,
Which does not always fall on Saturday
When the world looks for wages. Anyhow,
He found this infamy triumphant. Well:
Sagacity suggested, make this speech!
" The work was none of mine : suppose wrong wait,
Stand over for redressing? Mine for me,
My predecessors' work on their own head!
Meantime, there's plain advantage, should we leave
Things as we find them. Keep Rome manacled
Hand and foot: no fear of unruliness!
Her foes consent to even seem our friends
So long, no longer. Then, there's glory got
By boldness and bravado to the world:
The disconcerted world must grin and bear
The old saucy writing, — ' Grunt thereat who may,
So shall things be, for such my pleasure is —

Hohenstiel-Schwangau's.' How that reads in Rome,
I' the capitol where Brennus broke his pate,
And lends a flourish to our journalists!"
Only, it was nor read nor flourished of,
Since, not a moment did such glory stay
Excision of the canker! Out it came,
Root and branch, with much roaring, and some blood,
And plentiful abuse of him from friend
And foe. Who cared? Not Nature, who assuaged
The pain and set the patient on his legs
Promptly: the better! had it been the worse,
'T is Nature you must try conclusions with,
Not he, since nursing canker kills the sick
For certain, while to cut may cure, at least.
" Ah," groaned a second time Sagacity,
" Again the little mind, precipitate,
Rash, rude, when even in the right, as here!
The great mind knows the power of gentleness,
Only tries force because persuasion fails.
Had this man, by prelusive trumpet-blast,
Signified, 'Truth and Justice mean to come,
Nay, fast approach your threshold! Ere they knock,
See that the house be set in order, swept
And garnished, windows shut, and doors thrown wide!
The free State comes to visit the free Church:
Receive her! or . . . or . . . never mind what else!'
Thus moral suasion heralding brute force,
How had he seen the old abuses die,
And new life kindle here, there, everywhere,
Roused simply by that mild yet potent spell —
Beyond or beat of drum or stroke of sword —
Public opinion!"

"How, indeed?" he asked,
" When all to see, after some twenty years,
Were your own fool-face waiting for the sight,
Faced by as wide a grin from ear to ear
O' the knaves who, while the fools were waiting, worked —
Broke yet another generation's heart —
Twenty years' respite helping! Teach your nurse
'Compliance with, before you suck, the teat!'
Find what that means, and meanwhile hold your tongue!"

Whereof the war came which he knew must be.

Now, this had proved the dry-rot of the race
He ruled o'er, that, i' the old day, when was need

They fought for their own liberty and life,
Well did they fight, none better: whence, such love
Of fighting somehow still for fighting's sake
Against no matter whose the liberty
And life, so long as self-conceit should crow
And clap the wing, while justice sheathed her claw, —
That what had been the glory of the world
When thereby came the world's good, grew its plague
Now that the champion-armor, donned to dare
The dragon once, was clattered up and down
Highway and by-path of the world at peace,
Merely to mask marauding, or for sake
O' the shine and rattle that apprised the fields
Hohenstiel-Schwangau was a fighter yet,
And would be, till the weary world suppressed
Her peccant humors out of fashion now.
Accordingly the world spoke plain at last,
Promised to punish who next played with fire.

So, at his advent, such discomfiture
Taking its true shape of beneficence,
Hohenstiel-Schwangau, half-sad and part-wise,
Sat: if with wistful eye reverting oft
To each pet weapon, rusty on its peg,
Yet, with a sigh of satisfaction too
That, peacefulness become the law, herself
Got the due share of godsends in its train,
Cried shame and took advantage quietly.
Still, so the dry-rot had been nursed into
Blood, bones and marrow, that, from worst to best,
All, — clearest brains and soundest hearts save here, —
All had this lie acceptable for law
Plain as the sun at noonday — " War is best,
Peace is worst; peace we only tolerate
As needful preparation for new war:
War may be for whatever end we will —
Peace only as the proper help thereto.
Such is the law of right and wrong for us
Hohenstiel-Schwangau: for the other world,
As naturally, quite another law.
Are we content? The world is satisfied.
Discontent? Then the world must give us leave
To strike right, left, and exercise our arm
Torpid of late through overmuch repose,
And show its strength is still superlative
At somebody's expense in life or limb:

Which done, — let peace succeed and last a year!"
Such devil's-doctrine so was judged God's law,
We say, when this man stepped upon the stage,
That it had seemed a venial fault at most
Had he once more obeyed Sagacity.
"You come i' the happy interval of peace,
The favorable weariness from war:
Prolong it! artfully, as if intent
On ending peace as soon as possible.
Quietly so increase the sweets of ease
And safety, so employ the multitude,
Put hod and trowel so in idle hands,
So stuff and stop up wagging jaws with bread,
That selfishness shall surreptitiously
Do wisdom's office, whisper in the ear
Of Hohenstiel-Schwangau, there's a pleasant feel
In being gently forced down, pinioned fast
To the easy arm-chair by the pleading arms
O' the world beseeching her to there abide
Content with all the harm done hitherto,
And let herself be petted in return,
Free to re-wage, in speech and prose and verse,
The old unjust wars, nay — in verse and prose
And speech, — to vaunt new victories, shall prove
A plague o' the future, — so that words suffice
For present comfort, and no deeds denote
That — tired of illimitable line on line
Of boulevard-building, tired o' the theatre
With the tuneful thousand in their thrones above,
For glory of the male intelligence,
And Nakedness in her due niche below,
For illustration of the female use —
That she, 'twixt yawn and sigh, prepares to slip
Out of the arm-chair, wants fresh blood again
From over the boundary, to color-up
The sheeny sameness, keep the world aware
Hohenstiel-Schwangau's arm needs exercise
Despite the petting of the universe!
Come, you're a city-builder: what's the way
Wisdom takes when time needs that she entice
Some fierce tribe, castled on the mountain-peak,
Into the quiet and amenity
O' the meadow-land below? By crying 'Done
With fight now, down with fortress'? Rather — 'Dare
On, dare ever, not a stone displaced!'
Cries Wisdom: 'Cradle of our ancestors,

Be bulwark, give our children safety still!
Who of our children please may stoop and taste
O' the valley-fatness, unafraid, — for why?
At first alarm they have thy mother-ribs
To run upon for refuge; foes forget
Scarcely that Terror on her vantage-coign,
Couchant supreme among the powers of air,
Watches — prepared to pounce — the country wide!
Meanwhile the encouraged valley holds its own,
From the first hut's adventure in descent,
Half home, half hiding-place, — to dome and spire
Befitting the assured metropolis:
Nor means offence to the fort which caps the crag,
All undismantled of a turret-stone,
And bears the banner-pole that creaks at times
Embarrassed by the old emblazonment,
When festal days are to commemorate:
Otherwise left untenanted, no doubt,
Since, never fear, our myriads from below
Would rush, if needs were, man the walls again,
Renew the exploits of the earlier time
At moment's notice! But till notice sound,
Inhabit we in ease and opulence!'
And so, till one day thus a notice sounds,
Not trumpeted, but in a whisper-gust
Fitfully playing through mute city streets
At midnight weary of day's feast and game —
'Friends, your famed fort's a ruin past repair!
Its use is — to proclaim it had a use
Obsolete long since. Climb and study there
How to paint barbican and battlement
I' the scenes of our new theatre! We fight
Now — by forbidding neighbors to sell steel
Or buy wine, not by blowing out their brains!
Moreover, while we let time sap the strength
O' the walls omnipotent in menace once,
Neighbors would seem to have prepared surprise —
Run up defences in a mushroom-growth,
For all the world like what we boasted: brief —
Hohenstiel-Schwangau's policy is peace!'"

Ay, so Sagacity advised him filch
Folly from fools: handsomely substitute
The dagger o' lath, while gay they sang and danced,
For that long dangerous sword they liked to feel,
Even at feast-time, clink and make friends start.

No! he said: "Hear the truth, and bear the truth,
And bring the truth to bear on all you are
And do, assured that only good comes thence
Whate'er the shape good take! While I have rule,
Understand!— war for war's sake, war for sake
O' the good war gets you as war's sole excuse,
Is damnable and damned shall be. You want
Glory? Why so do I, and so does God.
Where is it found,— in this paraded shame, —
One particle of glory? Once you warred
For liberty against the world, and won:
There was the glory. Now, you fain would war
Because the neighbor prospers overmuch, —
Because there has been silence half-an-hour,
Like Heaven on earth, without a cannon-shot
Announcing Hohenstielers-Schwanganese
Are minded to disturb the jubilee,—
Because the loud tradition echoes faint,
And who knows but posterity may doubt
If the great deeds were ever done at all,
Much less believe, were such to do again,
So the event would follow: therefore, prove
The old power, at the expense of somebody!
Oh, Glory,— gilded bubble, bard and sage
So nickname rightly,— would thy dance endure
One moment, would thy vaunting make believe
Only one eye thy ball was solid gold,
Hadst thou less breath to buoy thy vacancy
Than a whole multitude expends in praise,
Less range for roaming than from head to head
Of a whole people? Flit, fall, fly again,
Only, fix never where the resolute hand
May prick thee, prove the glassy lie thou art!
Give me real intellect to reason with,
No multitude, no entity that apes
One wise man, being but a million fools!
How and whence wishest glory, thou wise one?
Wouldst get it, — didst thyself guide Providence, —
By stinting of his due each neighbor round
In strength and knowledge and dexterity
So as to have thy littleness grow large
By all those somethings once, turned nothings now,
As children make a molehill mountainous
By scooping out a trench around their pile,
And saving so the mudwork from approach?
Quite otherwise the cheery game of life,

True yet mimetic warfare, whereby man
Does his best with his utmost, and so ends
The victor most of all in fair defeat.
Who thinks, — would he have no one think beside?
Who knows, who does, — save his must learning die
And action cease? Why, so our giant proves
No better than a dwarf, once rivalry
Prostrate around him. Let the whole race stand
For him to try conclusions fairly with!
Show me the great man would engage his peer
Rather by grinning ' Cheat, thy gold is brass!'
Than granting ' Perfect piece of purest ore!
Still, is it less good mintage, this of mine?'
Well, and these right and sound results of soul
I' the strong and healthy one wise man, — shall such
Be vainly sought for, scornfully renounced
I' the multitude that make the entity —
The people? — to what purpose, if no less,
In power and purity of soul, below
The reach of the unit than, by multiplied
Might of the body, vulgarized the more,
Above, in thick and threefold brutishness?
See! you accept such one wise man, myself:
Wiser or less wise, still I operate
From my own stock of wisdom, nor exact
Of other sort of natures you admire,
That whoso rhymes a sonnet pays a tax,
Who paints a landscape dips brush at his cost,
Who scores a septett true for strings and wind
Mulcted must be — else how should I impose
Properly, attitudinize aright,
Did such conflicting claims as these divert
Hohenstiel-Schwangau from observing me?
Therefore, what I find facile, you be sure,
With effort or without it, you shall dare —
You, I aspire to make my better self
And truly the Great Nation. No more war
For war's sake, then! and, — seeing, wickedness
Springs out of folly, — no more foolish dread
O' the neighbor waxing too inordinate
A rival, through his gain of wealth and ease!
What? — keep me patient, Powers! — the people here,
Earth presses to her heart, nor owns a pride
Above her pride i' the race all flame and air
And aspiration to the boundless Great,
The incommensurably Beautiful —

Whose very falterings groundward come of flight
Urged by a pinion all too passionate
For heaven and what it holds of gloom and glow :
Bravest of thinkers, bravest of the brave
Doers, exalt in Science, rapturous
In Art, the — more than all — magnetic race
To fascinate their fellows, mould mankind
Hohenstiel-Schwangau-fashion, — these, what ? —these
Will have to abdicate their primacy
Should such a nation sell them steel untaxed,
And such another take itself, on hire
For the natural sennight, somebody for lord
Unpatronized by me whose back was turned ?
Or such another yet would fain build bridge,
Lay rail, drive tunnel, busy its poor self
With its appropriate fancy : so there's — flash —
Hohenstiel-Schwangau up in arms at once !
Genius has somewhat of the infantine :
But of the childish, not a touch nor taint
Except through self-will, which, being foolishness,
Is certain, soon or late, of punishment.
Which Providence avert ! — and that it may
Avert what both of us would so deserve,
No foolish dread o' the neighbor, I enjoin !
By consequence, no wicked war with him,
While I rule !

     " Does that mean — no war at all
When just the wickedness I here proscribe
Comes, haply, from the neighbor ? Does my speech
Precede the praying that you beat the sword
To ploughshare, and the spear to pruning-hook,
And sit down henceforth under your own vine
And fig-tree through the sleepy summer month,
Letting what hurly-burly please explode
On the other side the mountain-frontier ? No,
Beloved ! I foresee and I announce
Necessity of warfare in one case,
For one cause : one way, I bid broach the blood
O' the world. For truth and right, and only right
And truth, — right, truth, on the absolute scale of God,
No pettiness of man's admeasurement, —
In such case only, and for such one cause,
Fight your hearts out, whatever fate betide
Hands energetic to the uttermost !
Lie not ! Endure no lie which needs your heart

And hand to push it out of mankind's path —
No lie that lets the natural forces work
Too long ere lay it plain and pulverized —
Seeing man's life lasts only twenty years!
And such a lie, before both man and God,
Proving, at this time present, Austria's rule
O'er Italy, — for Austria's sake the first,
Italy's next, and our sake last of all,
Come with me and deliver Italy!
Smite hip and thigh until the oppressor leave
Free from the Adriatic to the Alps
The oppressed one! We were they who laid her low
In the old bad day when Villany braved Truth
And Right, and laughed 'Henceforward, God deposed,
Satan we set to rule forevermore
I' the world!' — whereof to stop the consequence,
And for atonement of false glory there
Gaped at and gabbled over by the world,
I purpose to get God enthroned again
For what the world will gird at as sheer shame
I' the cost of blood and treasure. 'All for nought —
Not even, say, some patch of province, splice
O' the frontier? — some snug honorarium-fee
Shut into glove and pocketed apace?'
(Questions Sagacity) 'in deference
To the natural susceptibility
Of folks at home, unwitting of that pitch
You soar to, and misdoubting if Truth, Right
And the other such augustnesses repay
Expenditure in coin o' the realm, — but prompt
To recognize the cession of Savoy
And Nice as marketable value!' No,
Sagacity, go preach to Metternich,
And, sermon ended, stay where he resides!
Hohenstiel-Schwangau, you and I must march
The other road! war for the hate of war,
Not love, this once!" So Italy was free.

What else noteworthy and commendable
I' the man's career? — that he was resolute —
No trepidation, much less treachery
On his part, should imperil from its poise
The ball o' the world, heaved up at such expense
Of pains so far, and ready to rebound,
Let but a finger maladroitly fall,
Under pretence of making fast and sure

The inch gained by late volubility,
And run itself back to the ancient rest
At foot o' the mountain. Thus he ruled, gave proof
The world had gained a point, progressive so,
By choice, this time, as will and power concurred,
O' the fittest man to rule ; not chance of birth,
Or such-like dice-throw. Oft Sagacity
Was at his ear : " Confirm this clear advance,
Support this wise procedure ! You, elect
O' the people, mean to justify their choice
And out-king all the kingly imbeciles ;
But that's just half the enterprise : remains
You find them a successor like yourself,
In head and heart and eye and hand and aim,
Or all done's undone ; and whom hope to mould
So like you as the pupil Nature sends,
The son and heir's completeness which you lack?
Lack it no longer ! Wed the pick o' the world,
Where'er you think you find it. Should she be
A queen, — tell Hohenstielers-Schwangauese,
' So do the old enthroned decrepitudes
Acknowledge, in the rotten hearts of them,
Their knell is knolled, they hasten to make peace
With the new order, recognize in me
Your right to constitute what king you will,
Cringe therefore crown in hand and bride on arm,
To both of us : we triumph, I suppose ! '
Is it the other sort of rank ? — bright eye,
Soft smile, and so forth, all her queenly boast ?
Undaunted the exordium — ' I, the man
O' the people, with the people mate myself :
So stand, so fall. Kings, keep your crowns and brides !
Our progeny (if Providence agree)
Shall live to tread the baubles underfoot
And bid the scarecrows consort with their kin.
For son, as for his sire, be the free wife
In the free state ! ' "

                    That is, Sagacity
Would prop up one more lie, the most of all
Pernicious fancy that the son and heir
Receives the genius from the sire, himself
Transmits as surely, — ask experience else !
Which answers, — never was so plain a truth
As that God drops his seed of heavenly flame
Just where He wills on earth : sometimes where man

Seems to tempt — such the accumulated store
Of faculties — one spark to fire the heap;
Sometimes where, fire-ball-like, it falls upon
The naked unpreparedness of rock,
Burns, beaconing the nations through their night.
Faculties, fuel for the flame? All helps
Come, ought to come, or come not, crossed by chance,
From culture and transmission. What's your want
I' the son and heir? Sympathy, aptitude,
Teachableness, the fuel for the flame?
You'll have them for your pains: but the flame's self,
The novel thought of God shall light the world?
No, poet, though your offspring rhyme and chime
I' the cradle, — painter, no, for all your pet
Draws his first eye, beats Salvatore's boy,—
And thrice no, statesman, should your progeny
Tie bib and tucker with no tape but red,
And make a foolscap-kite of protocols!
Critic and copyist and bureaucrat
To heart's content! The seed o' the apple-tree
Brings forth another tree which bears a crab :
'Tis the great gardener grafts the excellence
On wildings where he will.

                    "How plain I view,
Across those misty years 'twixt me and Rome" —
(Such the man's answer to Sagacity) —
"The little wayside temple, halfway down
To a mild river that makes oxen white
Miraculously, un-mouse-colors skin,
Or so the Roman country people dream!
I view that sweet small shrub-imbedded shrine
On the declivity, was sacred once
To a transmuting Genius of the land,
Could touch and turn its dunnest natures bright,
— Since Italy means the Land of the Ox, we know.
Well, how was it the due succession fell
From priest to priest who ministered i' the cool
Calm fane o' the Clitumnian god? The sire
Brought forth a son and sacerdotal sprout,
Endowed instinctively with good and grace
To suit the gliding gentleness below —
Did he? Tradition tells another tale.
Each priest obtained his predecessor's staff,·
Robe, fillet and insignia, blamelessly,
By springing out of ambush, soon or late,

And slaying him: the initiative rite
Simply was murder, save that murder took,
I' the case, another and religious name.
So it was once, is now, shall ever be
With genius and its priesthood in this world:
The new power slays the old — but handsomely.
There he lies, not diminished by an inch
Of stature that he graced the altar with,
Though somebody of other bulk and build
Cries, ' What a goodly personage lies here
Reddening the water where the bulrush roots !
May I conduct the service in his place,
Decently and in order, as did he,
And, as he did not, keep a wary watch
When meditating 'neath yon willow shade ! '
Find out your best man, sure the son of him
Will prove best man again, and, better still
Somehow than best, the grandson-prodigy !
You think the world would last another day
Did we so make us masters of the trick
Whereby the works go, we could pre-arrange
Their play and reach perfection when we please ?
Depend on it, the change and the surprise
Are part o' the plan : 't is we wish steadiness ;
Nature prefers a motion by unrest,
Advancement through this force which jostles that.
And so, since much remains i' the world to see,
Here 's the world still, affording God the sight."
Thus did the man refute Sagacity,
Ever at this old whisper in his ear:
" Here are you picked out, by a miracle,
And placed conspicuously enough, folks say
And you believe, by Providence outright
Taking a new way — nor without success —
To put the world upon its mettle : good !
But Fortune alternates with Providence ;
Resource is soon exhausted.   Never count
On such a happy hit occurring twice !
Try the old method next time ! "

" Old enough,"
(At whisper in his ear, the laugh outbroke,)
" And mode the most discredited of all,
By just the men and women who make boast
They are kings and queens thereby !   Mere self-defence
Should teach them, on one chapter of the law

Must be no sort of trifling — chastity:
They stand or fall, as their progenitors
Were chaste or unchaste. Now, run eye around
My crowned acquaintance, give each life its look
And no more, — why, you'd think each life was led
Purposely for example of what pains
Who leads it took to cure the prejudice,
And prove there's nothing so unprovable
As who is who, what son of what a sire,
And — inferentially — how faint the chance
That the next generation needs to fear
Another fool o' the selfsame type as he
Happily regnant now by right divine
And luck o' the pillow! No: select your lord
By the direct employment of your brains
As best you may, — bad as the blunder prove,
A far worse evil stank beneath the sun
When some legitimate blockhead managed so
Matters that high time was to interfere,
Though interference came from hell itself
And not the blind mad miserable mob
Happily ruled so long by pillow-luck
And divine right, — by lies in short, not truth.
And meanwhile use the allotted minute . . . "

                 One, —
Two, three, four, five — yes, five the pendule warns!
Eh? Why, this wild work wanders past all bound
And bearing! Exile, Leicester Square, the life
I' the old gay miserable time, rehearsed,
Tried on again like cast clothes, still to serve
At a pinch, perhaps? "Who's who?" was aptly asked,
Since certainly I am not I! since when?
Where is the bud-mouthed arbitress? A nod
Out-Homering Homer! Stay — there flits the clue
I fain would find the end of! Yes, — "Meanwhile,
Use the allotted minute!" Well, you see,
(Veracious and imaginary Thiers,
Who map out thus the life I might have led,
But did not, — all the worse for earth and me, —
Doff spectacles, wipe pen, shut book, decamp!)
You see 't is easy in heroics! Plain
Pedestrian speech shall help me perorate.
Ah, if one had no need to use the tongue!

How obvious and how easy 't is to talk
Inside the soul, a ghostly dialogue —
Instincts with guesses, — instinct, guess, again
With dubious knowledge, half-experience : each
And all the interlocutors alike
Subordinating, — as decorum bids,
Oh, never fear! but still decisively, —
Claims from without that take too high a tone,
—(" God wills this, man wants that, the dignity
Prescribed a prince would wish the other thing ") —
Putting them back to insignificance
Beside one intimatest fact — myself
Am first to be considered, since I live
Twenty years longer and then end, perhaps!
But, where one ceases to soliloquize,
Somehow the motives, that did well enough
I' the darkness, when you bring them into light
Are found, like those famed cave-fish, to lack eye
And organ for the upper magnitudes.
The other common creatures, of less fine
Existence, that acknowledge earth and heaven,
Have it their own way in the argument.
Yes, forced to speak, one stoops to say — one's aim
Was — what it peradventure should have been :
To renovate a people, mend or end
That bane come of a blessing meant the world —
Inordinate culture of the sense made quick
By soul, — the lust o' the flesh, lust of the eye,
And pride of life, — and, consequent on these,
The worship of that prince o' the power o' the air
Who paints the cloud and fills the emptiness
And bids his votaries, famishing for truth,
Feed on a lie.

   Alack, one lies one's self
Even in the stating that one's end was truth,
Truth only, if one states as much in words!
Give me the inner chamber of the soul
For obvious easy argument! 't is there
One pits the silent truth against a lie —
Truth which breaks shell a careless simple bird,
Nor wants a gorget nor a beak filed fine,
Steel spurs and the whole armory o' the tongue,
To equalize the odds. But, do your best,
Words have to come : and somehow words deflect
As the best cannon ever rifled will.

"Deflect" indeed! nor merely words from thoughts
But names from facts : "Clitumnus" did I say?
As if it had been his ox-whitening wave
Whereby folk practised that grim cult of old —
The murder of their temple's priest by who
Would qualify for his succession.   Sure —
Nemi was the true lake's style.   Dream had need
Of the ox-whitening peace of prettiness
And so confused names, well known once awake.

So, i' the Residenz yet, not Leicester Square,
Alone, — no such congenial intercourse! —
My reverie concludes, as dreaming should,
With daybreak : nothing done and over yet,
Except cigars!   The adventure thus may be,
Or never needs to be at all : who knows?
My Cousin-Duke, perhaps, at whose hard head
— Is it, now — is this letter to be launched,
The sight of whose gray oblong, whose grim seal,
Set all these fancies floating for an hour?

Twenty years are good gain, come what come will!
Double or quits!   The letter goes!   Or stays?

FIFINE AT THE FAIR

[1872]

DONE ELVIRE.

Vous plaît-il, don Juan, nous éclaircir ces beaux mystères ?

DON JUAN.

Madame, à vous dire la vérité . . .

DONE ELVIRE.

Ah ! que vous savez mal vous défendre pour un homme de cour, et qui doit être accoutumé à ces sortes de choses ! J'ai pitié de vous voir la confusion que vous avez. Que ne vous armez-vous le front d'une noble effronterie ? Que ne me jurez-vous que vous êtes toujours dans les mêmes sentimens pour moi, que vous m'aimez toujours avec une ardeur sans égale, et que rien n'est capable de vous détacher de moi que la mort ? — (*Molière, Don Juan*, Act 1ᵉʳ. Scène 3e.)

DONNA ELVIRA.

Don Juan, might you please to help one give a guess,
Hold up a candle, clear this fine mysteriousness ?

DON JUAN.

Madam, if needs I must declare the truth, — in short . . .

DONNA ELVIRA.

Fie, for a man of mode, accustomed at the court
To such a style of thing, how awkwardly my lord
Attempts defence ! You move compassion, that's the word —
Dumb-foundered and chapfallen ! Why don't you arm your brow
With noble impudence ? Why don't you swear and vow
No sort of change is come to any sentiment
You ever had for me ? Affection holds the bent,
You love me now as erst, with passion that makes pale
All ardor else : nor aught in nature can avail
To separate us two, save what, in stopping breath,
May peradventure stop devotion likewise — death !

PROLOGUE.

AMPHIBIAN.

THE fancy I had to-day,
    Fancy which turned a fear!
I swam far out in the bay,
    Since waves laughed warm and clear.

I lay and looked at the sun,
    The noon-sun looked at me:
Between us two, no one
    Live creature, that I could see.

Yes! There came floating by
    Me, who lay floating too,
Such a strange butterfly!
    Creature as dear as new:

Because the membraned wings
    So wonderful, so wide,
So sun-suffused, were things
    Like soul and nought beside.

A handbreadth overhead!
    All of the sea my own,
It owned the sky instead;
    Both of us were alone.

I never shall join its flight,
    For, nought buoys flesh in air.
If it touch the sea — good night!
    Death sure and swift waits there.

Can the insect feel the better
    For watching the uncouth play
Of limbs that slip the fetter,
    Pretend as they were not clay?

Undoubtedly I rejoice
    That the air comports so well
With a creature which had the choice
    Of the land once. Who can tell?

What if a certain soul
    Which early slipped its sheath,

And has for its home the whole
    Of heaven, thus look beneath,

Thus watch one who, in the world,
    Both lives and likes life's way,
Nor wishes the wings unfurled
    That sleep in the worm, they say?

But sometimes when the weather
    Is blue, and warm waves tempt
To free oneself of tether,
    And try a life exempt

From worldly noise and dust,
    In the sphere which overbrims
With passion and thought, — why, just
    Unable to fly, one swims!

By passion and thought upborne,
    One smiles to one's self — " They fare
Scarce better, they need not scorn
    Our sea, who live in the air!"

Emancipate through passion
    And thought, with sea for sky,
We substitute, in a fashion,
    For heaven — poetry:

Which sea, to all intent,
    Gives flesh such noon-disport
As a finer element
    Affords the spirit-sort.

Whatever they are, we seem:
    Imagine the thing they know;
All deeds they do, we dream;
    Can heaven be else but so?

And meantime, yonder streak
    Meets the horizon's verge;
That is the land, to seek
    If we tire or dread the surge:

Land the solid and safe —
    To welcome again (confess!)
When, high and dry, we chafe
    The body, and don the dress.

Does she look, pity, wonder
At one who mimics flight,
Swims — heaven above, sea under,
Yet always earth in sight?

FIFINE AT THE FAIR.

I.

O TRIP and skip, Elvire! Link arm in arm with me!
Like husband and like wife, together let us see
The tumbling-troop arrayed, the strollers on their stage,
Drawn up and under arms, and ready to engage.

II.

Now, who supposed the night would play us such a prank?
— That what was raw and brown, rough pole and shaven plank,
Mere bit of hoarding, half by trestle propped, half tub,
Would flaunt it forth as brisk as butterfly from grub?
This comes of sun and air, of Autumn afternoon,
And Pornic and Saint Gille, whose feast affords the boon —
This scaffold turned parterre, this flower-bed in full blow,
Bateleurs, baladines! We shall not miss the show!
They pace and promenade; they presently will dance:
What good were else i' the drum and fife? O pleasant land of
  France!

III.

Who saw them make their entry? At wink of eve, be sure!
They love to steal a march, nor lightly risk the lure.
They keep their treasure hid, nor stale (improvident)
Before the time is ripe, each wonder of their tent —
Yon six-legged sheep, to wit, and he who beats a gong,
Lifts cap and waves salute, exhilarates the throng —
Their ape of many years and much adventure, grim
And gray with pitying fools who find a joke in him.
Or, best, the human beauty, Mimi, Toinette, Fifine,
Tricot fines down if fat, padding plumps up if lean,
Ere, shedding petticoat, modesty, and such toys,
They bounce forth, squalid girls transformed to gamesome boys.

IV.

No, no, thrice, Pornic, no! Perpend the authentic tale!
'T was not for every Gawain to gaze upon the Grail!
But whoso went his rounds, when flew bat, flitted midge,

Might hear across the dusk, — where both roads join the bridge,
Hard by the little port, — creak a slow caravan,
A chimneyed house on wheels; so shyly-sheathed, began
To broaden out the bud which, bursting unaware,
Now takes away our breath, queen-tulip of the Fair!

V.

Yet morning promised much: for, pitched and slung and
    reared
On terrace 'neath the tower, 'twixt tree and tree appeared
An airy structure; how the pennon from its dome,
Frenetic to be free, makes one red stretch for home!
The home far and away, the distance where lives joy,
The cure, at once and ever, of world and world's annoy;
Since, what lolls full in front, a furlong from the booth,
But ocean-idleness, sky-blue and millpond-smooth?

VI.

Frenetic to be free! And, do you know, there beats
Something within my breast, as sensitive? — repeats
The fever of the flag? My heart makes just the same
Passionate stretch, fires up for lawlessness, lays claim
To share the life they lead: losels, who have and use
The hour what way they will, — applaud them or abuse
Society, whereof myself am at the beck,
Whose call obey, and stoop to burden stiffest neck!

VII.

Why is it that whene'er a faithful few combine
To cast allegiance off, play truant, nor repine,
Agree to bear the worst, forego the best in store
For us who, left behind, do duty as of yore, —
Why is it that, disgraced, they seem to relish life the more?
— Seem as they said, "We know a secret passing praise
Or blame of such as you! Remain! we go our ways
With something you o'erlooked, forgot or chose to sweep
Clean out of door: our pearl picked from your rubbish-heap.
You care not for your loss, we calculate our gain.
All's right. Are you content? Why, so let things remain!
To the wood then, to the wild: free life, full liberty!"
And when they rendezvous beneath the inclement sky,
House by the hedge, reduced to brute-companionship,
— Misguided ones who gave society the slip,
And find too late how boon a parent they despised,
What ministration spurned, how sweet and civilized —
Then, left alone at last with self-sought wretchedness,

No interloper else! — why is it, can we guess? —
At somebody's expense, goes up so frank a laugh?
As though they held the corn, and left us only chaff
From garners crammed and closed. And we indeed are clever
If we get grain as good, by threshing straw forever!

VIII.

Still, truants as they are and purpose yet to be,
That nowise needs forbid they venture — as you see —
To cross confine, approach the once familiar roof
O' the kindly race their flight estranged: stand half aloof,
Sidle half up, press near, and proffer wares for sale
— In their phrase, — make, in ours, white levy of black mail.
They, of the wild, require some touch of us the tame,
Since clothing, meat and drink, mean money all the same.

IX.

If hunger, proverbs say, allures the wolf from wood,
Much more the bird must dare a dash at something good:
Must snatch up, bear away in beak, the trifle-treasure
To wood and wild, and then — O how enjoy at leisure!
Was never tree-built nest, you climbed and took, of bird,
(Rare city-visitant, talked of, scarce seen or heard,)
But, when you would dissect the structure, piece by piece,
You found, enwreathed amid the country-product — fleece
And feather, thistle-fluffs and bearded windlestraws —
Some shred of foreign silk, unravelling of gauze,
Bit, maybe, of brocade, mid fur and blow-bell-down:
Filched plainly from mankind, dear tribute paid by town,
Which proved how oft the bird had plucked up heart of grace,
Swooped down at waif and stray, made furtively our place
Pay tax and toll, then borne the booty to enrich
Her paradise i' the waste; the how and why of which,
That is the secret, there the mystery that stings!

X.

For, what they traffic in, consists of just the things
We, — proud ones who so scorn dwellers without the pale,
Bateleurs, baladines, white leviers of black mail, —
I say, they sell what we most pique us that we keep!
How comes it, all we hold so dear they count so cheap?

XI.

What price should you impose, for instance, on repute,
Good fame, your own good fame and family's to boot?
Stay start of quick moustache, arrest the angry rise

Of eyebrow! All I asked is answered by surprise.
Now tell me: are you worth the cost of a cigar?
Go boldly, enter booth, disburse the coin at bar
Of doorway where presides the master of the troop,
And forthwith you survey his Graces in a group,
Live Picture, picturesque no doubt and close to life:
His sisters, right and left; the Grace in front, his wife.
Next, who is this performs the feat of the Trapeze?
Lo, she is launched, look — fie, the fairy! — how she flees
O'er all those heads thrust back, — mouths, eyes, one gape and
    stare, —
No scrap of skirt impedes free passage through the air,
Till, plumb on the other side, she lights and laughs again,
That fairy-form, whereof each muscle, nay, each vein
The curious may inspect, — his daughter that he sells
Each rustic for five sous. Desiderate aught else
O' the vendor? As you leave his show, why, joke the man!
"You cheat: your six-legged sheep, I recollect, began
Both life and trade, last year, trimmed properly and clipt,
As the Twin-headed Babe, and Human Nondescript!"
What does he care? You paid his price, may pass your jest.
So values he repute, good fame, and all the rest!

XII.

But try another tack; say: "I indulge caprice,
Who am Don and Duke, and Knight, beside, o' the Golden
    Fleece,
And, never mind how rich. Abandon this career!
Have hearth and home, nor let your womankind appear
Without as multiplied a coating as protects
An onion from the eye! Become, in all respects,
God-fearing householder, subsistent by brain-skill,
Hand-labor; win your bread whatever way you will,
So it be honestly, — and, while I have a purse,
Means shall not lack!" — his thanks will be the roundest
    curse
That ever rolled from lip.

XIII.

              Now, what is it? — returns
The question — heartens so this losel that he spurns
All we so prize? I want, put down in black and white,
What compensating joy, unknown and infinite,
Turns lawlessness to law, makes destitution — wealth,
Vice — virtue, and disease of soul and body — health?

XIV.

Ah, the slow shake of head, the melancholy smile,
The sigh almost a sob! What's wrong, was right erewhile?
Why are we two at once such ocean-width apart?
Pale fingers press my arm, and sad eyes probe my heart.
Why is the wife in trouble?

XV.

This way, this way, Fifine!
Here's she, shall make my thoughts be surer what they mean!
First let me read the signs, portray you past mistake
The gypsy's foreign self, no swarth our sun could bake.
Yet where's a woolly trace degrades the wiry hair?
And note the Greek-nymph nose, and — oh, my Hebrew pair
Of eye and eye — o'erarched by velvet of the mole —
That swim as in a sea, that dip and rise and roll,
Spilling the light around! While either ear is cut
Thin as a dusk-leaved rose carved from a cocoa-nut.
And then, her neck! now, grant you had the power to deck,
Just as your fancy pleased, the bistre-length of neck,
Could lay, to shine against its shade, a moonlike row
Of pearls, each round and white as bubble Cupids blow
Big out of mother's milk, — what pearl-moon would surpass
That string of mock-turquoise, those almandines of glass,
Where girlhood terminates? for with breasts'-birth commence
The boy, and page-costume, till pink and impudence
End admirably all: complete the creature trips -
Our way now, brings sunshine upon her spangled hips,
As here she fronts us full, with pose half-frank, half-fierce!

XVI.

Words urged in vain, Elvire! You waste your quarte and
    tierce,
Lunge at a phantom here, try fence in fairy-land.
For me, I own defeat, ask but to understand
The acknowledged victory of whom I call my queen,
Sexless and bloodless sprite: though mischievous and mean,
Yet free and flower-like too, with loveliness for law,
And self-sustainment made morality.

XVII.

A flaw
Do you account i' the lily, of lands which travellers know,
That, just as golden gloom supersedes Northern snow
I' the chalice, so, about each pistil, spice is packed, —

Deliriously-drugged scent, in lieu of odor lacked,
With us, by bee and moth, their banquet to enhance
At morn and eve, when dew, the chilly sustenance,
Needs mixture of some chaste and temperate perfume?
I ask, is she in fault who guards such golden gloom,
Such dear and damning scent, by who cares what devices,
And takes the idle life of insects she entices
When, drowned to heart's desire, they satiate the inside
O' the lily, mark her wealth and manifest her pride?

XVIII.

But, wiser, we keep off, nor tempt the acrid juice;
Discreet we peer and praise, put rich things to right use.
No flavorous venomed bell, — the rose it is, I wot,
Only the rose, we pluck and place, unwronged a jot,
No worse for homage done by every devotee,
I' the proper loyal throne, on breast where rose should be.
Or if the simpler sweets we have to choose among,
Would taste between our teeth, and give its to/ the tongue, —
O gorgeous poison-plague, on thee no hearts are set!
We gather daisy meek, or maiden violet:
I think it is Elvire we love, and not Fifine.

XIX.

"How does she make my thoughts be sure of what they
       mean?"
Judge and be just! Suppose, an age and time long past
Renew for our behoof one pageant more, the last
O' the kind, sick Louis liked to see defile between
Him and the yawning grave, its passage served to screen.
With eye as gray as lead, with cheek as brown as bronze,
Here where we stand, shall sit and suffer Louis Onze:
The while from yonder tent parade forth, not — oh, no —
Bateleurs, baladines! but range themselves a-row
Those well-sung women-worthies whereof loud fame still finds
Some echo linger faint, less in our hearts than minds.

XX.

See, Helen! pushed in front o' the world's worst night and
   storm,
By Lady Venus' hand on shoulder: the sweet form
Shrinkingly prominent, though mighty, like a moon
Outbreaking from a cloud, to put harsh things in tune,
And magically bring mankind to acquiesce
In its own ravage, — call no curse upon, but bless
(Beldame, a moment since) the outbreaking beauty, now,

That casts o'er all the blood a candor from her brow.
See, Cleopatra! bared, the entire and sinuous wealth
O' the shining shape; each orb of indolent ripe health,
Captured, just where it finds a fellow-orb as fine
I' the body: traced about by jewels which outline,
Fire-frame, and keep distinct, perfections — lest they melt
To soft smooth unity ere half their hold be felt:
Yet, o'er that white and wonder, a soul's predominance
I' the head so high and haught — except one thievish glance,
From back of oblong eye, intent to count the slain.
Hush, — O I know, Elvire! Be patient, more remain!
What say you to Saint? . . . Pish! Whatever Saint you please,
Cold-pinnacled aloft o' the spire, prays calm the seas
From Pornic Church, and oft at midnight (peasants say)
Goes walking out to save from shipwreck: well she may!
For think how many a year has she been conversant
With nought but winds and rains, sharp courtesy and scant
O' the wintry snow that coats the pent-house of her shrine,
Covers each knee, climbs near, but spares the smile benign
Which seems to say, "I looked for scarce so much from earth!"
She follows, one long thin pure finger in the girth
O' the girdle — whence the folds of garment, eye and eye,
Besprent with fleurs-de-lys, flow down and multiply
Around her feet, — and one, pressed hushingly to lip:
As if, while thus we made her march, some foundering ship
Might miss her from her post, nearer to God halfway
In heaven, and she inquired, "Who that treads earth can pray?
I doubt if even she, the unashamed! though, sure,
She must have stripped herself only to clothe the poor."

XXI.

This time, enough's a feast, not one more form, Elvire!
Provided you allow that, bringing up the rear
O' the bevy I am loth to — by one bird — curtail,
First note may lead to last, an octave crown the scale,
And this feminity be followed — do not flout! —
By — who concludes the masque with curtsey, smile and pout,
Submissive-mutinous? No other than Fifine
Points toe, imposes haunch, and pleads with tambourine!

XXII.

"Well, what's the meaning here, what does the masque
  intend,
Which, unabridged, we saw file past us, with no end
Of fair ones, till Fifine came, closed the catalogue?"

XXIII.

Task fancy yet again! Suppose you cast this clog
Of flesh away (that weeps, upbraids, withstands my arm)
And pass to join your peers, paragon charm with charm,
As I shall show you may, — prove best of beauty there!
Yourself confront yourself! This, help me to declare
That yonder-you, who stand beside these, braving each
And blinking none, beat her who lured to Troy-town beach
The purple prows of Greece, — nay, beat Fifine; whose face,
Mark how I will inflame, when seigneur-like I place
I' the tambourine, to spot the strained and piteous blank
Of pleading parchment, see, no less than a whole franc!

XXIV.

Ah, do you mark the brown o' the cloud, made bright with
    fire
Through and through? as, old wiles succeeding to desire,
Quality (you and I) once more compassionate
A hapless infant, doomed (fie on such partial fate!)
To sink the inborn shame, waive privilege of sex,
And posture as you see, support the nods and becks
Of clowns that have their stare, nor always pay its price;
An infant born perchance as sensitive and nice
As any soul of you, proud dames, whom destiny
Keeps uncontaminate from stigma of the sty
She wallows in! You draw back skirts from filth like her
Who, possibly, braves scorn, if, scorned, she minister
To age, want, and disease of parents one or both;
Nay, peradventure, stoops to degradation, loth
That some just-budding sister, the dew yet on the rose,
Should have to share in turn the ignoble trade, — who knows?

XXV.

Ay, who indeed! Myself know nothing, but dare guess
That off she trips in haste to hand the booty ... yes,
'Twixt fold and fold of tent, there looms he, dim-discerned,
The ogre, lord of all those lavish limbs have earned!
— Brute-beast-face, — ravage, scar, scowl and malignancy, —
O' the Strong Man, whom (no doubt, her husband) by and by
You shall behold do feats: lift up nor quail beneath
A quintal in each hand, a cart-wheel 'twixt his teeth.
Oh, she prefers sheer strength to ineffective grace,
Breeding and culture! seeks the essential in the case!
To him has flown my franc; and welcome, if that squint
O' the diabolic eye so soften through absinthe,

That, for once, tambourine, tunic and tricot 'scape
Their customary curse "Not half the gain o' the ape!"
Ay, they go in together!

XXVI.

Yet still her phantom stays
Opposite, where you stand : as steady 'neath our gaze, —
The live Elvire's and mine, — though fancy-stuff and mere
Illusion ; to be judged — dream-figures — without fear
Or favor, those the false, by you and me the true.

XXVII.

"What puts it in my head to make yourself judge you?"
Well, it may be, the name of Helen brought to mind
A certain myth I mused in years long left behind:
How she that fled from Greece with Paris whom she loved,
And came to Troy, and there found shelter, and so proved
Such cause of the world's woe, — how she, old stories call
This creature, Helen's self, never saw Troy at all.
Jove had his fancy-fit, must needs take empty air,
Fashion her likeness forth, and set the phantom there
I' the midst for sport, to try conclusions with the blind
And blundering race, the game create for Gods, mankind :
Experiment on these, — establish who would yearn
To give up life for her, who, other-minded, spurn
The best her eyes could smile, — make half the world sublime,
And half absurd, for just a phantom all the time !
Meanwhile true Helen's self sat, safe and far away,
By a great river-side, beneath a purer day,
With solitude around, tranquillity within ;
Was able to lean forth, look, listen, through the din
And stir ; could estimate the worthlessness or worth
Of Helen who inspired such passion to the earth,
A phantom all the time ! That put it in my head
To make yourself judge you — the phantom-wife instead
O' the tearful true Elvire !

XXVIII.

I thank the smile at last
Which thins away the tear ! Our sky was overcast,
And something fell ; but day clears up : if there chanced rain,
The landscape glistens more. I have not vexed in vain
Elvire : because she knows, now she has stood the test,
How, this and this being good, herself may still be best
O' the beauty in review ; because the flesh that claimed
Unduly my regard, she thought, the taste, she blamed

In me, for things externe, was all mistake, she finds, —
Or will find, when I prove that bodies show me minds,
That, through the outward sign, the inward grace allures,
And sparks from heaven transpierce earth's coarsest covertures,
All by demonstrating the value of Fifine!

XXIX.

Partake my confidence! No creature's made so mean
But that, some way, it boasts, could we investigate,
Its supreme worth: fulfils, by ordinance of fate,
Its momentary task, gets glory all its own,
Tastes triumph in the world, pre-eminent, alone.
Where is the single grain of sand, 'mid millions heaped
Confusedly on the beach, but, did we know, has leaped
Or will leap, would we wait, i' the century, some once,
To the very throne of things? — earth's brightest for the nonce,
When sunshine shall impinge on just that grain's facette
Which fronts him fullest, first, returns his ray with jet
Of promptest praise, thanks God best in creation's name!
As firm is my belief, quick sense perceives the same
Self-vindicating flash illustrate every man
And woman of our mass, and prove, throughout the plan,
No detail but, in place allotted it, was prime
And perfect.

XXX.

Witness her, kept waiting all this time!
What happy angle makes Fifine reverberate
Sunshine, least sand-grain, she, of shadiest social state?
No adamantine shield, polished like Helen there,
Fit to absorb the sun, regorge him till the glare,
Dazing the universe, draw Troy-ward those blind beaks
Of equal-sided ships rowed by the well-greaved Greeks!
No Asian mirror, like you Ptolemaic witch
Able to fix sun fast and tame sun down, enrich,
Not burn the world with beams thus flatteringly rolled
About her, head to foot, turned slavish snakes of gold!
And oh, no tinted pane of oriel sanctity,
Does our Fifine afford, such as permits supply
Of lustrous heaven, revealed, far more than mundane sight
Could master, to thy cell, pure Saint! where, else too bright,
So suits thy sense the orb, that, what outside was noon,
Pales, through thy lozenged blue, to meek benefic moon!
What then? does that prevent each dunghill, we may pass
Daily, from boasting too its bit of looking-glass,
Its sherd which, sun-smit, shines, shoots arrowy fire beyond
That satin-muffled mope, your sulky diamond?

XXXI.

And now, the mingled ray she shoots, I decompose.
Her antecedents, take for execrable! Gloze
No whit on your premiss: let be, there was no worst
Of degradation spared Fifine: ordained from first
To last, in body and soul, for one life-long debauch,
The Pariah of the North, the European Nautch!
This, far from seek to hide, she puts in evidence
Calmly, displays the brand, bids pry without offence
Your finger on the place. You comment, " Fancy us
So operated on, maltreated, mangled thus!
Such torture in our case, had we survived an hour?
Some other sort of flesh and blood must be, with power
Appropriate to the vile, unsensitive, tough-thonged,
In lieu of our fine nerve! Be sure, she was not wronged
Too much: you must not think she winced at prick as we!"
Come, come, that's what you say, or would, were thoughts but
   free.

XXXII.

Well then, thus much confessed, what wonder if there steal
Unchallenged to my heart the force of one appeal
She makes, and justice stamp the sole claim she asserts?
So absolutely good is truth, truth never hurts
The teller, whose worst crime gets somehow grace, avowed.
To me, that silent pose and prayer proclaimed aloud:
" Know all of me outside, the rest be emptiness
For such as you! I call attention to my dress,
Coiffure, outlandish features, lithe memorable limbs,
Piquant entreaty, all that eye-glance overskims.
Does this give pleasure? Then, repay the pleasure, put
Its price i' the tambourine! Do you seek further? Tut!
I'm just my instrument,—sound hollow: mere smooth skin
Stretched o'er gilt framework, I: rub-dub, nought else within—
Always, for such as you!—if I have use elsewhere,—
If certain bells, now mute, can jingle, need you care?
Be it enough, there's truth i' the pleading, which comports
With no word spoken out in cottages or courts,
Since all I plead is, 'Pay for just the sight you see,
And give no credit to another charm in me!'
Do I say, like your Love? 'To praise my face is well,
But, who would know my worth, must search my heart to tell!
Do I say, like your Wife? 'Had I passed in review
The produce of the globe, my man of men were — you!'
Do I say, like your Helen? 'Yield yourself up, obey

Implicitly, nor pause to question, to survey
Even the worshipful ! prostrate you at my shrine !
Shall you dare controvert what the world counts divine ?
Array your private taste, own liking of the sense,
Own longing of the soul, against the impudence
Of history, the blare and bullying of verse ?
As if man ever yet saw reason to disburse
The amount of what sense liked, soul longed for, — given, devised
As love, forsooth, — until the price was recognized
As moderate enough by divers fellow-men !
Then, with his warrant safe that these would love too, then,
Sure that particular gain implies a public loss,
And that no smile he buys but proves a slash across
The face, a stab into the side of somebody —
Sure that, along with love's main-purchase, he will buy
Up the whole stock of earth's uncharitableness,
Envy and hatred, — then, decides he to profess
His estimate of one, by love discerned, though dim
To all the world beside : since what's the world to him ? '
Do I say, like your Queen of Egypt ?   ' Who foregoes
My cup of witchcraft — fault be on the fool !   He knows
Nothing of how I pack my wine-press, turn its winch
Three-times-three, all the time to song and dance, nor flinch
From charming on and on, till at the last I squeeze
Out the exhaustive drop that leaves behind mere lees
And dregs, vapidity, thought essence heretofore !
Sup of my sorcery, old pleasures please no more !
Be great, be good, love, learn, have potency of hand
Or heart or head, — what boots ?   You die, nor understand
What bliss might be in life : you ate the grapes, but knew
Never the taste of wine, such vintage as I brew ! '.
Do I say, like your Saint ?   ' An exquisitest touch
Bides in the birth of things : no after-time can much
Enhance that fine, that faint, fugitive first of all !
What color paints the cup o' the May-rose, like the small
Suspicion of a blush which doubtfully begins ?
What sound out-warbles brook, while, at the source, it wins
That moss and stone dispart, allow its bubblings breathe ?
What taste excels the fruit, just where sharp flavors sheathe
Their sting, and let encroach the honey that allays ?
And so with soul and sense ; when sanctity betrays
First fear lest earth below seem real as heaven above,
And holy worship, late, change soon to sinful love —
Where is the plenitude of passion which endures
Comparison with that, I ask of amateurs ? '
Do I say, like Elvire " . . .

XXXIII.

(Your husband holds you fast,
Will have you listen, learn your character at last!)
" Do I say ?—like her mixed unrest and discontent,
Reproachfulness and scorn, with that submission blent
So strangely, in the face, by sad smiles and gay tears, —
Quiescence which attacks, rebellion which endears, —
Say?   ' As you loved me once, could you but love me now!
Years probably have graved their passage on my brow,
Lips turn more rarely red, eyes sparkle less than erst ;
Such tribute body pays to time ; but, unamerced,
The soul retains, nay, boasts old treasure multiplied.
Though dew-prime flee, — mature at noonday, love defied
Chance, the wind, change, the rain : love, strenuous all the more
For storm, struck deeper root and choicer fruitage bore,
Despite the rocking world ; yet truth struck root in vain :
While tenderness bears fruit, you praise, not taste again.
Why ? They are yours, which once were hardly yours, might g
To grace another's ground : and then — the hopes we know,
The fears we keep in mind ! — when, ours to arbitrate,
Your part was to bow neck, bid full decree of fate.
Then, O the knotty point — white-night's work to revolve —
What meant that smile, that sigh? Not Solon's self could
    solve!
Then, O the deep surmise what one word might express,
And if what seemed her "No" may not have meant her "Yes!"
Then, such annoy, for cause — calm welcome, such acquist
Of rapture if, refused her arm, hand touched her wrist !
Now, what 's a smile to you? Poor candle that lights up
The decent household gloom which sends you out to sup.
A tear ? worse ! warns that health requires you keep aloof
From nuptial chamber, since rain penetrates the roof !
Soul, body got and gained, inalienably safe
Your own, become despised ; more worth has any waif
Or stray from neighbor's pale : pouch that, — 't is pleasure,
    pride,
Novelty, property, and larceny beside !
Preposterous thought ! to find no value fixed in things,
To covet all you see, hear, dream of, till fate brings
About that, what you want, you gain ; then follows change.
Give you the sun to keep, forthwith must fancy range :
A goodly lamp, no doubt, — yet might you catch her hair
And capture, as she frisks, the fen-fire dancing there !
What do I say ? at least a meteor 's half in heaven ;
Provided filth but shine, my husband hankers even

After putridity that's phosphorescent, cribs
The rustic's tallow-rush, makes spoil of urchins' squibs,
In short, prefers to me — chaste, temperate, serene —
What sputters green and blue, this fizgig called Fifine!'"

XXXIV

So all your sex mistake! Strange that so plain a fact
Should raise such dire debate! Few families were racked
By torture self-supplied, did Nature grant but this —
That women comprehend mental analysis!

XXXV.

Elvire, do you recall when, years ago, our home
The intimation reached, a certain pride of Rome,
Authenticated piece, in the third, last and best
Manner, — whatever fools and connoisseurs contest, —
No particle disturbed by rude restorer's touch,
The palaced picture-pearl, so long eluding clutch
Of creditor, at last, the Rafael might — could we
But come to terms — change lord, pass from the Prince to me?
I think you recollect my fever of a year:
How the Prince would, and how he would not; now, — too dear
That promise was, he made his grandsire so long since,
Rather to boast "I own a Rafael" than "am Prince!"
And now, the fancy soothed — if really sell he must
His birthright for a mess of pottage — such a thrust
I' the vitals of the Prince were mollified by balm,
Could he prevail upon his stomach to bear qualm,
And bequeath Liberty (because a purchaser
Was ready with the sum — a trifle!) yes, transfer
His heart at all events to that land where, at least,
Free institutions reign! And so, its price increased
Fivefold (Americans are such importunates!),
Soon must his Rafael start for the United States.
O alternating bursts of hope now, then despair!
At last, the bargain's struck, I'm all but beggared, there
The Rafael faces me, in fine, no dream at all,
My housemate, evermore to glorify my wall.
A week must pass, before heart-palpitations sink,
In gloating o'er my gain, so late I edged the brink
Of doom; a fortnight more, I spend in Paradise:
"Was outline e'er so true, could coloring entice
So calm, did harmony and quiet so avail?
How right, how resolute, the action tells the tale!"
A month, I bid my friends congratulate their best:
"You happy Don!" (to me): "The blockhead!" (to the rest):

"No doubt he thinks his daub original, poor dupe!"
Then I resume my life: one chamber must not coop
Man's life in, though it boast a marvel like my prize.
Next year, I saunter past with unaverted eyes,
Nay, loll and turn my back: perchance to overlook
With relish, leaf by leaf, Doré's last picture-book.

XXXVI.

Imagine that a voice reproached me from its frame:
"Here do I hang, and may! Your Rafael, just the same,
'T is only you that change: no ecstasies of yore!
No purposed suicide distracts you any more!"
Prompt would my answer meet such frivolous attack:
"You misappropriate sensations. What men lack,
And labor to obtain, is hoped and feared about
After a fashion; what they once obtain, makes doubt,
Expectancy's old fret and fume, henceforward void.
But do they think to hold such havings unalloyed
By novel hopes and fears, of fashion just as new,
To correspond i' the scale? Nowise, I promise you!
Mine you are, therefore mine will be, as fit to cheer
My soul and glad my sense to-day as this-day-year.
So, any sketch or scrap, pochade, caricature,
Made in a moment, meant a moment to endure,
I snap at, seize, enjoy, then tire of, throw aside,
Find you in your old place. But if a servant cried
'Fire in the gallery!' — methinks, were I engaged
In Doré, elbow-deep, picture-books million-paged
To the four winds would pack, sped by the heartiest curse
Was ever launched from lip, to strew the universe.
Would not I brave the best o' the burning, bear away
Either my perfect piece in safety, or else stay
And share its fate, be made its martyr, nor repine?
Inextricably wed, such ashes mixed with mine!"

XXXVII.

For which I get the eye, the hand, the heart, the whole
O' the wondrous wife again!

XXXVIII.

But no, play out your rôle
I' the pageant! 'T is not fit your phantom leave the stage:
I want you, there, to make you, here, confess you wage
Successful warfare, pique those proud ones, and advance
Claim to . . . equality? nay, but predominance
In physique o'er them all, where Helen heads the scene

Closed by its tiniest of tail-tips, pert Fifine.
How ravishingly pure you stand in pale constraint!
My new-created shape, without or touch or taint,
Inviolate of life and worldliness and sin —
Fettered, I hold my flower, her own cup's weight would win
From off the tall slight stalk a-top of which she turns
And trembles, makes appeal to one who roughly earns
Her thanks instead of blame, (did lily only know,)
By thus constraining length of lily, letting snow
Of cup-crown, that's her face, look from its guardian stake,
Superb on all that crawls beneath, and mutely make
Defiance, with the mouth's white movement of disdain,
To all that stoops, retires, and hovers round again!
How windingly the limbs delay to lead up, reach
Where, crowned, the head waits calm: as if reluctant, each,
That eye should traverse quick such lengths of loveliness,
From feet, which just are found embedded in the dress
Deep swathed about with folds and flowings virginal,
Up to the pleated breasts, rebellious 'neath their pall,
As if the vesture's snow were moulding sleep not death,
Must melt and so release; whereat, from the fine sheath,
The flower-cup-crown starts free, the face is unconcealed,
And what shall now divert me, once the sweet face revealed,
From all I loved so long, so lingeringly left?

XXXIX.

Because indeed your face fits into just the cleft
O' the heart of me, Elvire, makes right and whole once more
All that was half itself without you! As before,
My truant finds its place! Doubtlessly sea-shells yearn,
If plundered by sad chance: would pray their pearls return,
Let negligently slip away into the wave!
Never may eyes desist, those eyes so gray and grave,
From their slow sure supply of the effluent soul within!
And, would you humor me? I dare to ask, unpin
The web of that brown hair! O'erwash o' the sudden, but
As promptly, too, disclose, on either side, the jut
Of alabaster brow! So part rich rillets dyed
Deep by the woodland leaf, when down they pour, each side
O' the rock-top, pushed by Spring!

XL.

" And where i' the world is all
This wonder, you detail so trippingly, espied?
My mirror would reflect a tall, thin, pale, deep-eyed
Personage, pretty once, it may be, doubtless still

Loving, — a certain grace yet lingers, if you will, —
But all this wonder, where?"

XLI.

Why, where but in the sense
And soul of me, Art's judge? Art is my evidence
That something was, is, might be; but no more thing itself,
Than flame is fuel. Once the verse-book laid on shelf,
The picture turned to wall, the music fled from ear, —
Each beauty, born of each, grows clearer and more clear,
Mine henceforth, ever mine!

XLII.

But if I would retrace
Effect, in Art, to cause, — corroborate, erase
What's right or wrong i' the lines, test fancy in my brain
By fact which gave it birth? I re-peruse in vain
The verse, I fail to find that vision of delight
I' the Bazzi's lost-profile, eye-edge so exquisite.
And, music: what? that burst of pillared cloud by day
And pillared fire by night, was product, must we say,
Of modulating just, by enharmonic change, —
The augmented sixth resolved, — from out the straighter range
Of D sharp minor — leap of disimprisoned thrall —
Into thy light and life, D major natural?

XLIII.

Elvire, will you partake in what I shall impart?
I seem to understand the way heart chooses heart
By help of the outside form, — a reason for our wild
Diversity in choice, — why each grows reconciled
To what is absent, what superfluous in the mask
Of flesh that's meant to yield, — did nature ply her task
As artist should, — precise the features of the soul,
Which, if in any case they found expression, whole
I' the traits, would give a type, undoubtedly display
A novel, true, distinct perfection in its way.
Never shall I believe any two souls were made
Similar; granting, then, each soul of every grade
Was meant to be itself, prove in itself complete,
And, in completion, good, — nay, best o' the kind, — as meet
Needs must it be that show on the outside correspond
With inward substance, — flesh, the dress which soul has donned,
Exactly reproduce, — were only justice done
Inside and outside too, — types perfect every one.

How happens it that here we meet a mystery
Insoluble to man, a plaguy puzzle? Why
Each soul is either made imperfect, and deserves
As rude a face to match; or else a bungler swerves,
And nature, on a soul worth rendering aright,
Works ill, or proves perverse, or, in her own despite,
— Here too much, there too little, — bids each face, more or
    less,
Retire from beauty, make approach to ugliness?
And yet succeeds the same: since, what is wanting to success,
If somehow every face, no matter how deform,
Evidence, to some one of hearts on earth, that, warm
Beneath the veriest ash, there hides a spark of soul
Which, quickened by love's breath, may yet pervade the whole
O' the gray, and, free again, be fire? — of worth the same,
Howe'er produced, for, great or little, flame is flame.
A mystery, whereof solution is to seek.

XLIV.

I find it in the fact that each soul, just as weak
Its own way as its fellow, — departure from design
As flagrant in the flesh, — goes striving to combine
With what shall right the wrong, the under or above
The standard: supplement unloveliness by love.
— Ask Plato else! And this corroborates the sage,
That Art, — which I may style the love of loving, rage
Of knowing, seeing, feeling the absolute truth of things
For truth's sake, whole and sole, not any good, truth brings
The knower, seer, feeler, beside, — instinctive Art
Must fumble for the whole, once fixing on a part
However poor, surpass the fragment, and aspire
To reconstruct thereby the ultimate entire.
Art, working with a will, discards the superflux,
Contributes to defect, toils on till, — *fiat lux*, —
There 's the restored, the prime, the individual type!

XLV.

Look, for example now! This piece of broken pipe
(Some shipman's solace erst) shall act as crayon; and
What tablet better serves my purpose than the sand?
— Smooth slab whereon I draw, no matter with what skill,
A face, and yet another, and yet another still.
There lie my three prime types of beauty!

XLVI.

                            Laugh your best!
"Exaggeration and absurdity?" Confessed!

Yet, what may that face mean, no matter for its nose,
A yard long, or its chin, a foot short?

XLVII.

                              " You suppose,
Horror?" Exactly! What's the odds if, more or less
By yard or foot, the features do manage to express
Such meaning in the main? Were I of Gérôme's force,
Nor feeble as you see, quick should my crayon course
O'er outline, curb, excite, till, — so completion speeds
With Gérôme well at work, — observe how brow recedes,
Head shudders back on spine, as if one haled the hair,
Would have the full-face front what pin-point eye's sharp stare
Announces; mouth agape to drink the flowing fate,
While chin protrudes to meet the burst o' the wave : elate
Almost, spurred on to brave necessity, expend
All life left, in one flash, as fire does at its end.
Retrenchment and addition effect a masterpiece,
Not change i' the motive: here diminish, there increase —
And who wants Horror, has it.

XLVIII.

                              Who wants some other show
Of soul, may seek elsewhere — this second of the row?
What does it give for germ, monadic mere intent
Of mind in face, faint first of meanings ever meant?
Why, possibly, a grin, that, strengthened, grows a laugh;
That, softened, leaves a smile; that, tempered, bids you quaff
At such a magic cup as English Reynolds once
Compounded : for the witch pulls out of you response
Like Garrick's to Thalia, however due may be
Your homage claimed by that stiff-stoled Melpomene!

XLIX.

  And just this one face more! Pardon the bold pretence!
May there not lurk some hint, struggle toward evidence
In that compressed mouth, those strained nostrils, steadfast eyes
Of utter passion, absolute self-sacrifice,
Which — could I but subdue the wild grotesque. refine
That bulge of brow, make blunt that nose's aquiline,
And let, although compressed, a point of pulp appear
I' the mouth — would give at last the portrait of Elvire?

L.

  Well, and if so succeed hand-practice on awry
Preposterous art-mistake, shall soul-proficiency

Despair, — when exercised on nature, which at worst
Always implies success, — however crossed and curst
By failure, — such as art would emulate in vain?
Shall any soul despair of setting free again
Trait after trait, until the type as wholly start
Forth, visible to sense, as that minutest part,
(Whate'er the chance,) which first arresting eye, warned soul
That, under wrong enough and ravage, lay the whole
O' the loveliness it "loved" — I take the accepted phrase?

LI.

So I account for tastes : each chooses, none gainsays
The fancy of his fellow, a paradise for him,
A hell for all beside. You can but crown the brim
O' the cup ; if it be full, what matters less or more?
Let each, i' the world, amend his love, as I, o' the shore,
My sketch, and the result as undisputed be!
Their handiwork to them, and my Elvire to me :
— Result more beautiful than beauty's self, when lo,
What was my Rafael turns my Michelagnolo!

LII.

For, we two boast, beside our pearl, a diamond.
I' the palace-gallery, the corridor beyond,
Upheaves itself a marble, a magnitude man-shaped
As snow might be. One hand — the Master's — smoothed and
    scraped
That mass, he hammered on and hewed at, till he hurled
Life out of death, and left a challenge: for the world,
Death still, — since who shall dare, close to the image, say
If this be purposed Art, or mere mimetic play
Of Nature? — wont to deal with crag or cloud, as stuff
To fashion novel forms, like forms we know, enough
For recognition, but enough unlike the same,
To leave no hope ourselves may profit by her game ;
Death therefore to the world. Step back a pace or two!
And then, who dares dispute the gradual birth its due
Of breathing life, or breathless immortality,
Where out she stands, and yet stops short, half bold, half shy,
Hesitates on the threshold of things, since partly blent
With stuff she needs must quit, her native element
I' the mind o' the Master, — what's the creature, dear-divine
Yet earthly-awful too, so manly-feminine,
Pretends this white advance? What startling brain-escape
Of Michelagnolo takes elemental shape?
I think he meant the daughter of the old man o' the sea,

Emerging from her wave, goddess Eidotheé —
She who, in elvish sport, spite with benevolence
Mixed Mab-wise up, must needs instruct the Hero whence
Salvation dawns o'er that mad misery of his isle.
Yes, she imparts to him, by what a pranksome wile
He may surprise her sire, asleep beneath a rock,
When he has told their tale, amid his webfoot flock
Of sea-beasts, "fine fat seals with bitter breath!" laughs she
At whom she likes to save, no less: Eidotheé, ·
Whom you shall never face evolved, in earth, in air,
In wave; but, manifest i' the soul's domain, why, there
She ravishingly moves to meet you, all through aid
O' the soul! Bid shine what should, dismiss into the shade
What should not be, — and there triumphs the paramount
Emprise o' the Master! But, attempt to make account
Of what the sense, without soul's help perceives? I bought
That work — (despite plain proof, whose hand it was had wrought
I' the rough: I think we trace the tool of triple tooth,
Here, there, and everywhere) — bought dearly that uncouth
Unwieldy bulk, for just ten dollars — "Bulk, would fetch —
Converted into lime — some five pauls!" grinned a wretch,
Who, bound on business, paused to hear the bargaining,
And would have pitied me "but for the fun o' the thing!"

LIII.

Shall such a wretch be — you? Must — while I show Elvire
Shaming all other forms, seen as I see her here
I' the soul, — this other-you perversely look outside,
And ask me, "Where i' the world is charm to be descried
I' the tall thin personage, with paled eye, pensive face,
Any amount of love, and some remains of grace?"
See yourself in my soul!

LIV.

And what a world for each
Must somehow be i' the soul, — accept that mode of speech, —
Whether an aura gird the soul, wherein it seems
To float and move, a belt of all the glints and gleams
It struck from out that world, its weaklier fellows found
So dead and cold; or whether these not so much surround,
As pass into the soul itself, add worth to worth,
As wine enriches blood, and straightway send it forth,
Conquering and to conquer, through all eternity,
That's battle without end.

LV.

    I search but cannot see
What purpose serves the soul that strives, or world it tries
Conclusions with, unless the fruit of victories
Stay, one and all, stored up and guaranteed its own
Forever, by some mode whereby shall be made known
The gain of every life. Death reads the title clear —
What each soul for itself conquered from out things here :
Since, in the seeing soul, all worth lies, I assert, —
And nought i' the world, which, save for soul that sees, inert
Was, is, and would be ever, — stuff for transmuting, — null
And void until man's breath evoke the beautiful —
But, touched aright, prompt yields each particle its tongue
Of elemental flame, — no matter whence flame sprung
From gums and spice, or else from straw and rottenness,
So long as soul has power to make them burn, express
What lights and warms henceforth, leaves only ash behind,
Howe'er the chance : if soul be privileged to find
Food so soon that, by first snatch of eye, suck of breath,
It can absorb pure life : or, rather, meeting death
I' the shape of ugliness, by fortunate recoil
So put on its resource, it find therein a foil
For a new birth of life, the challenged soul's response
To ugliness and death, — creation for the nonce.

LVI.

  I gather heart through just such conquests of the soul,
Through evocation out of that which, on the whole,
Was rough, ungainly, partial accomplishment, at best,
And — what, at worst, save failure to spit at and detest ? —
— Through transference of all, achieved in visible things,
To where, secured from wrong, rest soul's imaginings —
Through ardor to bring help just where completion halts,
Do justice to the purpose, ignore the slips and faults —
And, last, through waging with deformity a fight
Which wrings thence, at the end, precise its opposite.
I praise the loyalty o' the scholar, — stung by taunt
Of fools, " Does this evince thy Master men so vaunt ?
Did he then perpetrate the plain abortion here ? " —
Who cries, " His work am I ! full fraught by him, I clear
His fame from each result of accident and time,
Myself restore his work to its fresh morning-prime,
Not daring touch the mass of marble, fools deride,
But putting my idea in plaster by its side,
His, since mine ; I, he made, vindicate who made me ! "

LVII.

For, you must know, I too achieved Eidotheé,
In silence and by night — dared justify the lines
Plain to my soul, although, to sense, that triple-tine's
Achievement halt halfway, break down, or leave a blank.
If she stood forth at last, the Master was to thank!
Yet may there not have smiled approval in his eyes —
That one at least was left who, born to recognize
Perfection in the piece imperfect, worked, that night,
In silence, such his faith, until the apposite
Design was out of him, truth palpable once more?
And then — for at one blow, its fragments strewed the floor —
Recalled the same to live within his soul as heretofore.

LVIII.

And, even as I hold and have Eidotheé,
I say, I cannot think that gain, — which would not be
Except a special soul had gained it, — that such gain
Can ever be estranged, do aught but appertain
Immortally, by right firm, indefeasible,
To who performed the feat, through God's grace and man's will!
Gain, never shared by those who practised with earth's stuff,
And spoiled whate'er they touched, leaving its roughness rough,
Its blankness bare, and, when the ugliness opposed,
Either struck work or laughed "He doted or he dozed!"

LIX.

While, oh, how all the more will love become intense
Hereafter, when "to love" means yearning to dispense,
Each soul, its own amount of gain through its own mode
Of practising with life, upon some soul which owed
Its treasure, all diverse and yet in worth the same,
To new work and changed way! Things furnish you rose-flame,
Which burn up red, green, blue, nay, yellow more than needs,
For me, I nowise doubt; why doubt a time succeeds
When each one may impart, and each receive, both share
The chemic secret, learn, — where I lit force, why there
You drew forth lambent pity, — where I found only food
For self-indulgence, you still blew a spark at brood
I' the grayest ember, stopped not till self-sacrifice imbued
Heaven's face with flame? What joy, when each may supplement
The other, changing each, as changed, till, wholly blent,
Our old things shall be new, and, what we both ignite,
Fuse, lose the varicolor in achromatic white!

Exemplifying law, apparent even now
In the eternal progress, — love's law, which I avow
And thus would formulate: each soul lives, longs and works
For itself, by itself, because a lodestar lurks,
An other than itself, — in whatsoe'er the niche
Of mistiest heaven it hide, whoe'er the Glumdalclich
May grasp the Gulliver: or it, or he, or she —
Theosutos e broteios eper kekramene, —
(For fun's sake, where the phrase has fastened, leave it fixed!
So soft it says, — God, man, or both together mixed!)
This, guessed at through the flesh, by parts which prove the whole,
This constitutes the soul discernible by soul
— Elvire, by me!

LX.

"And then" — (pray you, permit remain
This hand upon my arm! — your cheek dried, if you deign,
Choosing my shoulder) — "then!" — (Stand up for, boldly state
The objection in its length and breadth!) "You abdicate,
With boast yet on your lip, soul's empire, and accept
The rule of sense; the Man, from monarch's throne has stept —
Leapt, rather, at one bound, to base, and there lies, Brute.
You talk of soul, — how soul, in search of soul to suit,
Must needs review the sex, the army, rank and file
Of womankind, report no face nor form so vile
But that a certain worth, by certain signs, may thence
Evolve itself and stand confessed — to soul — by sense.
Sense? Oh, the loyal bee endeavors for the hive!
Disinterested hunts the flower-field through, alive
Not one mean moment, no, — suppose on flower he light, —
To his peculiar drop, petal-dew perquisite,
Matter-of-course snatched snack: unless he taste, how try?
This, light on tongue-tip laid, allows him pack his thigh,
Transport all he counts prize, provision for the comb,
Food for the future day, — a banquet, but at home!
Soul? Ere you reach Fifine's, some flesh may be to pass!
That bombéd brow, that eye, a kindling chrysopras,
Beneath its stiff black lash, inquisitive how speeds
Each functionary limb, how play of foot succeeds,
And how you let escape or duly sympathize
With gastro-knemian grace, — true, your soul tastes and tries,
And trifles time with those, but, fear not, will arrive
At essence in the core, bring honey home to hive,
Brain-stock and heart-stuff both — to strike objectors dumb —
Since only soul affords the soul fit pabulum!

Be frank for charity! Who is it you deceive —
Yourself or me or God, with all this make-believe?"

LXI.

And frank I will respond as you interrogate.
Ah, Music, wouldst thou help! Words struggle with the weight
So feebly of the False, thick element between
Our soul, the True, and Truth! which, but that intervene
False shows of things, were reached as easily by thought
Reducible to word, as now by yearnings wrought
Up with thy fine free force, O Music, that canst thrid,
Electrically win a passage through the lid
Of earthly sepulchre, our words may push against,
Hardly transpierce as thou! Not dissipate, thou deign'st,
So much as tricksily elude what words attempt
To heave away, i' the mass, and let the soul, exempt
From all that vapory obstruction, view, instead
Of glimmer underneath, a glory overhead.
Not feebly, like our phrase, against the barrier go
In suspirative swell the authentic notes I know,
By help whereof, I would our souls were found without
The pale, above the dense and dim which breeds the doubt!
But Music, dumb for you, withdraws her help from me;
And, since to weary words recourse again must be,
At least permit they rest their burden here and there,
Music-like: cover space! My answer, — need you care
If it exceed the bounds, reply to questioning
You never meant should plague? Once fairly on the wing,
Let me flap far and wide!

LXII.

For this is just the time,
The place, the mood in you and me, when all things chime.
Clash forth life's common chord, whence, list how there ascend
Harmonics far and faint, till our perception end, —
Reverberated notes whence we construct the scale
Embracing what we know and feel and are! How fail
To find or, better, lose your question, in this quick
Reply which nature yields, ample and catholic?
For, arm in arm, we two have reached, nay, passed, you see,
The village-precinct; sun sets mild on Sainte-Marie —
We only catch the spire, and yet I seem to know
What's hid i' the turn o' the hill: how all the graves must glow
Soberly, as each warms its little iron cross,
Flourished about with gold, and graced (if private loss
Be fresh) with stiff rope-wreath of yellow crisp bead-blooms

Which tempt down birds to pay their supper, 'mid the tombs,
With prattle good as song, amuse the dead awhile,
If couched they hear beneath the matted camomile!

LXIII.

Bid them good-bye before last friend has sung and supped!
Because we pick our path and need our eyes, — abrupt
Descent enough, — but here's the beach, and there's the bay,
And, opposite, the streak of Île Noirmoutier.
Thither the waters tend; they freshen as they haste,
At feel o' the night-wind, though, by cliff and cliff embraced,
This breadth of blue retains its self-possession still;
As you and I intend to do, who take our fill
Of sights and sounds — soft sound, the countless hum and skip
Of insects we disturb, and that good fellowship
Of rabbits our footfall sends huddling, each to hide
He best knows how and where; and what whirred past, wings
 wide?
That was an owl, their young may justlier apprehend!
Though you refuse to speak, your beating heart, my friend,
I feel against my arm, — though your bent head forbids
A look into your eyes, yet, on my cheek, their lids
That ope and shut, soft send a silken thrill the same.
Well, out of all and each these nothings, comes — what came
Often enough before, the something that would aim
Once more at the old mark: the impulse to at last
Succeed where hitherto was failure in the past,
And yet again essay the adventure. Clearlier sings
No bird to its couched corpse, "Into the truth of things —
Out of their falseness rise, and reach thou, and remain!"

LXIV.

"That rise into the true out of the false — explain?"
May an example serve? In yonder bay I bathed,
This sunny morning: swam my best, then hung, half swathed
With chill, and half with warmth, i' the channel's midmost deep:
You know how one — not treads, but stands in water? Keep
Body and limbs below, hold head back, uplift chin,
And, for the rest, leave care! If brow, eyes, mouth, should
 win
Their freedom, — excellent! If they must brook the surge,
No matter though they sink, let but the nose emerge.
So, all of me in brine lay soaking: did I care
One jot? I kept alive by man's due breath of air
I' the nostrils, high and dry. At times, o'er these would run
The ripple, even wash the wavelet, — morning's sun

Tempted advance, no doubt : and always flash of froth,
Fish-outbreak, bubbling by, would find me nothing loth
To rise and look around ; then all was overswept
With dark and death at once. But trust the old adept !
Back went again the head, a merest motion made,
Fin-fashion, either hand, and nostril soon conveyed
Assurance light and life were still in reach as erst :
Always the last and — wait and watch — sometimes the first.
Try to ascend breast-high ? wave arms wide free of tether ?
Be in the air and leave the water altogether ?
Under went all again, till I resigned myself
To only breathe the air, that's footed by an elf,
And only swim the water, that's native to a fish.
But there is no denying that, ere I curbed my wish,
And schooled my restive arms, salt entered mouth and eyes
Often enough — sun, sky, and air so tantalize !
Still, the adept swims, this accorded, that denied ;
Can always breathe, sometimes see and be satisfied !

LXV.

I liken to this play o' the body — fruitless strife
To slip the sea and hold the heaven — my spirit's life
'Twixt false, whence it would break, and true, where it would
    bide.
I move in, yet resist, am upborne every side
By what I beat against, an element too gross
To live in, did not soul duly obtain her dose
Of life-breath, and inhale from truth's pure plenitude
Above her, snatch and gain enough to just illude
With hope that some brave bound may baffle evermore
The obstructing medium, make who swam henceforward soar :
— Gain scarcely snatched when, foiled by the very effort, souse,
Underneath ducks the soul, her truthward yearnings dowse
Deeper in falsehood ! ay, but fitted less and less
To bear in nose and mouth old briny bitterness
Proved alien more and more : since each experience proves
Air — the essential good, not sea, wherein who moves
Must thence, in the act, escape, apart from will or wish.
Move a mere hand to take water-weed, jelly-fish,
Upward you tend ! And yet our business with the sea
Is not with air, but just o' the water, watery :
We must endure the false, no particle of which
Do we acquaint us with, but up we mount a pitch
Above it, find our head reach truth, while hands explore
The false below : so much while here we bathe, — no more !

LXVI.

Now, there is one prime point (hear and be edified!)
One truth more true for me than any truth beside —
To-wit, that I am I, who have the power to swim,
The skill to understand the law whereby each limb
May bear to keep immersed, since, in return, made sure
That its mere movement lifts head clean through coverture.
By practice with the false, I reach the true? Why, thence
It follows, that the more I gain self-confidence,
Get proof I know the trick, can float, sink, rise, at will,
The better I submit to what I have the skill
To conquer in my turn, even now, and by and by
Leave wholly for the land, and there laugh, shake me dry
To last drop, saturate with noonday — no need more
Of wet and fret, plagued once: on Pornic's placid shore,
Abundant air to breathe, sufficient sun to feel!
Meantime I buoy myself: no whit my senses reel
When over me there breaks a billow; nor, elate
Too much by some brief taste, I quaff intemperate
The air, o'ertop breast-high the wave-environment.
Full well I know the thing I grasp, as if intent
To hold, — my wandering wave, — will not be grasped at all:
The solid-seeming grasped, the handful great or small
Must go to nothing, glide through fingers fast enough;
But none the less, to treat liquidity as stuff —
Though failure — certainly succeeds beyond its aim,
Sends head above, past thing that hands miss, or the same.

LXVII.

So with this wash o' the world, wherein life-long we drift;
We push and paddle through the foam by making shift
To breathe above at whiles when, after deepest duck
Down underneath the show, we put forth hand and pluck
At what seems somehow like reality — a soul.
I catch at this and that, to capture and control,
Presume I hold a prize, discover that my pains
Are run to nought: my hands are balked, my head regains
The surface where I breathe and look about, a space.
The soul that helped me mount? Swallowed up in the race
O' the tide, come who knows whence, gone gayly who knows
    where!
I thought the prize was mine; I flattered myself there.
It did its duty, though: I felt it, it felt me;
Or, where I look about and breathe, I should not be.
The main point is — the false fluidity was bound

Acknowledge that it frothed o'er substance, nowise found
Fluid, but firm and true. Man, outcast, " howls," — at rods ? —
If " sent in playful spray a-shivering to his gods ! "
Childishest childe, man makes thereby no bad exchange.
Stay with the flat-fish, thou ! We like the upper range
Where the " gods " live, perchance the dæmons also dwell:
Where operates a Power, which every throb and swell
Of human heart invites that human soul approach,
" Sent " near and nearer still, however " spray " encroach
On " shivering " flesh below, to altitudes, which gained,
Evil proves good, wrong right, obscurity explained,
And " howling " childishness. Whose howl have we to thank,
If all the dogs 'gan bark and puppies whine, till sank
Each yelper's tail 'twixt legs ? for Huntsman Commonsense
Came to the rescue, bade prompt thwack of thong dispense
Quiet i' the kennel; taught that ocean might be blue,
And rolling and much more, and yet the soul have, too,
Its touch of God's own flame, which He may so expand,
" Who measurèd the waters i' the hollow of His hand,"
That ocean's self shall dry, turn dewdrop in respect
Of all-triumphant fire, matter with intellect
Once fairly matched ; bade him who egged on hounds to bay
Go curse, i' the poultry yard, his kind: " there let him lay "
The swan's one addled egg : which yet shall put to use,
Rub breast-bone warm against, so many a sterile goose !

LXVIII.

No, I want sky not sea, prefer the larks to shrimps,
And never dive so deep but that I get a glimpse
O' the blue above, a breath of the air around. Elvire,
I seize — by catching at the melted beryl here,
The tawny hair that just has trickled off, — Fifine !
Did not we two trip forth to just enjoy the scene,
The tumbling-troop arrayed, the strollers on their stage,
Drawn up and under arms, and ready to engage —
Dabble, and there an end, with foam and froth o'er face,
Till suddenly Fifine suggested change of place ?
Now we taste æther, scorn the wave, and interchange apace
No ordinary thoughts, but such as evidence
The cultivated mind in both. On what pretence
Are you and I to sneer at who lent help to hand,
And gave the lucky lift ?

LXIX.

Still sour ? I understand !
One ugly circumstance discredits my fair plan —

That Woman does the work : I waive the help of Man.
" Why should experiment be tried with only waves,
When solid spars float round ?   Still some Thalassia saves
Too pertinaciously, as though no Triton, bluff
As e'er blew brine from conch, were free to help enough !
Surely, to recognize a man, his mates serve best !
Why is there not the same or greater interest
In the strong spouse as in the pretty partner, pray,
Were recognition just your object, as you say,
Amid this element o' the false ? "

LXX.

      We come to terms.
I need to be proved true ; and nothing so confirms
One's faith in the prime point that one 's alive, not dead,
In all Descents to Hell whereof I ever read,
As when a phantom there, male enemy or friend,
Or merely stranger-shade, is struck, is forced suspend
His passage : "You that breathe, along with us the ghosts ? "
Here, why must it be still a woman that accosts ?

LXXI.

 Because, one woman's worth, in that respect, such hairy hosts
Of the other sex and sort !   Men ?   Say you have the power
To make them yours, rule men, throughout life's little hour,
According to the phrase ; what follows ?   Men, you make,
By ruling them, your own : each man for his own sake
Accepts you as his guide, avails him of what worth
He apprehends in you to sublimate his earth
With fire : content, if so you convoy him through night,
That you shall play the sun, and he, the satellite,
Pilfer your light and heat and virtue, starry pelf,
While, caught up by your course, he turns upon himself.
Women rush into you, and there remain absorbed.
Beside, 't is only men completely formed, full-orbed,
Are fit to follow track, keep pace, illustrate so
The leader : any sort of woman may bestow
Her atom on the star, or clod she counts for such, —
Each little making less bigger by just that much.
Women grow you, while men depend on you at best.
And what dependence !   Bring and put him to the test,
Your specimen disciple, a handbreadth separate
From you, he almost seemed to touch before !   Abate
Complacency you will, I judge, at what 's divulged !
Some flabbiness you fixed, some vacancy out-bulged,
Some — much — nay, all, perhaps, the outward man 's your
   work :

But, inside man ? — find him, wherever he may lurk,
And where 's a touch of you in his true self ?

LXXII.

              I wish
Some wind would waft this way a glassy bubble-fish
O' the kind the sea inflates, and show you, once detached
From wave . . . or no, the event is better told than watched :
Still may the thing float free, globose and opaline
All over, save where just the amethysts combine
To blue their best, rim-round the sea-flower with a tinge
Earth's violet never knew ! Well, 'neath that gem-tipped fringe,
A head lurks — of a kind — that acts as stomach too ;
Then comes the emptiness which out the water blew
So big and belly-like, but, dry of water drained,
Withers away nine-tenths. Ah, but a tenth remained !
That was the creature's self : no more akin to sea,
Poor rudimental head and stomach, you agree,
Than sea 's akin to sun who yonder dips his edge.

LXXIII.

 But take the rill which ends a race o'er yonder ledge
O' the fissured cliff, to find its fate in smoke below !
Disengage that, and ask — what news of life, you know
It led, that long lone way, through pasture, plain and waste ?
All 's gone to give the sea ! no touch of earth, no taste
Of air, reserved to tell how rushes used to bring
The butterfly and bee, and fisher-bird that 's king
O' the purple kind, about the snow-soft silver-sweet
Infant of mist and dew ; only these atoms fleet,
Embittered evermore, to make the sea one drop
More big thereby — if thought keep count where sense must
 stop.

LXXIV.

 The full-blown ingrate, mere recipient of the brine,
That takes all and gives nought, is Man ; the feminine
Rillet that, taking all and giving nought in turn,
Goes headlong to her death i' the sea, without concern
For the old inland life, snow-soft and silver-clear,
That 's woman — typified from Fifine to Elvire.

LXXV.

 Then, how diverse the modes prescribed to who would deal
With either kind of creature ! 'T is Man, you seek to seal
Your very own ? Resolve, for first step, to discard

Nine-tenths of what you are! To make, you must be marred, —
To raise your race, must stoop, — to teach them aught, must
    learn
Ignorance, meet halfway what most you hope to spurn
I' the sequel. Change yourself, dissimulate the thought
And vulgarize the word, and see the deed be brought
To look like nothing done with any such intent
As teach men — though perchance it teach, by accident!
So may you master men : assured that if you show
One point of mastery, departure from the low
And level, — head or heart-revolt at long disguise,
Immurement, stifling soul in mediocrities, —
If inadvertently a gesture, much more, word
Reveal the hunter no companion for the herd,
His chance of capture's gone. Success means, they may snuff,
Examine, and report, — a brother, sure enough,
Disports him in brute-guise ; for skin is truly skin,
Horns, hoofs, are hoofs and horns, and all, outside and in,
Is veritable beast, whom fellow-beasts resigned
May follow, made a prize in honest pride, behind
One of themselves and not creation's upstart lord!
Well, there's your prize i' the pound — much joy may it afford
My Indian! Make survey and tell me, — was it worth
You acted part so well, went all-fours upon earth
The live-long day, brayed, belled, and all to bring to pass
That stags should deign eat hay when winter stints them grass?

LXXVI.

    So much for men, and how disguise may make them mind
Their master. But you have to deal with womankind?
Abandon stratagem for strategy! Cast quite
The vile disguise away, try truth clean-opposite
Such creep-and-crawl, stand forth all man and, might it chance,
Somewhat of angel too! — whate'er inheritance,
Actual on earth, in heaven prospective, be your boast,
Lay claim to! Your best self revealed at uttermost, —
That's the wise way o' the strong! And e'en should falsehood
    tempt
The weaker sort to swerve, — at least the lie's exempt
From slur, that's loathlier still, of aiming to debase
Rather than elevate its object. Mimic grace,
Not make deformity your mask! Be sick by stealth,
Nor traffic with disease — malingering in health!
No more of : "Countrymen, I boast me one like you —
My lot, the common strength, the common weakness too!
I think the thoughts you think ; and if I have the knack

Of fitting thoughts to words, you peradventure lack,
Envy me not the chance, yourselves more fortunate!
Many the loaded ship self-sunk through treasure-freight,
Many the pregnant brain brought never child to birth,
Many the great heart broke beneath its girdle-girth!
Be mine the privilege to supplement defect,
Give dumbness voice, and let the laboring intellect
Find utterance in word, or possibly in deed!
What though I seem to go before? 't is you that lead!
I follow what I see so plain — the general mind
Projected pillar-wise, flame kindled by the kind.
Which dwarfs the unit — me — to insignificance!
Halt you, I stop forthwith, — proceed, I too advance!"

LXXVII.

Ay, that's the way to take with men you wish to lead,
Instruct, and benefit. Small prospect you succeed
With women so! Be all that's great and good and wise,
August, sublime — swell out your frog the right ox-size —
He's buoyed like a balloon, to soar, not burst, you'll see!
The more you prove yourself, less fear the prize will flee
The captor. Here you start after no pompous stag
Who condescends be snared, with toss of horn, and brag
Of bray, and ramp of hoof; you have not to subdue
The foe through letting him imagine he snares you!
'T is rather with . . .

LXXVIII.

Ah, thanks! quick — where the dipping disk
Shows red against the rise and fall o' the fin! there frisk
In shoal the — porpoises? Dolphins, they shall and must
Cut through the freshening clear — dolphins, my instance just!
'T is fable, therefore truth: who has to do with these,
Needs never practise trick of going hands and knees
As beasts require. Art fain the fish to captivate?
Gather thy greatness round, Arion! Stand in state,
As when the banqueting thrilled conscious — like a rose
Throughout its hundred leaves at that approach it knows
Of music in the bird — while Corinth grew one breast
A-throb for song and thee; nay, Periander pressed
The Methymnæan hand, and felt a king indeed, and guessed
How Phœbus' self might give that great mouth of the gods
Such a magnificence of song! The pillar nods,
Rocks roof, and trembles door, gigantic, post and jamb,
As harp and voice rend air — the shattering dithyramb!
So stand thou, and assume the robe that tingles yet

With triumph; strike the harp, whose every golden fret
Still smoulders with the flame, was late at fingers' end —
So, standing on the bench o' the ship, let voice expend
Thy soul, sing, unalloyed by meaner mode, thine own,
The Orthian lay; then leap from music's lofty throne
Into the lowest surge, make fearlessly thy launch!
Whatever storm may threat, some dolphin will be stanch!
Whatever roughness rage, some exquisite sea-thing
Will surely rise to save, will bear — palpitating —
One proud humility of love beneath its load —
Stem tide, part wave, till both roll on, thy jewell'd road
Of triumph, and the grim o' the gulf grow wonder-white
I' the phosphorescent wake; and still the exquisite
Sea-thing stems on, saves still, palpitatingly thus,
Lands safe at length its load of love at Tænarus,
True woman-creature!

LXXIX.

Man? Ah, would you prove what power
Marks man, — what fruit his tree may yield, beyond the sour
And stinted crab, he calls love-apple, which remains
After you toil and moil your utmost, — all, love gains
By lavishing manure? — try quite the other plan!
And, to obtain the strong true product of a man,
Set him to hate a little! Leave cherishing his root,
And rather prune his branch, nip off the pettiest shoot
Superfluous on his bough! I promise, you shall learn
By what grace came the goat, of all beasts else, to earn
Such favor with the god o' the grape: 't was only he
Who, browsing on its tops, first stung fertility
Into the stock's heart, stayed much growth of tendril-twine,
Some faintish flower, perhaps, but gained the indignant wine,
Wrath of the red press! Catch the puniest of the kind —
Man-animalcule, starved body, stunted mind,
And, as you nip the blotch 'twixt thumb and finger-nail,
Admire how heaven above and earth below avail
No jot to soothe the mite, sore at God's prime offence
In making mites at all, — coax from its impotence
One virile drop of thought, or word, or deed, by strain
To propagate for once — which nature rendered vain,
Who lets first failure stay, yet cares not to record
Mistake that seems to cast opprobrium on the Lord!
Such were the gain from love's best pains! But let the elf
Be touched with hate, because some real man bears himself
Manlike in body and soul, and, since he lives, must thwart
And furify and set a-fizz this counterpart

O' the pismire that's surprised to effervescence, if,
By chance, black bottle come in contact with chalk cliff,
Acid with alkali! Then thrice the bulk, out blows
Our insect, does its kind, and cuckoo-spits some rose!

LXXX.

No — 't is ungainly work, the ruling men, at best!
The graceful instinct 's right: 't is women stand confessed
Auxiliary, the gain that never goes away,
Takes nothing and gives all: Elvire, Fifine, 't is they
Convince, — if little, much, no matter! — one degree
The more, at least, convince unreasonable me
That I am, anyhow, a truth, though all else seem
And be not: if I dream, at least I know I dream.
The falsity, beside, is fleeting: I can stand
Still, and let truth come back, — your steadying touch of hand
Assists me to remain self-centred, fixed amid
All on the move. Believe in me, at once you bid
Myself believe that, since one soul has disengaged
Mine from the shows of things, so much is fact: I waged
No foolish warfare, then, with shades, myself a shade,
Here in the world — may hope my pains will be repaid!
How false things are, I judge: how changeable, I learn:
When, where, and how it is I shall see truth return,
That I expect to know, because Fifine knows me! —
How much more, if Elvire!

LXXXI.

"And why not, only she?
Since there can be for each, one Best, no more, such Best,
For body and mind of him, abolishes the rest
O' the simply Good and Better. You please select Elvire
To give you this belief in truth, dispel the fear
Yourself are, after all, as false as what surrounds:
And why not be content? When we two watched the rounds
The boatman made, 'twixt shoal and sandbank, yesterday,
As, at dead slack of tide, he chose to push his way,
With oar and pole, across the creek, and reach the isle
After a world of pains — my word provoked your smile,
Yet none the less deserved reply: ''T were wiser wait
The turn o' the tide, and find conveyance for his freight —
How easily—within the ship to purpose moored,
Managed by sails, not oars! But no, — the man 's allured
By liking for the new and hard in his exploit!
First come shall serve! He makes — courageous and adroit —
The merest willow-leaf of boat do duty, bear

His merchandise across: once over, needs he care
If folk arrive by ship, six hours hence, fresh and gay?'
No: he scorns commonplace, affects the unusual way;
And good Elvire is moored, with not a breath to flap
The yards of her, no lift of ripple to o'erlap
Keel, much less, prow. What care? since here's a cockle-shell,
Fifine, that's taut and crank, and carries just as well
Such seamanship as yours!"

LXXXII.

Alack, our life is lent,
From first to last, the whole, for this experiment
Of proving what I say — that we ourselves are true!
I would there were one voyage, and then no more to do
But tread the firm land, tempt the uncertain sea no more.
I would we might dispense with change of shore for shore
To evidence our skill, demonstrate — in no dream
It was, we tided o'er the trouble of the stream.
I would the steady voyage, and not the fitful trip, —
Elvire, and not Fifine, — might test our seamanship.
But why expend one's breath to tell you, change of boat
Means change of tactics too? Come see the same afloat
To-morrow, all the change, new stowage fore and aft
O' the cargo; then, to cross requires new sailor-craft!
To-day, one step from stern to bow keeps boat in trim:
To-morrow, some big stone — or woe to boat and him! —
Must ballast both. That man stands for Mind, paramount
Throughout the adventure: ay, howe'er you make account,
'T is mind that navigates, — skips over, twists between
The bales i' the boat, — now gives importance to the mean,
And now abates the pride of life, accepts all fact,
Discards all fiction, — steers Fifine, and cries, i' the act,
"Thou art so bad, and yet so delicate a brown!
Wouldst tell no end of lies: I talk to smile or frown!
Wouldst rob me: do men blame a squirrel, lithe and sly,
For pilfering the nut she adds to hoard? Nor I.
Elvire is true, as truth, honesty's self, alack!
The worse! too safe the ship, the transport there and back
Too certain! one may loll and lounge and leave the helm,
Let wind and tide do work: no fear that waves o'erwhelm
The steady-going bark, as sure to feel her way
Blindfold across, reach land, next year as yesterday!
How can I but suspect, the true feat were to slip
Down side, transfer myself to cockle-shell from ship,
And try if, trusting to sea-tracklessness, I class
With those around whose breast grew oak and triple brass:

Who dreaded no degree of death, but, with dry eyes,
Surveyed the turgid main and its monstrosities —
And rendered futile so, the prudent Power's decree
Of separate earth and disassociating sea;
Since, how is it observed, if impious vessels leap
Across, and tempt a thing they should not touch — the deep?
(See Horace to the boat, wherein, for Athens bound,
When Virgil must embark — Jove keep him safe and sound! —
The poet bade his friend start on the watery road,
Much reassured by this so comfortable ode.)

LXXXIII.

Then, never grudge my poor Fifine her compliment!
The rakish craft could slip her moorings in the tent,
And, hoisting every stitch of spangled canvas, steer
Through divers rocks and shoals, — in fine, deposit here
Your Virgil of a spouse, in Attica: yea, thrid
The mob of men, select the special virtue hid
In him, forsooth, and say — or rather, smile so sweet,
"Of all the multitude, you — I prefer to cheat!
Are you for Athens bound? I can perform the trip,
Shove little pinnace off, while yon superior ship,
The Elvire, refits in port!" So, off we push from beach
Of Pornic town, and lo, ere eye can wink, we reach
The Long Walls, and I prove that Athens is no dream,
For there the temples rise! they are, they nowise seem!
Earth is not all one lie, this truth attests me true!
Thanks therefore to Fifine! Elvire, I 'm back with you!
Share in the memories! Embark I trust we shall
Together some fine day, and so, for good and all,
Bid Pornic Town adieu, — then, just the strait to cross,
And we reach harbor, safe, in Iostephanos!

LXXXIV.

How quickly night comes! Lo, already 't is the land
Turns sea-like; overcrept by gray, the plains expand,
Assume significance; while ocean dwindles, shrinks
Into a pettier bound: its plash and plaint, methinks,
Six steps away, how both retire, as if their part
Were played, another force were free to prove her art,
Protagonist in turn! Are you unterrified?
All false, all fleeting too! And nowhere things abide,
And everywhere we strain that things should stay, — the one
Truth, that ourselves are true!

LXXXV.

       A word, and I have done.
Is it not just our hate of falsehood, fleetingness,
And the mere part, things play, that constitutes express
The inmost charm of this Fifine and all her tribe?
Actors! We also act, but only they inscribe
Their style and title so, and preface, only they,
Performance with "A lie is all we do or say."
Wherein but there can be the attraction, Falsehood's bribe,
That wins so surely o'er to Fifine and her tribe
The liking, nay the love of who hate Falsehood most,
Except that these alone of mankind make their boast
"Frankly, we simulate!" To feign, means — to have grace
And so get gratitude! This ruler of the race,
Crowned, sceptred, stoled to suit, — 't is not that you detect
The cobbler in the king, but that he makes effect
By seeming the reverse of what you know to be
The man, the mind, whole form, fashion, and quality.
Mistake his false for true, one minute, — there's an end
Of the admiration! Truth, we grieve at or rejoice:
'T is only falsehood, plain in gesture, look and voice,
That brings the praise desired, since profit comes thereby.
The histrionic truth is in the natural lie.
Because the man who wept the tears was, all the time,
Happy enough; because the other man, a-grime
With guilt, was, at the least, as white as I and you;
Because the timid type of bashful maidhood, who
Starts at her own pure shade, already numbers seven
Born babes and, in a month, will turn their odd to even;
Because the saucy prince would prove, could you unfurl
Some yards of wrap, a meek and meritorious girl —
Precisely as you see success attained by each
O' the mimes, do you approve, not foolishly impeach
The falsehood!

LXXXVI.

 That's the first o' the truths found: all things, slow
Or quick i' the passage, come at last to that, you know!
Each has a false outside, whereby a truth is forced
To issue from within: truth, falsehood, are divorced
By the excepted eye, at the rare season, for
The happy moment. Life means — learning to abhor
The false, and love the true, truth treasured snatch by snatch,
Waifs counted at their worth. And when with strays they
  match

I' the particolored world, — when, under foul, shines fair,
And truth, displayed i' the point, flashes forth everywhere
I' the circle, manifest to soul, though hid from sense,
And no obstruction more affects this confidence, —
When faith is ripe for sight, — why, reasonably, then
Comes the great clearing-up. Wait threescore years and ten!

LXXXVII.

Therefore I prize stage-play, the honest cheating; thence
The impulse pricked, when fife and drum bade Fair commence,
To bid you trip and skip, link arm in arm with me,
Like husband and like wife, and so together see
The tumbling-troop arrayed, the strollers on their stage
Drawn up and under arms, and ready to engage.
And if I started thence upon abstruser themes . . .
Well, 't was a dream, pricked too!

LXXXVIII.

A poet never dreams:
We prose-folk always do: we miss the proper duct
For thoughts on things unseen, which stagnate and obstruct
The system, therefore; mind, sound in a body sane,
Keeps thoughts apart from facts, and to one flowing vein
Confines its sense of that which is not, but might be,
And leaves the rest alone. What ghosts do poets see?
What dæmons fear? what man or thing misapprehend?
Unchoked, the channel 's flush, the fancy 's free to spend
Its special self aright in manner, time, and place.
Never believe that who create the busy race
O' the brain, bring poetry to birth, such act performed,
Feel trouble them, the same, such residue as warmed
My prosy blood, this morn, — intrusive fancies, meant
For outbreak and escape by quite another vent!
Whence follows that, asleep, my dreamings oft exceed
The bound. But you shall hear.

LXXXIX.

I smoked. The webs o' the weed,
With many a break i' the mesh, were floating to re-form
Cupola-wise above: chased thither by soft warm
Inflow of air without; since I — of mind to muse, to clench
The gain of soul and body, got by their noonday drench
In sun and sea — had flung both frames o' the window wide,
To soak my body still and let soul soar beside.
In came the country sounds and sights and smells — that fine
Sharp needle in the nose from o' fermenting wine!

In came a dragon-fly with whir and stir, then out,
Off and away: in came, — kept coming, rather, — pout
Succeeding smile, and take-away still close on give, —
One loose long creeper-branch, tremblingly sensitive
To risks, which blooms and leaves,— each leaf tongue-broad, each
    bloom
Midfinger-deep, — must run by prying in the room
Of one who loves and grasps and spoils and speculates.
All so far plain enough to sight and sense: but, weights,
Measures and numbers, — ah, could one apply such test
To other visitants that came at no request
Of who kept open house, — to fancies manifold
From this four-cornered world, the memories new and old,
The antenatal prime experience — what know I? —
The initiatory love preparing us to die —
Such were a crowd to count, a sight to see, a prize
To turn to profit, were but fleshly ears and eyes
Able to cope with those o' the spirit!

XC.

                        Therefore, — since
Thought hankers after speech, while no speech may evince
Feeling like music, — mine, o'erburdened with each gift
From every visitant, at last resolved to shift
Its burden to the back of some musician dead
And gone, who feeling once what I feel now, instead
Of words, sought sounds, and saved forever, in the same,
Truth that escapes prose, — nay, puts poetry to shame.
I read the note, I strike the key, I bid *record*
The instrument — thanks greet the veritable word!
And not in vain I urge: "O dead and gone away,
Assist who struggles yet, thy strength become my stay,
Thy record serve as well to register — I felt
And knew thus much of truth! With me, must knowledge melt
Into surmise and doubt and disbelief, unless
Thy music reassure — I gave no idle guess,
But gained a certitude, I yet may hardly keep!
What care? since round is piled a monumental heap
Of music that conserves the assurance, thou as well
Wast certain of the same! thou, master of the spell,
Mad'st moonbeams marble, didst *record* what other men
Feel only to forget!" Who was it helped me, then?
What master's work first came responsive to my call,
Found my eye, fixed my choice?

XCI.

Why, Schumann's "Carnival!"
My choice chimed in, you see, exactly with the sounds
And sights of yestereve, when, going on my rounds,
Where both roads join the bridge, I heard across the dusk
Creak a slow caravan, and saw arrive the husk
O' the spice-nut, which peeled off this morning, and displayed,
'Twixt tree and tree, a tent whence the red pennon made
Its vivid reach for home and ocean-idleness —
And where, my heart surmised, at that same moment, — yes, —
Tugging her tricot on, — yet tenderly, lest stitch
Announce the crack of doom, reveal disaster which
Our Pornic's modest stock of merceries in vain
Were ransacked to retrieve, — there, cautiously a-strain,
(My heart surmised) must crouch in that tent's corner, curved
Like Spring-month's russet moon, some girl by fate reserved
To give me once again the electric snap and spark
Which prove, when finger finds out finger in the dark
O' the world, there's fire and life and truth there, link but hands
And pass the secret on. Lo, link by link, expands
The circle, lengthens out the chain, till one embrace
Of high with low is found uniting the whole race,
Not simply you and me and our Fifine, but all
The world: the Fair expands into the Carnival,
And Carnival again to . . . ah, but that's my dream!

XCII.

I somehow played the piece: remarked on each old theme
I' the new dress; saw how food o' the soul, the stuff that's made
To furnish man with thought and feeling, is purveyed
Substantially the same from age to age, with change
Of the outside only for successive feasters. Range
The banquet-room o' the world, from the dim farthest head
O' the table, to its foot, for you and me bespread,
This merry morn, we find sufficient fare, I trow.
But, novel? Scrape away the sauce; and taste, below,
The verity o' the viand, — you shall perceive there went
To board-head just the dish which other condiment
Makes palatable now: guests came, sat down, fell-to,
Rose up, wiped mouth, went way, — lived, died, — and never knew
That generations yet should, seeking sustenance,
Still find the selfsame fare, with somewhat to enhance
Its flavor, in the kind of cooking. As with hates

And loves and fears and hopes, so with what emulates
The same, expresses hates, loves, fears, and hopes in Art:
The forms, the themes — no one without its counterpart
Ages ago; no one but, mumbled the due time
I' the mouth of the eater, needs be cooked again in rhyme,
Dished up anew in paint, sauce-smothered fresh in sound,
To suit the wisdom-tooth, just cut, of the age, that's found
With gums obtuse to gust and smack which relished so
The meat o' the meal folk made some fifty years ago.
But don't suppose the new was able to efface
The old without a struggle, a pang! The commonplace
Still clung about his heart, long after all the rest
O' the natural man, at eye and ear, was caught, confessed
The charm of change, although wry lip and wrinkled nose
Owned ancient virtue more conducive to repose
Than modern nothings roused to somethings by some shred
Of pungency, perchance garlic in amber's stead.
And so on, till one day, another age, by due
Rotation, pries, sniffs, smacks, discovers old is new,
And sauce, our sires pronounced insipid, proves again
Sole piquant, may resume its titillating reign —
With music, most of all the arts, since change is there
The law, and not the lapse: the precious means the rare,
And not the absolute in all good save surprise.
So I remarked upon our Schumann's victories
Over the commonplace, how faded phrase grew fine,
And pallid perfection — piqued, up-startled by that brine,
His pickle — bit the mouth and burnt the tongue aright,
Beyond the merely good no longer exquisite:
Then took things as I found, and thanked without demur
The pretty piece — played through that movement, you prefer,
Where dance and shuffle past, — he scolding while she pouts,
She canting while he calms, — in those eternal bouts
Of age, the dog — with youth, the cat — by rose-festoon
Tied teasingly enough — Columbine, Pantaloon:
She, toe-tips and *staccato*, — *legato*, shakes his poll
And shambles in pursuit, the senior. *Fi la folle!*
Lie to him! get his gold and pay its price! begin
Your trade betimes, nor wait till you've wed Harlequin
And need, at the week's end, to play the duteous wife,
And swear you still love slaps and leapings more than life!
Pretty! I say.

XCIII.

And so, I somehow-nohow played
The whole o' the pretty piece; and then . . . whatever weighed

My eyes down, furled the films about my wits? suppose,
The morning-bath, — the sweet monotony of those
Three keys, flat, flat and flat, never a sharp at all. —
Or else the brain's fatigue, forced even here to fall
Into the same old track, and recognize the shift
From old to new, and back to old again, and, — swift
Or slow, no matter, — still the certainty of change,
Conviction we shall find the false, where'er we range,
In art no less than nature : or what if wrist were numb,
And over-tense the muscle, abductor of the thumb,
Taxed by those tenths' and twelfths' unconscionable stretch?
Howe'er it came to pass, I soon was far to fetch —
Gone off in company with Music!

XCIV.

      Whither bound
Except for Venice? She it was, by instinct found
Carnival-country proper, who far below the perch
Where I was pinnacled, showed, opposite, Mark's Church,
And, underneath, Mark's Square, with those two lines of street,
Procuratié-sides, each leading to my feet —
Since from above I gazed, however I got there.

XCV.

  And what I gazed upon was a prodigious Fair,
Concourse immense of men and women, crowned or casqued,
Turbaned or tiar'd, wreathed, plumed, hatted or wigged, but
  masked —
Always masked, — only, how? No face-shape, beast or bird,
Nay, fish and reptile even, but someone had preferred,
From out its frontispiece, feathered or scaled or curled,
To make the vizard whence himself should view the world,
And where the world believed himself was manifest.
Yet when you came to look, mixed up among the rest
More funnily by far, were masks to imitate
Humanity's mishap : the wrinkled brow, bald pate,
And rheumy eyes of Age, peak'd chin and parchment chap,
Were signs of day-work done, and wage-time near. — mishap
Merely ; but, Age reduced to simple greed and guile,
Worn apathetic else as some smooth slab, erewhile
A clear-cut man-at-arms i' the pavement, till foot's tread
Effaced the sculpture, left the stone you saw instead, —
Was not that terrible beyond the mere uncouth?
Well, and perhaps the next revolting you was Youth,
Stark ignorance and crude conceit, half smirk, half stare
On that frank fool-face, gay beneath its head of hair
Which covers nothing.

XCVI.

These, you are to understand,
Were the mere hard and sharp distinctions. On each hand,
I soon became aware, flocked the infinitude
Of passions, loves and hates, man pampers till his mood
Becomes himself, the whole sole face we name him by,
Nor want denotement else, if age or youth supply
The rest of him: old, young, — classed creature: in the main
A love, a hate, a hope, a fear, each soul a-strain
Some one way through the flesh — the face, an evidence
O' the soul at work inside; and, all the more intense,
So much the more grotesque.

XCVII.

"Why should each soul be tasked
Some one way, by one love or else one hate?" I asked.
When it occurred to me, from all these sights beneath
There rose not any sound: a crowd, yet dumb as death!

XCVIII.

Soon I knew why. (Propose a riddle, and 't is solved
Forthwith — in dream!) They spoke; but, since on me devolved
To see, and understand by sight, — the vulgar speech
Might be dispensed with. "He who cannot see, must reach
As best he may the truth of men by help of words
They please to speak, must fare at will of who affords
The banquet," — so I thought. "Who sees not, hears and so
Gets to believe; myself it is that, seeing, know,
And, knowing, can dispense with voice and vanity
Of speech. What hinders then, that, drawing closer, I
Put privilege to use, see and know better still
These *simulacra*, taste the profit of my skill,
Down in the midst?"

XCIX.

And plumb I pitched into the square —
A groundling like the rest. What think you happened there?
Precise the contrary of what one would expect!
For, — whereas, so much more monstrosities deflect
From nature and the type, as you the more approach
Their precinct, — here, I found brutality encroach
Less on the human, lie the lightlier as I looked
The nearlier on these faces that seemed but now so crook'd
And clawed away from God's prime purpose. They diverged
A little from the type, but somehow rather urged

To pity than disgust: the prominent, before,
Now dwindled into mere distinctness, nothing more.
Still, at first sight, stood forth undoubtedly the fact
Some deviation was: in no one case there lacked
The certain sign and mark, say hint, say, trick of lip
Or twist of nose, that proved a fault in workmanship,
Change in the prime design, some hesitancy here
And there, which checked the man and let the beast appear;
But that was all.

C.

     All; yet enough to bid each tongue
Lie in abeyance still. They talked, themselves among,
Of themselves, to themselves; I saw the mouths at play,
The gesture that enforced, the eye that strove to say
The same thing as the voice, and seldom gained its point
— That this was so, I saw; but all seemed out of joint
I' the vocal medium 'twixt the world and me. I gained
Knowledge by notice, not by giving ear, — attained
To truth by what men seemed, not said: to me one glance
Was worth whole histories of noisy utterance,
— At least, to me in dream.

CI.

     And presently I found
That, just as ugliness had withered, so unwound
Itself, and perished off, repugnance to what wrong
Might linger yet i' the make of man. My will was strong
I' the matter; I could pick and choose, project my weight:
(Remember how we saw the boatman trim his freight!)
Determine to observe, or manage to escape,
Or make divergency assume another shape
By shift of point of sight in me the observer: thus
Corrected, added to, subtracted from, — discuss
Each variant quality, and brute-beast touch was turned
Into mankind's safeguard! Force, guile, were arms which
  earned
My praise, not blame at all: for we must learn to live,
Case-hardened at all points, not bare and sensitive,
But plated for defence, nay, furnished for attack,
With spikes at the due place, that neither front nor back
May suffer in that squeeze with nature, we find — life.
Are we not here to learn the good of peace through strife,
Of love through hate, and reach knowledge by ignorance?
Why, those are helps thereto, which late we eyed askance,
And nicknamed unaware! Just so, a sword we call

Superfluous, and cry out against, at festival :
Wear it in time of war, its clink and clatter grate
O' the ear to purpose then !

CII.

                         I found, one must abate
One's scorn of the soul's casing, distinct from the soul's self —
Which is the centre-drop : whereas the pride in pelf,
The lust to seem the thing it cannot be, the greed
For praise, and all the rest seen outside, — these indeed
Are the hard polished cold crystal environment
Of those strange orbs unearthed i' the Druid temple, meant
For divination (so the learned please to think)
Wherein you may admire one dewdrop roll and wink,
All unaffected by — quite alien to — what sealed
And saved it long ago : though how it got congealed
I shall not give a guess, nor how, by power occult,
The solid surface-shield was outcome and result
Of simple dew at work to save itself amid
The unwatery force around ; protected thus, dew slid
Safe through all opposites, impatient to absorb
Its spot of life, and lasts forever in the orb
We, now, from hand to hand pass with impunity.

CIII.

   And the delight wherewith I watch this crowd must be
Akin to that which crowns the chemist when he winds
Thread up and up, till clue be fairly clutched, — unbinds
The composite, ties fast the simple to its mate,
And, tracing each effect back to its cause, elate,
Constructs in fancy, from the fewest primitives,
The complex and complete, all diverse life, that lives
Not only in beast, bird, fish, reptile, insect, but
The very plants and earths and ores. Just so I glut
My hunger both to be and know the thing I am,
By contrast with the thing I am not ; so, through sham
And outside, I arrive at inmost real, probe
And prove how the nude form obtained the checkered robe.

CIV.

— Experience, I am glad to master soon or late,
Here, there, and everywhere i' the world, without debate !
Only, in Venice why ? What reason for Mark's Square
Rather than Timbuctoo ?

CV.

And I became aware,
Scarcely the word escaped my lips, that swift ensued
In silence and by stealth, and yet with certitude,
A formidable change of the amphitheatre
Which held the Carnival; although the human stir
Continued just the same amid that shift of scene.

CVI.

For as on edifice of cloud i' the gray and green
Of evening, — built about some glory of the west,
To barricade the sun's departure, — manifest,
He plays, pre-eminently gold, gilds vapor, crag and crest
Which bend in rapt suspense above the act and deed
They cluster round and keep their very own, nor heed
The world at watch; while we, breathlessly at the base
O' the castellated bulk, note momently the mace
Of nightfall here, fall there, bring change with every blow,
Alike to sharpened shaft and broadened portico
I' the structure: heights and depths, beneath the leaden stress,
Crumble and melt and mix together, coalesce,
Re-form, but sadder still, subdued yet more and more
By every fresh defeat, till wearied eyes need pore
No longer on the dull impoverished decadence
Of all that pomp of pile in towering evidence
So lately: —

CVII.

Even thus nor otherwise, meseemed
That if I fixed my gaze awhile on what I dreamed
Was Venice' Square, Mark's Church, the scheme was straight unschemed,
A subtle something had its way within the heart
Of each and every house I watched, with counterpart
Of tremor through the front and outward face, until
Mutation was at end; impassive and stock-still
Stood now the ancient house, grown — new, is scarce the phrase,
Since older, in a sense, — altered to . . . what i' the ways,
Ourselves are wont to see, coerced by city, town,
Or village, anywhere i' the world, pace up or down
Europe! In all the maze, no single tenement
I saw, but I could claim acquaintance with.

CVIII.

There went
Conviction to my soul, that what I took of late
For Venice was the world; its Carnival — the state
Of mankind, masquerade in life-long permanence
For all time, and no one particular feast-day. Whence
'T was easy to infer what meant my late disgust
At the brute-pageant, each grotesque of greed and lust
And idle hate, and love as impotent for good —
When from my pride of place I passed the interlude
In critical review; and what, the wonder that ensued
When, from such pinnacled pre-eminence, I found
Somehow the proper goal for wisdom was the ground
And not the sky, — so, slid sagaciously betimes
Down heaven's baluster-rope, to reach the mob of mimes
And mummers; whereby came discovery there was just
Enough and not too much of hate, love, greed and lust,
Could one discerningly but hold the balance, shift
The weight from scale to scale, do justice to the drift
Of nature, and explain the glories by the shames
Mixed up in man, one stuff miscalled by different names
According to what stage i' the process turned his rough,
Even as I gazed, to smooth — only get close enough!
— What was all this except the lesson of a life?

CIX.

And — consequent upon the learning how from strife
Grew peace — from evil, good — came knowledge that, to get
Acquaintance with the way o' the world, we must nor fret
Nor fume, on altitudes of self-sufficiency,
But bid a frank farewell to what — we think — should be,
And, with as good a grace, welcome what is — we find.

CX.

Is — for the hour, observe! Since something to my mind
Suggested soon the fancy, nay, certitude that change,
Never suspending touch, continued to derange
What architecture, we, walled up within the cirque
O' the world, consider fixed as fate, not fairy-work.
For those were temples, sure, which tremblingly grew blank
From bright, then broke afresh in triumph, — ah, but sank
As soon, for liquid change through artery and vein
O' the very marble wound its way! And first a stain
Would startle and offend amid the glory; next,
Spot swift succeeded spot, but found me less perplexed

By portents; then, as 't were, a sleepiness soft stole
Over the stately fane, and shadow sucked the whole
Façade into itself, made uniformly earth
What was a piece of heaven; till, lo, a second birth,
And the veil broke away because of something new
Inside, that pushed to gain an outlet, paused in view
At last, and proved a growth of stone or brick or wood
Which, alien to the aim o' the Builder, somehow stood
The test, could satisfy, if not the early race
For whom he built, at least our present populace,
Who must not bear the blame for what, blamed, proves mishap
Of the Artist: his work gone, another fills the gap,
Serves the prime purpose so. Undoubtedly there spreads
Building around, above, which makes men lift their heads
To look at, or look through, or look — for aught I care —
Over: if only up, it is, not down, they stare,
" Commercing with the skies," and not the pavement in the
  Square.

CXI.

But are they only temples that subdivide, collapse,
And tower again, transformed? Academies, perhaps!
Domes where dwells Learning, seats of Science, bower and hall
Which house Philosophy — do these, too, rise and fall,
Based though foundations be on steadfast mother-earth,
With no chimeric claim to supermundane birth,
No boast that, dropped from cloud, they did not grow from
  ground?
Why, these fare worst of all! these vanish and are found
Nowhere, by who tasks eye some twice within his term
Of threescore years and ten, for tidings what each germ
Has burgeoned out into, whereof the promise stunned
His ear with such acclaim, — praise-payment to refund
The praisers, never doubt, some twice before they die
Whose days are long i' the land.

CXII.

                    Alack, Philosophy!
Despite the chop and change, diminished or increased,
Patched-up and plastered-o'er, Religion stands at least
I' the temple-type. But thou? Here gape I, all agog
These thirty years, to learn how tadpole turns to frog;
And thrice at least have gazed with mild astonishment,
As, skyward up and up, some fire-new fabric sent
Its challenge to mankind, that, clustered underneath
To hear the word, they straight believe, ay, in the teeth

O' the Past, clap hands, and hail triumphant Truth's outbreak —
Tadpole-frog-theory propounded past mistake!
In vain! A something ails the edifice, it bends,
It bows, it buries . . . Haste! cry "Heads below" to friends —
But have no fear they find, when smother shall subside,
Some substitution perk with unabated pride
I' the predecessor's place!

CXIII.

        No, — the one voice which failed
Never, the preachment's coigne of vantage nothing ailed, —
That had the luck to lodge i' the house not made with hands!
And all it preached was this: "Truth builds upon the sands,
Though stationed on a rock: and so her work decays,
And so she builds afresh, with like result. Nought stays
But just the fact that Truth not only is, but fain
Would have men know she needs must be, by each so plain
Attempt to visibly inhabit where they dwell."
Her works are work, while she is she; that work does well
Which lasts mankind their lifetime through, and lets believe
One generation more, that, though sand run through sieve,
Yet earth now reached is rock, and what we moderns find
Erected here is Truth, who, 'stablished to her mind
I' the fulness of the days, will never change in show
More than in substance erst: men thought they knew; we know!

CXIV.

Do you, my generation? Well, let the blocks prove mist
I' the main enclosure, — church and college, if they list,
Be something for a time, and everything anon,
And anything awhile, as fit is off or on,
Till they grow nothing, soon to reappear no less
As something, — shape reshaped, till out of shapelessness
Come shape again as sure! no doubt, or round or square
Or polygon its front, some building will be there,
Do duty in that nook o' the wall o' the world where once
The Architect saw fit precisely to ensconce
College or church, and bid such bulwark guard the line
O' the barrier round about, humanity's confine.

CXV.

Leave watching change at work i' the greater scale, on these
The main supports, and turn to their interstices
Filled up by fabrics too, less costly and less rare,

Yet of importance, yet essential to the Fair
They help to circumscribe, instruct, and regulate !
See, where each booth-front boasts, in letters small or great,
Its specialty, proclaims its privilege to stop
A breach, beside the best !

CXVI.

       Here History keeps shop,
Tells how past deeds were done, so and not otherwise :
" Man ! hold truth evermore ! forget the early lies ! "
There sits Morality, demure behind her stall,
Dealing out life and death : " This is the thing to call
Right, and this other, wrong ; thus think, thus do, thus say,
Thus joy, thus suffer ! — not to-day as yesterday —
Yesterday's doctrine dead, this only shall endure !
Obey its voice and live ! " — enjoins the dame demure.
While Art gives flag to breeze, bids drum beat, trumpet blow,
Inviting eye and ear to yonder raree-show.
Up goes the canvas, hauled to height of pole. I think,
We know the way — long lost, late learned — to paint ! A wink
Of eye, and lo, the pose ! the statue on its plinth !
How could we moderns miss the heart o' the labyrinth
Perversely all these years, permit the Greek seclude
His secret till to-day ? And here 's another feud
Now happily composed : inspect this quartet-score !
Got long past melody, no word has Music more
To say to mortal man ! But is the bard to be
Behindhand ? Here 's his book, and now perhaps you see
At length what poetry can do !

CXVII.

       Why, that 's stability
Itself, that change on change we sorrowfully saw
Creep o'er the prouder piles ! We acquiesced in law
When the fine gold grew dim i' the temple, when the brass
Which pillared that so brave abode where Knowledge was,
Bowed and resigned the trust ; but, bear all this caprice,
Harlequinade where swift to birth succeeds decease
Of hue at every turn o' the tinsel-flag which flames
While Art holds booth in Fair ? Such glories chased by shames
Like these, distract beyond the solemn and august
Procedure to decay, evanishment in dust,
Of those marmoreal domes, — above vicissitude,
We used to hope !

CXVIII.

"So, all is change, in fine," pursued
The preachment to a pause. When — "All is permanence!"
Returned a voice. Within? without? No matter whence
The explanation came: for, understand, I ought
To simply say — " I saw," each thing I say " I thought."
Since ever, as, unrolled, the strange scene-picture grew
Before me, sight flashed first, though mental comment too
Would follow in a trice, come hobblingly to halt.

CXIX.

So, what did I see next but, — much as when the vault
I' the west, — wherein we watch the vapory, manifold
Transfiguration, — tired turns blaze to black, — behold,
Peak reconciled to base, dark ending feud with bright,
The multiform subsides, becomes the definite.
Contrasting life and strife, where battle they i' the blank
Severity of peace in death, for which we thank
One wind that comes to quell the concourse, drive at last
Things to a shape which suits the close of things, and cast
Palpably o'er vexed earth heaven's mantle of repose?

CXX.

Just so, in Venice' Square, that things were at the close
Was signalled to my sense; for I perceived arrest
O' the change all round about. As if some impulse pressed
Each gently into each, what was distinctness, late,
Grew vague, and, line from line no longer separate,
No matter what its style, edifice . . . shall I say,
Died into edifice? I find no simpler way
Of saying how, without or dash or shock or trace
Of violence, I found unity in the place
Of temple, tower, — nay, hall and house and hut, — one blank
Severity of peace in death; to which they sank
Resigned enough, till . . . ah, conjecture, I beseech,
What special blank did they agree to, all and each?
What common shape was that wherein they mutely merged
Likes and dislikes of form, so plain before?

CXXI.

I urged
Your step this way, prolonged our path of enterprise
To where we stand at last, in order that your eyes
Might see the very thing, and save my tongue describe
The Druid monument which fronts you. Could I bribe

Nature to come in aid, illustrate what I mean,
What wants there she should lend to solemnize the scene?

CXXII.

How does it strike you, this construction gaunt and gray —
Sole object, these piled stones, that gleam unground-away
By twilight's hungry jaw, which champs fine all beside
I' the solitary waste we grope through? Oh, no guide,
Need we to grope our way and reach the monstrous door
Of granite! Take my word, the deeper you explore
That caverned passage, filled with fancies to the brim,
The less will you approve the adventure! such a grim
Bar-sinister soon blocks abrupt your path, and ends
All with a cold dread shape, — shape whereon Learning spends
Labor, and leaves the text obscurer for the gloss,
While Ignorance reads right — recoiling from that Cross!
Whence came the mass and mass, strange quality of stone
Unquarried anywhere i' the region round? Unknown!
Just as unknown, how such enormity could be
Conveyed by land, or else transported over sea,
And laid in order, so, precisely each on each,
As you and I would build a grotto where the beach
Sheds shell — to last an hour: this building lasts from age
To age the same. But why?

CXXIII.

Ask Learning! I engage
You get a prosy wherefore, shall help you to advance
In knowledge just as much as helps you Ignorance
Surmising, in the mouth of peasant-lad or lass,
"I heard my father say he understood it was
A building, people built as soon as earth was made
Almost, because they might forget (they were afraid)
Earth did not make itself, but came of Somebody.
They labored that their work might last, and show thereby
He stays, while we and earth, and all things come and go.
Come whence? Go whither? That, when come and gone, we
    know
Perhaps, but not while earth and all things need our best
Attention: we must wait and die to know the rest.
Ask, if that's true, what use in setting up the pile?
To make one fear and hope: remind us, all the while
We come and go, outside there's Somebody that stays;
A circumstance which ought to make us mind our ways,
Because, — whatever end we answer by this life, —
Next time, best chance must be for who, with toil and strife,

Manages now to live most like what he was meant
Become : since who succeeds so far, 't is evident,
Stands foremost on the file ; who fails, has less to hope
From new promotion. That 's the rule — with even a rope
Of mushrooms, like this rope I dangle! those that grew
Greatest and roundest, all in life they had to do,
Gain a reward, a grace they never dreamed, I think ;
Since, outside white as milk and inside black as ink,
They go to the Great House to make a dainty dish
For Don and Donna; while this basket-load, I wish
Well off my arm, it breaks, — no starveling of the heap
But had his share of dew, his proper length of sleep
I' the sunshine : yet, of all, the outcome is — this queer
Cribbed quantity of dwarfs which burden basket here
Till I reach home ; 't is there that, having run their rigs,
They end their earthly race, are flung as food for pigs.
Any more use I see ? Well, you must know, there lies
Something, the Curé says, that points to mysteries
Above our grasp : a huge stone pillar, once upright,
Now laid at length, half-lost — discreetly shunning sight
I' the bush and brier, because of stories in the air —
Hints what it signified, and why was stationed there,
Once on a time. In vain the Curé tasked his lungs —
Showed, in a preachment, how, at bottom of the rungs
O' the ladder, Jacob saw, where heavenly angels stept
Up and down, lay a stone which served him, while he slept,
For pillow ; when he woke, he set the same upright
As pillar, and a-top poured oil : things requisite
To instruct posterity, there mounts from floor to roof,
A staircase, earth to heaven ; and also put in proof,
When we have scaled the sky, we well may let alone
What raised us from the ground, and — paying to the stone
Proper respect, of course — take staff and go our way,
Leaving the Pagan night for Christian break of day.
' For,' preached he, ' what they dreamed, these Pagans, wide-
    awake
We Christians may behold. How strange, then, were mistake
Did anybody style the stone, — because of drop
Remaining there from oil which Jacob poured a-top, —
Itself the Gate of Heaven, itself the end, and not
The means thereto ! ' Thus preached the Curé, and no jot
The more persuaded people but that, what once a thing
Meant and had right to mean, it still must mean. So cling
Folk somehow to the prime authoritative speech,
And so distrust report, it seems as they could reach
Far better the arch-word, whereon their fate depends,

Through rude charactery, than all the grace it lends,
That lettering of your scribes! who flourish pen apace
And ornament the text, they say — we say, efface.
Hence, when the earth began its life afresh in May,
And fruit-trees bloomed, and waves would wanton, and the bay
Ruffle its wealth of weed, and stranger-birds arrive,
And beasts take each a mate, — folk, too, found sensitive,
Surmised the old gray stone upright there, through such tracts
Of solitariness and silence, kept the facts
Entrusted it, could deal out doctrine, did it please:
No fresh and frothy draught, but liquor on the lees,
Strong, savage, and sincere: first bleedings from a vine
Whereof the product now do Curés so refine
To insipidity, that, when heart sinks, we strive
And strike from the old stone the old restorative.
'Which is?' — why, go and ask our grandames how they used
To dance around it, till the Curé disabused
Their ignorance, and bade the parish in a band
Lay flat the obtrusive thing that cumbered so the land!
And there, accordingly, in bush and brier it — 'bides
Its time to rise again!' (so somebody derides,
That's pert from Paris,) 'since, yon spire, you keep erect
Yonder, and pray beneath, is nothing, I suspect,
But just the symbol's self, expressed in slate for rock,
Art's smooth for Nature's rough, new chip from the old block!
There, sir, my say is said! Thanks, and Saint Gille increase
The wealth bestowed so well!" — wherewith he pockets piece,
Doffs cap, and takes the road. I leave in Learning's clutch
More money for his book, but scarcely gain as much.

CXXIV.

To this it was, this same primeval monument,
That, in my dream, I saw building with building blent
Fall: each on each they fast and founderingly went
Confusion-ward; but thence again subsided fast,
Became the mound you see. Magnificently massed
Indeed, those mammoth-stones, piled by the Protoplast
Temple-wise in my dream! beyond compare with fanes
Which, solid-looking late, had left no least remains
I' the bald and blank, now sole usurper of the plains
Of heaven, diversified and beautiful before.
And yet simplicity appeared to speak no more
Nor less to me than spoke the compound. At the core,
One and no other word, as in the crust of late,
Whispered, which, audible through the transition-state,
Was no loud utterance in even the ultimate

Disposure. For as some imperial chord subsists,
Steadily underlies the accidental mists
Of music springing thence, that run their mazy race
Around, and sink, absorbed, back to the triad base, —
So, out of that one word, each variant rose and fell
And left the same " All 's change, but permanence as well."
— Grave note whence — list aloft! — harmonics sound, that
    mean :
" Truth inside, and outside, truth also ; and between
Each, falsehood that is change, as truth is permanence.
The individual soul works through the shows of sense
(Which, ever proving false, still promise to be true)
Up to an outer soul as individual too ;
And, through the fleeting, lives to die into the fixed,
And reach at length 'God, man, or both together mixed,'
Transparent through the flesh, by parts which prove a whole,
By hints which make the soul discernible by soul —
Let only soul look up, not down, not hate but love,
As truth successively takes shape, one grade above
Its last presentment, tempts as it were truth indeed
Revealed this time ; so tempts, till we attain to read
The signs aright, and learn, by failure, truth is forced
To manifest itself through falsehood ; whence divorced
By the excepted eye, at the rare season, for
The happy moment, truth instructs us to abhor
The false, and prize the true, obtainable thereby.
Then do we understand the value of a lie ;
Its purpose served, its truth once safe deposited,
Each lie, superfluous now, leaves, in the singer's stead,
The indubitable song ; the historic personage
Put by, leaves prominent the impulse of his age ;
Truth sets aside speech, act, time, place, indeed, but brings
Nakedly forward now the principle of things
Highest and least."

CXXV.

        Wherewith change ends. What change to dread
When, disengaged at last from every veil, instead
Of type remains the truth ? once — falsehood : but anon
Theosuton e broteion eper kekramenon,
Something as true as soul is true, though veils between
Prove false and fleet away. As I mean, did he mean,
The poet whose bird-phrase sits, singing in my ear
A mystery not unlike ? What through the dark and drear
Brought comfort to the Titan ? Emerging from the lymph,

"God, man, or mixture" proved only to be a nymph:
"From whom the clink on clink of metal" (money, judged
Abundant in my purse) "struck" (bumped at, till it budged)
"The modesty, her soul's habitual resident"
(Where late the sisterhood were lively in their tent)
"As out of wingèd car" (that caravan on wheels)
"Impulsively she rushed, no slippers to her heels,"
And "Fear not, friends we flock!" soft smiled the sea-Fifine—
Primitive of the veils (if he meant what I mean)
The poet's Titan learned to lift, ere "Three-formed Fate,
Moirai Trimorphoi," stood unmasked the Ultimate.

CXXVI.

Enough o' the dream! You see how poetry turns prose.
Announcing wonder-work, I dwindle at the close
Down to mere commonplace old facts which everybody knows.
So dreaming disappoints! The fresh and strange at first,
Soon wears to trite and tame, nor warrants the outburst
Of heart with which we hail those heights, at very brink
Of heaven, whereto one least of lifts would lead, we think,
But wherefrom quick decline conducts our step, we find,
To homely earth, old facts familiar left behind.
Did not this monument, for instance, long ago
Say all it had to say, show all it had to show,
Nor promise to do duty more in dream?

CXXVII.

                    Awaking so,
What if we, homeward-bound, all peace and some fatigue,
Trudge, soberly complete our tramp of near a league,
Last little mile which makes the circuit just, Elvire?
We end where we began: that consequence is clear.
All peace and some fatigue, wherever we were nursed
To life, we bosom us on death, find last is first
And thenceforth final too.

CXXVIII.

            "Why final? Why the more
Worth credence now than when such truth proved false before?"
Because a novel point impresses now: each lie
Redounded to the praise of man, was victory
Man's nature had both right to get, and might to gain,
And by no means implied submission to the reign
Of other quite as real a nature, that saw fit
To have its way with man, not man his way with it.
This time, acknowledgment and acquiescence quell

Their contrary in man; promotion proves as well
Defeat: and Truth, unlike the False with Truth's outside,
Neither plumes up his will nor puffs him out with pride.
I fancy, there must lurk some cogency i' the claim,
Man, such abatement made, submits to, all the same.
Soul finds no triumph, here, to register like Sense
With whom 't is ask and have, — the want, the evidence
That the thing wanted, soon or late, will be supplied.
This indeed plumes up will; this, sure, puffs out with pride,
When, reading records right, man's instincts still attest
Promotion comes to Sense because Sense likes it best;
For bodies sprouted legs, through a desire to run:
While hands, when fain to filch, got fingers one by one,
And nature, that's ourself, accommodative brings
To bear that, tired of legs which walk, we now bud wings
Since of a mind to fly. Such savor in the nose
Of Sense, would stimulate Soul sweetly, I suppose,
Soul with its proper itch of instinct, prompting clear
To recognize soul's self soul's only master here
Alike from first to last. But if time's pressure, light's
Or rather dark's, approach, wrest thoroughly the rights
Of rule away, and bid the soul submissive bear
Another soul than it play master everywhere
In great and small, — this time, I fancy, none disputes
There's something in the fact that such conclusion suits
Nowise the pride of man, nor yet chimes in with attributes
Conspicuous in the lord of nature. He receives
And not demands — not first likes faith and then believes.

CXXIX.

And as with the last essence, so with its first faint type.
Inconstancy means raw, 't is faith alone means ripe
I' the soul which runs its round: no matter how it range
From Helen to Fifine, Elvire bids back the change
To permanence. Here, too, love ends where love began.
Such ending looks like law, because the natural man
Inclines the other way, feels lordlier free than bound.
Poor pabulum for pride when the first love is found
Last also! and, so far from realizing gain,
Each step aside just proves divergency in vain.
The wanderer brings home no profit from his quest
Beyond the sad surmise that keeping house were best
Could life begin anew. His problem posed aright
Was — "From the given point evolve the infinite!"
Not — " Spend thyself in space, endeavoring to joint
Together, and so make infinite, point and point:

Fix into one Elvire a Fair-ful of Fifines!"
Fifine, the foam-flake, she: Elvire, the sea's self, means
Capacity at need to shower how many such!
And yet we left her calm profundity, to clutch
Foam-flutter, bell on bell, that, bursting at a touch,
Blistered us for our pains. But wise, we want no more
O' the fickle element. Enough of foam and roar!
Land-locked, we live and die henceforth: for here's the villa
 door.

CXXX.

How pallidly you pause o' the threshold! Hardly night,
Which drapes you, ought to make real flesh and blood so white!
Touch me, and so appear alive to all intents!
Will the saint vanish from the sinner that repents?
Suppose you are a ghost! A memory, a hope,
A fear, a conscience! Quick! Give back the hand I grope
I' the dusk for!

CXXXI.

That is well. Our double horoscope
I cast, while you concur. Discard that simile
O' the fickle element! Elvire is land not sea —
The solid land, the safe. All these word-bubbles came
O' the sea, and bite like salt. The unlucky bath 's to blame.
This hand of yours on heart of mine, no more the bay
I beat, nor bask beneath the blue! In Pornic, say,
The Mayor shall catalogue me duly domiciled,
Contributable, good-companion of the guild
And mystery of marriage. I stickle for the town,
And not this tower apart; because, though, halfway down,
Its mullions wink o'erwebbed with bloomy greenness, yet
Who mounts to staircase top may tempt the parapet,
And sudden there's the sea! No memories to arouse:
No fancies to delude! Our honest civic house
Of the earth be earthy too! — or graced perchance with shell
Made prize of long ago, picked haply where the swell
Menaced a little once — or seaweed-branch that yet
Dampens and softens, notes a freak of wind, a fret
Of wave: though, why on earth should sea-change mend or mar
The calm contemplative householders that we are?
So shall the seasons fleet, while our two selves abide:
E'en past astonishment how sunrise and springtide
Could tempt one forth to swim; the more if time appoints
That swimming grow a task for one's rheumatic joints.
Such honest civic house, behold, I constitute

Our villa! Be but flesh and blood, and smile to boot!
Enter for good and all! then fate bolt fast the door,
Shut you and me inside, never to wander more!

CXXXII.

Only, — you do not use to apprehend attack!
No doubt, the way I march, one idle arm, thrown slack
Behind me, leaves the open hand defenceless at the back,
Should an impertinent on tiptoe steal, and stuff
— Whatever can it be? A letter sure enough,
Pushed betwixt palm and glove! That largess of a franc?
Perhaps inconsciously, — to better help the blank
O' the nest, her tambourine, and, laying egg, persuade
A family to follow, the nest-egg that I laid
May have contained — but just to foil suspicious folk —
Between two silver whites a yellow double yolk!
Oh, threaten no farewell! five minutes shall suffice
To clear the matter up. I go, and in a trice
Return; five minutes past, expect me! If in vain —
Why, slip from flesh and blood, and play the ghost again!

EPILOGUE.

The Householder.

Savage I was sitting in my house, late, lone:
   Dreary, weary with the long day's work:
Head of me, heart of me, stupid as a stone:
   Tongue-tied now, now blaspheming like a Turk;
When, in a moment, just a knock, call, cry,
   Half a pang and all a rapture, there again were we! —
"What, and is it really you again?" quoth I:
   "I again, what else did you expect?" quoth She.

"Never mind, hie away from this old house —
   Every crumbling brick embrowned with sin and shame!
Quick, in its corners ere certain shapes arouse!
   Let them — every devil of the night — lay claim,
Make and mend, or rap and rend, for me! Good-bye!
   God be their guard from disturbance at their glee,
Till, crash, comes down the carcass in a heap!" quoth I:
   "Nay, but there's a decency required!" quoth She.

"Ah, but if you knew how time has dragged, days, nights!
  All the neighbor-talk with man and maid — such men!
All the fuss and trouble of street-sounds, window-sights:
  All the worry of flapping door and echoing roof; and then,
All the fancies . . . Who were they had leave, dared try
  Darker arts that almost struck despair in me?
If you knew but how I dwelt down here!." quoth I:
  "And was I so better off up there?" quoth She.

"Help and get it over! . *Reunited to his wife*
  (How draw up the paper lets the parish-people know?)
Lies M or N, departed from this life,
  Day the this or that, month and year the so and so.
What i' the way of final flourish? Prose, verse? Try!
  Affliction sore long time he bore, or, what is it to be?
Till God did please to grant him ease. Do end!" quoth I:
  "I end with — Love is all, and Death is nought!" quoth She.

www.ingramcontent.com/pod-product-compliance
Lightning Source LLC
Chambersburg PA
CBHW022142300426
44115CB00006B/305